EDUCATING PEOPLE TO BE EMOTIONALLY INTELLIGENT

EDUCATING PEOPLE TO BE EMOTIONALLY INTELLIGENT

Edited by

Reuven Bar-On, J.G. Maree and
Maurice Jesse Elias

Westport, Connecticut
London

Library of Congress Cataloging-in-Publication Data

Educating people to be emotionally intelligent / edited by Reuven Bar-On, J.G. Maree, and Maurice Jesse Elias ; foreword by Daniel Goleman.
  p. cm.
Includes bibliographical references and index.
ISBN-10: 0–275–99363–9 (alk. paper)
ISBN-13: 978–0–275–99363–4 (alk. paper)
 1. Emotional intelligence. I. Bar-On, Reuven, 1944– II. Maree, Kobus, 1951– III. Elias, Maurice J.
BF576.E378 2007
152.4071—dc22   2006100464

British Library Cataloguing in Publication Data is available.

Library of Congress Catalog Card Number:
ISBN-10: 0–275–99363–9
ISBN-13: 978–0–275–99363–4

First published in 2007

Praeger Publishers, 88 Post Road West, Westport, CT 06881
An imprint of Greenwood Publishing Group, Inc.
www.praeger.com

Printed in the United States of America

The paper used in this book complies with the Permanent Paper Standard issued by the National Information Standards Organization (Z39.48-1984).

10 9 8 7 6 5 4 3 2 1

Contents

Foreword

In a sense, this book represents the healing of a long-standing wound in Western civilization, one caused by the chasm between thought and feeling. While Eastern thought has never split the two concepts—the Chinese have a word that translates as 'heart-mind', and there is no word for 'emotion', the meaning of which is separate from cognition in Sanskrit or Tibetan—Western thought has long posited rational thought as inevitably opposed to the irrationality of emotion.

Some scholars see historical footprints of this philosophical split as far back as the 12th century, when the first European universities emerged as centers of learning distinct from monasteries. The pedagogic assumption of scholasticism in the West has been that education was for the rational mind; emotions were out of place—and, implicitly, unschoolable.

While some might argue that the model has worked well—few people question the excellence of modern institutions of learning—there are signs that we have been inadvertently short-changing our children because of this split between thought and feeling. Traditionally, in focusing on the skills of literacy and the like, schools have ignored basic skills that children need for life.

With the faltering in recent decades of other institutions in society, children in America and many other countries in the developed world had began to suffer from a range of problems, such as violence, substance abuse, school dropout and unwanted pregnancy, at unprecedented rates. In response to these social crises, there has been a succession of school-based 'wars on...', each targeting one or another of these problems. When the WT Grant Foundation commissioned a study of these programs, it was found that the active ingredients in the successful programs comprised helping children to acquire mastery in life skills such as self-awareness and emotional self-regulation, empathy and social interaction (see Hawkins, J.D. et al. 1992. *Communities that care,* San Francisco: Jossey-Bass).

In their seminal article on emotional intelligence, published in 1990, Peter Salovey and John Mayer articulate a framework for thinking about an expanded range of essential skills for life, and what it might mean to educate the 'whole child' (see Salovey, P. and Mayer, J.D. 1990. *Emotional intelligence.* Imagination, Cognition, and Personality, 9:185–211). Educators have been quick to take up the challenge of educating children in this domain. At the University of Illinois in Chicago, the Collaborative for Academic, Social and Emotional Learning (CASEL) lists on its website more than 80 school-based programs that follow best-practice guidelines, 21 of these being designated as 'CASEL Select Programs' in that they are considered to meet the highest standards of social-emotional learning (SEL).

It is particularly heartening that this educational movement has been gathering solid empirical evidence to demonstrate the efficacy of education in emotional and social intelligence abilities. The most impressive data come from a meta-analysis of 668 independent studies of SEL programs and their outcomes, conducted by Roger Weissberg and his associates at CASEL. The definitive dataset shows substantial benefits from this approach to educating children, ranging from reductions in suspension rates and improvements in school discipline and pro-social behavior to greater emotional bonding with the school. And perhaps most telling is that educating children to enhance their emotional and social abilities had an academic payoff: a sizeable increase in all indicators of academic achievement.

Another recent finding in the Promoting Alternative Thinking Strategies (PATHS) program, a pioneering SEL curriculum for elementary school students, relates some of the boost in academic achievement directly to enhanced function in the prefrontal cortex. Specifically, this suggests that neuroplasticity—the shaping of the brain through experience—plays a key role in the benefits to be derived from SEL in children.

This book attests to the remarkable growth and contributions of a field that was virtually unknown a decade ago. The resulting expertise touches many aspects of life, including our efficacy as individuals and as parents. More fundamentally, this volume establishes a key point: emotional intelligence—unlike IQ—is not fixed, but rather can be systematically cultivated. We now understand the neuroanatomy that mediates this domain of human performance, and have begun to establish models and principles of learning that take its unique neural dynamics into account.

Most striking is the rapid emergence of a community of practice centering on educating people to be emotionally intelligent. As in other domains of expertise, this informal network shares ideas and experiences, and tests and refines methods, thus contributing to an ever-expanding communal body of knowledge. The first members of this community were the many pioneers who independently designed curricula in what is now known as 'SEL'—but who did so long before the existence of a critical mass of practitioners. Other early contributors were those in child development who began to study emotional competence and its emergence in childhood.

As schools increasingly began to adopt SEL programs, an ancillary expertise emerged—one well represented in this book. Practitioners recognized the need to train teachers and to engage parents and family as partners with schools, and explored how best to go about these essential tasks. Methods for assessing the efficacy of SEL have been developed and provide invaluable feedback for improving future iterations of curricula, best practices for implementation and model programs that embody them.

In addition to educating children to be emotionally intelligent, there is also adult education in the form of organizations and individual practitioners offering the 'grown-up' equivalent of SEL in the workplace. Here the expertise resides largely among the burgeoning ranks of executive coaches, and in the organizations that have successfully trained large numbers of their own employees in emotional intelligence abilities.

Finally, emotional intelligence is also being applied in treating people with psychiatric disorders, many of whom exhibit deficiencies in emotional and social abilities among their major symptoms. Here the spill-over from other SEL efforts proves fruitful in developing skill-building interventions that can supplement current treatments.

Hopefully, the publication of this book will add another substantial contribution to support the case for educating the human heart.

Daniel Goleman

What This Book Is About

Our primary purpose in publishing *Educating People to Be Emotionally Intelligent* is to create a book that recognizes and reflects the rapidly growing global interest in scientifically based applications of emotional intelligence (EI) in education. Educators and parents, corporate coaches and trainers, health care and psychological service providers, academicians, researchers and students are all striving to learn more about applying EI in various educational settings in order to enhance individual performance as well as group efficacy and organizational productivity. This book is the first to bring together the work of such a wide range of scholars, theorists, researchers and practitioners, representing the main schools of EI, as well as the key approaches to social-emotional learning (SEL) and closely related fields.

The decision to publish this book was inspired by the extensive positive international reaction to a special issue of *Perspectives in Education* entitled 'Educating people to be emotionally and socially intelligent', published in 2003. From many quarters, we received requests for a comprehensive overview of this field, grounded in theory, research and best practice—and also accessible to a wide readership. Consequently, we recruited the international roster of experts that you can see in the table of contents to work with us to meet this challenge and need.

From the beginning, we sought to create a readable book that was accessible to the widest possible audience, including those who may not be interested in extensive information on any one aspect of applying EI in education and also those who may want a more well-rounded perspective within a specific area and across areas. The intended readership of this book comprises parents, educators, psychologists, counsellors, educational planners, trainers and corporate coaches,

HR and OD professionals, mental health practitioners and health care providers, as well as scholars, students and researchers in the fields of human development, psychology, education and emotional intelligence and all others interested in the application of EI in various educational settings.

The spirit of this endeavor was trans- and inter-disciplinary, multi-theoretical and international. We attempted to weave this spirit into the fabric of the book by stressing the importance of learning about and using a wide variety of approaches based on diverse theoretical backgrounds.

You will note that the term 'emotional intelligence' is used throughout this book to encompass an incisive, broad and diverse approach to describing this construct including closely related terms most widely used in the literature, such as 'emotional awareness', 'emotional literacy', 'emotional competence', 'alexithymia', 'psychological mindedness', 'social intelligence', 'social-emotional learning', 'personal intelligences', 'practical intelligence' and 'emotional-social intelligence'. A burgeoning body of literature suggests that most of these terms and conceptualizations have been used to describe a common construct or different aspects of that construct. Moreover, they tend to focus on the following competencies:

- The ability to recognize and understand emotions and to express feelings non-destructively.
- The ability to understand how others feel and relate with them cooperatively.
- The ability to manage and control emotions effectively.
- The ability to manage change and the emotions generated by change, and to adapt and solve problems of a personal and interpersonal nature.
- The ability to generate positive affect and be self-motivated.

All of the chapters in this book relate to one or more of these competencies and associated skills in one form or another. In light of the fact that the boundaries of this construct are still being studied, as has been the case with many scientific disciplines, we thought that it was imperative to adopt a wide and inclusive approach to what is currently encompassed in the term 'emotional intelligence'.

Along with providing a forum for discussing various approaches to applying EI in education, we also wanted to bring together, in a single volume, chapters that review and evaluate the most valid and reliable of these approaches. Each chapter is a gateway to the extensive additional information available regarding the particular approaches being used by the authors and their colleagues. Ideally, the information presented in this book will help you to decide which educational application, or specific aspect of a particular application, might prove useful for you to explore further and eventually apply based on the particular interests and needs of the end-user.

The resulting material covers the landscape of important aspects of educating people to be emotionally intelligent. Moreover, the chapters appear in a comparatively logical order, and you will note that the book can be roughly divided into seven distinguishable parts that will give you a wealth of information related to various forms of education throughout a person's life and based on the major approaches of EI as we know it today. The chapters also follow a common framework that allowed the authors to convey their unique information and perspectives in a way that facilitated the book being coherent across the various domains included.

The first part of this book is represented by one chapter (Chapter 1), which is axiomatic in nature in that it begins by asking if it is important to be emotionally intelligent and if people can be educated to be emotionally intelligent. This chapter empirically addresses these two questions, thus setting the stage for the chapters that follow.

The second part of the book provides information on the development of emotional competence in children (Chapter 2), and describes how best to raise children to be emotionally intelligent (Chapter 3).

Following this foundation, strategically positioned in child development and parenting, the third part of the book explores a wide array of approaches to educating children to be emotionally intelligent (Chapters 4 to 10), including many developed, reviewed and recommended by the Collaborative for Academic, Social and Emotional Learning (CASEL), which is recognized as the preeminent international and objective authority on applications of EI in educational contexts.

The fourth part of the book comprises four chapters (Chapters 11 to 14) that focus on the adult version of this approach to education—in the form of EI training and coaching in the workplace. Here, a great deal of input is based on the work of the Consortium for Research on Emotional Intelligence in Organizations, co-founded by Daniel Goleman and Cary Cherniss as a counterpart to CASEL in the workplace domain. There is a natural progression from educating children to be emotionally intelligent to educating adults to be emotionally intelligent. As with children, numerous studies and approaches are cited in these chapters showing that improving the EI of adults in the workplace, and creating a climate conducive to so doing, increases occupational performance and organizational productivity. Both social and economic capital become enhanced.

In the fifth part of this book, Chapters 15 and 16 represent the growing realization that counselling individuals with physical and psychological disturbances in the clinical setting can be heuristically conceptualized as another form of EI education. As the chapters show, various theories of emotional intelligence actually serve as a valuable guide to intervention in this area and point out key skill areas that are essential for the individuals' recovery—in order for them not only to survive but to thrive emotionally as well.

The sixth and penultimate part of the book comprises three chapters that provide the reader with a comprehensive description of EI assessment issues and tools (Chapters 17 and 18) as well as the neurological foundation of this construct (Chapter 19) with potential application in educating people to be emotionally intelligent. Although Chapter 17's survey of EI assessment methods for children is extensive, it is important to point out that this survey was completed even as other promising measures, such as the Mayer-Salovey-Caruso Emotional Intelligence Test (MSCEIT) for children and adolescents, were becoming more prominent. Indeed, we should expect the assessment area to be a constant source of innovative work because every arena in which we endeavor to educate people to be emotionally intelligent brings with it the responsibility to evaluate those efforts competently and efficiently.

The seventh and concluding part of the book, Chapter 20, comprises an integrative summary of the entire volume, in which Peter Salovey sums up the major contributions made in each of the chapters to critically evaluate what we have learned, how best to use this knowledge and what still needs to be empirically explored so that it can be more confidently applied to help educate people to be emotionally intelligent. The inclusive content of this book provides a unique platform that allows the chapter to begin to set the agenda for the next generation of work in this field.

We hope that this book will represent a significant contribution to the field of emotional intelligence and become a benchmark for future researchers and practitioners who wish to apply this construct in various educational endeavors.

We would like to express our gratitude to Heinemann Educational Publishers and Praeger Publishers, who have agreed to co-publish this volume. We have enjoyed working with them and the direct contact with Sujata Pillay, Chris Reinders, Debra Primo, Pumlani Xaba and Deborah Carvalko. We would also like to thank Graham Shaw, who was instrumental in creating a partnership between the two publishers for the purpose of publishing our book.

We conclude by conveying our special thanks to the contributors of this book. These world-renowned theorists, researchers and practitioners share our commitment to developing this field in responsible, practical, feasible and scientifically sound ways. Many of the contributors are both colleagues and friends with whom we have been in contact for a number of years. Similarly, the work has benefited from the input of formal and informal reviewers over the course of the book's evolution. We would like to thank them personally for sharing their experience and knowledge with us and you. Being part of a team like this, our editorial task was relatively simple, besides being thoroughly enjoyable.

Reuven Bar-On
Jacobus G. Maree
Maurice J. Elias
June 30, 2006

─── 1 ───

How Important Is It to Educate People to Be Emotionally Intelligent, and Can It Be Done?

Reuven Bar-On

Introduction

For many years, education has emphasized the strengthening of cognitive skills such as acquiring knowledge, recalling learned information and applying that information to understand our world, to reason and to solve problems. Our capacity for using these skills is measured by 'intelligence tests' that render an intelligence quotient or 'IQ' score. The more adept we are at performing these skills, the higher our IQ is expected to be as well as our performance in school, which traditionally has been measured by grades and grade point averages. The higher our IQ, the greater are the chances that we will perform these cognitive skills better and receive higher grades in school.

But what happens *after* school? While IQ scores are useful for predicting how we will do in school, they tell us little about our performance once we leave school. IQ proves to be a weak predictor of how well we relate with others, perform at work and cope with a wide variety of daily challenges (Sternberg 1985; Wagner 1997).

It has been argued for nearly a century that something else is missing in the **human performance formula** that makes it difficult for us to understand why some people do well in life while others do not, irrespective of how cognitively intelligent they are. For almost as long as psychologists have been studying and measuring cognitive intelligence, they have also been looking for additional predictors of various types of performance. Based on his work in the area of 'social intelligence', as he defined it, Edward Thorndike (1920) made one of the first attempts by psychologists to identify these predictors. But this search for the missing component in the human performance formula took place in other fields of science as well, and even earlier than the 20th century. In 1872, Charles Darwin published the first known scientific work on what I refer to as 'emotional-social intelligence' or, simply, 'emotional intelligence' (EI), as it is more popularly termed today. Darwin's publication summarizes work that began in 1837 on the role of emotional expression in survival and adaptation (see Darwin 1872/1965).

With respect to the theme of this book, which focuses on educating people to be emotionally intelligent, it is fitting to begin by asking the following questions:

1. What does it mean for people to be emotionally intelligent?
2. Is it important for people to be emotionally intelligent?
3. Can we educate people to be emotionally intelligent?

I address these questions in this chapter.

What Does It Mean for People to Be Emotionally Intelligent?

Based on my conceptualization of this construct, people who are emotionally and socially intelligent are able to understand and express themselves, to understand and relate well to others, and to successfully cope with the demands of daily life (Bar-On 1997b; 2000; 2005a). This is based, first and foremost, on the ability to be aware of their emotions and of themselves in general, to understand their strengths and weaknesses, and to be able to express feelings non-destructively. Furthermore, to be emotionally and socially intelligent is to be aware of the feelings and needs of others, and to be able to establish and maintain cooperative, constructive and mutually satisfying relationships. Ultimately, emotionally intelligent people are able to effectively manage personal, social and environmental change by realistically and flexibly coping with the immediate situation and solving problems of an interpersonal nature. To do this, they need to manage emotions effectively and be sufficiently optimistic, positive and self-motivated.

Our ability to scientifically measure the construct of emotional-social intelligence enables us to demonstrate the importance of this type of intelligence and to show that people can be educated to be emotionally intelligent.

There are a number of ways to assess EI. Chapters 17 and 18 of this book review the most popular psychometric instruments used today to measure this construct. According to the *Encyclopedia of Applied Psychology* (Spielberger 2004), the three most commonly used EI instruments are:

1. the Mayer-Salovey-Caruso Emotional Intelligence Test (MSCEIT) (Mayer, Salovey & Caruso 2002)

2. the Emotional Competence Inventory (ECI) (Boyatzis, Goleman & HayGroup 2001)

3. the Bar-On Emotional Quotient Inventory (EQ-i) (Bar-On 1997a).

As most of the findings presented in this chapter are based on results generated by the EQ-i, I will briefly describe this instrument. The MSCEIT and ECI are described in Chapter 18.

The EQ-i is a self-report measure of emotionally and socially intelligent behavior which provides an estimate of the underlying construct of emotional-social intelligence. The EQ-i was developed over a period of 17 years and originally normed on 3,831 adults in the United States (US) and Canada. It has been translated into more than 30 languages, and normative data have been collected in numerous settings around the world. The EQ-i was the first EI measure to be published by a psychological test publisher and to be peer-reviewed in the *Buros Mental Measurement Yearbook* (Plake& Impara 1999). Since its publication in 1997, the EQ-i has been consistently described in the literature as the most widely used EI measure. For a more detailed description of the psychometric properties of this measure and how it was developed, normed and validated, you can refer to other sources (see, for example, Bar-On 1997b; 2000; 2004).

Briefly, the EQ-i contains 133 items and employs a five-point response format with responses ranging from 'very seldom or not true of me' (1) to 'very often true of me or true of me' (5). A list of the EQ-i items is found in the instrument's technical manual (Bar-On 1997b). The subject's responses render a total EQ score, 5 composite scale scores and 15 subscale scores. Table 1.1 summarizes the EI competencies, skills and facilitators measured by this instrument.

Raw scores are computer tabulated and converted into standard scores based on a mean of 100 and standard deviations of 15. The EQ-i has a built-in correction factor which automatically adjusts the scale scores based on scores obtained from two of the instrument's validity indices. This is an important psychometric feature for self-report measures because it reduces the potentially distorting effects of response bias by increasing the accuracy of the results obtained. I have recently published a summary of 60 studies conducted on this instrument (Bar-On 2004).

Various versions of the EQ-i are available, including:

- a semi-structured interview—the Bar-On EQ-Interview (Bar-On & Handley 2003a)

- a multi-rater assessment instrument—the Bar-On EQ-360 (Bar-On & Handley 2003 b)

- a youth version of the EQ-i—the Bar-On EQ-i:YV (Bar-On & Parker 2000).

Table 1.1   The Bar-On EQ-i scales and what they assess

EQ-i Scales		The EI competency assessed by each scale:
Intrapersonal	Self-regard	To accurately perceive, understand and accept oneself
	Emotional Self-awareness	To be aware of and understand one's emotions and feelings
	Assertiveness	To effectively and constructively express one's feelings
	Independence	To be self-reliant and free of emotional dependency on others
	Self-actualization	To strive to achieve personal goals and actualize one's potential
Interpersonal	Empathy	To be aware of and understand how others feel
	Social Responsibility	To identify with one's social group and cooperate with others
	Interpersonal Relationship	To establish mutually satisfying relationships and relate well with others
Stress Management	Stress Tolerance	To effectively and constructively manage emotions
	Impulse Control	To effectively and constructively control emotions
Adaptability	Reality Testing	To objectively validate one's feelings and thinking with external reality
	Flexibility	To adapt and adjust one's feelings and thinking to new situations
	Problem-solving	To effectively solve problems of a personal and interpersonal nature
General Mood	Optimism	To be positive and look at the brighter side of life
	Happiness	To feel content with oneself, others and life in general

Is It Important for People to Be Emotionally Intelligent?

One way to demonstrate that it is important to be emotionally intelligent is by showing that emotionally intelligent people tend to perform better in various aspects of life than do people who are less emotionally intelligent. The approach is based essentially on examining the construct's predictive ability, and therefore this section of the chapter focuses on what EI is able to predict and how well.

In other publications, I have described more than 20 predictive validity studies that have been conducted on more than 23,000 individuals (Bar-On 1997b; 2001;

2003; 2004; 2005; 2006; Bar-On, Handley & Fund 2005; Krivoy, Weyl Ben-Arush & Bar-On 2000). These findings illuminate the predictive validity of emotional-social intelligence by examining its impact on physical and psychological health, social interaction, performance at school and in the workplace, self-actualization, and overall subjective well-being. The findings reveal that the average predictive validity coefficient is .59, for the studies conducted, which suggests that this construct has a substantial impact on human performance. The figure is based on averaging the correlation coefficients that surfaced in the above mentioned predictive validity studies, and it represents a rough estimate, or meta-analysis, of the construct's overall predictive validity. The estimate becomes more accurate as additional findings from larger and more diverse studies are analyzed and as the results are generated by a wider variety of EI instruments. Below, I summarize the major findings that went into this interim analysis.

The impact of EI on physical health

The three studies that I describe below suggest that there is a moderate but statistically significant relationship between emotional-social intelligence and physical health.

In the first study (Krivoy et al. 2000), the EQ-i results of 35 adolescent cancer survivors were compared with those of a control group comprising 35 adolescents matched for age and gender from the local normative population sample. In addition to revealing significant differences between the two groups with respect to overall emotional-social intelligence, the results indicated that the EQ-i subscale that was able to most significantly distinguish between the experimental and control groups was Optimism, which measures an important facilitator of emotionally and socially intelligent behavior (Bar-On 2000).

In another study (Bar-On 2004), 3,571 adults completed the EQ-i and were asked to respond to the following statement using a five-point scale: 'I feel good about my health in general'. This approach was thought to provide a fairly good estimate of the participants' general physical condition, in that self-perceived health has been shown to correlate significantly with clinically assessed health (Shadbolt, Barresi & Craft 2002). The results of a multiple regression analysis rendered an overall correlation of .49, indicating a moderate relationship.

In a recent study (Bar-On 2006), a sample of 2,514 male recruits in the Israeli Defence Force (IDF) completed the EQ-i at the beginning of their tour of duty. Ninety-one recruits were identified as having received medical profiles that indicated minor to mild health problems. Forty-two were identified with more severe medical problems, and an additional group of 42 was randomly selected from the sample as not having received a medical profile and thus considered to be physically healthy. A multiple regression analysis was applied to the data; it rendered an overall correlation of .37, suggesting a low-moderate yet statistically significant relationship between EI and physical health.

The impact of EI on psychological health

In one of the first studies that directly examined the relationship between EI and psychological health, the EQ-i scores of 418 psychiatric patients were compared with randomly selected non-clinical samples in Argentina, Israel, South Africa and the US (Bar-On 1997b). In addition to statistically significant differences in overall emotional-social intelligence, significant differences on most of the EQ-i scales were also revealed between the clinical and non-clinical samples.

In another study (Bar-On 2003), a sample of 2,514 males completed the EQ-i at the time of their induction into the military. In this sample, 152 recruits were identified as having been discharged from active service for psychiatric reasons. An additional group of 152 individuals was randomly selected from a sample of 241 who were diagnosed with less severe psychiatric disturbances that allowed them to complete their tour of duty with relatively few limitations. The EQ-i scores of these two groups were compared with a group of 152 recruits, randomly selected from the same sample, who did not receive a psychiatric profile during the entire period of their military service. A multiple regression analysis of the data revealed a moderate yet significant relationship of .39 between EI and psychological health.

Studies conducted by Brackett and Salovey (2004) have generated statistically significant correlations between the MSCEIT and measures of anxiety and depression, which also suggests that there is a relationship between EI and psychological health.

The impact of EI on social interaction

In addition to a number of earlier studies that have suggested a relationship between EI and social interaction (Bar-On 1997b; 2000), a recent examination of an older dataset sheds new light on the nature of this relationship (Bar-On 2006). When the EQ-i was normed in the US and Canada (Bar-On 1997b), 533 participants in the normative sample completed the Sixteen Personality Factor Questionnaire (16PF) in addition to the EQ-i. A multiple regression analysis of the relationship between the 15 EQ-i subfactors and Factor H on the 16PF, which assesses the desire for 'genial and positive social relationships' (Cattell, Eber & Tatsuoka 1970), suggested that EI relates significantly—at .69—to social interaction. Brackett and his colleagues have also found statistically significant correlations, but in the low to moderate range, between the MSCEIT and the 'quality of interpersonal relationships' (Brackett & Mayer 2003).

The impact of EI on performance at school

Four studies conducted in South Africa, Canada and the US have indicated that EI has an impact on performance at school. Performance was assessed by the students' grade point average (GPA) in all four studies.

In a path analysis conducted by James Parker and his colleagues on 667 Canadian high-school students, the overall degree of correlation between emotional-social intelligence and scholastic performance was found to be .41, which indicates a moderate yet statistically significant relationship (Parker, Creque, Barnhart et al. 2004).

Findings from a study conducted on 448 university students in South Africa also indicate that there was a significant difference in EI between academically successful and unsuccessful students (Swart 1996). These results were confirmed by a study carried out on 1,125 university students in the US (Bar-On 1997b). In both studies, the successful students were found to be the more emotionally intelligent.

Claude Marchessault recently examined the impact of EQ-i scores on the GPA of 106 first-year university students in the US (Bar-On 2006). The students completed the EQ-i at the beginning of the academic year, and their GPA was calculated during the middle of the year. Multiple regression analysis revealed a correlation of .45, which additionally confirms a significant relationship between EI and performance at school.

Brackett and Salovey also describe statistically significant correlations between the MSCEIT and performance at school (2004).

The impact of EI on performance in the workplace

In the six studies described below, the EQ-i clearly demonstrates that there is a significant relationship between EI and various aspects of occupational performance.

In the first known study that directly examined the relationship between EI and occupational performance, the EQ-i scores of 1,171 US Air Force (USAF) recruiters were compared with their ability to meet annual recruitment quotas (Bar-On et al. 2005; Handley 1997). Based on USAF criteria, the recruiters were divided into 'high performers' (those who were able to meet at least 100% of their annual quota), and 'low performers' (those who met less than 80% of the quota). A discriminant function analysis indicated that EQ-i scores were able to identify fairly accurately high and low performers based on a regression correlation of .53, which demonstrates that the relationship between EI and occupational performance is moderately high.

In two other studies, performance in highly stressful and potentially dangerous occupations was studied by comparing EQ-i scores with externally rated performance for a sample of 335 regular combat soldiers in the IDF and for an additional sample of 240 soldiers in an elite IDF unit (Bar-On et al. 2005). Both studies revealed a significant relationship between EI and this specific type of performance; the predictive validity coefficient in the former study was .55 and .51 in the latter.

In three additional studies (Bar-On 2004; Bar-On et al. 2005), leadership capability was studied by:

- examining the relationship between EQ-i scores and peer nomination—new recruits in the IDF considered to possess leadership ability
- examining criterion group membership—IDF recruits who were accepted for officer training versus those who were not
- using multi-rater evaluations conducted at the Center for Creative Leadership in the US—ratings on 21 leadership criteria made by an average of seven to eight co-workers.

The results indicated that there is a moderate to high relationship between EI and leadership based on the respective predictive validity coefficients of .39 (n=536), .49 (n=940) and .82 (n=236).

The average predictive validity coefficient for the six studies I described above is .54, meaning that nearly 30% of the variance in occupational performance is based on EI. When compared with Wagner's extensive meta-analysis (1997), which reveals that cognitive intelligence accounts for approximately 6% of occupational performance, the findings presented here suggest that EQ accounts for five times more variance than IQ when explaining this specific type of performance.

Correlations between MSCEIT scores and various aspects of occupational performance were also found to be statistically significant, albeit in the low to moderate range (Brackett & Salovey 2004). Similarly, Boyatzis and Sala (2004) summarize a number of studies suggesting that EI, as assessed with the ECI, significantly impacts occupational performance, including leadership.

The impact of EI on self-actualization

Self-actualization is the process of striving to actualize our potential capacity, capabilities and talents. It requires the ability and drive to set and achieve our goals, and it is characterized by being involved in various interests and pursuits. It is not merely 'adequate' performance but an attempt to do our best.

In the re-examination of an older dataset used in my doctoral research (Bar-On 1988), I recently ran a multiple regression analysis on the impact of EI competencies and skills on self-actualization (Bar-On 2005). A subset of 67 South African university students were identified within this dataset as having concomitantly completed an earlier version of the EQ-i and the Personal Orientation Inventory (POI) (Shostrom 1974). The POI is a self-actualization measure based on Abraham Maslow's conceptualization of this construct. The results indicated that EI has a significant impact on self-actualization based on the correlation of .64.

Three other studies have also examined the relationship between EI and self-actualization (Bar-On 2001). Large samples were studied in the Netherlands (n=1,639), Israel (n=2,702) and North America (n=3,831). The results confirmed the above mentioned South African study, which indicates that emotional-social intelligence has a strong impact on self-actualization, with multiple regression correlations reaching levels of .78, .75 and .80 respectively. Although a measure of cognitive intelligence was not administered to all of the samples studied, the relationship between cognitive intelligence and self-actualization for the Dutch and Israeli samples was not revealed to be statistically significant. The implication of these findings is that EQ more than IQ affects our ability to do our best, to accomplish goals and to actualize our potential to its fullest.

The impact of EI on subjective well-being

In a recent study (Bar-On 2005), it was revealed that emotional-social intelligence also has an impact on overall subjective well-being. In this study, **well-being** was defined as a subjective state that emerges from our general feeling of satisfaction with:

- our physical health and ourselves in general
- our close interpersonal relationships
- the nature of our occupations and financial situation.

A measure of subjective well-being was constructed from nine questions that tap into these three areas; it was administered with the EQ-i to 3,571 individuals in the US and Canada. The relationship between EI and well-being was examined with multiple regression analysis, and the results indicated that the two constructs are highly correlated based on a correlation of .76. Significant correlations were also obtained between the MSCEIT and two measures of subjective well-being (Brackett & Mayer 2003).

Can We Educate People to Be Emotionally Intelligent?

After demonstrating, in the previous section, that EI has a significant impact on various aspects of human performance, we can now ask whether emotionally and socially intelligent behavior can be enhanced in order to improve performance as well as self-actualization and overall subjective well-being. To address this question, I will summarize the findings from four studies in this section, demonstrating that such behavior can indeed be enhanced at school, at work and in the clinical setting.

Enhancing EI at school

A growing number of children worldwide are being introduced to EI-enhancing educational programs such as the 'Self-Science' curriculum. Karen McCown and her colleagues (McCown, Jensen, Freedman & Rideout 1998) developed this particular program over 40 years ago. In light of the fact that an extensive evaluation of the impact of this program is currently under way, I will focus on only one subset of the preliminary results to exemplify the potential of programs like these. This example is of a 7th grade class of 26 children whose average age was 12 years when the study began in the US (Freedman 2003). The children were tested with the EQ-i:YV at the beginning of the school year, before they were exposed to Self-Science, and again at the end of the school year, when they had participated in the curriculum for nine to ten months.

A comparison of the pre- and post-intervention assessments suggests that the children's emotional-social intelligence increased significantly. At the end of the first year, the children were better able to understand and express themselves, to understand and relate with others, to manage and control their emotions, and to adapt to their immediate school environment. These important changes suggest that this program is viable. The Self-Science curriculum is described in detail in Chapter 8, and other EI-enhancing programs for school-age children are presented in Chapters 4, 5, 6, 7, 9 and 10.

Future studies related to EI-enhancing programs need to examine pre- and post-implementation behavioral parameters on larger and more diverse samples in order to assess the extent to which these programs help, for example, to increase school attendance, improve scholastic performance, curb violence, reduce drug abuse and decrease teen pregnancy.

Enhancing EI in the workplace

Sjölund and Gustafsson (2001) conducted a study in Sweden illustrating that emotionally and socially intelligent behavior can be enhanced in adults as well as in children. The researchers compared the EQ-i scores of 29 managers at a Stockholm construction company before and after they participated in a work-shop designed to increase managerial skills. As part of the workshop curriculum, they were taught techniques designed to strengthen EI competencies and skills thought to be important for their work as managers. Not only did their total EQ score increase from a mean of 97 to 106 (p-level $< .001$), but 9 out of the 15 EQ-i subscales increased significantly as well. The two EI competencies that increased the most were emotional self-awareness and empathy, which many consider to be the two most important components of EI. Furthermore, the partic-ipants who began the workshop with the lowest EQ-i scores were found to be the ones who made the most progress. Kate Cannon, the developer of the EI compo-nent of this workshop, reported similar findings based on her experience in the US (Bar-On 2003). This is particularly encouraging, because the people with the lowest scores are the ones who need to improve their EI skills the most.

At an EI conference in 2003, Geetu Bharwaney presented preliminary findings from the individual coaching she has been providing to corporate executives in the United Kingdom (UK) since 1999. In the sample presented, she assessed 47 executives from the same company with the EQ-i before she began coaching them and approximately two months after they completed the intervention.

The five EQ-i subscale scores that revealed the most significant changes were as follows:

1. Self-regard—87 to 95.
2. Self-actualization—92 to 102.
3. Stress tolerance—97 to 102.
4. Reality-testing—97 to 109.
5. Happiness—93 to 100.

These and other related findings are presented in Chapter 13. In Chapters 11, 12 and 14, detailed information is provided on similar programs that have been specifically designed to enhance EI in order to increase individual and organizational performance in the workplace.

Enhancing EI in the clinical setting

In addition to the classroom and workplace, there is evidence suggesting that EI skills can also be enhanced in the clinical setting.

Using an earlier version of the EQ-i, a graduate student at the University of Pretoria tested a group of 58 patients within 10 days of being hospitalized for myocardial infarction (Dunkley 1996). Subsequently, 22 of these patients were randomly selected to participate in a stress management program. The program included instructions on how to identify sources of stress in their lives and how to cope with these situations more effectively. The patients were administered the EQ-i a second time five weeks after they completed the program. In addition to significant changes in the total EQ score—92 versus 102 (t-value = −5.47, p-level < .001)—nine of the subscale scores revealed statistically significant changes. Taking into consideration the primary purpose of this program, which was to reduce stress, it is not surprising that the EQ-i factor that changed the most was Stress tolerance. This specific change is extremely important in light of the fact that stress represents one of the major psychosocial factors that has an impact on cardiovascular disturbances like myocardial infarction. Lastly, most of the EQ-i scores received by the participants in the program were significantly higher than those obtained by patients who did not participate in the program.

In Chapters 15 and 16, further information is provided on ways of enhancing EI competencies and skills as a potential adjunct to medical and psychiatric treatment.

Conclusions

In this chapter, I presented a number of findings demonstrating that it is both important and possible to educate people to be emotionally intelligent.

With regard to researchers and practitioners who have been working and will be working in this area, there are a number of issues that must be addressed in order to maximize the successful application of EI in education. Based on my experience, I am convinced that there are four basic goals that need to be achieved before more serious progress can be made:

1. We need to *continue to study the impact of emotional-social intelligence* on a wider variety of human performance using a number of different EI assessment instruments. This will provide us with more information on the various types of performance and behavior that are affected by EI.

2. We need to *develop more educational programs,* designed to improve emotionally and socially intelligent behavior, that are based on scientific observations and empirical findings rather than on unsubstantiated theories. Continued research on how EI affects various aspects of human performance and behavior should guide the development of these programs. Organizations such as CASEL, the Center for Social and Emotional Education (CSEE) and Six Seconds should continue with an aggressive policy of developing, conducting, evaluating and promoting the educational programs that get the best results.

3. We need to *recruit emotionally intelligent individuals* to educate people to become more emotionally intelligent, simply because they make the most effective teachers (Haskett 2002).

4. To continue studying the impact of EI on various aspects of human performance and behavior, to guide the development of EI-enhancing curricula, and to recruit emotionally intelligent teachers, we need to *access a wide variety of multidimensional EI assessment instruments* that are scientifically developed, normed and validated. The outcome of our work and progress in this area depends, in part, on the validity and reliability of these instruments. Without the use of valid and reliable psychometric instruments, we will not know for certain if our efforts are effective, ineffective or even counterproductive, and to what extent and why.

In closing, it is reasonable to assume that if we succeed in raising and educating more emotionally and socially intelligent children, we will help to build more effective, productive and humane organizations, communities and societies.

References

Bar-On, R. 1988. *The development of a concept of psychological well-being.* Unpublished doctoral dissertation, Rhodes University, South Africa.

———. 1997a. *The Bar-On Emotional Quotient Inventory (EQ-i): A Test of Emotional Intelligence.* Toronto, Canada: Multi-Health Systems.

———. 1997b. *Bar-On Emotional Quotient Inventory (EQ-i): Technical Manual.* Toronto, Canada: Multi-Health Systems.

———. 2000. Emotional and social intelligence: Insights from the Emotional Quotient Inventory (EQ-i). In *Handbook of emotional intelligence,* Ed. Reuven Bar-On and James D.A. Parker. San Francisco: Jossey-Bass.

———. 2001. Emotional intelligence and self-actualization. In *Emotional intelligence in everyday life: A scientific inquiry,* Ed. Joseph Ciarrochi, Joe Forgas, and John D. Mayer. New York: Psychology Press.

———. 2003. How important is it to educate people to be emotionally and socially intelligent, and can it be done? *Perspectives in Education* 21 (4): 3–13.

———. 2004. The Bar-On Emotional Quotient Inventory (EQ-i): Rationale, description, and summary of psychometric properties. In *Measuring emotional intelligence:*

Common ground and controversy, Ed. Glenn Geher, pp. 111–42. Hauppauge, NY: Nova Science Publishers.

———. 2005a. The Bar-On model of Emotional–Social Intelligence (ESI). *Psicothema* 17.

———. 2005b. The impact of emotional-social intelligence on subjective well-being. *Perspectives in Education* 23(2).

———. 2006. The Bar-On model of emotional-social intelligence (ESI). *Psicothema* 18.

Bar-On, R., and R. Handley. 2003a. *The Bar-On EQ-360.* Toronto, Canada: Multi-Health Systems.

———. 2003b. *The Bar-On EQ-Interview.* Toronto, Canada: Multi-Health Systems.

Bar-On, R., R. Handley, and S. Fund. 2005. The impact of emotional and social intelligence on performance. In *Linking emotional intelligence and performance at work: Current research evidence,* Ed. Vanessa Druskat, Fabio Sala, and Gerald Mount. Mahwah, NJ: Lawrence Erlbaum.

Bar-On, R., and J.D.A. Parker. 2000. *Emotional Quotient Inventory: Youth Version (EQ-i: YV).* Toronto, Canada: Multi-Health Systems.

Bharwaney, G. 2003. Emotional intelligence: The cutting edge of interventions in corporate and educational settings. Paper presented on the 29th of May 2003 at the Nexus EQ Conference, Halifax, Nova Scotia, Canada.

Boyatzis, R.E., D. Goleman, and Hay Group 2001. *The Emotional Competence Inventory (ECI).* Boston: HayGroup.

Boyatzis, R.E., and F. Sala, 2004. The Emotional competence Inventory (ECI). In *Measuring emotional intelligence: Common ground and controversy.* Hauppauge, NY: Nova Science. pp. 147–80.

Brackett, M.A., and J.D. Mayer. 2003. Convergent, discriminant, and incremental validity of competing measures of emotional intelligence. *Personality and Social Psychology Bulletin* 29 (9): 1147–58.

Brackett, M.A., and P. Salovey. 2004. Measuring emotional intelligence with the Mayer-Salovey-Caruso Emotional Intelligence Test (MSCEIT). In *Measuring emotional intelligence.*

Brackett, M.A., R.M. Warner, , and J. S. Bosco. 2005. Emotional intelligence and relationship satisfaction among couples. *Personal Relationships* 12:197–212.

Cattell, R.B., H.W. Eber, and M.M. Tatsuoka, 1970. *Handbook for the Sixteen Personality Factor Questionnaire (16PF).* Champaign, Illinois: Institute for Personality and Ability Testing.

Darwin, C. 1872. *The expression of the emotions in man and animals.* Repr. Chicago: University of Chicago Press, 1965.

Dunkley, J. 1996. The psychological well-being of coronary heart disease patients before and after an intervention program. Unpublished master's thesis. University of Pretoria, South Africa.

Freedman, J. 2003. Key lessons from 35 years of social-emotional education: How Self-Science builds self-awareness, positive relationships, and healthy decision-making. *Perspectives in Education* 21 (4): 69–80.

Handley, R. 1997, April. AFRS rates emotional intelligence. *Air Force Recruiter News.*

Haskett, R.A. 2002. Emotional intelligence and teaching success in higher education. Unpublished doctoral dissertation, Indiana University.

Krivoy, E., M. Weyl Ben-Arush, and R. Bar-On. 2000. Comparing the emotional intelligence of adolescent cancer survivors with a matched sample from the normative population. *Medical & Pediatric Oncology* 35 (3): 382.

Mayer, J.D., P. Salovey, and D.R. Caruso. 2002. *Mayer-Salovey-Caruso Emotional Intelligence Test (MSCEIT)*. Toronto, Canada: Multi-Health Systems, Inc.

McCown, K., A.L. Jensen, J.M. Freedman, and M.C. Rideout. 1998. *Self-Science: The emotional intelligence curriculum*. San Mateo, CA: Six Seconds.

Parker, J.D.A., R.E. Creque, D.L. Barnhart, J.I. Harris, S.A. Majeski, L.M. Wood, B.J. Bond, and M.J. Hogan. 2004. Academic achievement in high school: Does emotional intelligence matter? *Personality and Individual Differences* 37: 1321–30.

Plake, B.S., and J.C. Impara, eds. 1999. The Bar-On Emotional Quotient Inventory (EQ-i). *Supplement to the thirteenth mental measurement yearbook*. Lincoln, NE: Buros Institute for Mental Measurement.

Shadbolt, B., J. Barresi, and P. Craft. 2002. Self-rated health as a predictor of survival among patients with advanced cancer. *Journal of Clinical Oncology* 20 (10): 2514–19.

Shostrom, E.L. 1974. *Personal Orientation Inventory: An Inventory for the Measurement of Self-Actualization*. San Diego, CA: Educational Industrial Testing Service.

Sjölund, M., & H. Gustafsson. 2001. *Outcome study of a leadership development assessment and training program based on emotional intelligence*. An internal report prepared for the Skanska Management Institute in Stockholm, Sweden.

Spielberger, C., ed. 2004. *Encyclopedia of Applied Psychology*. San Diego, CA: Academic Press.

Sternberg, R.J. 1985. *Beyond IQ: A triarchic theory of human intelligence*. New York: Cambridge University Press.

Stone-McCown, K., A.L. Jensen, J. M. Freedman, and M.C. Rideout. 1998. *Self science: The emotional intelligence curriculum*. San Mateo, CA: Six Seconds.

Swart, A. 1996. *The relationship between well-being and academic performance*. Unpublished master's thesis, University of Pretoria, South Aftrica.

Thorndike, E.L. 1920. Intelligence and its uses. *Harper's Magazine* 140:227–35.

Wagner R.K. 1997. Intelligence, training, and employment. *American Psychologist* 52 (10): 1059–69.

— 2 —

The Development of Emotional Competence: Pathways for Helping Children to Become Emotionally Intelligent

Carolyn Saarni

Introduction

As other contributions to this book make clear, there are at least two distinct conceptualizations of EI. Mayer and Salovey (1997) have developed an approach emphasizing abilities that promote reasoning about emotions, and Bar-On (2004; 2005) focuses on a set of abilities relating to managing emotions and social relationships. Both approaches are concerned with the measurement of individual differences relative to how much or to what extent an individual exhibits EI aptitude or traits. While social and personality psychologists were refining their conceptualizations of EI, a separate strand of research and theory was emerging within developmental psychology. The strand was concerned with emotional development and its manifestations in behavior, cognition and feeling (Denham 1999; Gordon 1989; Saarni, Mumme & Campos 1998). Theorists focused on the functional effects of emotion on infants and children, and therefore concentrated on the kinds of contexts that facilitated or inhibited adaptive emotional development.

In this chapter, I summarize some of the main features of this context-oriented approach to the development of emotional competence, which is complementary to the more adult-focused approach found within the various investigations of

EI. Halberstadt, Denham and Dunsmore (2001) have also provided a useful comparison of the theoretical differences between EI, emotional competence and affective competence, which is their own construct—you can refer to their text for the discussion.

Let us consider the following examples of emotionally competent behavior relative to the developmental stage of the child:

1. Joey is ten months old. His gaze follows his mother's movements toward Fred. Fred is her older brother, but a stranger to Joey. Mom smiles broadly, and enthusiastically greets and hugs Fred. She calls out to Joey and brings the tall and unfamiliar male figure to him. Joey keeps scanning his mother's happy expressions and allows the man to pick him up, albeit warily. Mom lovingly puts her arms around both of them. Joey relaxes and smiles at Fred.

2. Four-year-old Natalia attends pre-school. George, three-and-a-half, runs into her as he races around on a tricycle. Natalia falls to the ground, quickly looks around for a caregiver, sees none, and angrily tells George that he has hurt her. George looks blankly at her. Then a caregiver appears, and Natalia starts to howl loudly, throwing herself on the ground again.

3. Nine-year-old Andrew has had a tough day: he was disappointed at being the last child to be chosen for the kick-ball team, his teacher criticized him about something, and now he has to go with his mother to take their dog to the vet. Old Sammy is going to be put down. Andrew is misty-eyed about it as he approaches home. He walks in and sees his mom weeping next to old Sammy. He walks up to her and hugs her, saying, 'Mommy, Sammy loves you too, and he knows he's going to die soon. He wants you to know it's okay for him to go now.' Mom reciprocates his comforting hug, and then they both turn their attention to the sick dog.

4. Fifteen-year-old Susan is outraged that one of the school's social clubs had put up a banner that advertises a rage-rock band known for its anti-female and gay-bashing lyrics. She stomps over to one of the boys at the table and demands that they not advertise the band on the school grounds because the band is discriminatory and contributes to harassment at the school. The boy gives her the finger, which proves her point. She writes up the incident for the school newspaper, sparking a lively debate among the students about free speech and respect.

Each of the above examples shows the growing child's ability to learn from her or his social environment and to figure out how emotions work. This means they learn how to:

1. use the environment as a source of emotional meaning—Joey's social referencing behavior with his mother and Uncle Fred

2. manage emotional expressiveness to their advantage—Natalia's strategic use of exaggerated distress to get attention

3. access their own emotional experience to connect empathically with another— Andrew's action of comforting his mother

4. coordinate their values with their emotional responses, which allows them to facilitate a desired emotional communication with others—Susan's outrage energized her to promote a more desired emotional exchange at her school.

A developmental perspective adds depth and richness to our understanding of emotional processes. It especially highlights the profound importance of contextual influence on the way in which we generate emotions and give them meaning. For further theoretical ideas on this, see Lerner (1998) and Saarni (2000b).

Skills of Emotional Competence

My own work and the work of others who write and conduct developmental research on the construct of emotional competence emphasizes that such competence is a superordinate construct—within this construct, we can examine a number of skills along a developmental trajectory. The skills are interdependent; they dynamically influence the development of other skills of emotional competence. Therefore the skills listed below do not follow a specific sequence. Moreover, each skill is embedded in its social context, which includes the cultural values and beliefs of an individual's society.

The eight skills of emotional competence, as I have formulated them, are as follows (Saarni 1999):

1. *Awareness of our emotional state,* including the possibility that we are experiencing multiple emotions. At more mature levels, awareness that we might *not* be consciously aware of our emotions owing to unconscious dynamics or selective inattention.

2. *skill in discerning and understanding the emotions of others,* based on situational and expressive cues that have a degree of cultural consensus as to their emotional meaning.

3. *skill in using the vocabulary of emotion and expression of terms commonly available* in our subculture. At more mature levels, skill in acquiring cultural scripts that link emotion with social roles.

4. *Capacity for empathic and sympathetic involvement* in others' emotional experiences.

5. *skill in understanding that inner emotional states need not correspond to outer expression,* both in ourselves and in others. At more mature levels, understanding that our emotional-expressive behavior may impact on others and taking this into account in our self-presentation strategies.

6. *skill in adaptive coping with aversive emotions and distressing circumstances* by using self-regulatory strategies that lessen the intensity or temporal duration of such emotional states and by employing effective problem-solving strategies for dealing with problematic situations.

7. *Awareness that the structure or nature of relationships* is largely defined by how emotions are communicated within the relationship.

8. *Capacity for emotional self-efficacy,* in which we view our emotional experience as justified and in accord with our moral beliefs.

We will return to a more detailed discussion of skills 1 to 6, particularly in terms of what facilitates their development and what may hinder their acquisition. I do not address skills 7 and 8 in this chapter because there is little empirical research on what may be the facilitating or inhibiting factors in their acquisition and development. For more information, you can read Saarni, Campos, Camras and Witherington (in press); or Saarni (1999).

We now briefly explore the theoretical foundations of emotional competence. **Mature emotional competence** is the demonstration of self-efficacy in emotion-eliciting social transactions. **Self-efficacy** means that the individual has the capacity and skills to achieve a desired outcome (Bandura 1977). When we apply the notion of self-efficacy to emotion-eliciting social transactions, we are talking about how people can constructively regulate their evoked emotions so that they can simultaneously and strategically apply their knowledge about emotions and their emotional expressiveness to their relationships with others. The outcome is that they can negotiate their way through challenging interpersonal exchanges and manage both their ongoing elicited emotions and their socially communicative expressive behavior. This explanation of mature emotional competence is similar to the description Bar-On gives of emotional intelligence (2004; 2005). However, the developmental perspective emphasizes that the above mentioned desired outcome is based on the moral and cultural values that the individual has acquired through socialization. **Socialization,** by definition, implies development over time as well as a dynamic interaction between what the infant, child, teen or adult contributes to a transaction and what are the social-environmental 'demands' or constraints. This viewpoint is consistent with a functionalist theory of emotion (Campos, Mumme, Kermoian & Campos 1994), which we explore below.

The eight skills of emotional competence are derived from a careful perusal of the developmental research literature on emotion. There are cultural constraints on the degree to which these skills are present or useful across differently structured societies (Chen, Hastings, Rubin et al. 1998). Moreover, there is no single summary score 'test' for emotional competence skills—the skills are not seen as a collective trait or aptitude that children and youth uniformly display across situations. Bar-On's Emotional Quotient Inventory (EQ-i) for school-age children and youth comes closest to providing a combined social-emotional and personality attribute assessment of children's self-reported emotion-related functioning (Bar-On & Parker 2000). The different skills noted above have typically been evaluated in children and youth:

- by having them respond to tasks, like puppet play, designed to elicit their implicit or explicit understanding of emotion-related processes

- by having their parents or teachers systematically rate their emotion-related behavior (see further discussion below, and Chapter 17)

- by interviewing them about their emotional experience, using hypothetical narrative or video vignettes or self-report (Casey 1993; Saarni 1997; Shipman, Zeman, Nesin & Fitzgerald 2003; Zeman & Shipman 1997)
- by observing them directly in emotion-eliciting situations (Saarni 1984; Underwood, Hurley, Johanson & Mosley 1999; Wilton, Craig & Pepler 2000).

There are various caregiver-completed tests that examine young children's general social-emotional adaptation. The outcomes of the tests are influenced by children's temperament, family functioning and cultural context, and by caregiver beliefs, knowledge and bias (Carter, Briggs-Gowan & Ornstein Davis, 2004; M. Lewis 2000). Noteworthy tests are the Vineland Adaptive Behavior Scales (Sparrow, Balla & Cicchetti 1984) and the downward extension of the Child Behavior Checklist (Achenbach & Rescorla 2000). But these inventories are more often used to screen for developmental delay, pathology or school readiness rather than for specific skills of emotional functioning. Carter et al. (2004) have reviewed social-emotional assessment of young children; you can refer to their text for recommendations for practice.

Functionalist Theory of Emotion

A theory of emotion is critical to our understanding of how individuals apply the skills of emotionally competent behavior in their emotionally evocative transactions with the environment. The functionalist theoretical perspective, closely allied with Lazarus' adaptational model of emotion (1991), proposes that emotion is generated when something significant impacts on an individual and thus elicits a readiness to act; in other words, when the individual has a stake in the outcome (Campos et al. 1994). As a consequence, goals and motivation are closely allied with emotion generation: What is the outcome that is desired or that needs to be avoided? Social signals from others are also critical to emotion generation, for they define how some event is meaningful, for example Joey's encounter with Uncle Fred. Social signals are also powerful influences on the generation of emotions such as pride, shame and guilt through the effects of signalled approval or disapproval from others who are considered important. Another influence is hedonic experience: pleasurable stimulation motivates action for repeated experience, and aversive stimulation motivates avoidance. Lastly, our emotion is obviously influenced by memory processes—our emotion-laden recall of an event influences our anticipated emotional reaction to a similar impending event.

The functionalist perspective on emotion helps us to understand that a particular child can develop many different responses that 'serve' a given emotion. For example, Andrew felt sad about the impending loss of the family's dog. He could simply have cried alongside his mother at the prospect, but instead he chose to focus on comforting her in her grief. We could argue that he coped with his own sadness by transforming it through sympathy with his mother, or that he expressed his sadness in a mutually supportive fashion with his mother. Andrew might also feel sad on other occasions and choose to express it by withdrawing for a while as he reminisces about his loss. We all respond to particular emotions in ways that take into account the context in which they were evoked and the particular nuances of our goals in combination with other goals and concerns that confront us as well. By adolescence, youth are well aware that there is considerable variability between a particular evoked emotion and how they express it facially, vocally or kinesthetically, or how they undertake particular actions to remedy the evocative circumstances. As many youth readily explain, 'It depends on whom you're with and what's happening at the time.'

The Power of Social Context

As mentioned, the social context includes cultural beliefs and values, which profoundly influence the meaning that children learn to give to their own emotions and to the situations in which the emotions are elicited. Our very engagement with a particular situation means that we change the context's implications for ourselves. We do this by ignoring some aspects and focusing on other aspects of the situation, or we may alter the situation by assigning to it our own meanings.

We cannot separate emotional experience from the interpersonal context that we have experienced or are currently engaged in. The construct of attachment is an example of this, and we find that under duress, supportive relationships mean a great deal for young children in order for them to be able to access their early manifestations of emotional competence skills (Denham 1999). Frequently, developmental psychologists find that children who have not had secure attachments tend to show weakness in one or more emotional competence skills. For example, Shipman and Zeman (2001) compared matched samples of maltreating and non-maltreating mother-child dyads. The maltreated children expected less support from their mothers and generated fewer constructive strategies for coping with anger as compared to the non-maltreated children. In turn, the maltreating mothers demonstrated less understanding of their children's emotional expressive displays and generated fewer effective strategies for helping their children to cope with emotionally challenging situations in comparison with the non-maltreating mothers.

Furthermore, the physically maltreated children were not as readily able to access coping strategies when they were emotionally aroused; their emotion management skills (see skill 6 below) were restricted in comparison with the children who had more supportive mothers. The interpersonal context in which children live has highly significant implications for the way in which they develop emotional competence skills. And it is important to bear in mind, as we shall examine below, that children also bring something to the equation: their own temperament or disposition (Lengua, Wolchik, Sandler & West 2000).

Developmental Advances and the Skills of Emotional Competence

Next, I review some of the developmental advantages that children gain as they master each of the above mentioned skills over time. We do not focus on infancy and toddlerhood, although many of the emotional competence skills can be inferred as 'proto-manifestations' in the age period of birth to two years. See Saarni et al. (in press) for a discussion of infant emotional development as well as a more detailed discussion of the following emotional competence skills.

Skill 1: Awareness of our emotional state

Children who know what they are feeling also tend to be more able to verbalize what they want; they can articulate what they are happy or angry about and indicate what their goals are. They are more able to negotiate with others when there is a conflict or a need to assert themselves, assuming that they can also modulate their emotional arousal so as to respond to the social exchange. By adolescence, well-functioning youth develop the confidence to disclose their feelings and opinions to others, thereby taking into account their 'true self', and they may choose to express feelings that maintain their sense of dignity, despite negative interpersonal consequences. Moreover, in an early study it was determined that some pre-adolescents recognized that although negative social consequences could occur if they expressed their genuine emotions, they argued that they would still express these emotions because they considered the emotions to be important. From this perspective, the young teens viewed their emotional experience as part of their developing definition of self (see also Harter 1999).

The capacity to be aware of ourselves and our emotional responses is also relevant to the development of the self-conscious emotions of pride, shame, guilt and embarrassment. Owing to their attachment to their parents, children two years old, for example, come to care about their parents' emotionally charged responses toward them, and thus begin to internalize the parental standards for desired behavior. With corresponding cognitive development, young children begin to evaluate whether their performance has met these standards. We can then observe their emotionally expressive behavior display shame, embarrassment or pride in situations that elicit the expected standards. Although the former body of research views the self-conscious emotions as desirable and pivotal to pro-social development (Kochanska & Thompson 1997), there is another situation in which the internalization of standards puts some children at risk. Young children who grow up with chronically depressed mothers appear to develop excessive 'accountability' for their mothers' mood states. The children appear extremely careful in their interaction with others, as though others were fragile, and their behavior includes higher levels of appeasement, apologizing and suppression of negative emotion when compared to young children with non-depressed mothers (Zahn-Waxler 2000; Zahn-Waxler, Kochanska, Krupnick & McKnew 1990).

Research on young adults has shown that personal shame experiences are often associated with a sense of powerlessness and having less control over the situation, as well as feeling exposed to others' negative judgements (Tangney 1995). Furthermore, shame-prone individuals were more likely to externalize blame onto others or onto events, whereas guilt was more often associated with repair. Interestingly, Barrett, Zahn-Waxler and Cole (1993) also found, with regard to toddlers, that the 'amenders' appeared to be feeling guilt over a misdeed rather than the more avoidant behavior displayed by toddlers who appeared to be feeling shame.

Lastly, as touched on above, we must consider whether we can be aware of feeling several emotions at once or in rapid oscillation as we assess a complex situation from various viewpoints and see how our goals are differently affected (Stein, Trabasso & Liwag 2000). The emotional experience of ambivalence is a case in point; for example, in the situation of a family experiencing divorce the child may say, 'I'm glad I get to live with my dad, but I'm sad about not living with my mom too' or 'I love my dad, but right now I'm angry with him for leaving me'. Children can articulate such movement from one emotional response to the other balenced response in late childhood (Harter & Whitesell 1989).

Relative to these factors that facilitate or impede children's learning to become aware of what they experience emotionally, family discourse about emotions has proven to be important for children to acquire emotion concepts (Chambers 1999). In the case of parents who are disengaged, non-supportive, hostile and fragmented in their parenting practices, we also find that the children have difficulties adjusting, and, by implication, difficulties with being able to use their awareness of how they feel in order to regulate their emotional arousal and interaction with their peers (see, for example, Katz & Gottman 1993; Katz & Woodin 2002; McHale, Johnson & Sinclair 1999).

Skill 2: Understanding of the emotions of others

In order to understand others' emotions, children must be able to use situational and expressive cues—both verbal and non-verbal—to infer what others are feeling. This skill requires engagement with others, and thus we find that autistic children, for example, are generally unlikely to develop this skill (Charman, Swettenham, Baron-Cohen et al. 1997; Harris 1989). Moreover, children need to realize that others have minds, intentions, beliefs and inner states (Wellman & Banerjee 1991). Thus children and youth must take into account others' unique personal information and apply that information when inferring others' emotional state (Gnepp 1989).

Sensitivity to others' expressive behavior across different expressive channels begins early in infancy (Thompson, Easterbrooks & Padilla-Walker 2003). Such development allows for the social referencing phenomenon that we see in the example of Joey meeting his uncle for the first time. Joey is able to 'read' his mother's emotional-expressive behavior for meaningful cues as to how he could respond to Fred, in spite of some stranger wariness having developed by that age. Children also learn what the common situational elicitors of emotions are (Gross & Bailif 1991), and when facial expressions and situational elicitors are seemingly contradictory, they opt for whichever cue is presented more clearly or intensely; for example, children looking at a picture of a boy about to get an injection correctly conclude that the boy is feeling scared in spite of the fact that he is smiling weakly (Wiggers & Van Lieshout 1985).

Regrettably, some children grow up in families in which they are often the targets of a high degree of expression of negative emotion by their parents. Isley, O'Neil, Clatfelter and Parke (1999) found that such children were subsequently impaired in their social functioning with their peers. Similarly, Schultz, Izard and Ackerman (2000) found that parental depression and family instability predicted pre-school children's anger attribution bias, which in turn was associated with peer rejection. Their teachers also rated these children as prone to aggression, that is, if they perceived anger in a peer and believed it was directed at themselves, they were more likely to react with preemptive aggression. Furthermore, maltreated children are more likely to show poor ability in understanding others' facial expression cues (Pollack et al. 2000). Finally, children who grow up in homes scarred by domestic violence and spousal abuse also show deficits in emotion understanding and are frequently rated by teachers as aggressive, more often in the case of boys, or depressed, more often in the case of girls. Thus, exposure to chronic adult hostility and anger places a child at risk for aversive emotion socialization experience, which also affects negatively their relations with peers (Katz & Woodin 2002; Kolbo 1996; Osofsky 1999).

By contrast, social competence has been found to be greater when children are more accurate in understanding others' emotional experience (Cassidy, Parke, Butkovsky & Braungart 1992; Denham, McKinley, Couchoud & Holt 1990; Denham, Mitchell-Copeland, Strandberg et al. 1997). Likewise, when children were skillful in taking others' perspectives and understanding others' beliefs and feelings, they were also better able to coordinate their conversations with peers (Slomkowski & Dunn 1996). The implication that I draw from these results is that these children are better negotiators—a skill that is particularly useful in situations characterized by disagreement or conflict. This conclusion is also suggested by research undertaken by Garner and Estep (2001), who found that pre-school children's ability to provide explanations for the causes and consequences of others' emotions was a significant predictor of the children initiating social interaction as well as being chosen as recipients of social bids. In short, these children were more often engaged with their peers in mutually satisfying play.

Not surprisingly, what promotes children's social competence and their parallel understanding of others' emotional experience appears to be family life that is supportive of the children's developing awareness of their own emotions. The children are not mocked for experiencing the 'vulnerable' emotions of sadness and fear. Supportive parents talk about emotions, model the appropriate self-regulation when they themselves experience strong affect, and do not invalidate or dismiss their own or their children's feelings (Gottman 1998; Gottman, Katz & Hooven 1997).

Skill 3: Use of an emotion lexicon

Using language and symbols, children can travel through time and space to communicate with others about their own and others' emotions. Modern technology promotes this exchange. Youth are especially keen to take advantage of the communication afforded by cellphones, 'instant messaging', web log sites or 'blogs', and email, for example. When children communicate their emotions to another, they learn that the other's response to them may modify their subjective feeling state for better or for worse. They can feel comforted or they may also risk being shamed (Barrett 1997). Research on family discourse, especially conversations between parents and their children, has been found to be pivotal for children's acquisition of emotion-descriptive language, for their understanding of the social influences involved in emotion communication (Denham & Auerbach 1995) and for their comprehension of the causes of emotion (Dunn, Bretherton & Munn 1987). This last investigation also indicated that access to an adult who is interested in their emotional reactions may be highly significant in children's willingness to talk about emotions and have their understanding of emotions elaborated. Mothers tended to use conversations about emotional responses as a functional way of guiding or explaining something to their children, whereas the children were more likely to use emotion-descriptive words simply to comment on their own reaction or observation of another. Thus, they were learning to communicate their own self-awareness of emotion states to their mothers, who in turn were likely to communicate meaningfulness to their children by using guiding, persuading, clarifying or otherwise interpretive emotion-related language.

Another study sheds further light on the issue. Dunn and Brown (1994) found that families in which there was considerable anger and distress had children who were less likely to be engaged in discourse about emotional experience. By contrast, if families were low in frequency of negative emotion expression, then when an emotional event that was negative for the child did occur, there was a greater likelihood of an emotion-related conversation ensuing between child and parent. Thus this research suggests that children's acquisition of emotion-descriptive language is anchored in relationship contexts—if everyone is angry or distressed much of the time, an instance of the child displaying distress may be viewed as trivial; the family may meta-communicate that the child's emotional reaction is not very important. Indeed, other studies confirm that differences in the families' emotional milieus provide varying preparatory stages for their children's later emotional experiences in the world beyond the home (Du Rocher Schudlich, Shamir & Cummings 2004; Laible 2004).

Children's ever-maturing skill at representation allows them to develop complex links between emotional experience and socially communicated scripts that facilitate a shared understanding of expectations of how people will act and respond emotionally (Russell & Ridgeway 1983; Russell, Fernández-Dols, Manstead & Wellenkamp 1996). In her illustrative developmental research, Fivush (1991) found that mothers in the US tended to talk with greater elaboration about sadness with their daughters and about anger with their sons. She also found that when anger was involved, the mothers tended to emphasize relationship repair with their daughters, but were more accepting of retaliation by their angry sons. Lastly, in cases of severely abused and traumatized children and youth, research has indicated that there may well be a deficit in representing emotional experience. Thus, these children and youth are unable to access their emotional experience in ways that would permit them to work through the trauma by verbally sharing it with a therapist. Clinicians have described this as 'alexithymia', and substantiating research has been undertaken by Camras, Sachs-Alter and Ribordy (1996) with regard to maltreated children.

Skill 4: Capacity for empathy and sympathy

Attentiveness to emotional-expressive cues begins early in infancy and thus appears to pave the way for the development of empathy and sympathy. **Empathy** is an immediate emotional response that the observer experiences on witnessing another's emotional state. With empathy, we vicariously experience a similar emotional reaction as the target. **Sympathy** can be elicited by responding to both witnessed emotional experience and purely symbolic information about the other's emotional plight. Sympathy also contains elements of sorrow or concern for the distressed person. When feeling sympathetic, we do not necessarily vicariously experience the identical negative affect as the target (Eisenberg 2003).

In a number of studies, Eisenberg and her colleagues have found that children need to establish psychological boundaries so that they can respond sympathetically and not be overwhelmed by their vicarious emotional response. If such response distresses them, they could become preoccupied with coping with their own arousal and can no longer focus on the needs of the other. Sympathy and any accompanying pro-social behavior are short-circuited in this situation. Zahn-Waxler and Robinson (1995) suggest that personal distress reactions are most likely to occur when the other's emotional-expressive behavior is particularly vivid and intense, and if there appears to be little that the child can do to improve the other's distressing situation.

We need to address how empathy and sympathy combine with our personal values to predict socially responsible behavior that is accompanied by compassion. Children whose parents model compassion and believe that people should help others in distress are more likely to behave pro-socially (Chapman, Zahn-Waxler, Cooperman & Iannotti 1987). Adolescents with

conduct disorder are particularly noteworthy for failing to respond empathically (Cohen & Strayer 1996), and are more likely to have had negative family
experiences.

From a developmental perspective, empathy is based on the attachment
relationships that the infant has with its caregivers. Joint attention, social
exchange and cooperative turn-taking between caregiver and the infant create
'a world of shared meaning, empathic understanding and appropriate linking
of one's own emotions with those of others that then generalize beyond
the parent-child dyad' (Zahn-Waxler 1991:156). More recently, Strayer and
Roberts (2004) found that parental empathy predicted child empathy, but
not directly—it was mediated by the child's frequency and intensity of
anger. Empathic parents had children who were not angry, but low-empathy
parents were controlling of their children, with the result that the children
were more prone to anger and, in their own turn, unlikely to be empathic.
Thus, it was a cycle of the child's anger and the parents' resulting controlling disciplinary style that was associated with reduced empathy in their
children.

The socialization of sympathy seems to be influenced by parental modelling
of sympathetic responses and also by the parents' attitudes toward controlling
their children's emotional displays. Parents applying restrictive parental
attitudes toward their children's expression of vulnerable emotions such as
sadness or fear were more likely to have young children who reacted with
personal distress rather than with sympathy (Eisenberg, Fabes, Schaller et al.
2004). More recently, Valiente and colleagues also found that a high level
of parental negative expressive style was associated with their children's
likelihood of experiencing personal distress rather than sympathy (Valiente,
Eisenberg, Fabes et al. 2004). Once again we see that parental derogation
of their child ill-prepares the child for harmonious relationships with others.
This outcome was further substantiated in a longitudinal study that followed children into adulthood (Koestner, Franz & Weinberger 1990).
These investigators found that empathic concern in adulthood was most
strongly related to fathers' involvement in childcare, parental affection
expressed toward their children and parental inhibition of children's
aggression.

The development of empathy and its link, through sympathy, with altruistic
behavior clearly promotes the well-being of others in distress. The well-being
of children and youth who respond empathically and sympathetically is also
facilitated—they enjoy more favorable relations with others, they themselves
may become more effective parents, and they are able to regulate their emotional
arousal such that they can effectively intervene to assist others. Empathy and
sympathy work together with the skills we have examined thus far to provide
for the development of cooperative behavior, thereby facilitating social-
emotional competence. (See also Arsenio and Lemerise (2001) for a discussion
of poor empathy and weak social values in bullies.)

Skill 5: Management of emotional expressiveness

Children learn to manage their expressive behavior by taking into account relationship dimensions such as closeness of the relationship, power or status similarity/difference, and the degree to which they are exposed, for example a public versus private situation. Older children are also more likely to report that both dissembled and genuine emotional-expressive behavior is regulated (see research reviewed in Saarni 1999). Evaluation of school-age children's responses to interview questions about hypothetical vignettes yielded the following four general categories for when children expected the protagonists to dissemble the expression of how they felt (Saarni 1979):

1. Avoidance of a negative outcome, for example getting in trouble, getting hurt.

2. Protection of their self-esteem, for example adopting the stoic emotional 'front' or acting cool, and avoidance of expressing vulnerable feelings such as fear or sadness so that they would not be teased.

3. Maintenance or enhancement of relationships, for example concealing their real feelings so that another's feelings will not be hurt by their otherwise blunt honesty.

4. Observance of norms and conventions, for example being polite or observing etiquette scripts like 'You should smile when you receive a gift, even if you don't like it'.

Whether children actually manage their expressive behavior according to these motivational categories is likely to be dependent on how intense their genuine feelings are, as well as on their relationship with the interactant. In the same early research study, I found that children believed it would be acceptable to express genuine feelings with almost anyone if they were obviously physically hurt or if a catastrophe had occurred. In short, intensity of felt emotion—as appropriate to the eliciting situation—moderated whether the children would express it directly or not, regardless of audience.

Children's skill at self-presentation includes their ability to manage how they express their emotional reactions. Controlling angry arousal and limiting their aggression and hostile feelings is obviously appropriate for harmonious peer interactions; once again, we find that children are influenced by the emotion socialization processes in their families of origin. Children living with parents—who themselves have difficulty with anger management, who behave toward their partners and children with hostility and contempt, and who inadequately provide support and encouragement for their children's experience of emotionally challenging situations—have difficulty acquiring the social skills and emotional communicative strategies necessary for friendship development and behavior adjustment (Davies, Forman, Rasi & Stevens 2002; Katz & Woodin 2002). Children learn to manage their emotional-expressive behavior when they grow up in a family that talks about and appropriately models emotions, and their elicitation and consequences. Moreover, management is facilitated by a supportive parent being available in a situation that emotionally challenges the child—a parent who sympathetically hears what the child has to say, provides reasoned alternatives and helps the child to modulate their emotional arousal so that the child can begin to learn how to manage their self-presentation effectively. Essentially, an effective emotion-socializing parent is a good emotion coach. (See Gottman, Katz and Hooven (1997) for an elaboration of parental coaching on emotion.)

Skill 6: Effective emotion regulation and adaptive coping

When children effectively regulate their emotional arousal, they use strategies that modify its intensity, duration or aversiveness. Thereby, they exert 'effortful control' over their disposition to react emotionally in ways that might otherwise not be adaptive for them. For example, among adults, reacting with road rage to a driver who cuts sharply into the lane is not effective emotion regulation. We can feel exasperated with the rude driver, but by adulthood an emotionally competent driver would react to the situation with humor, by distracting themselves from it, or by simply taking some deep breaths and soothing their initial disposition to becoming angry. An instance that children often encounter is how to cope with an injection. Most children report that they do not like injections, but the variability in their emotional responses to the prospect of having to get an injection is considerable. A supportive parent and an understanding medical professional help to 'scaffold' for the child: they think of ways for the child to endure the unpleasant event and to recover as quickly as possible afterwards. Shaming or deceiving the child are not appropriate scaffolding strategies. Providing a health rationale, coaching the child in breathing or counting strategies, telling a distracting story or simply providing sympathetic reassurance are all more helpful to the young child.

Closely linked to emotion regulation is the action of coping with distressing circumstances. We must regulate our emotional arousal so that we can pay attention to the situation at hand requiring a response. As children mature, they increasingly make more accurate appraisals of the problematic situation and what is realistically under their control regarding it. They learn societal values about effective and ineffective coping (Saarni 1997a). However, this does not mean that in a moment of intense negative affect children (or adults) will remember to cope effectively, especially if they fail to calm their emotional arousal. Being able to access their awareness of how they feel and to verbalize that feeling can be helpful to children (and adults) as a way of containing the emotional arousal and then considering how to cope with the aversive circumstances. This modulation of emotional arousal allows the child to continue attending to what is going on socially or to the challenges they face (Gottman, Katz & Hooven 1997). In some situations, children can avoid negative emotional escalation by circumventing problems (Eisenberg, Spinrad, Fabes et al. 2004). Effective coping provides the child or youth with a sense of mastery and enhances their resilience should they be faced with similarly aversive circumstances in the future (Luthar, Doernberger & Zigler 1993).

The primary facilitator of children's acquisition of adaptive emotion regulation and coping is, once again, family support—it allows children to explore a range of emotions without condemnation (Ramsden & Hubbard 2002). Such support, as well as secure attachments, is associated with less likelihood of substance abuse and less stress as reported by adolescents (Howard & Medway 2004). Moreover, family structure provides a safe and predictable place in which children can experience diverse emotions (Valiente et al. 2004). Parents who use inductive discipline strategies also promote more effective coping in their children insofar as such children are also more pro-social (Krevans & Gibbs 1996). Lastly, research has shown that children who enjoy both family support and structure have a larger repertoire of coping strategies (Hardy, Power & Jaedicke 1993). Clearly, having access to such a repertoire permits children to adapt to a wider variety of emotion-provoking circumstances.

Children also contribute to the acquisition of this sixth skill: their temperament-related dispositions influence not only their responses to emotionally evocative situations—such as threshold and latency—but also the ways in which their caregivers respond to them. To the extent that a child is temperamentally 'soothable' (Thompson et al. 2003) and to the degree that the older child can access effortful control in resisting impulsive behavior (Eisenberg et al. 2004), parents and teachers alike find it easier to provide guidance and scaffolding support. Young children who can self-soothe or respond to the soothing actions of others are more able to learn how to regulate their emotional arousal. With adequate emotional regulation, they learn how to exert effortful control over challenging situations, which enhances their mastery and ultimately promotes their learning of the skills of emotional competence. Unfortunately, research by Lawson and Ruff (2004) suggests that there was a temperamental 'double hazard' comprising young children who exhibited a proneness to negative emotionality and also demonstrated difficulty in their ability to pay attention. Such children were more likely to show a decline in cognitive functioning over time as well as to have more problems with behavioral adjustment in the pre-school years. A child presenting with this 'double hazard' requires better attuned parenting, greater environmental consistency and support, and caring support for their learning to regulate their proneness to negative emotional arousal and to sustain their attention.

Conclusion

There are many links between the skills of emotional competence and the broad models of adult EI described by Bar-On (2004; 2005; Bar-On & Parker 2000) and Mayer and Salovey (1997; Mayer, Salovey, Caruso & Siarenios 2001). Emotional self-awareness, perception of the emotions of others, access to empathic concern for others, management of emotional-expressive behavior and modulation of emotional reactivity are relevant both to EI and emotional competence skills. The developmental perspective that I presented here emphasizes the dynamic interplay between the socializing influences of families and peers and that which the children themselves contribute to acquiring these skills. Furthermore, these skills are not acquired sequentially—each skill reciprocally influences the differentiation of the other skills. It would be simplistic to state that awareness of our own emotions appears normatively at age 18 months, for example. Indeed, our awareness of our emotional states is refined and becomes more complex throughout childhood and adolescence, and is influenced by our growing emotion lexicon, and our ability to regulate emotional arousal, to manage our expressiveness and to be open to the emotional experiences of others.

In light of the interdependence of the emotional competence skills, parents and teachers can be reassured that their efforts to provide guidance, support and opportunities for conceptual elaboration and exploration of emotional experience will bolster the development of *every* skill. By contrast, chronic shaming and exposure to family violence and hostility are now well-documented risk factors for children in the acquisition of the basic skills of competent emotional functioning.

In summary, talking about emotions with children provides children with cognitive learning opportunities; modelling emotional competence skills provides children with experiential and concrete exposure, and constitutes an excellent way for adults to be 'emotion coaches'; treating children with respect for their developmentally appropriate emotional experience while giving them sensitive and supportive scaffolding facilitates their further acquisition of emotional competence skills. Broad cultural values and specific moral and ethical concerns are also part of learning these skills, and children and youth are responsive to adult influence when adults themselves live their lives with dignity and authenticity. It is likely that these adults have mastered EI and apply their talent and attributes in interactions with their children and youth.

References

Achenbach, T., & L. Rescorla. 2000. Manual for the ASEBA preschool forms and profiles. Burlington, VT: University of Vermont.

Arsenio, W., & E. Lemerise. 2001. Varieties of childhood bullying: Values, emotion processes, and social competence. *Social Development* 10:59–73.

Bandura, A. 1977. Self-efficacy: Toward a unifying theory of behavioral change. *Psychological Review* 84:191–215.

Bar-On, R. 2004. The Bar-On Emotional Quotient Inventory (EQ-i): Rationale, description and summary of psychometric properties. In *Measurement of emotional intelligence: Common ground and controversy.* Ed. G. Geher, pp. 115–45. Hauppauge, NY: Nova Science Publishers.

———. 2006. The Bar-On model of emotional-social intelligence (ESI). *Psicothema* 18.

Bar-On, R., & J.D. Parker, 2000. *The Bar-On Emotional Quotient Inventory: Youth Version (EQ-i:YV).* Toronto, Canada: Multi-Health Systems.

Barrett, K.C. 1997. Emotion communication and the development of the social emotions. *New Directions for Child Development* 77:69–88.

Barrett, K.C., C. Zahn-Waxler, and P.M. Cole. 1993. Avoiders versus amenders: Implications for the investigation of guilt and shame during toddlerhood. *Cognition and Emotion* 7:481–505.

Campos, J.J., D. Mumme, R. Kermoian, and R.G. Campos. 1994. A functionalist perspective on the nature of emotion. In Fox, vol. 59, pp. 284–303.

Camras, L., E. Sachs-Alter, and S. Ribordy. 1996. Emotion understanding in maltreated children: Recognition of facial expressions and integration with other emotion cues. In Lewis and Sullivan, pp. 203–25.

Carter, A.S., M. Briggs-Gowan. and N. Ornstein Davis.. 2004. Assessment of young children's social-emotional development and psychopathology: Recent advances and recommendations for practice. *Journal of Child Psychology and Psychiatry* 45:109–34.

Casey, R. 1993. Children's emotional experience: Relations among expression, self-report, and understanding. *Developmental Psychology* 29:119–29.

Cassidy, J. 1994. Emotion regulation: Influences of attachment relationships. In Fox, Vol. 59, pp. 228–49.

Cassidy, J., R. Parke, L. Butkovsky, and J. Braungart. 1992. Family-peer connections: The roles of emotional expressiveness within the family and children's understanding of emotions. *Child Development* 63:603–18.

Chambers, S.M. 1999. The effect of family talk on young children's development and coping. In *Learning to cope: Developing as a person in complex societies*. Ed. E. Frydenberg, pp. 130–49. Oxford, U.K.: Oxford University Press.

Chapman, M., C. Zahn-Waxler, G. Cooperman, and R. Iannotti. 1987. Empathy and responsibility in the motivation of children's helping. *Developmental Psychology* 23:140–45.

Charman, T., J. Swettenham, S. Baron-Cohen, A. Cox, G. Baird, and A. Drew. 1997. Infants with autism: An investigation of empathy, pretend play, joint attention, and imitation. *Developmental Psychology* 33:781–89.

Chen, X., P. Hastings, K. Rubin, H. Chen, G. Cen, and S. Stewart. 1998. Child-rearing attitudes and behavioral inhibition in Chinese and Canadian toddlers: A cross-cultural study. *Developmental Psychology* 34:677–86.

Cohen, D., and J. Strayer. 1996. Empathy in conduct disordered and comparison youth. *Developmental Psychology* 32:988–98.

Davies, P.T., E.N. Forman,, J. Rasi, and K. Stevens. 2002. Assessing children's emotional security in the interparental relationship: the security in the interparental subsystem scales. *Child Development* 73:544–63.

Denham, S., and S. Auerbach. 1995. Mother-child dialogue about emotions. *Genetic, Social, and General Psychology Monographs* 121:311–38.

Denham, S., M. McKinley, E. Couchoud, and R. Holt. 1990. Emotional and behavioral predictors of preschool peer ratings. *Child Development* 61:1145–52.

Denham, S., J. Mitchell-Copeland, K. Strandberg, S. Auerbach, and K. Blair. 1997. Parental contributions to preschoolers' emotion competence: Direct and indirect effects. *Motivation and Emotion* 21:65–86.

Denham, S.A. 1999. *Emotional development in young children.* New York: Guilford.

Du Rocher Schudlich, T., H. Shamir, and E.M. Cummings. 2004. Marital conflict, children's representations of family relationships, and children's dispositions towards peer conflict strategies. *Social Development* 13:171–92.

Dunn, J., I. Bretherton, and P. Munn. 1987. Conversations about feeling states between mothers and their young children. *Developmental Psychology* 23:132–39.

Dunn, J., and J. Brown. 1994. Affect expression in the family: Children's understanding of emotions, and their interactions with others. *Merrill-Palmer Quarterly,* 40:120–137.

Eisenberg, N. 2003. Prosocial behavior, empathy, and sympathy. In *Well-being: Positive development across the lifecourse.* Ed. M. Bornstein and L. Davidson, pp. 253–65. Mahwah, NJ: Erlbaum.

Eisenberg, N., R. Fabes, M. Schaller, G. Carlo, and P.A. Miller. 1991. The relations of parental characteristics and practices to children's vicarious emotional responding. *Child Development* 62:1393–1408.

Eisenberg, N., T. Spinrad, R. Fabes, M. Reiser, A. Cumberland, S. Shepard, C. Valiente, S. Losoya, I. Guthrie, and M. Thompson. 2004. The relations of effortful control and impulsivity to children's resiliency and adjustment. *Child Development* 75:25–46.

Fivush, R. 1991. The social construction of personal narratives. *Merrill-Palmer Quarterly* 37:59–82.

Fox, N. Ed. 1994. *The development of emotion regulation. Monographs of the Society for Research in Child Development.* Chicago: University of Chicago Press.

Garner, P. W., and K. Estep. 2001. Emotional competence, emotion socialization, and young children's peer-related social competence. *Early Education and Development* 12:29–48.

Gnepp, J. 1989. Children's use of personal information to understand other people's feelings. In Saarni and Harris, pp. 151–80.

Gordon, S.L. 1989. The socialization of children's emotions: Emotional culture, competence, and exposure. In Saarni and Harris, pp. 319–49.

Gottman, J. 1998. *Raising an emotionally intelligent child.* New York: Fireside (Simon & Schuster).

Gottman, J., L.F. Katz, and C. Hooven. 1997. *Meta-emotion.* Hillsdale, NJ: Erlbaum.

Gross, A. L., and B. Bailif. 1991. Children's understanding of emotion from facial expressions and situations: A review. *Developmental Review* 11:368–98.

Halberstadt, A.., S. Denham, and J. Dunsmore. 2001. Affective social competence. *Social Development* 10:79–119.

Hardy, D., T. Power, and S. Jaedicke. 1993. Examining the relation of parenting to children's coping with everyday stress. *Child Development* 64:1829–41.

Harris, P. L. 1989. *Children and emotion: The development of psychological understanding.* Oxford, U.K.: Basil Blackwell.

Harter, S. 1999. *The construction of the self.* New York: Guilford Press.

Harter, S., and N. Whitesell. 1989. Developmental changes in children's understanding of single, multiple and blended emotion concepts. In Saarni and Harris, pp. 81–116.

Howard, M. S., and F. Medway. 2004. Adolescents' attachment and coping with stress. *Psychology in the Schools* 41:391–402.

Isley, S.L., R. O'Neil, D. Clatfelter, and R.D. Parke. 1999. Parent and child expressed affect and children's social competence: Modeling direct and indirect pathways. *Developmental Psychology* 35:547–60.

Katz, L. F., and J. Gottman. 1993. Patterns of marital conflict predict children's internalizing and externalizing behaviors. *Developmental Psychology* 29:940–50.

Katz, L.F., and E.M. Woodin. 2002. Hostility, hostile detachment, and conflict engagement in marriages: Effects on child and family functioning. *Child Development* 73:636–52.

Kochanska, G., and R. Thompson. 1997. The emergence and development of conscience in toddlerhood and early childhood. In *Parenting and children's internalization of values: A handbook of contemporary theory.* Ed. J. Grusec & L. Kuczynski, pp. 53–77. New York: Wiley.

Koestner, R., C. Franz, and J. Weinberger. 1990. The family origins of empathic concern: A 26-year longitudinal study. *Journal of Personality and Social Psychology* 58:709–17.

Kolbo, J. R. 1996. Risk and resilience among children exposed to family violence. *Violence and Victims* 11(2): 113–28.

Krevans, J., and J. Gibbs. 1996. Parents' use of inductive discipline: Relations to children's use of empathy and prosocial behavior. *Child Development* 67:3263–77.

Laible, D. 2004. Mother-child discourse in two contexts: Links with child temperament, attachment security, and socioemotional competence. *Developmental Psychology* 40:979–92.

Lawson, K.R., and H.A. Ruff. 2004. Early attention and negative emotionality predict later cognitive and behavioural function. *International Journal of Behavioral Development* 28(2): 157–65.

Lazarus, R.S. 1991. *Emotion and adaptation.* New York: Oxford University Press.

Lengua, L. J., S.A. Wolchik, I.N. Sandler, and S.G. West. 2000. The additive and interactive effects of parenting and temperament in predicting adjustment problems in children. *Journal of Clinical Child Psychology* 29:232–44.

Lerner, R.M. 1998. Theories of human development: Contemporary perspectives. In *Handbook of child psychology,* vol. 1, *Theoretical models of human development.* 5th ed. Ed. R.M. Lerner, pp. 1–24. New York: Wiley.

Lewis, M. 2000. Self-conscious emotions: Embarrassment, pride, shame, and guilt. In Lewis and Haviland-Jones, pp. 623–36.

Lewis, M.L. 2000. The cultural context of infant mental health: The developmental niche of infant-caregiver relationships. In *Handbook of infant mental health.* Ed. C. H. Zeanah, pp. 91–107. NY: Guilford.

Lewis, M., and J. Haviland-Jones, Eds. 2000. *Handbook of Emotions* 2nd ed. New York: Guilford Press.

Lewis, M., and M.W. Sullivan, Eds. 1996. *Emotional development in atypical children.* Mahway, NJ: Erlbaum.

Luthar, S., C. Doernberger, and E. Zigler. 1993. Resilience is not a unidimensional construct: Insights from a prospective study of inner-city adolescents. *Development and Psychopathology* 5:703–17.

McHale, J.P., D. Johnson, D., and R. Sinclair. 1999. Family dynamics, preschoolers' family representations, and preschool peer relationships. *Early Education and Development* 10:373–401.

Mayer, J.D., and P. Salovey. 1997. What is emotional intelligence? In *Emotional development and emotional intelligence: Educational implications.* Ed. P. Salovey and D.J. Sluyter. New York: Basic Books.

Mayer, J.D., P. Salovey, D. Caruso, and G. Siarenios. 2001. Emotional intelligence as a standard intelligence. *Emotion* 1.232–42.

Osofsky, J. 1999. The impact of violence on children. *The Future of Children* 9(3): 33–49.

Pollack, S.D., D. Cicchetti, K. Hornung, A. Reed. 2000. Recognizing emotion in faces: Developmental effects of child abuse and neglect. *Developmental Psychology* 36:679–88.

Ramsden, S., and J. Hubbard. 2002. Family expressiveness and parental emotion coaching: Their role in children's emotion regulation and aggression. *Journal of Abnormal Child Psychology* 30:657–67.

Russell, J.A. 1991. Culture and the categorization of emotion. *Psychological Bulletin* 110:426–50.

Russell, J., and D. Ridgeway. 1983. Dimensions underlying children's emotion concepts. *Developmental Psychology* 19(6): 795–804.

Russell, J.A., J.M. Fernández-Dols, A. Manstead, and J. Wellenkamp. (Eds.). 1996. *Everyday conceptions of emotion: An introduction to the psychology, anthropology, and linguistics of emotions.* Hingham, MA: Kluwer.

Saarni, C. 1979. Children's understanding of display rules for expressive behavior. *Developmental Psychology* 15:424–29.

———. 1984. An observational study of children's attempts to monitor their expressive behavior. *Child Development* 55:1504–13.

———. 1997. Coping with aversive feelings. *Motivation and Emotion* 21:45–63.

———. 1999. *The development of emotional competence.* New York: Guilford Press.

———. 2000. The social context of emotional development. In Lewis and Haviland-Jones, pp. 306–22.

Saarni, C., J. Campos, L. Camras, and D. Witherington. in press. Emotional development: Action, communication, and understanding. In *Handbook of child psychology,* vol. 3, *Social, emotional, and personality development* 6th ed. Ed. N. Eisenberg. New York: Wiley.

Saarni, C., and P.L. Harris. Eds. 1989. *Children's understanding of emotion.* New York: Cambridge University Press.

Saarni, C., D. Mumme, and J. Campos. 1998. Emotional development: Action, communication, and understanding. In *Handbook of child psychology* vol. 3, *Social, emotional, and personality development.* 5th ed. Ed. N. Eisenberg, pp. 237–309. New York: Wiley.

Schultz, D., C. Izard, and B. Ackerman. 2000. Children's anger attribution bias: Relations to family environment and social adjustment. *Social Development* 9:284–301.

Shipman, K., and J. Zeman. 2001. Socialization of children's emotion regulation in mother-child dyads: A development psychopathology perspective. *Development and Psychopathology* 13:317–36.

Shipman, K., J. Zeman, A. Nesin, and M. Fitzgerald. 2003. Children's strategies for displaying anger and sadness: What works with whom? *Merrill-Palmer Quarterly* 49:100–22.

Slomkowski, C., and J. Dunn. 1996. Young children's understanding of other people's beliefs and feelings and their connected communication with friends. *Developmental Psychology* 32:442–47.

Sparrow, S., D. Balla., and D. Cicchetti. 1984. *Vineland Adaptive Behavior Scales: Expanded form manual.* Circle Pines, MN: American Guidance Service.

Stein, N., T. Trabasso, and M. Liwag. 2000. A goal appraisal theory of emotional understanding: Implications for development and learning. In Lewis and Haviland-Jones, pp. 436–57.

Strayer, J., and W.L. Roberts. 2004. Children's anger, emotional expressiveness, and empathy: Relations with parents' empathy, emotional expressiveness, and parenting practices. *Social Development* 13:229–54.

Tangney, J.P. 1995. Shame and guilt in interpersonal relationships. In Tangney and Fischer, pp. 114–39.

Tangney, J.P. and K. Fischer. Eds. 1995. *Self-conscious emotions: The psychology of shame, guilt, embarrassment, and pride.* New York: Guilford Press.

Thompson, R., M.A. Easterbrooks, and L. Padilla-Walker. 2003. Social and emotional development in infancy. In *Handbook of Psychology*, vol. 6, *Developmental Psychology.* Ed. R. Lerner, M.A. Easterbrooks, and J. Mistry, pp. 91–112. New York: Wiley.

Underwood, M., J. Hurley, C. Johanson, and J. Mosley. 1999. An experimental, observational investigation of children's responses to peer provocation: Developmental and gender differences in middle childhood. *Child Development* 70(6): 1428–46.

Valiente, C.,N. Eisenberg, R. Fabes, S. Shepard, A. Cumberland, and S. Losoya. 2004. Prediction of children's empathy-related responding from their effortful control and parents' expressivity. *Developmental Psychology* 40:911–26.

Wellman, H., and M. Banerjee. 1991. Mind and emotion: Children's understanding of the emotional consequences of beliefs and desires. *British Journal of Developmental Psychology* 9:191–214.

Wiggers, M., and C. van Lieshout. 1985. Development of recognition of emotions: Children's reliance on situational and facial expressive cues. *Developmental Psychology* 21:338–49.

Wilton, M., W. Craig, and D. Pepler. 2000. Emotional regulation and display in classroom victims of bullying: Characteristic expressions of affect, coping styles and relevant contextual factors. *Social Development* 9:226–45.

Zahn-Waxler, C. 1991. The case for empathy: A developmental review. *Psychological Inquiry* 2:155–58.

———, C. 2000. The development of empathy, guilt, and internalization of distress: Implications for gender differences in internalizing and externalizing problems. In *Anxiety, depression, and emotion.* Ed. R.J. Davidson, pp. 222–65. New York: Oxford University Press.

Zahn-Waxler, C., G. Kochanska, J. Krupnick, and D. McKnew. 1990. Patterns of guilt in children of depressed and well mothers. *Developmental Psychology* 26:51–59.

Zahn-Waxler, C., and J. Robinson. 1995. Empathy and guilt: Early origins of feelings of responsibility. In Tangney and Fischer, pp. 143–73.

Zeman, J., and K. Shipman. 1997. Social-contextual influences on expectancies for managing anger and sadness: The transition from middle childhood to adolescence. *Developmental Psychology* 33:917–24.

—— 3 ——

Emotionally Intelligent Parenting

Robin Stern and Maurice J. Elias

Introduction

In this chapter, we address two aspects of EI that are integral to parenting: on the one hand, the most important competencies of EI for parents to teach their children and, on the other hand, the most important competencies of EI for parents to embody as daily role models for their children. These aspects become intertwined in the course of most parenting decisions and action. However, in order for us to understand each aspect and its importance to parenting more deeply, we look at the aspects separately. Working from an ecological theory which sees individual behavior as resulting from influences at multiple levels—from immediate, small group contexts to organizations to national customs—we recognize that the most powerful influences on children are in their microsystems, and, within those, the most salient figures are the parents or guardians with whom they live. Hence, we focus on how EI theory and practice can make these essential interactions more likely to affect children's emotional growth in beneficial ways. Certainly, the accumulated evidence with regard to influences on children's behavior suggests that modelling EI is a powerful way of teaching children how to be aware of and manage their own social-emotional lives—a key to success in life. It begins at home.

Key Arenas for Emotionally Intelligent Parenting

Most EI theories cover several emotional and social domains. Typically, these include:

- recognizing, understanding and regulating strong emotions
- expressing feelings non-destructively
- recognizing and understanding how others feel
- relating well interpersonally
- solving problems of a personal and interpersonal nature as they arise.

(Bar-On 1997; 2005; Elias, Zins, Weissberg et al. 1997; Shelton & Stern 2003)

Children learn these skills by interacting with others, especially those with whom they have the most frequent face-to-face contact. The contexts for the inter-actions—households, childcare settings, classrooms, playgroups, camps, after-school programs and religious institutions—are microsystems, and these are the most powerful levels of socialization (Belsky 1984). As children grow up, their parents serve as the key gatekeepers with regard to their experiences within most microsystems. Yet parents' own EI skills are likely to exercise a strong influence on how they deal with the microsystems through which their children pass.

Thus we propose that there is a strong connection between the EI skills that parents demonstrate every day and the EI skills that they teach their children. From EI theory and our own experience, parents' ability to impart EI skills to their children is most often thwarted when parents get emotionally derailed in the course of parenting (Elias, Tobias & Friedlander 2000; Shelton & Stern 2003). This in turn has a negative impact on microsystems in ways that further impede the likelihood of enhancing children's EI skills. In this chapter, we use three arenas to show how parents can better manage their strong feelings and thereby create more opportunities for children to develop their EI skills. The arenas are limit setting, parent-child communication and children's friendships.

Limit setting: The emotional strain of saying no

Imagine this: a six-year-old asks for a cookie before dinner. His mother doesn't usually like her children to have sugar, especially just before a meal, but she agrees because the boy has been at home with the sniffles and is feeling grumpy. He has the cookie, and then wants another. His mother says, 'No, one was a special treat for today and that's it.' But he goes straight to the jar, takes another cookie and stuffs it into his mouth. What is his mother to do? It is not the end of the world, but he did violate a limit that she set. Should she ignore it? Should she punish him? Should she make an exception? After all, there are exceptions in life.

Here is another common scenario: Craig, father of two, has clear rules around bedtime. His daughter watches a TV show at 8:00, then he reads her a story and she goes to bed at 8:30. It's a Thursday night. At 8:45, Craig is exhausted, his wife is not at home, and his daughter has firmly planted herself on the couch sobbing and begging to watch 'one more show'. Craig barely has the energy to pick up the remote to turn off the power. What should he do?

One of the most essential and, at the same time, challenging aspects of emotionally intelligent parenting—or *any* approach to parenting, for that matter—is limit setting. It is imperative that parents demonstrate the importance of having emotional boundaries in relationships; boundaries with regard to health and wellness, and, perhaps the most contested of all, boundaries when it comes to consumption and entertainment.

It seems as if setting limits should be easy for parents: they decide what they think is best, they tell the child the parameters, and if the child violates those parameters, the parents enforce a consequence. But in fact setting limits, and sticking to them, is probably one of the most difficult jobs in parenting. No matter how much parents have read about limit setting and no matter how practiced they are at articulating those limits, it simply will not work if they cannot tolerate the feelings that inevitably arise when they say no. Most parents know these feelings well: discomfort, exhaustion, frustration, sadness and anger, among others.

Parents need to be aware that setting limits, whether for a child of 3 or 13, is a challenge. This is because parents want to give their children everything, they want to be there for them at all times, and they don't want them to be uncomfortable or unhappy. Children find limits difficult too, because they are new at delaying gratification. Study after study shows that it is this new and developing ability—to want and to delay; to manage impulses, desires and emotions—that predicts success later in life (Mischel, Shoda & Rodriguez 1989). Consequently, parents are doing children a great disservice if they respond to their needs and concerns immediately and do not give them the chance to develop a capacity for emotional self-control.

Initially, setting limits can be fairly straightforward. Parents often begin by setting limits for children based on definitions of safety. Telling a three-year-old not to stick his toy in a light socket is clear enough. Likewise, ensuring that a little girl has a healthy lunch for kindergarten is something within a parent's control and is based on shared knowledge about nutrition.

But as children mature, limit setting becomes increasingly subjective and challenging. During preteen and teen years, parents set limits for a variety of reasons, such as health, safety, achievement, values and religion. Sometimes parents do not agree with a decision their teenagers are making, or they see them as endangering their emotional safety. At this level, parents can continue to exert their choices over their children's choices. Parents need to be the ones ultimately in charge and setting the limits. It is natural that children come up against these limits and try to challenge them.

For this reason, parents may know a great deal about setting limits and even may be well practiced at articulating those limits, but they will struggle to *carry out* the limit setting if they cannot tolerate what they feel while saying no to their child. As mentioned above, limit setting is complicated because it conflicts with other powerful parental motivations, which mainly are to give their children things rather than to be a source of restriction, to want to be there for them, and not to be the cause of their children's discomfort or unhappiness.

When limits are made around safety issues, parents have less trouble setting or defending them because they feel more conviction and less doubt. When parents must defend limits that are not associated directly with safety issues, they are likely to be less firmly convinced. And it is here that children may press their advantage. It is uncomfortable and often exhausting to deal with a child who challenges us. It can wear a parent out.

It is worth reiterating that the most difficult and crucial aspect of limit setting is standing firm and following through.

As parents, you can set and maintain effective boundaries using these guidelines:

- Think about your limits before setting them.
- Be clear about the limits with your children, so that boundaries do not become an issue.
- Explain your reasoning behind the limits whenever possible—'Because I said so' is not an effective and long-lasting explanation for children.
- Be clear about the consequences when children violate the limits.
- Make sure that these consequences are equal for each of your children.
- *Always* follow through on the consequences—if you say you are going to do something, do it. But if you said something in anger and you have no plan of enforcing it, tell your child that you spoke in haste and anger and then provide a consequence on which you indeed plan to follow up.
- When possible, enforce the consequences yourself.
- Involve your children, when appropriate, in defining and defending limits within the household.
- Make sure all parental figures and caregivers are aware of the boundaries in your family.
- When your children have respected the boundaries, let them know how much you appreciate their actions.
- Demonstrate respect for boundaries and limits in your own life. You are the model!

Undoubtedly, parents have a great responsibility to help their children to define and defend boundaries in their own lives on a daily basis. The process of setting and maintaining limits is central to this task. The more children practice setting these boundaries collaboratively and creatively in a supportive environment, the more they will develop the skill to set limits effectively as they negotiate their own lives.

Emotionally intelligent parenting ultimately recognizes the powerful emotions that parents experience in limit setting and other key parenting arenas, and focuses on helping parents to manage these emotions rather than allowing themselves to get emotionally hijacked. In such circumstances, parents are least likely to function in ways they will be proud of and from which children will learn the best socialization messages. Furthermore, key EI skills are necessary for both parents and children to successfully resolve the challenges that limit setting and related situations pose.

As mentioned above, addressing both the process and the consequences of limit setting depends on key components of EI theory. Establishing, explaining and maintaining limit setting are all closely related to parents regulating strong emotions and using creative problem-solving methods. Concomitantly, respecting limits requires children to exercise emotional self-control, express feelings non-destructively and think of alternative solutions to problems. Parenting focused on EI recognizes that parents are most likely to employ their highest level of skills when they have their strong emotions under control.

Of course, there will be times when children persist in defying limits, putting themselves or others in harm's way. In this case, parents can approach counsellors, school psychologists or social workers, or teachers for their perceptions of the child's actions. They can also consider a referral for professional assistance in and/or outside school.

Careful and accurate listening

There are many compelling reasons for parents to listen to their children actively and to create meaningful dialogue. For example, the literature on substance abuse prevention illustrates that parents need to know what is happening in children's key microsystems, such as classmates and friends, in order to support their children to 'just say no' (Greenberg, Weissberg, O'Brien et al. 2003).

Here is another scenario: Sarah, 14, arrives home after an afternoon with friends and seems sullen and distracted. As her father is preparing dinner, he notices Sarah sulking around the kitchen, opening and closing the refrigerator door, checking and rechecking her cellphone for new messages. 'What's wrong, honey?' he asks, concerned. 'Nothing,' Sarah immediately replies. Why is this scene so familiar to many parents? Why do children often have such a hard time opening up to parents when they are obviously upset? How can parents overcome the frustration of this lack of communication and encourage their children to tell them when things go wrong?

Children feel reluctant to talk to parents for many reasons. Though parents may be excellent listeners in workplace situations, with friends or colleagues and with spouses, they often do not apply the most basic rules of active listening in their communications with their children. Parents can become overly outcome-oriented, focusing more on finding out specific kinds of information or simply wanting to hear that things are okay, rather than having a meaningful exchange. Releasing expectations is one of the first steps to a good dialogue taking place between parents and children. The goal is for parents to get to know their children, not to interview or interrogate them.

Thus, it is critical that parents show authentic interest in having a conversation with their children only when they actually have the time to listen. For example, parents should not ask a child how a relationship break-up is going while reading the mail. Emotional subjects like these can be deeply upsetting and difficult for youth to open up about—a parent must respect the depth and complexity of these feelings, especially with regard to social situations. Furthermore, instead of asking pointed questions about a child's grade on a quiz, a parent is likely to learn more by letting their child talk about what is important *to them* at the time. A question like, 'So how are things going with your friends?' lets a child lead the discussion and may even uncover issues the parent did not know existed. It also avoids the child becoming irritated with the parent for failing, in their view, to keep up to date with their daily lives.

A parent also can model sharing about their life by telling carefully chosen stories from the day or week. In this case, parents must be sure to avoid long-winded anecdotes that might alleviate their frustration but could well bore the children! Parents who share consistently teach children that sharing is a part of beneficial communication between people. Furthermore, children learn the value and process of reflection from hearing their parents reflect as they talk about their lives. These days, many people lament the loss of civility among communities and families, and attribute it to the transfer of storytelling—a significant form of reflection—from grandparents, extended family members and close friends to less personal media outlets.

Sharing stories from our own lives is also a powerful way of teaching EI skills to children. Specifically, storytelling invokes the skills of recognizing and understanding how others feel, expressing feelings clearly, and communicating in understandable, sequential ways. Indeed, emotionally intelligent parenting highlights the key role of emotion in all communication. Careful and accurate listening requires an individual to have sufficient emotional self-control not to talk and adequate emotional self-awareness to effectively understand how others feel. (We call this empathy, and Carolyn Saarni discussed this in Chapter 2.) As children observe and participate in effective listening, they will gradually come to appreciate how the interpersonal world works. This includes learning that:

- they cannot have effective social interactions without being able to recognize and understand feelings in others
- they cannot recognize and understand the feelings of others if they are unable to recognize and understand those feelings in themselves
- good emotional self-regulation is important as it helps them to listen without talking, when necessary, and to talk when it is important to do so.

This skill building does not occur didactically—it occurs in the course of everyday communication. And adult-child communication is asymmetrical: adults have to pay more attention to children's developmental perspective than vice versa. If considering tension with a friend, for example, a parent can mention it to her child in this way: 'I'm trying to figure out how to let my friend know that she's hurting my feelings. It got me down today.' A parent should not assume that the 'stuff' of their life is over the child's head. Parents should not burden children with the details of office politics, divorce or illness, but letting their children know that they too are working through challenges or feeling good about a recent success shows the children that these conversations, and the bonding that results, is at the heart of family life.

In this regard, however, parents need to be careful not to see themselves as therapists. Instead, best practice dictates that parents can be effective when they give advice *if asked for it,* but they should not assume, or appear to assume, that they have the answers to all of life's problems. The 'I'm the parent and I know it all' kind of approach will only serve to make a child feel disempowered, or even judged. Instead, the best path for a parent eager to hear from their children involves giving thoughtful feedback when asked, being reflective, and—authentically but rarely—thinking of parallel examples from their own life. It is important that children know that parents faced adolescence too...and survived!

It is also crucial that parents manage their own expectations about when and how an exchange should happen. Think about Karen, who has a 7-year-old son and a 14-year-old daughter. Karen may wish for an intimate talk when she says goodnight to her children, but they are exhausted from a long day at school and on the sports field. Karen needs to find out her children's best times to open up to conversation. Some parents try to chat with their children over breakfast. This is usually unsuccessful as many youth and teenagers are groggy and irritable at this time of the morning. Again, parents need to know their children, and be aware that their best times of day may not always coincide. For example, Karen might have more success if she chose lunchtime or dinnertime in which to elicit a conversation with her children. Whenever a family finds time, they should make sure that it is conducive to both parent and child giving their undivided attention.

Parents sometimes find it torturous to wait for the right time to ask the right questions. The EI skill of self-management is critical here, along with empathy and creative problem-solving methods. Karen needs to be aware that what she wants to know about her daughter may emerge when they are making dinner together and casually chatting, and not when Karen says outright, 'How was your day?'. Sarah's father in the scenario above was frustrated when he heard her brief reply of 'okay' to his question, 'How are things going with your friends?'. But by managing his own feelings and waiting for her to approach him, he was able to have an intimate and meaningful conversation with her about some tough social issues.

Building bonds: Supporting children in making and maintaining friendships

Think about this scenario: Merette, a nine-year-old with bright eyes, comes home from school. In the afternoon, her mother notices that she wanders around the house or watches TV without really paying attention. 'What's the matter, honey?' her mother asks. 'Nothing,' Merette mumbles. Mom repeats the question. This time, Merette tentatively replies, 'Nobody wanted to play with me today.' Her eyes fill with tears. Her mother feels upset. What should she say?

Parents are often faced with disconcerting moments in which they need to support their children through challenging social situations. It is crucial for Merette's mother, and any parent in this kind of situation, to be self-reflective, to think about her own social style and history before reacting to her daughter's social struggle with a gut-level response. Parents need to ask themselves: What were my childhood friendships like? Was it easy or difficult for me to make new friends or maintain friendships? Do I thrive in social situations or do I prefer to be alone? Has that changed since I was young, or have I always felt that way?

This kind of soul searching is the significant first step for parents concerned with helping their children to form and maintain good friendships. Merette's mother may reflect and realize that she was always the center of her group of friends, surrounded by people who were eager to spend time with her. If she goes into a conversation with her daughter assuming that Merette will be the same, she will be making a grave mistake and will fail to learn more about her daughter. It is all too common, and destructive, for parents to project their histories or preferences onto their children. Instead, they should reflect on and use their history with careful consideration.

To this end, parents must ask themselves: What is my social style and how is this similar, or different, from my child's social style? It can happen that outgoing parents will have children who desire and feel comfortable with time spent alone, while parents who prefer their own company can have children who are happiest in a large group of friends. It is the parents' responsibility to closely self-examine their assumptions and judgements about their child's social style, and act appropriately.

It is also important that parents practice the habit of self-reflection during an interaction with their children. Merette's mother should analyze her gut reaction to Merette's problem while they are talking about the issue. This type of reaction can be deeply connected to her historical experiences and will certainly affect the way she is able to support Merette in this difficult time. She needs to pay attention to Merette's social style, considering whether Merette wants to be the center of attention or would prefer to be alone.

Self-awareness is a skill that we can learn, just as it is a skill for parents to manage the emotions that arise when they and their children discuss problems that the children may be experiencing. Parents need to bear in mind that these conversations are about the children, not about themselves. This is an essential part of effective parenting. It takes a self-aware parent to give a child guidance without projecting and support without assuming. Being patient and reasonable will also facilitate the conversation.

Conversations about friendship that parents and children can have hold many opportunities for teaching. Parents can show their children how to read non-verbal cues, how to enter a group and start a dialogue, and how to handle silence. These conversations can serve as building blocks for children's social skills, as well as a chance for intimacy between parents and their children to be enhanced.

It is vital for parents to foster their children's emotional and social intelligence in order to help them to improve their friendships, or to become more 'befriend-able' (Elias et al. 2000). Building bonds is basic to every relationship as well as other social and vocational commitments. Friendship encompasses the skills we discussed in the parenting arenas of limit setting and active listening, and emphasizes social awareness, or empathy, as the basis for interactions and relationships to be effective, cooperative, constructive and mutually satisfying. Friendship is extremely difficult, if not impossible, to achieve and sustain if we cannot recognize and understand how others feel. For adults and children alike, this skill adds value because the relationships that it facilitates are extremely rewarding and make our lives richer and more fulfilling than they are when we exist in isolation.

Children can do things that will help others to like them, or prevent others from liking them. With children, parents can discuss the following points in an effort to build the emotional and social competencies that lead to true friendships:

- Think about how they have made friends in the past. What did they do that helped the relationship to be successful?

- Be brave—make the first move. For some children, it is easier to make friends on a one-to-one basis than in groups. Parents should encourage the child to identify a person with whom they would like to be friends, and think about what they both would enjoy doing, such as watch a movie, play a game or listen to music. Then they can invite the person to do this. Parents can suggest that, when they are together, the child asks questions to find out what the person does and does not like.

- Try new activities. Particularly in the case of preteens and adolescents, good friendships come out of shared experiences. This tends to work best with new groups of children other than their classmates or those in the community. Parents should encourage their children to sign up for social clubs, sports teams and events, school performances, extracurricular activities, library programs, religious institution groups, or group lessons in music or dance. In groups, people share their interests, work together and start to care about each other. Activities in these groups can continue over quite some time, which allows good friendships to be cemented.

As research on EI in the workplace strongly suggests, some skills play a role in a person getting a job and others that are involved in the person keeping that job and managing difficult work situations (Druskat, Sala & Mount 2005). This is also true of friendships (Brackett, Warner & Bosco 2005). Friendships evolve over time. With their children, parents can discuss the following points for addressing tensions within new and old friendships and helping these relationships to flourish:

- When there is a **problem:** Parents can help their children to realize that everyone experiences good and bad days, and that friends can experience them together. Children should be encouraged to consider what has happened, and think about restoring the relationship rather than holding a grudge. Some children find it easier to express friendship difficulties and disappointments in the form of a letter or email to a parent or other trusted person. Whether the letter or message is sent or not, the child may find that simply putting their feelings into words can be cathartic or clarifying.

- When the friendship is becoming **boring or repetitive:** Parents should encourage their children to find out about their friends' likes and dislikes, the places they have been to and want to go to, their favorite foods and books and movies, and so on. Similarly, children should share their own preferences and experiences with their friends. In this way, it should be easy for the children to think of something new to do or even simply to talk about together.

- When the child **spends time alone** because they cannot think of anything exciting to do with their friends: Children do not always need to do exciting things—one of the good things about a friendship can be simply spending time together. This is one of the vital messages of the emotionally intelligent approach to parenting: relationships matter more than activities.

- When **interpersonal issues** arise: A troubled friendship can elicit powerful emotions. Parents can help their children in this situation by enacting a kind of role reversal. The parent can pretend that the problem the child is having is a problem that another child is having. The parent can say, for example: 'My friend's son is nine. His friends at school teased him about his torn shirt. What do you think I should say to her that she can tell her son?'. The child will probably know that the parent is actually referring to them, but they will usually play along and try to think of a solution to the issue.

- When **rumors and gossip** arise: This can be one of the most important tests of a friendship. Our emotional fight-and-flight centers are highly attuned to betrayal. Therefore, parents need to advise children to be loyal and not to gossip in their friendships. Parents may overhear their children gossiping or see rumors being spread by email or cellphone messages, in which case they should wait for a quiet moment in which to discuss the matter with their child. They need to point out that gossip is a negative action, whether it is spoken or written. Because email allows people to communicate without being face to face, children may succumb to the temptation to gossip first because they do not see the harm they may cause to the person about whom they are gossiping, and second because they may feel they will not be found out. In this way, the potential for anonymity in email can be as problematic as peer pressure—both can make it challenging for children to behave as true friends should. With attention to building children's EI skills, especially empathy, parents can help them to realize the implications of what they say about others and can guide them in developing rewarding and lasting friendships.

- When children **feel used:** Friendship requires equal participation and effort from all members of the relationship. Children will feel used if their friends visit them and play with their toys in the afternoons but ignore them at school, for instance. Parents can help their children to recognize when they are being used, and at the same time to have the consideration not to do this to others.

Fostering children's emotional intelligence

Fortunately, it is within the reach of many parents to provide their children with everything they need for social, emotional and academic growth, as well as for the development of sound character. CASEL, available on the internet at www.casel.org, plays a leading role in identifying these factors and is an excellent resource for educators and parents. According to Elias, Tobias and Friedlander (2002), parents should pay attention to these suggestions:

- **Appreciation:** Praise children for trying new things, for not conforming to what their peers are doing, and for taking care of household or school responsibilities, no matter how small.

- **Sense of belonging:** Help children to participate in local sports events, extracurricular activities and group hobbies, but avoid overload. Focus on activities that are meaningful and have the potential to be lasting.

- **Confidence:** Encourage children to make an effort with regard to tasks and projects, and to follow through their commitments. Notice and celebrate their accomplishments.

- **Competencies:** Help children to build skills necessary for meeting household and family responsibilities, working in groups and teams, and exercising leadership. Encourage them to view doing chores as preparation for adult life. Help them to build their study and planning skills for projects and assignments.

- **Contributions:** Involve children in family decisions about helping others, encouraging them to give some of the gifts they receive to those in greater need. In this way, they will learn about the benefits of being involved in the community.

When parents and guardians focus on these factors, they engender positive, lasting, caring and respectful relationships with their children. These factors also serve as important guidelines for educators as they structure the classrooms, formulate the school rules, and consider extracurricular opportunities for their students.

Conclusion

We suggest that parents who wish to raise their children to be emotionally intelligent would do well to use the tenets of EI to guide their parenting. We have explored three prominent arenas in which parent-child interactions take place to illustrate how parents can respond to situations in ways that will foster their children's emotional and social competencies. The examples that we provided reflect our experience that parents should not underestimate the potential of their children for emotional and social growth. We have witnessed remarkable progress, especially when parents open their minds and hearts to the possibilities of change in their children and in themselves. The reward can be a marked improvement in the quality of and satisfaction with their family life.

While there is comprehensive anecdotal and practice-based support for the techniques we have put forward, we recognize that controlled research studies are lacking. This is a valuable arena for future work, especially from a cross-cultural and international perspective. While further knowledge is gathered, however, we urge parents and guardians to become increasingly aware of their own EI capabilities and to use this chapter and related resources when interacting with their children. In so doing, they can help their children to be well prepared for the joys and challenges of life in an ever-more complex adulthood.

References

Bar-On, R. 1997. *The Bar-On Emotional Quotient Inventory (EQ-i): Technical manual.* Toronto, Canada: Multi-Health Systems.

———. 2006. The Bar-On model of emotional-social intelligence (ESI). *Psicothema* 18.

Belsky, J. 1984. The determinants of parenting. A process model. *Child Development* 55:83–96.

Brackett, M.A., R.M. Warner, and J.S. Bosco. 2005. Emotional intelligence and relationship satisfaction among couples. *Personal Relationships* 12:197–212.

Druskat, V., F. Sala, and G. Mount. Eds. 2005. *Linking emotional intelligence and performance at work: Current research evidence.* Mahwah, NJ: Lawrence Erlbaum.

Elias, M.J., S.E. Tobias, and B.S. Friedlander. 2000. *Emotionally intelligent parenting: How to raise a self-disciplined, responsible, socially skilled child.* New York: Three Rivers Press/Random House.

———. 2002. *Raising emotionally intelligent teenagers.* New York: Three Rivers Press/Random House.

Elias, M. J., J.E. Zins, R.P. Weissberg, K.S. Frey, M.T. Greenberg, N.M. Haynes, R. Kessler, M.E. Schwab-Stone, and T.P. Shriver. 1997. *Promoting social and emotional learning: Guidelines for educators.* Alexandria, VA: Association for Supervision and Curriculum Development.

Greenberg, M.T., R.P. Weissberg, M.U. O'Brien, J.E. Zins, L. Fredericks, H. Resnik, and M.J. Elias. 2003. School-based prevention: promoting positive social development through social and emotional learning. *American Psychologist* 58(6/7): 466–74.

Mischel, W., Y. Shoda, and M. Rodriguez. 1989. Delay of gratification in children. *Science* 26:933–38.

Shelton, C. and R. Stern. 2003 *Understanding emotions in the classroom: Differentiating teaching strategies for optima teaching.* Port Chester, NY: National Professional Resources.

—— 4 ——

School-Family Partnerships to Enhance Children's Social, Emotional and Academic Learning

Evanthia N. Patrikakou and Roger P. Weissberg

Introduction

Parents and educators want children to be knowledgeable, responsible and caring. They want children to have the foundational social, emotional and academic skills to succeed in school and life. The realization of such potential depends, to a great degree, on the contexts within which children develop and learn, as well as on the connections linking those contexts (Christenson & Sheridan 2001; Epstein 2001; Patrikakou, Weissberg, Redding & Walberg 2005).

From the onset of a child's life, the context of the family and the relationships formed among family members are profound catalysts of cognitive, emotional and social development. From the critical bonding of infancy to the later years of development and citizenship, families are the first context and socialization system in which a child's skills interact with the immediate environment and result in personal and social growth. (See Chapters 2 and 3 for factors that impact on emotional development and suggestions for parents to enhance their children's social-emotional competence.)

Society and the nature of life experiences of children and youth changed dramatically during the 20th century. In addition to dynamic demographics, changes include:

- increased economic and social pressures on families
- weakening of community institutions that nurture children's emotional, moral and social development
- unmediated access to media, such as the internet, that potentially encourages behavior that can damage health.

(Weissberg, Walberg, O'Brien & Kuster 2003)

Such changes make it critical that schools work effectively with families to address children's academic, social, emotional and character development (Christenson & Havsey 2004). In fact, parent involvement and social-emotional learning are being included in educational policies today, and several federal and state mandates are calling for increased parent involvement or include SEL standards along with the various academic ones (Moles 2005; Redding & Sheley 2005). Unfortunately, many educators have been better prepared to work directly with children rather than collaboratively with families. Furthermore, they are not nearly as well prepared to enhance children's social-emotional competence as they are to teach reading and math, for example (Chavkin 2005).

The importance of school-family partnerships to foster children's full development has also been underlined by decades of work in social competence promotion and EI that have indicated that children develop social-emotional skills both through instruction and by observing how adults interact with each other (Bar-On & Parker 2000; Elias, Zins, Weissberg et al. 1997; Goleman 1995; Greenberg, Weissberg, O'Brien et al. 2003; Zins, Weissberg, Wang & Walberg 2004). Therefore, given today's social milieu, collaboration and communication between home and school are critical to ensure that parents and teachers provide children with common and mutually reinforcing messages about the importance of learning and pro-social, responsible behavior (Christenson & Sheridan 2001; Fantuzzo, Tighe & Childs 2000). When parents and teachers work meaningfully together, they both extend children's learning opportunities and demonstrate crucial relationship skills which children can emulate.

In light of this increased need to better understand school-family partnerships and how they can enhance children's social-emotional development and academic performance across several developmental stages, in this chapter we explore:

- social-emotional learning
- school-based SEL programming that involves parents in meaningful ways
- the common important ingredients that SEL programs include to best reach out to parents.

Children's Social-Emotional Learning

SEL is the process through which children:

- develop awareness and management of their emotions

- set and achieve important personal and academic goals
- use social awareness skills and interpersonal skills to establish and maintain positive relationships
- demonstrate decision-making and responsible behaviors to achieve success in school and life.

(CASEL 2003; Elias et al. 1997; Payton, Wardlaw, Graczyk et al. 2000)

Social-emotional education provides a framework for the coordination of school, family and community prevention of problem behaviors and promotion of positive youth development efforts (CASEL 2003; Elias et al. 1997). Critical components of effective programs include:

- developmentally and culturally appropriate SEL classroom instruction
- student engagement in constructive activities in the classroom, school and community
- ongoing student, family and teacher involvement in planning, implementing and evaluating the program.

(Greenberg et al. 2003)

SEL contributes to children's positive psychological development, social relationships, health and academic performance. For example, research indicates that developing children's SEL skills not only enhances peer acceptance but also improves their sense of self-worth, their self-confidence and their competence in handling daily responsibilities and stresses (Greenberg et al. 2003; Zins et al. 2004). Furthermore, SEL programming improves academic performance, grade retention, attendance and graduation rates, as well as reduces suspensions and expulsions (Durlak & Weissberg 2005; Zins et al. 2004). By enhancing SEL competencies, we also help to prevent high risk behaviors, such as drug use and violence (see, for example, Greenberg et al. 2003; Wilson, Gottfredson & Najaka 2001). Because these psychosocial, academic and health behaviors share many risk and protective factors, and can be addressed by similar intervention strategies, there is growing national support for implementing better coordinated approaches that prevent these behaviors and promote positive youth development (Catalano, Berglund, Ryan et al. 2002).

The most important SEL skills

According to CASEL (2003), the following five core sets of competencies are essential for success in school and life:

1. **Self-awareness**—recognizing our emotions and values, and being able to realistically assess our strengths and limitations.
2. **Self-management**—being able to set and achieve goals, and handling our emotions so that they facilitate rather than interfere with the task at hand.
3. **Social awareness**—showing understanding and empathy for the thoughts and feelings of others.

4. **Relationship skills**—establishing and maintaining healthy relationships, working effectively in groups, and dealing constructively with conflict.
5. **Responsible decision-making**—making ethical, constructive choices about personal and social behavior.

CASEL is working with the State of Illinois in the US to provide national leadership in defining and setting standards for quality education to promote children's social-emotional development. Recently, the Illinois legislature and governor passed the Children's Mental Health Act of 2003. This legislation called upon the Illinois State Board of Education (ISBE) to develop and implement a plan for incorporating social-emotional development as part of the Illinois Learning Standards. The ISBE convened a broadly representative group of educators and parents with expertise in instruction, curriculum design and child development to craft these standards, which have been approved and posted on ISBE's website (ISBE 2005).

The Illinois SEL standards, which are based on CASEL's framework, are organized around three goals:

1. Develop self-awareness and self-management skills to achieve school and life success.
2. Use social awareness and interpersonal skills to establish and maintain positive relationships.
3. Apply decision-making skills and responsible behaviors in personal, school and community contexts.

Table 4.1 lists the standards for these goals.

The 10 SEL standards are specific statements of the knowledge and skills that pre-school to high-school students should be able to demonstrate. Each standard includes five benchmarks, or learning targets, that specify developmentally appropriate knowledge and skills for the following levels, used in the US:

1. Early elementary—Grades K–3.
2. Late elementary—Grades 4–5.
3. Middle/junior high—Grades 6–8.
4. Early high school—Grades 9–10.
5. Late high school—Grades 11–12.

As teaching SEL skills becomes an increasingly important part of the educational landscape, it is important for us to explore practical and evidence-based ways through which these skills can be integrated in school curricula and reinforced at home. Next, we present a general description of evidence-based programs that educators use to enhance their students' SEL and the coordinated strategies they provide to involve families in the process.

School-Based SEL Programming and Family Involvement

There are many school-based SEL programs that claim to promote SEL skills. Some of the programs systematically involve parents in order to enhance the generalizability of student-acquired SEL skills and strengthen the home-school interconnection. Unfortunately, most do not actually do so. The best SEL practices involve students, parents, community members and educators as partners in program planning, implementation and evaluation. Increasingly, parents are collaborating with schools to select and maintain planned, systematic, social-emotional education from pre-school to high school. When educators and parents adopt SEL programs, it is important for all concerned to remember that effective programs:

- teach children to apply SEL skills and ethical values in daily life
- build connection to school through caring, engaging classroom and school practices
- provide developmentally and culturally appropriate instruction
- are multi-year efforts that address academic performance, health, social relationships and citizenship in coordinated ways.

Table 4.1   Illinois State Board of Education learning standards for SEL

Goal	Corresponding Standards
Develop self-awareness and self-management skills to achieve school and life success.	• Identify and manage one's emotions and behavior. • Recognize personal qualities and external supports. • Demonstrate skills related to achieving personal and academic goals.
Use social-awareness and interpersonal skills to establish and maintain positive relationships.	• Recognize the feelings and perspectives of others. • Recognize individual and group similarities and differences. • Use communication and social skills to interact effectively with others. • Demonstrate an ability to prevent, manage, and resolve interpersonal conflicts in constructive ways.
Demonstrate decision-making skills and responsible behaviors in personal, school and community contexts.	• Consider ethical, safety, and societal factors in making decisions. • Apply decision-making skills to deal responsibly with daily academic and social situations. • Contribute to the well-being of one's school and community.

(Source: www.isbe.net/ils/social_emotional/standards.htm)

CASEL (2003) examined 242 nationally available prevention and positive youth development programs, and systematically evaluated the quality of 80 multi-year programs. Ratings focused on the following:

- The instructional practices that each program used to promote student application of SEL skills beyond classroom lessons.
- Program benefits on student behavior as documented by rigorous research.
- Professional development and technical assistance to support program implementation.
- The coordination of instruction with school-wide, family involvement and community involvement practices.

CASEL (2003) rated 22 of the programs 'high' across these dimensions and named them 'CASEL Select Programs'.

Because home involvement is so important for the generalizability and sustainability of SEL skills, CASEL (2003) applied a four-point rating scale to evaluate the extent and quality of each program's efforts to make family involvement an integral part of its content and implementation. The scale points ranged from 'no structured family involvement' to 'structure provided for consistent family involvement through use of multiple well-designed strategies'.

Twelve CASEL Select Programs received the highest rating for involving parents through a comprehensive outreach approach. Table 4.2 lists the programs and describes the parent component.

When we review the family component of these programs, three common themes arise that we need to be bear in mind when searching for a comprehensive SEL program that goes beyond classroom instruction to integrate other social environments crucial for a child's healthy development. We will now briefly explore each theme (Henderson & Mapp 2002; Patrikakou et al. 2005):

1. **Communication between home and school:** Program designers and practitioners recognize that two-way communication between home and school is the most important factor promoting children's social competence. Communication needs to be positive, ongoing, consistent and persistent in order to yield a solid home-school collaboration and family participation in meeting SEL goals. *General communication* entails information about the program's goals; *specific communication* involves the child's actual progress in the program. Whether general or specific, communication is the key to forming and maintaining meaningful and productive home-school connections. Usually, communication is embedded in the programs as the main ingredient in multiple levels and units. Thus, parents are kept informed about the curriculum, about their children's progress, and about ways in which they can reinforce what their children are learning in the classroom to promote positive development and prevent diverse problem behaviors.

For example, the PATHS program provides teachers with specific suggestions about ways to involve parents throughout the program and encourages

Table 4.2 SEL programs with exemplary parent involvement components

Program Name	Grades	Parent Component Description
Caring School Community www.devsu.org	K–6	• Includes a component with extensive family activities • A guide, *Homeside Activities*, for each grade level involves parents and encourages parent-child interactions • English and Spanish versions are available • Pre- and post-activity discussions in class around *Homeside Activities*
Know Your Body www.kendallhunt.com	K–6	• Each of the program modules at all grade levels has interactive family activities • Letters are sent home at the beginning of each module to inform parents of the content discussed in class
Lions-Quest ("Skills Series") www.lions-quest.org	K–12	• Program includes parent workshops, materials, interactive home activities, and other family resources • English and Spanish versions are available for certain materials • *Family Connections*, a guide for K–5, details parent meetings for each grade • *The Surprise Years: Understanding you Changing Adolescents*, a book for parents of older students detailing the changes that occur in early adolescence and ways parents can be supportive
Michigan Model of Comprehensive Health Education www.emc.emich.edu	K–12	• Several lessons include *family resources* informing parents of program content and how to reinforce learning at home • Provides materials and activities for family meetings

Program	Grades	Description
PATHS (Promoting Alternative Thinking) www.preventionscience.com	K–6	• Provides parent handbooks with information about the curriculum and ways parents can reinforce school-based SEL learning at home • Teachers' instructional manual includes specific suggestions for ways to involve parents throughout the program • Program encourages orientation meeting for parents, annual or semiannual follow-up meetings, and classroom parent visits to observe or volunteer during a PATHS lesson
Peace Works www.peaceeducation.org	K–12	• Parent component offers informational materials and training in conflict resolution • A parent guide, *Fighting Fair for Families*, offers families with information on conflict resolution and the creation of a positive, nurturing environment • Implementation manual for the parent component includes large group presentations, small group, interactive activities, and training sessions for the entire family
Reach out to Schools: Social Competency Program www.open-circle.org	K–5	• Parent component with multiple sessions aims to familiarize families with skills and language children are learning in the program • Implementation manual for the parent component includes several handouts and a parent workbook • Frequent newsletters keep parents apprised of program content and vocabulary
Resolving Conflict Creatively Program www.esrnational.org	K–8	• Parent component with multiple units to introduce parents to creative conflict resolution and the promotion of peace through effective communication • Several handouts assist teachers to communicate with families
Responsive Classroom www.responsiveclassroom.org	K–6	• Includes parent reports as part of the main program components • Offers family letters to keep parents apprised • Encourages parent visits during the *morning meeting*

Program	Grade	Description
Second Step www.cfchildren.org	Pre-K–9	• Family component with multimedia resources to involve parents in the process of building children's social and emotional skills • Includes a multi-session parent workshop on the skills children learn • Frequent letters home inform and encourage parents to practice at home the skills learned in class • Invitations to parents to participate in classroom program lessons • Encourages the integration of social and emotional learning aspects in parent-teacher conferences
Skills, Opportunities, and Recognition (SOAR) www.preventionscience.com	K–6	• Family component includes newsletters, tips for parents, and outreach services • Multi-session family workshops promote bonding to the family, improve parent-child communication, create a positive home learning environment, and enhance children's school success, and ways to reduce risk factors and strengthen protective factors related to substance abuse in children
Voices: A Comprehensive Reading, Writing, and Character Education Program www.aboutvlf.com	K–6	• All thematic units include a wide variety of family activities in discussing books and practicing literacy and social skills • Provides letters home informing families what children are studying in each theme and suggesting specific ways in which parents could be involved • Family members are invited at school to participate in certain activities

(Source: CASEL 2003)

orientation and follow-up meetings to keep parents actively informed. Other programs, such as Reach Out to Schools and Second Step, offer multiple sessions or workshops to familiarize families with the skills and language that their children are learning in class. In general, during the implementation of these programs, information is shared with families in a variety of ways—ranging from newsletters, workshops, big and small group meetings to one-to-one parent-teacher meetings—and most offer opportunities for family involvement at home and at school.

2. **Parent involvement at home:** CASEL Select Programs provide specific strategies and support through which teachers can involve parents, such as activities and materials that reinforce and extend classroom learning at home. Such structures help teachers to facilitate the process in a more efficient way, and provide parents with the specificity needed to make their involvement meaningful in light of the complexity of the school curriculum and demands on their time. For example, the Caring School Community program provides educators with a guide for each grade level that involves parents and encourages parent-child interaction. The program also facilitates parent involvement at home and parent-child-school communication by including pre- and post-activity discussions in class around the relevant activities. Parent-child interaction encouraged by SEL programs yields multiple benefits as it fosters improved children's applications of SEL skills to daily problems and challenges at school and home, as well as socially competent communication and interaction among family members. It is important to emphasize the bi-directional nature of family involvement. It is the outcome of school outreach. In turn, it also informs classroom-based work in various ways, such as classroom presentations based on the family activity that was completed at home, and feedback from parents about the child's progress. This keeps the programmatic activities grounded in the realities of the specific school and the families that it serves.

3. **Parent involvement at school:** Given the demands of modern life, involving families at school presents greater challenges than involvement at home. Often, both parents work extended hours and struggle to attend school meetings or activities. Select Programs offer various opportunities for families to get involved in school- or classroom-based activities. For example, parent workshops are offered at convenient times to inform parents about SEL in general, about the program's goals, and about specific family activities that enhance children's learning and development. Programs such as Second Step extend invitations families to visit the classroom during one of the program's sessions, or even to participate in program lessons. Second Step also encourages the integration of social-emotional aspects of a student's school progress in parent-teacher conferences, highlighting the importance of the development of such skills and the involvement of parents in the process. We have found that this experience reinforces family involvement and creates a sense of 'ownership' that instills in parents a desire to continue being involved.

A Cautionary Note

Although SEL programs offer educators and parents a set of resources to help them to foster self-awareness, social awareness, self-management, relationship skills and responsible decision making, we must also recognize their limitations. To date, there have been relatively few studies that offer robust scientific evidence indicating program impact beyond the benefits of school-based programming alone (Kumpfer, Alvarado, Tait & Turner 2002). Furthermore, most programmatic work concentrates on elementary and middle-school children. The lack of programs for high-school students becomes even more pronounced when we search for teen SEL programs that include parents in systematic and developmentally appropriate ways (Elias, Bryan, Patrikakou & Weissberg 2003). Finally, frequently programs do not address the hard-to-reach parents; for example, parents who do not read, do not speak English, or require additional support that is not always included in the program design. (See Table 4.2 for programs that include materials in Spanish and check program websites for updated information.)

Conclusion

SEL programs that include a well-structured parent involvement component provide an essential framework for us to foster the healthy development and school success of our children and youth. However, to improve our efforts in future, we need additional and better:

- evaluation studies to examine outcomes and benefits of SEL programming— particularly investigating the differences between those that include a strong parent involvement component and those that do not

- developmentally appropriate programming for adolescents and their families

- culturally diverse and innovative programs that connect with a larger percentage of the hard-to-reach families

- resources that sustain programming efforts and support implementation for educators and families

- professional development for teachers and school administrators in school-family collaboration and SEL.

In summary, we would like children to develop in healthy and positive ways. There is powerful evidence showing that when schools and families collaborate students enjoy academic and behavioral benefits (Henderson & Mapp 2002). In recent years, pioneering programs that foster the development of social-emotional skills have recognized the importance of school-family partnerships and have begun to include such partnerships in their frameworks. During the next decade, we anticipate the development of more innovative programmatic efforts, more evaluations to demonstrate efficacy, and enhanced teacher training to better prepare educators to promote SEL skills and school-family partnerships.

By building greater capacity for schools to partner with parents more productively, we will accept the challenge of better preparing our children for a rapidly evolving world. It is critical that we rise to these challenges sooner rather than later for the benefit of all our children.

Acknowledgements

We acknowledge the support of the US Department of Education through a grant to the Mid-Atlantic Regional Educational Laboratory for Student Success at Temple University.

References

Bar-On, R., and J.D.A. Parker, eds. 2000. *The handbook of emotional intelligence.* San Francisco, CA: Jossey Bass.

Catalano, R.F., M.L. Berglund, J.A.M. Ryan, H.S. Lonczak, and J.D. Hawkins. 2002. Positive youth development in the United States: Research findings on evaluations of positive youth development programs. *Prevention & Treatment,* 5, Article 15. Retrieved from http:journals.apa.org/prevention/volume5/pre0050015a.html.

Chavkin, N.F. 2005. Preparing educators for school-family partnerships: Challenges and opportunities. In Patrikakou, Weissberg, Redding, and Walberg. pp. 164–80.

Christenson, S.L., and L.H. Havsey. 2004. Family-school-peer relationships: Significance for social, emotional, and academic learning. In Zins, Weissberg, Wang, and Walberg, pp. 59–75.

Christenson, S.L., and S.M. Sheridan. 2001. *Schools and families: Creating essential connections for learning.* New York: Guildford.

Collaborative for Academic, Social, and Emotional Learning (CASEL). 2003. *Safe and sound: An educational leader's guide to evidence-based social and emotional learning programs.* Chicago: Author.

Durlak, J.A., and R.P. Weissberg. 2005, August. *A major meta-analysis of positive youth development programs.* Invited presentation at the Annual Meeting of the American Psychological Association. Washington, DC.

Elias, M.J., K. Bryan, E.N. Patrikakou, and R.P Weissberg. 2003. Challenges in creating effective home-school partnerships in adolescence: Promising paths of collaboration. *School-Community Journal* 13(1): 133–53.

Elias, M.J., J.E. Zins, R.P Weissberg, K.S. Frey, M.T. Greenberg, N.M. Haynes, R. Kessler, M.E. Schwab-Stone, and T.P Shriver. 1997. *Promoting social and emotional learning: Guidelines for Educators.* Alexandria, VA: Association for Supervision and Curriculum Development.

Epstein, J.L. 2001. *School, family, and community partnerships: Preparing educators and improving schools.* Boulder, CO: Westview Press.

Fantuzzo, J., E. Tighe, and S. Childs. 2000. Family Involvement Questionnaire: A multivariate assessment of family participation in early childhood education. *Journal of Educational Psychology* 92:367–76.

Goleman, D. 1995. *Emotional intelligence.* New York, NY: Bantam.

Greenberg, M.T., R.P. Weissberg, M.U. O'Brien, J.E. Zins, L. Fredericks, H. Resnik, and M.J. Elias. 2003. Enhancing school-based prevention and youth development through coordinated social, emotional, and academic learning. *American Psychologist* 58: 466–74.

Henderson, A.T., and K.L. Mapp. 2002. *A new wave of evidence.* Austin, TX: National Center for Family and Community Connections with Schools.

Illinois State Board of Education (ISBE). 2005. Illinois Learning Standards. Social/Emotional Learning (http://www.isbe.net/ils/social_emotional/standards.htm).

Kumpfer, K.L., R. Alvarado, C. Tait, and C. Turner. 2002. Effectiveness of school-based family and children's skills training for substance abuse prevention among 6–8 year old rural children. *Psychology of Addictive Behaviors* 16:565–71.

Moles, O. 2005. School-family relations and student learning: Federal education initiatives. In Patrikakou, Weissberg, Redding, and Walberg. pp. 131–47.

Patrikakou, E.N., R.P. Weissberg, S. Redding, and H.J. Walberg,eds. 2005. *School-family partnerships for children's success.* New York, NY: Teachers College Press.

Payton, J.W., D.M. Wardlaw, P.A. Graczyk, M.A. Bloodworth, C.J. Tompsett, and R.P. Weissberg. 2000. Social and emotional learning: A framework for promoting mental health and reducing risk behaviors in children and youth. *Journal of School Health* 70:179–85.

Redding, S., and P. Sheley. 2005. Grass roots from the top down: The state's role in family-school relationships. In Patrikakou, Weissberg, Redding, and Walberg. pp. 148–63.

Weissberg, R.P., H.J. Walberg, M.U. O'Brien, and C.B. Kuster, eds. 2003. *Long-term trends in the well-being of children and youth.* Washington, DC: Child Welfare League of America Press.

Wilson, D.B., D.C. Gottfredson, and S.S. Najaka. 2001. School-based prevention of problem behaviors: A meta-analysis. *Journal of Quantitative Criminology* 17:247–72.

Zins, J.E., R.P. Weissberg, M.C. Wang, and H.J. Walberg,eds. 2004. *Building academic success on social and emotional learning. What does the research say?* New York: Teachers College Press.

— 5 —

The Social, Emotional and Academic Education of Children: Theories, Goals, Methods and Assessments

Jonathan Cohen and Sandra V. Sandy

Introduction

As adults, whether we are parents and/or teachers, what role do we want to play in developing social and emotional, ethical and traditional 'academic' skills in children? What 'lessons' or sets of skills, knowledge and dispositions are most important for children and adolescents to learn? Whatever the priorities, as parents and teachers we do not serve only to shape children's linguistic competencies or 'intelligence', we *always* teach social-emotional competencies and ethical dispositions as well. Teaching techniques vary to the extent that we are conscious, thoughtful and clear about our goals and methods. Educational or therapeutic interventions can be defined on the basis of theories, goals (also the process and techniques that yield those goals), and modes of evaluation. Theory always shapes goals which in turn suggests methods to actualize the goal. How we evaluate process and outcome determines learning. There is considerable variation in the extent to which we are invested in being conscious and effective social-emotional learners as well as teachers. For example, how we listen and talk with children, solve problems, cooperate, and manage internal and interpersonal moments are ongoing 'lessons' from which children learn.

Social-emotional education (SEE) refers to the process of teaching and learning the skills, knowledge and dispositions that allow people to understand, process, manage and express the social-emotional aspects of their lives (Cohen 2002). In this chapter, we will use the terms 'social, emotional and academic education' (SEAE), 'social-emotional learning' (SEL) and 'character education' (CE) as having overlapping meaning. But there are certain important differences between them. For example, proponents of CE have historically, currently and explicitly recognized the great importance of promoting moral or ethical dispositions much more than many leaders in SEL. And the field of SEL has emphasized the fundamental importance of skill-based teaching and learning more than many leaders in CE. But research from both spheres has shown that effective efforts involve the coordination of the following two processes over three to five years:

1. Purposefully promoting students' and adults' social and emotional competencies.
2. Systemically intervening to create safe, caring, participatory and responsive schools, homes and communities.

(Berkowitz & Bier 2004; Cohen 2001; Catalano, Berglund, Ryan et al. 2002; Greenberg, Weissberg, O'Brien et al. 2003; Sandy 2001; Zins, Weissberg, Wang & Walberg 2004)

In this chapter we will summarize and critique the range of theories, goals, methods and evaluation procedures that currently shape efforts in SEE.

Current Theory, Goals, Methods and Assessment

Theories

When we consider school or individual change, our theory always shapes our goals, which in turn suggests methods to actualize these goals. Over the last hundred years, there has been a range of theories, goals and linked methods from education and mental heath that have shaped theory and practice in SEAE (For a more detailed description of these precursors, see www.csee.net/SEE/roots.aspx).

Curiously, there has been relatively little discussion about the theoretical frameworks for current work in SEE. Various theories in child development have certainly provided a theoretical framework for many aspects of CE (Berkowitz & Bier in press). Cognitive behavioral theory has been a major approach to much of the important skill-based, primary prevention work as well as teaching and learning that shapes the SEL curriculum (Greenberg et al. 2003; Zins et al. 2004). Systems theory underlies a great deal of this work. When we consider the creation of safer, more caring and responsive schools, school-family partnerships and the coordination of existing health promotion and risk prevention efforts, we are working with systems. The school is an 'open system'—it is embedded in the larger community. We need to think systemically to create a 'comprehensive' climate for social, emotional and/or traditional 'academic' learning.

Psychoanalytic theory is another implicit, or sometimes explicit, theoretical model (Kusché & Greenberg 2001; Marans & Cohen 1999; Twemlow, Fonagy, Sacco et al. 2001). The model proposes that:

- conscious and unconscious, or unrecognized, emotions and thoughts shape who we are, how we act and what we learn
- conscious and unconscious meanings that children attribute to experiences shape learning and how we create conscious and unrecognized meanings over time.

Goals and core principles

Regardless of theory, social-emotional educational goals in work done with pre-K–12 students have always focused on the promotion of social-emotional competencies, as well as, on the one hand and to a greater or lesser extent, ethical dispositions, and on the other hand the creation of a climate for learning and safety.

As we outline in the appendix on pages 82 to 84, there have been various interesting attempts to define the core principles and practices that characterize efforts in SEL and CE. The Character Education Partnership delineates 11 principles of CE (Likona, Schaps & Lewis 1996), while Cohen (2001) suggests that there are five principles that characterize effective SEE efforts. CASEL (2003) review evidence-based SEE programs and suggest that ten core dimensions represent key principles of effective SEE programming. Goleman's model (1998) is based on five clusters of SEL. Similarly, Bar-On's model (1997) consists of five key components. Finally, Elias (2003) summarizes his understanding of the ten key dimensions that characterize effective academic, social and emotional learning.

Although investigators have focused on different social and/or emotional competencies and used somewhat differing terms to describe them, there is considerable overlap among these models. Our review of the theorists' SEE principles suggests that the following competencies are the ones most longitudinal researchers (Cohen 2001) consider to be predictive of children's ability to learn and to solve problems non-violently, as well as of the fundamentally important work- and love-related outcomes we mentioned above:

- Awareness of self and others, or reflective and empathic abilities.
- Flexibility and creativity in problem-solving and decision-making.
- Ability to regulate impulses.
- Capacity to cooperate.
- Skills in communicating clearly and directly.
- Learning to be self-motivating.
- Forming and maintaining friendships.

Other models of SEL that show promise are the Salovey-Mayer model (which is discussed in several of the other chapters in this book) and Kornhaber's model which is based on Gardner's (1983) model of multiple intelligences.

SEL can serve three overlapping audiences:

1. All children as part of a regular education process.
2. Special-needs children in special education programs.
3. All adults in relationships with children, parents, school personnel and people in the community.

SEE programs for children without special needs represent an effective and vitally important primary prevention and health enhancement effort. Although some children grow up in families where SEE is an organizing center of family life, high-quality SEE is fundamentally beneficial to these children as well. Research studies have confirmed that virtually every child can learn to become more socially and emotionally competent, including children with special needs (Cohen, Bezsylko & Shepherd in preparation). However, there are exceptions—children who present with severe autistic disorders by definition are typically unable to learn in socially and emotionally substantive ways.

Methods and implementation strategies

There are many ways in which educators and school-based mental health professionals translate systemic and pedagogical goals into school practice. No curriculum or 'best package' can adequately address the complex series of issues involved in these interventions. Few of even the best evidence-based SEAE curricula, for example, incorporate important mental health guidelines and/or the systemic dimensions we noted above that will directly affect how safe people feel in school.

In practice, schools committed to SEAE-informed school reform tend to focus on the following five dimensions:

1. Planning and creating a school-home vision for change.
2. Creating a climate for learning within the school.
3. Forging a vital school-home partnership.
4. Adopting pedagogic practices that promote social, emotional, ethical and cognitive capacities.
5. Maintaining evaluation methods that support continuous improvement and an authentic learning community.

Although some practitioners focus exclusively on promoting social-emotional skills, and although CE practitioners may highlight the importance of ethical or moral competency in ways that SEE practitioners do not, virtually every effective SEE and CE effort is grounded in promoting social-emotional competencies and ethical dispositions. Systemically, both work to create a safe, caring and responsive school, home and community.

Assessment, or evaluation

Evaluation provides the foundation for learning. In public education it is well known that if we do not 'measure it', it does not count. On the one hand, expert practitioners and researchers agree that continuous evaluation or an action research model is an essential component of effective practice. On the other hand, how can we evaluate students' developing social-emotional competencies and ethical dispositions? And how can we most helpfully evaluate the school as a system and the climate it fosters in the classroom? Although there are various measures of social-emotional competence for pre-school and school-age children (see Chapter 17), the field needs better ways of evaluating individual ethical ability and school climate that recognizes student, school staff and parent 'voices'. (See Cohen (in press) for a more detailed discussion.) This is an important area of current research. However, there is a range of ways in which we can—and need to—evaluate both individual and systemic processes to promote authentic learning communities.

With regard to **SEE programs for students,** there is a range of ways in which we can translate these methods into action. Just as we teach language arts and social science as a standard part of the curriculum, we can teach SEL as a formal, stand-alone course of study. We find a fairly recent empirical example in the US: New Haven's Social Development Program, a K–12 curricular-based sequence of courses mandated by every school in the city. The program includes detailed lesson plans for every class (Shriver, Schwab-Stone & DeFalco 1999). Here, students are initially taught social and emotional skills in isolation. Just as some children need to learn the basic building blocks of reading—phoneme recognition—in isolation, some need to learn social-emotional skills in the same way. Our experience has been that in certain urban public schools, where many impoverished children experience less rather than more socialization, skill-based training in isolation is vital as the first step.

Among the ways that we can integrate SEL into school life, there are programs which present a more or less detailed perspective of child development in relation to SEE, with a variety of methods that can be integrated into the classroom. For example, the Social Problem-Solving/Decision-Making Program can be used as a stand-alone course or as an approach integrated into whatever the teacher is doing in a morning meeting, an academic class or a sports session (Elias & Tobias 1996). Although this program uses problem-solving and decision-making as organizing ideas, a range of skills and understandings are presented and taught. The Responsive Classroom approach (Charney 1992) is another example of an effort to present a point of view about learning, development and discipline—one that can be integrated into every facet of daily school life. CASEL (2003) has recently completed an important review of evidence-based SEE curricula (see Chapter 6). (See also Chapters 6 and 7 for a discussion of facilitating student success in school and in life through SEL.)

As linguistic and mathematical achievement is increasingly emphasized, there has been a growing interest in integrating SEE into the existing curriculum. Teachers can use existing language arts, social studies, history and arts courses as well as community service, advisory programs and athletics as 'a window and a mirror'. Providing an opportunity not only to look into the window, the curriculum asks participants to look at themselves (the mirror) and to learn socially and emotionally. Brackett's work describes one important method designed to further this goal (see Chapter 9). Moreover, the infusion of SEE into the curriculum has been a major focus in the Center for Social and Emotional Education's (CSEE) summer institutes and professional development activities.

SEE can also be integrated into non-academic aspects of school as well as home and community life. For example, the process of talking with children about 'what kind of classroom we want this to be' and/or 'what kinds of things we will discuss at the dinner-table' can lead to a shared sense of what children and adults want. An organizing idea that influences almost every SEE effort is: 'disagreement and mistakes are opportunities for us to learn'. To the extent that adults and children develop a shared vision, this can create the platform for reflection, discussion and learning rather than a punitive disciplinary response to children's misbehavior.

Some perspectives present a specific point of view about child development and social-emotional competence. Arts education, for example, represents a powerful point of view about how we can use analysis of and imagination about musical sounds or a depicted scene as a way of learning about ourselves (Burton, Horowitz & Ables 1999). Similarly, a psychoanalytically informed perspective about child development and learning suggests that discovering more about our *unrecognized* needs and motivation profoundly furthers educators' and parents' abilities to make sense of the world and to become more effective problem-solvers (Marans & Cohen 1999). Lastly, Saarni's work presents another important example of this framework (see Chapter 2).

At the other end of the SEE spectrum are systemic interventions to create safer, more caring, participatory and responsive relationships, schools, homes and communities. Feeling safe—socially and emotionally as well as physically—cared for and engaged is the optimal foundation for all learning. There is mounting evidence that healthy and caring relationships foster learning not only about ourselves and others but academically as well (CASEL 2003; Goleman 1998; Jensen 1998; Pianta 1999). SEE is a powerful systemic intervention when teachers, principals, athletic coaches, cafeteria workers and bus drivers consistently value caring and responsive relationships, the importance of modelling socially and emotionally competent behavior, and learning from the mistakes that inevitably are made. This process runs parallel to the way in which we explicitly and consistently value reading and practice. Making community service, other forms of service and experiential learning a vital facet of school life is another critically important systemic intervention (Elias, Zins, Weissberg et al. 1997). Coordinating risk prevention and health promotion is also part of this list.

Finally, the creation of long-term school-home learning partnerships is a critical, encompassing systemic intervention. It stands to reason that if children are learning about non-violent problem-solving and conflict resolution at school, but their parents act otherwise, SEE efforts will be undermined. Parents and educators need to reflect collaboratively on their goals and on how they can and need to reinforce one another in the education of children's 'minds and hearts'. The Peaceful Kids' Educating Communities in Social Emotional Learning (ECSEL) is an example of an evidence-based program and curriculum that explicitly integrates SEE into children's lives at home, in school and in the community. This program is for pre-school children aged two to six, parents and school staff (Sandy & Boardman 2000).

In practice, SEE varies in regard to which concepts and skills are the program's focus, its audience, and the way in which it seeks to infuse the particular skills and related sets of understandings into the academic and non-academic dimensions of school life. Effective SEE programs and perspectives aim to promote a wide range of social-emotional competencies on the one hand and, on the other, systemically aim to create safer, more caring and responsive schools and homes. In varying degrees, the programs focus on the above mentioned skills, understanding, will or motivation, and beliefs. Some explicitly focus on all the social-emotional competencies; others on only two or three skills, such as cooperative learning and being socially caring and responsive, while implicitly focusing on the others such as in order to be cooperative, we must also be reflective, empathic and flexible problem-solvers.

With regard to **SEE training for educators,** promoting educators' and parents' social-emotional competencies is an essential but often overlooked aspect of effective practice. The Bank Street College of Education is one of the few schools to have focused on the development of reflective educators and the whole child from its inception in 1931 (Shapiro 1991; see also the website at www.bankstreet.edu). Bank Street has long been one of the SEE leaders, even before we started to use the terms 'SEE' and 'SEL'. Specifically, the Advisement Program was established at Bank Street to enhance continuous self-reflection about theory and practice. It includes weekly meetings with groups of students on campus, biweekly individual student-advisor meetings throughout the year, and monthly half-day visits by the faculty advisor to the student's workplace.

Some SEE programs for educators are geared towards further effective teaching in the classroom. For example, the Annenberg Institute for School Reform has recently created a program called the Critical Friends Groups (Annenberg Institute 1998; see also the website at www.annenberginstitute.org). This program is structured to promote teachers' ability to effectively collaborate and sustain communities of adult learners. The Annenberg Institute has also taken the rare and necessary step of systematically testing the efficacy of the program in achieving its goals. One finding indicated a strong positive correlation between the existence of 'professional learning communities' in the school, the effectiveness of teachers and student achievement.

The primary focus of CSEE's work is education and professional development. In our institutes (see www.csee.net/climate/programsservices/summer_institute.html), CSEE and the City University of New York four-course, graduate-level sequence in SEAE (see www.csee.net/resources/ highered.aspx), our primary focus has always been the way in which we can promote adults' and students' social-emotional competencies.

Barriers to Effective Implementation of SEE

In the last 15 years, a growing body of educational and psychoeducational research from a number of overlapping but often fragmented fields—such as risk prevention, health/mental health promotion, CE and SEL—have shown that when we purposefully integrate social, emotional and cognitive teaching we promote students' ability to achieve academically, to solve problems non-violently and to foster the capacity to be effective citizens (Berkowitz & Bier 2004; Greenberg et al. 2003; Zins et al. 2004). Several recent research reports, including the American Psychological Association's 2003 *Presidential task force on prevention, promoting strength, resilience, and health in young people,* have concluded that we now have the knowledge and guidelines to direct effective, coordinated educational and health/mental health practice and policy.

But there are many reasons why most SEE and CE efforts fail to foster learning and behavioral change. In particular, three factors have undermined the efficacy of school-based practice:

1. Short-term and fragmented efforts.
2. Ill-conceived efforts.
3. Inadequate opportunities and support for adults to 'walk the talk'. We will now briefly explore each of them.

Most SEL and CE efforts are short term and/or fragmented. If we sought to teach children to read a book or to 'read themselves' in eight sessions, the activities would fail. Both activities entail a process that is necessarily a multi-year one that optimally includes parents, educators and children working in conjunction. Pedagogic research in recent years has underscored how powerfully helpful it is to coordinate teaching and learning across domains. When we teach a given period in history, academic achievement exponentially increases if we also assign meaningful novels and mathematical lessons linked to this period (Morris 2003). By emphasizing that learning to 'read ourselves' and to be creative problem-solvers is fundamentally important across academic and non-academic spheres in school, we promote learning and the recognition that these are important capacities that shape all learning, relationships and self-experience.

Many SEE efforts fail because long-term, coordinated plans and school-home partnerships are not developed. Too many of the efforts are ill conceived, for example developmentally and/or culturally inappropriate curricula, inadequate 'buy-in' from faculty, inadequate evaluation procedures as well as the fact that teachers sometimes inadvertently try to teach skills and knowledge that students are not yet able to master. Although we are yet to reach consensus about the appropriate social-emotional 'scope and sequence', there are four noteworthy resources in this area. The WT Grant Foundation Consortium worked on this topic and delineated a model (Elias, Weissberg, Dodge et al. 1994). Similarly, CSEE has synthesized several US Department of Education models of social-emotional health education's scope and sequence. You can look for details about the social-emotional skills and knowledge that children can and should learn on our website: www.csee.net. The Illinois State Department of Education has recently developed social-emotional standards with linked benchmarks (see their website at www.isbe.net/ils/social_emotional/standards.htm). Bar-On (personal communication 10 October 2005) has been involved with a longitudinal study of 23,000 youth from birth to adulthood. He is studying the development of key EI competencies over time and the factors they affect, such as biomedical, developmental, cognitive, social, educational and behavioral factors. (Refer to the website www.csee.netfor results and empirical guidelines.)

Lastly, the efforts of school-based practice falter because educators are not committed to being ongoing, vital SEL role models. SEL involves not just the students in schools but also the adults in their lives: teachers, parents and the wider community. We have discovered that educators who want to implement SEE programs in their classrooms report that they need to apply learning to their personal lives before they can effectively use it in the classroom. Children's accomplishments are always guided by the behavior and belief systems of the important adults in their lives. Regardless of their teaching expertise, adults are role models who influence children most strongly by the ways in which they behave towards each other and with the children in their care. If these adults lack social and emotional competency, children will quickly notice the discrepancy between behaviors that the adults advocate for children and the actions that the adults take themselves. Unfortunately, little attention has been given to the importance of adults being social-emotional learners themselves. In fact, most colleges and departments of education do not include SEAE as a vital and explicit dimension in teacher education. But there is growing interest in this area and it represents one of the most important 'next steps' that we can and need to take (Cohen in press).

Communication and sharing with regard to our colleagues, students and constituency, that is, parents and the community, are powerful tools for furthering our ability to understand, empathize and become effective educators and role models. There is evidence to suggest that teachers' lack of fundamental social-emotional support is a major contributor to teacher 'burnout' (Anderson & Iwanicki 1984). **Burnout** is demonstrated when teachers experience emotional exhaustion, a sense of little or no personal accomplishment, and depersonalization, which leads them to giving unfeeling and impersonal responses to students.

Conclusion

In this chapter, we have presented an overview of current social-emotional and CE work in pre-K–12 schools. For generations, parents and educators have intuitively known that how children feel about themselves and others, and how they manage the social and emotional aspects of their lives, is as important—if not more so—than school grades. We now have research-based guidelines for how pre-K–12 schools can integrate social, emotional and ethical education into traditional academic study as well as how to create a climate for learning that promotes students' ability to learn and develop in healthy ways. We have described the way in which various theoretical models provide a framework for practice. We have also outlined a range of ways that these goals are translated into classroom and school-wide practice.

Looking beyond our discussion of some of the common barriers to effective practice, we see a fundamental obstacle to integrating SEE into the teaching and learning process. Particularly problematic is the fact that US colleges and departments of education have failed to assimilate recent research and practice into their teacher and school-based mental health education programs. Such research provides guidelines supporting the idea that SEE infused systematically and developmentally into schools, districts and state departments of education predictably reduce school violence and increase school success in general, and academic achievement in particular. While there are other obstacles that further undermine the infusion of this work into pre-K–12 schools, we suggest that teacher education is one of the most important realms requiring our focus. To the extent that we educate teachers, school-based mental health professionals and parent educators in training, we affect generations of students.

References

American Psychological Association. 2003. Presidential Task Force on Prevention, *Promoting Strength, Resilience, and Health in Young People, American Psychologist.*

Anderson, M.B., and E.F. Iwanicki. 1984. Teacher motivation and its relationship to burnout. *Educational Administration Quarterly* 20:109–32.

Annenberg Institute for School Reform. 1998. *Critical Friends' Groups as a vehicle for improving student learning.* Providence, RI: The National School Reform Faculty.

Bar-On, R. (1997). *The Bar-On Emotional Quotient Inventory (EQ-i): Technical manual.* Toronto, Canada: Multi-Health Systems.

Berkowitz, M.W. and M.C. Bier. 2004. Research based character education. *Annals of the American Academy of Political and Social Science* 591(January): 72–85.

Berkowitz, M.W. and M. Bier. in press. The interpersonal roots of character education. In *Character psychology and character education.* Ed. D.K. Lapsley and F.C. Power. South Bend, In: University of Notre Dame Press.

Burton, J., R. Horowitz, and H. Ables. 1999. *Learning in and through the arts: The issue of transfer.* Article presented at the American Educational Research Association National Conference, Montreal, Canada.

Catalano, R.F., M.L. Berglund, J.A.M. Ryan, H.S. Lonczak, and J.D. Hawkins. 2002. Positive youth development in the United States: Research findings on evaluations of positive youth development programs. Available at URL: http:/journals.apa.org/prevention/volume5/pre0050015a.html. Accessed August 1, 2002.

Charney, R.S. 1992. *Teaching children to care: Management in the responsive classroom.* Greenfield, MA: Northeast Foundation for Children.

Cohen, J. 1999. Social and emotional learning past and present: A psychoeducational dialogue. In Cohen, *Educating minds and hearts.*

————, Ed. 1999. *Educating minds and hearts: Social emotional learning and the passage into adolescence.* New York: Teachers College Press.

————. 2001. Social and emotional education: Core principles and practices. In Cohen, *Caring classrooms/intelligent schools.*

————, 2001. *Caring classrooms/intelligent schools: The social emotional education of young children.* New York: Teachers College Press.

————. 2002. Psychoanalysis and the education of children. *Journal of Applied Psycho-analytic Studies,*4 (Special Issue): 1–4.

————. in press/2006. Social, emotional, ethical, and academic education: Creating a climate for learning, democratic participation and well-being. *Harvard Educational Review* 76(2): 201–37.

Cohen, J., S. Bezsylko, and M.J. Shepherd. (in preparation). Social emotional learning and the learning disabled student: Meeting the needs of students with disabilities. In *Building youth learning capacity and character: A training resource manual for educators* Ed. J. Zins and M. Elias.

Collaborative for Academic, Social and Emotional Learning (CASEL). 2003. *Safe and sound: An educational leader's guide to evidence-based SEL programs.* Available at URL: http:/www.casel.org. Accessed September 5, 2003.

Elias, M.J. 2003. *Academic and social-emotional learning.* Brussels, Belgium: International Academy of Education. Available at URL: http:/www.ibe.unesco.org. Accessed July 7, 2003.

Elias, M.J., and S.E. Tobias. 1996. *Social problem solving: Interventions in the schools.* New York: Guilford.

Elias, M.J., R. Weissberg, K. Dodge, J.D. Hawkins, P. Kendall, L. Jason, C. Perry, M.J. Rotheram-Borus, and J.E. Zins. 1994. The school-based promotion of social compe-tence: Theory, research, practice, and policy. In *Stress, risk, and resilience in children and adolescents.* Ed. R. Haggerty, L. Sherrod, N. Garmezy, and M. Rutter. New York: Cambridge University Press.

Elias, M, J.E. Zins, R.P. Weissberg, K.S. Frey, M.T. Greenberg, N.M. Haynes, R. Kessler, M.E. Schwab-Stone, and T.P. Shriver. 1997. *Promoting social and emotional learning: Guidelines for educators.* Alexandria, VA: Association for Supervision and Curricu-lum Development.

Gardner, H. 1983. *Frames of mind: The theory of multiple intelligences.* New York: Basic Books.

Goleman, D. 1998. *Emotional intelligence.* New York: Bantam Books.

————. 2000. *Working with emotional intelligence.* New York: Bantam Books.

Greenberg, M.T., R.P. Weissberg, M.U. O'Brien, J.E. Zins, L. Fredericks, H. Resnik, and M.J. Elias. 2003. Enhancing school-based prevention and youth development through coordinated social, emotional, and academic learning. *American Psychologist* 58 (6/7): 466–74.

Kusché, C.A., and M.T. Greenberg. 2001. *PATHS in your classroom: promoting emotional literacy and alleviating emotional distress.* In Cohen, *Caring Classrooms/ Intelligent Schools.*

Jensen, E. 1998. *Teaching with the brain in mind.* Alexandria, VA: Association for Supervision and Curriculum Development.

Likona, T., E. Schaps, and C. Lewis. 1996. *The eleven principles of effective character education.* Character Education Partnership. Available at URL http:// www.character.org. Accessed August 20, 2003.

Marans, S., and J. Cohen. 1999. Social emotional learning: A psychoanalytically informed perspective. In Cohen, *Educating minds and hearts.*

McClellan, B.E. (1999). *Moral education in America: Schools and the shaping of character from colonial times to the present.* New York: Teachers College Press.

Morris, R.C. 2003. A guide to curricular integration. *Kappa Delta Pi Record* Summer:164–67.

Northeast Foundation for Children. 2002. Evaluation of the 1999–2001 Courage to Teach Program. Reach Out to Schools: Social Competency Program: Wellesley College, Lesley University, Fetzer Institute, Center for Teacher Formation.

Pianta, R.C. 1999. *Enhancing relationships between children and teachers.* Washington, DC: American Psychological Association.

Sandy, S.V. 2001. Conflict resolution education in the schools: "Getting there." *Conflict Resolution Quarterly* 19(2): 237–50.

Sandy, S.V., and S.K. Boardman. 2000. The Peaceful Kids [ECSEL] conflict resolution program. *The International Journal of Conflict Management* 11(4): 337–57.

Shapiro, E.K. 1991. Teacher: Being and becoming. *Thought and Practice* 3(1): 5–24.

Shriver, T.P., M. Schwab-Stone, and K. DeFalco. 1999. Why SEL is the better way: The New Haven Social Development Program. In Cohen,. *Educating minds and hearts.*

Twemlow, S., P. Fonagy, F.C. Sacco, M. Gies, and D. Hess. 2001. Improving the social and intellectual climate in elementary schools by addressing bully-victim-bystander relationship power struggles. In Cohen, *Caring classrooms/Intelligent schools.*

Weist, M.D., S.W. Evans, and N.A. Lever. Eds. 2003. *Handbook of school mental health: Advancing practice and research.* New York: Kluwer Academic/Plenum Publishers.

Zins, J., R.W. Weissberg, M.C. Wang, and H. Walberg. Eds. 2004. *Building School Success on social emotional learning: What does the research say?* New York: Teachers College Press.

Appendix A

CASEL's 10 core dimensions that represent key elements of effective SEL programming (2003):

1. Incorporate approaches that are based on sound theories of child development and on scientific research.

2. Teach children to apply SEL skills and ethical values in daily life.

3. Use diverse teaching methods to engage students in creating a classroom atmosphere in which caring, responsibility and a commitment to learning thrive.

4. Offer developmentally appropriate classroom instruction, including clearly specified learning objectives for each grade level from pre-school through high school, emphasizing respect for diversity.

5. Help schools to coordinate and unify fragmented programs.

6. Build social and emotional skills that encourage classroom participation, positive interactions with teachers and good study habits.

7. Involve school staff, students, parents and community members in applying and modelling SEL-related skills in the home, school and community.

8. Ensure high-quality program implementation by addressing key factors such as leadership, adequate time and resources, and the inclusion of stakeholders in the planning process.

9. Offer well-planned professional development and support for all school personnel.

10. Conduct a needs assessment to establish a good fit between the SEL program and school concerns, and continue with data gathering to ensure accountability and continuous improvement.

The Character Education Partnership's 11 principles of CE (Likona et al. 1996):

1. CE promotes core ethical values as the basis of good character.

2. 'Character' must be comprehensively defined to include thinking, feeling and behavior.

3. CE requires an intentional, proactive and comprehensive approach that promotes the core values in all phases of school life.

4. The school must be a caring community.

5. To develop character, students need opportunities for moral action.

6. CE includes a meaningful and challenging academic curriculum that respects all learners and helps them to succeed.

7. CE should strive to develop students' intrinsic motivation.

8. School staff must create a learning and moral community in which everyone shares responsibility for CE and attempts to adhere to the core values advocated for students.

9. CE requires moral leadership from both staff and students.

10. The school must recruit parents and community members in the character-building effort.

11. Evaluation of CE should assess the school staff's functioning as character educators as well as the extent to which students manifest good character.

Cohen's five core principles and practices of effective SEL (2001):

1. Children and adults purposefully teaching and learning about reflective and empathic abilities—learning to become aware of feelings/experience, perspective taking, empathic abilities and active listening.

2. Using this awareness to become flexible and creative problem-solvers and decision-makers, for example by identifying and solving problems, and learning to set goals.

3. Using this awareness to become generative social-emotional learners, for example by regulating feelings, controlling impulses, cooperating, negotiating, saying no, seeking help, being responsible, recognizing and appreciating diversity, communicating clearly and directly, and accepting 'not knowing' or 'being confused' as normal.

4. Creating safe, caring and responsive homes, schools and communities.

5. Long-term collaborative school, community and home planning and learning.

Goleman's five clusters of SEL (1998), each of which is linked to a collection of skills:

1. Self-awareness.
2. Social awareness.
3. Responsible decision-making.
4. Relationship management.
5. Self-management.

Bar-On's five key components (1997):

1. The ability to be aware of, to understand and to express our emotions and feelings non-destructively.

2. The ability to understand how others feel and to use this information to relate with them.

3. The ability to manage and control emotions so they work for us and not against us.

4. The ability to manage change, and to adapt and solve problems of a personal and interpersonal nature.

5. The ability to generate positive affect to be self-motivated.

Elias's ten key dimensions that characterize effective academic, social and emotional learning (2003):

1. Learning requires caring.
2. Teaching everyday life skills.
3. Linking SEE to other school services.
4. Using goal-setting to focus instruction.
5. Using varied instructional procedures.
6. Promoting community service to build empathy.
7. Involving parents.
8. Building social-emotional skills gradually and systematically.
9. Preparing and supporting staff well.
10. Evaluating what we do.

6

School Practices to Build Social-Emotional Competence as the Foundation of Academic and Life Success

Joseph E. Zins, Maurice J. Elias and Mark T. Greenberg

Introduction

The children we are educating today will grow up to live in a culture and world that is different from ours. Worldwide, there have been significant changes in societal conditions and in the related needs of young people in the past few decades; for example, the numbers affected by HIV/Aids, the frequency with which violence and crime occur, and the prevalence of substance abuse have escalated. Homicide is now a leading cause of death among male adolescents, and both men and women have an unacceptably high probability of being exposed to violent crime (Federal Interagency Forum 2004). These issues have the potential to undermine the psychosocial well-being and educational attainment of our youth. Therefore, it is no longer optional for the educational and mental health establishments to address these issues.

To be successful in school and in life, students need not only to master academic content, but also to learn to understand and manage their emotions, be responsible and caring, exercise good judgement and make sound decisions, be able to make healthy choices and resolve conflicts, and be prepared to contribute to their community as constructive, committed and effective citizens. Likewise, a safe and supportive learning environment is needed to help them cope with the significant hurdles that may interfere with their education and well-being. Prevention and promotion activities must be employed more frequently, along with further traditional treatment services, as the roles that schools can take in helping students to meet today's challenges and deal with an increasingly complex world are more important than ever. Dryfoos (1994) cautions that a significant proportion of children will fail to grow into productive adults unless major changes take place in the way they are taught and nurtured. Recent world events make the scope and currency of these concerns increasingly significant.

In this chapter, we begin by asking these questions:

- What competencies and skills do young people need to develop to meet the challenges of local and global citizenship?
- How can schools ensure their success in developing these skills?
- How can youth avoid many of the potential pitfalls that may lead to negative outcomes?

We could discuss a variety of outcomes, such as enhanced physical and psychological health and appreciation of diversity. But we recognize that enacting the rights and responsibilities of citizenship involves making connections between emotional and social skills and between school and life success. Thus, we begin our discussion by defining the parameters of SEL and proceed to explore the links between SEL and success. We then review intervention strategies, and conclude with suggestions for key future issues.

What Is SEL?

CASEL introduced the field of SEL in the book *Promoting social and emotional learning* (Elias et al. 1997). As explained in Chapter 4, SEL refers to the educational process of acquiring knowledge, skills, attitudes and beliefs to recognize and manage emotions; to care about others; to make good decisions; to behave ethically and responsibly; to develop positive relationships, and to avoid negative behaviors. SEL represents the aspect of education that links academic achievement with the skills necessary for succeeding in school, in the family, in the community, in the workplace and, indeed, in life in general. Such learning is important to students because emotions affect how and what they learn, and relationships provide a foundation for learning (Elias, Zins, Weissberg et al. 1997).

In developing the concept of SEL, CASEL built on a foundation of research from groups such as the Consortium on the School-Based Promotion of Social Competence (1994) and the Conduct Problems Prevention Research Group (1992). This research was first widely popularized by Daniel Goleman in his book *Emotional Intelligence* (1995). From this research, CASEL identified a core set of social and emotional skills to be learned that influence and give direction for behavior in all aspects of life, and that underlie performance on a wide range of life tasks (Elias et al. 1997). As our CASEL colleagues elaborated in Chapter 4, the five skills comprise self-awareness, self-management, social awareness, relationship skills and responsive decision-making. Drawn from studies on brain functioning, motivation, child development and prevention science (see Chapters 1, 2, 17 and 19 for additional discussion of terminology), the skills are similar to the major EI factors listed by Bar-On (1997), Mayer and Salovey (1997), and Goleman (1995) (see Zins, Weissberg and Utne O'Brien (in press)).

The term 'social-emotional learning' is derived from a journey that has been both conceptual and practical. It began with a shift in thinking from prevention of mental illness and behavioral-emotional disorders as a goal toward the broader goal of promoting social competence. As applications of this work moved further toward education, and as research began to emphasize the role of emotions in children's well-being and in their learning, the term 'social-emotional learning' was invented to describe these elements. We must remember, however, that no term completely captures the domain of a psychological construct, and we recommend going beyond labels and looking in detail at how various theorists and researchers define and elaborate what they mean. Frequently, similar labels can disguise differences, and divergent labels can distract from underlying similarities; for example, see a critical analysis of SEL and EI by Matthews, Zeidner and Roberts (2003).

Equipped with such skills, attitudes and beliefs, young people are more likely to make healthy, caring, ethical and responsible decisions, and to avoid engaging in behaviors with negative consequences such as interpersonal violence, substance abuse and bullying (Elias et al. 1997; Lemerise & Arsenio 2000).

The Conceptual Link Between SEL and School and Life Success

To enhance educational and social-emotional outcomes for students, SEL instruction and the related skills, knowledge and attitude development should occur within a supportive, safe learning environment. Furthermore, the interventions should facilitate the development of this environment. Structural features of school environments found to produce beneficial outcomes are as follows:

- Teacher-family partnerships to encourage and reinforce learning commitment, engagement and positive behavior.
- Safe and orderly school and classroom environments.
- Caring relationships between students and teachers that foster commitment and connection to the school.
- The use of teaching approaches such as cooperative learning and proactive classroom management.

- Adult and peer norms that convey high expectations and support for high quality academic performance.

(Greenberg, Weissberg, O'Brien et al. 2003)

Conceptually, effective SEL instruction can be depicted as involving the following:

Individual skill building and problem resolution + environmental support + practice and applications = development of productive, responsible, healthy, ethical, non-violent, contributing citizens

In other words, SEL competencies are developed and reinforced in a supportive environment, which leads to asset-building, risk reduction, enhanced healthy behaviors, and greater attachment and engagement in school. Over the long term, students' performance in school and in life is likely to improve (Elias, Zins, Graczyk & Weissberg 2003).

SEL interventions help students to be better prepared for learning. For example, students develop self-management and interpersonal skills by managing their behaviors and communicating effectively to achieve goals. They are more engaged in learning, as they experience relationship-centered, supportive learning environments and a positive academic orientation. They gain subject mastery through the fostering of a greater depth of understanding of the material. And their participation in school increases when social and emotional instruction is integrated with academics. Moreover, the interventions help students to develop the SEL competencies for avoiding engaging in high-risk negative behaviors such as dropping out of school, being interpersonally violent, having unprotected sex and using illegal drugs.

Table 6.1 illustrates areas in which SEL programming is linked empirically to improved school attitudes, behavior and performance (Zins, Weissberg, Wang & Walberg 2004). The research indicates that students who become more self-aware and confident about their learning abilities try harder, and students who motivate themselves, set goals, effectively manage their stress and organize their approach to work perform better. Additionally, students who make responsible decisions about studying and completing their homework, and use problem-solving and relationship skills to overcome obstacles, achieve more. Put differently, a combination of interpersonal, instructional, climate and environmental supports produces improved outcomes (Zins, Bloodworth, Weissberg & Walberg 2004).

SEL Intervention Strategies

Evaluations of SEL interventions are becoming increasingly rigorous, with more sophisticated research designs. Larger and more diverse samples are being studied. More valid and reliable assessment measures are being applied. Greater

Table 6.1 Examples of SEL Outcomes Related to Success in School and Life

Outcome	Successes
Attitudes	• Higher sense of self-efficacy • Better sense of community (bonding) and view of school as caring • Stronger commitment to democratic values • More positive attitudes toward school and learning • Improved ethical attitudes and values • Higher academic motivation and educational aspirations • Greater trust and respect for teachers • Improved coping with school stressors • Increased understanding of consequences of behavior
Behaviors	• More pro-social behavior • Fewer absences and suspensions; maintained or improved attendance • More likely to work out own way of learning • Reductions in aggression, disruptions, and interpersonal violence • Fewer hostile negotiations; lower rate of conduct problems; better conflict resolution skills • More classroom participation and higher engagement • Greater effort to achieve; more frequent reading outside of school • Better transitions • Less drug, tobacco, and alcohol use and delinquent behavior • Decrease in sexually transmitted diseases, HIV/AIDS, suicide • More involvement in positive activities like sports
Performance	• Improved math, language arts, and social studies skills • Increases in achievement over time (elementary to middle school) • Higher achievement test scores and no decreases in scores • More progress in phonological awareness • Improved learning-to-learn skill • Better problem solving and planning • Improved nonverbal reasoning

(Source: Based on Consortium on the School-Based Promotion of Social Competence 1994; Elias et al. 1997; Fredericks 2003; US Department of Health and Human Services 2002; Wilson, Gottfredson and Najaka 2001; and Zins et al. 2004. Reprinted by permission from Zins, Elias and Greenberg 2003:59–60.)

concern is being expressed for implementation fidelity and sustainability. Longer follow-up studies are being conducted. Additionally, more thorough data analyses are being carried out.

We can organize the various approaches that are being applied according to the type of intervention strategy that is employed.

Categorically targeted skill building

Although general competence enhancement programs may improve children's critical thinking skills and social behaviors, the positive impact of these programs does not consistently generalize to more problem-specific domains such as substance use, high-risk sexual behavior and violence (Durlak 1995). Additional future studies need to examine this question more closely. Combining general personal and social skills training—for example in problem-solving and decision-making—with attempts to affect student knowledge, attitudes and behavioral competence in specific domains appears to be a more promising approach for preventing specific problem behaviors (Weissberg, Caplan & Sivo 1989).

Generic competence enhancement and ecological restructuring

SEL interventions focusing independently on children are not as effective as those that simultaneously educate children and instill positive changes in the environment, that is, 'ecological restructuring'. Consequently, we need to distinguish between person-centered and ecologically oriented competence enhancement efforts. Person-centered programs teach skills in the absence of creating environmental supports for continued skill application in daily interactions. By contrast, ecologically oriented programs emphasize the teaching of skills, the fostering of meaningful opportunities for children to use the skills, and the establishment of structures to reinforce effective skill application (Hawkins & Weis 1985). Combining classroom instruction with efforts to create environmental support and reinforcement from peers, family members, school personnel, health professionals, other concerned community members and the media increases the likelihood that students will adopt positive social and health practices (Perry & Jessor 1985). Such programs try to change not only the child's but also the teacher's behavior, the teacher-child relationship, and classroom and school-level resources and procedures (Weissberg et al. 1989).

School-wide systems-oriented environmental change

Programs in this category provide more comprehensive and coordinated social and emotional education. They contain many components from the above mentioned two areas, such as personal skill building and social/environmental support, and they target several problem behaviors. Moreover, they focus on school organizational change and restructuring, and have a well-developed process for integrating and systemically coordinating all of their components with academic instruction and with available student support services, such as school psychology, nutrition, guidance counselling, health education and nursing.

Examples of SEL Intervention Strategies

In Table 6.2, we provide an overview of programs arranged by intervention strategy, focal areas for SEL skill development and SEL-related outcomes. Because of the large number of programs that exist, we describe only a few here. You can find more extensive reviews in CASEL (2003).

The Life Skills Training (LST) program

LST is a classroom-based program that combines general and targeted skills training to prevent substance abuse (see their website at www.lifeskillstraining. com). Classroom teachers teach 3rd–7th-grade students cognitive-behavioral skills for building self-esteem, making responsible decisions, problem-solving, communicating effectively, developing interpersonal relationships and asserting personal rights. The program also emphasizes skills and knowledge specifically related to resisting social and media influences to use tobacco, alcohol or other drugs. These skills are taught through a variety of teaching methods including demonstration, role play and behavioral homework assignments for out-of-class practice, feedback and reinforcement for adaptive skill application. (See Botvin, Griffin, Diaz et al. (2000), and Botvin, Griffin, Paul and Macaulay (2003).)

Second Step: A Violence Prevention Curriculum

This program was developed by the Committee for Children specifically for children in pre-school through Grade 8 to help them change the attitudes and behaviors that contribute to interpersonal violence (see the website at www.cfchildren.org). It particularly attempts to reduce impulsive and aggressive behaviors and lead to higher levels of social competence, as part of a comprehensive plan to reduce violence. Teachers learn to recognize and deal with classroom behavioral issues, and students learn empathy, how to recognize and understand their feelings, how to make good choices and how to control their anger. It has been found that children who tend to engage in aggressive behaviors are deficient in these skills. The skills are taught throughout the curriculum, which lasts three to six months, and is accompanied by a parental component. (See Grossman, Neckerman, Koepsell et al. (1997), and McMahon, Washburn, Felix et al. (2000).)

The Social Decision-Making–Social Problem-Solving (SDM-SPS) project

Elias and colleagues designed a widely disseminated social competence enhancement curriculum for elementary school children in both regular and special education (Elias & Bruene 2005a, 2005b) (see the website at www.umdnj.edu/spsweb). During the instructional phase, teachers use scripted lessons to introduce classroom activities with the following format:

1. Group sharing of successes, interacting with others and resolving problem situations that children wish to share.
2. Overview of the cognitive, affective and behavioral skills that are going to be taught.

3. Written and video presentations of situations that call for it and model skill application.

4. Discussion of the situations and ways to use the new skills.

5. Role plays that encourage behavioral rehearsal of skills in diverse situations.

6. Summary and review.

During the application phase, teachers use problem-solving dialoguing methods to encourage students to use adaptive coping strategies in handling real-life problems effectively. (See Elias, Gara, Schuyler et al. (1991), and Elias, Gara, Ubriaco et al. (1986).)

The Promoting Alternative Thinking Strategies (PATHS) curriculum

This multi-year model for the elementary years is an extensive hybrid curriculum that combines models of self-control, emotional awareness and social problem-solving (Kusché & Greenberg 1995) (see the website at www. channing-bete.com/positiveyouth/pages/PATHS). Two unique features of PATHS are, first, its focus on emotion recognition and emotion regulation as necessary processes for effective coping and, second, its focus on ongoing generalization techniques used in the classroom throughout the day. Emotional awareness implies recognition of emotions in ourselves and in others, while emotion regulation entails self-control, frustration tolerance, and so on. Both are viewed as fundamental to triggering and guiding many subsequent intertwined interpersonal and cognitive processes. Thus, PATHS presents a developmental curricular model in which emotion awareness and regulation are seen as essential skills that children need to master in order to demonstrate effective problem-solving. PATHS has been shown not only to reduce behavior problems and improve social competence (Kam, Greenberg & Kusché 2004), but also to improve EI (Greenberg, Kusché, Cook & Quamma 1994).

The Seattle Social Development Project (SSDP)

Social Development Theory, which guides the SSDP, proposes that positive social bonds to family and school develop when:

• family and school experiences foster skills for successful participation

• children have opportunities for active involvement

• responsible adults and peers consistently reward children for constructive, pro-social involvement.

(Hawkins & Weis 1985) (see the website at www.depts.washington.edu/sdrg).

Children in elementary grades learn to be active participants in their learning, to bond to their family and school, and to engage in positive behaviors. (See

Table 6.2   Some effective SEL intervention strategies

SEL intervention strategy	Program	Focal areas for SEL skills development	SEL-related outcomes
Categorically targeted skill building	Life Skills Training (LST)	Cognitive-behavioral competencies; bonding; pro-social norms; resisting social and media pressure; stress management; knowledge about tobacco, alcohol and other drugs	Increases in interpersonal skills, knowledge of smoking and substance use consequences; decreases in cigarette and marijuana smoking, alcohol and polydrug use
	Second Step: A Violence Prevention Curriculum	Affective, cognitive, and behavioral competencies; pro-social norms; social skills related to empathy, impulse control, anger management	Increases in observed neutral and pro-social behavior; decreases in observed physical aggression
Generic competence enhancement & ecological restructuring	Social Decision Making– Social Problem Solving (SDM-SPS)	Affective, cognitive, and behavioral competencies; self-control; group participation and social awareness; recognition for positive behavior	Increases in problem solving, dealing with stressors; decreases in aggressiveness, self-destructive behavior, vandalism, use of alcohol and tobacco

	Promoting Alternative Thinking Strategies (PATHS)	Affective, cognitive, and behavioral competencies; bonding; self-control; emotional awareness; social problem solving; pro-social norms; self-efficacy; recognition for positive behavior; resilience	Increases in emotional understanding, social problem solving & planning, self-efficacy; decreases in aggressiveness, impulsivity, conduct problems
School-wide systems oriented environmental change	Seattle Social Development Project (SSDP)	Affective, cognitive and behavioral competencies; bonding; opportunities for positive involvement; pro-social norms; academic support; cooperative learning; parent training in behavior management	Increases in attachment and bonding to school, academic achievement; decreases in school conduct problems, rate of violent acts, alcohol use, sexual intercourse
	Child Development Project (CDP); now know as Caring School Community	Affective, cognitive and behavioral competencies; bonding; positive organizational structure and democratic values; pro-social norms; academic support in literacy; parent involvement activities	Improved attitudes toward school; more involvement in positive activities; higher self-efficacy; better conflict resolution skills; improved attitudes toward school; decreases in delinquency, drug use and misbehavior

(Source: Reprinted by permission from Zins, Elias and Greenberg 2003:61.)

Ayers, Williams, Hawkins et al. (1999), and O'Donnell, Hawkins, Catalano et al. (1995).)

The Caring School Community

This intervention operates on a school-wide basis in the elementary grades and addresses specific positive youth development constructs such as promoting bonding; fostering resilience; and promoting social, emotional, cognitive, behavioral and moral competence (see the website at www.devstu.org). These constructs enhance the social and moral development of children. The need to create changes is directed toward the classroom, school and home environments, and includes specific academic instruction and development of a positive school culture that is caring, nurturing and participatory. The program consists of several components including cooperative learning, a problem-solving approach to discipline, a values-based reading and language arts program, and school- and community-building activities. The goal is to build a 'caring community of learners' in which children care about learning and about each other. (See Lewis, Schaps and Watson (1996).)

Key Future Issues

During the last two decades, considerable progress has been made in SEL intervention development, evaluation design and demonstrations of its efficacy. As a result, a new generation of 'effective programs', such as CASEL (2003), illustrates the central role that social and emotional learning can play in enhancing developmental outcomes, as well as in decreasing problem behaviors and emotional difficulties. As a growing number of countries incorporate SEL into the fabric of their education systems, they have had to confront a uniform set of issues (Elias 2003), some of which we will now examine.

Assessment and outcome evaluation

The push for greater use of data and data analysis to guide practice and keep stakeholders informed points to the necessity of improving SEL assessment practices. Simply put: we need to know if the programming is working as it is being delivered, rather than waiting to make such a determination once the intervention is finished. Building an ongoing assessment and monitoring system into curriculum implementation is essential to provide timely feedback for continual program monitoring, revision and improvement. For SEL programming to become a mainstream aspect of education, it will be necessary to expand current efforts to document its effects on educational outcomes (Durlak and Weissberg 2005; Zins et al. 2004) and cost-effectiveness (Aos, Lieb, Mayfield et al. 2004). Indeed, the assessment of outcomes is crucial to every SEL project. For example, the key components of effective SEL interventions that we delineated earlier—such as skills development and problem solution + environmental support + opportunities for practice—could be assessed in pre- and post-intervention evaluations.

Professional preparation and networking

Most educators are not being prepared adequately to teach SEL in their classrooms. Further examination of the field indicates insufficient opportunities for teacher training either on a pre- or an in-service basis (Zins 2001). Few colleges of education provide specific training in the research, theory, content or pedagogy of SEL, and students typically receive minimal theory related to children's social and emotional development. Yet current and prospective educators are eager for this type of training, as CASEL has documented by monitoring the huge response to our books, website and conference presentations on SEL. Given the tremendous pressure on the education community to deal with the substantial problems that potentially may interfere with the psychosocial well-being and educational achievement of children, the flexible and efficient manner in which SEL can be incorporated into the academic curriculum makes it attractive as an intervention. Moreover, professionals are needed to support implementation and the scaling-up of sustainable interventions; to coordinate various programs related to SEL, prevention and health; and to integrate these areas within the academic endeavors of the school (Elias et al. 2003).

Educational models to train professionals in implementing SEL strategies and programs need to be developed, and further opportunities for current and future educators to obtain such preparation should be made available if SEL is to become an essential part of children's education (Elias 1994). Therefore, there is a need to ensure that SEL instruction in pre-school through secondary school, which promotes quality interventions, is readily available, broadly disseminated and widely practiced in elementary and secondary schools around the world.

Professionals involved in this work need to be able to communicate, support and learn from one another. Experienced interventionists have gained a great deal of knowledge in their daily work, and novices could avoid many errors by having access to those who have already dealt with similar problems. You can find a list of international resources that may be helpful in this regard in Elias (2003).

Sustainability

A growing body of literature suggests that in order for programs to be able to endure with fidelity, they must be adaptable to changes in their host settings while maintaining the essence of their efficacy (Elias et al. 2003). There must be what Greenberg, Domitrovich, Graczyk and Zins (in press) call an 'implementation support system'. This term refers to the resources available to support not only the programmatic efforts but also those who guide its functioning.

Moreover, sustainability includes networking with seasoned implementers who can help to anticipate pitfalls and lend wisdom from their experiences. To educators, this should bring to mind an upgraded version of cross-age peer tutoring—a pedagogy of demonstrated efficacy (Johnson & Johnson 1994).

As broader implementation of SEL interventions occurs, there is an even greater need for researchers to closely examine the issues of quality of implementation and fidelity in real-world circumstances. More effort to ensure implementation fidelity appears to be essential. Research findings suggest that children have limited capacities to transfer and generalize skills, attitudes and information for handling stressors in one domain to address problems in another (Dodge, Pettit, McClaskey & Brown 1986). Therefore, a major task for future research involves developing skills-attitudes-information training models that target multiple social and health outcomes in the context of the same intervention.

Conclusion

Educators are facing immense challenges worldwide. Among them are violence and HIV/Aids, huge numbers of people living in poverty, life becoming more complex technologically, political conditions changing almost daily, and media encouraging negative and high-risk behaviors in young people. At the same time, there are substantial opportunities for making a significant difference in the lives of today's children—who will be tomorrow's leaders. In the face of this continuing array of challenges, it becomes imperative for educators and those concerned about children to take advantage of every opportunity for strengthening our youth. The importance of SEL as a potential preventive and health-enhancing intervention that supports these efforts cannot be overstated. The growing empirical base indicating that well-designed, well-implemented and well-monitored SEL programming can positively influence a wide range of academic, emotional, social, behavioral and health outcomes is highly relevant for education globally (Zins et al. 2004).

Although currently the number of replication studies that examine program impacts is limited, the consistency of findings from multiple programs with similar mechanisms of action permits us to draw lessons for implementing and scaling up such efforts (Greenberg et al. 2003). There are organizations devoted specifically to SEL, like CASEL, along with professional guild organizations such as those for educational leaders, teachers and school psychologists. On both a national and an international level, these organizations have a major role to play in ensuring that the science behind the practice continues to grow. (See Elias (2003) for a partial international listing of these organizations.) In the near future, we need to establish forums for greater collaboration among all of these entities with the aim of ensuring that SEL approaches are disseminated widely, thereby moving education forward worldwide.

References

Aos, S., R. Lieb, J. Mayfield, M. Miller, and A. Pennucci. 2004. *Benefits and costs of prevention and early intervention programs for youth.* Olympia: Washington State Institute for Public Policy.

Ayers, C.D., J.H. Williams, J.D. Hawkins, P.L. Peterson, and R.D. Abbott. 1999. Assessing correlates of onset, escalation, de-escalation, and desistance of delinquent behavior. *Journal of Quantitative Criminology* 15(3): 277–306.

Bar-On, R. 1997. *The Emotional Intelligence Inventory (EQ-i): Technical manual.* Toronto: Multi-Health Services.

Botvin, G.J., K.W. Griffin, T. Diaz, L.M. Scheier, C. Williams, and J.A. Epstein. 2000. Preventing illicit drug use in adolescents: Long-term follow-up data from a randomized control trial of a school population. *Addictive Behaviors* 25:769–74.

Botvin, G.J., K.W. Griffin, E. Paul, and A.P. Macaulay. 2003. Preventing tobacco and alcohol use among elementary school students through Life Skills Training. *Journal of Child & Adolescent Substance Abuse* 12:1–18.

Collaborative for Academic, Social, and Emotional Learning (CASEL). 2003. *Safe and sound: An educational leader's guide to evidence-based social and emotional learning programs.* Chicago, IL: Author.

Conduct Problems Prevention Research Group. (1992). A developmental and clinical model for the prevention of conduct disorders: The FAST Track Program. *Development and Psychopathology* 4:509–27.

Consortium on the School-Based Promotion of Social Competence. (1994). The promotion of social competence: Theory, research, practice, and policy. In *Stress, risk, resilience in children and adolescents: Processes, mechanisms, and interaction.* Ed. R.J. Haggerty, L. Sherrod, N. Garmezy, and M. Rutter, pp. 268–316. New York: Cambridge University Press.

Dodge, K.A., G.S. Pettit, C.L. McClaskey, and M.M. Brown. 1986. Social competence in children. *Monographs of the Society for Research in Child Development* 51(2, Serial No. 213).

Dryfoos, J. 1994. *Full-service schools: A revolution in health and social services for children, youth, and families.* San Francisco: Jossey-Bass.

Durlak, J.A. 1995. *School-based prevention programs for children and adolescents.* Thousand Oaks, CA: Sage.

Durlak, J.A., and R.P. Weissberg. 2005. Paper presented at the annual convention of the American Psychological Association.

Elias, M.J.. 1994. Consulting in school and related settings to promote the socialization of responsible citizenship: A unifying approach to achieving social, health, and academic goals. *Journal of Educational and Psychological Consultation* 5:381–88.

————.. 2003. *Academic and social-emotional learning.* Educational Practices Series-11. UNESCO, International Academy of Education, International Bureau of Education.

Elias, M.J. , and L. Bruene. 2005a. *Social Decision Making/Social Problem Solving: A Curriculum for Academic, Social, and Emotional Learning, Grades 2–3 and 4–5.* Champaign, IL: Research Press.

————. 2005b. *Social Decision Making/Social Problem Solving for Middle School Students: Skills and Activities for Academic, Social, and Emotional Success.* Champaign, IL: Research Press.

Elias, M.J., M.A. Gara, T.F. Schuyler, L.R. Branden-Muller, and M.A. Sayette. 1991. The promotion of social competence: Longitudinal study of a preventative school-based program. *American Journal of Orthopsychiatry* 61:409–17.

Elias, M.J., M.A. Gara, M. Ubriaco, P.A. Rothbaum, J.F. Clabby, and T. Schuyler. 1986. The impact of a preventive social problem solving intervention on children's coping with middle school stressors. *American Journal of Community Psychology* 14:259–75.

Elias, M.J., J.E. Zins, P.A. Graczyk, and R.P. Weissberg. 2003. Implementation, sustainability, and scaling up of social-emotional and academic innovations in public schools. *School Psychology Review* 32:303–19.

Elias, M.J., J.E. Zins, R.P. Weissberg, K.S. Frey, M.T. Greenberg, N.M. Haynes, R. Kessler, M.E. Schwab-Stone, and T.P. Shriver. 1997. *Promoting social and emotional learning: Guidelines for educators.* Alexandria, VA: Association for Supervision and Curriculum Development.

Federal Interagency Forum on Child and Family Statistics. 2004. *America's children report: International comparisons.* Washington, DC: U.S. Government Printing Office. Available from http:/www.childstats.gov/intnlindex.asp.

Fredericks, L. 2003. *Social and emotional learning, service-learning, and educational leadership.* Chicago, IL: Collaborative for Academic, Social, and Emotional Learning.

Goleman, D. 1995. *Emotional intelligence.* New York: Bantam.

Greenberg, M.T., C. Domitrovich, P.A. Graczyk, and J.E. Zins. in press. *The study of implementation in school-based prevention research: Implications for theory, research, and practice.* Report submitted to The Center for Mental Health Services. Rockville, MD: Substance Abuse and Mental Health Services Administration.

Greenberg, M.T., C.A. Kusché, E.T. Cook, and J.P. Quamma. 1995. Promoting emotional competence in school-aged children: The effects of the PATHS curriculum. *Developmental Research and Psychopathology* 7:117–36.

Greenberg, M.T., R.P. Weissberg, M.U. O'Brien, J.E. Zins, L. Fredericks, H. Resnik, and M.J. Elias. 2003. Enhancing school-based prevention and youth development through coordinated social and emotional learning. *American Psychologist* 58:466–74.

Grossman, D.C., H.J. Neckerman, T.D. Koepsell, P.Y. Liu, K.N. Asher, K. Beland, K. Frey, and F.P. Rivara. 1997. The effectiveness of a violence prevention curriculum among children in elementary school. *Journal of the American Medical Association* 277:1605–11.

Hawkins, J.D., R.F. Catalano, D.M. Morrison, J. O'Donnell, R.D. Abbott, and L.E. Day. 1999. The Seattle Social Development Project: Effects of the first four years on protective factors and problem behaviors. In *Preventing antisocial behavior: Interventions from birth through adolescence.* Ed. J. McCord and R.E. Tremblay. New York: Guilford Press.

Hawkins, J.D., and J.G. Weis. 1985. The social development model: An integrated approach to delinquency prevention. *The Journal of Primary Prevention* 6:73–97.

Johnson, D.W., and R.T. Johnson. 1994. *Learning together and alone: Cooperative, competitive, and individualistic learning.* Needham Heights, MA: Allyn and Bacon.

Kam, C., M.T. Greenberg, and C.A. Kusché. 2004. Sustained effects of the PATHS curriculum on the social and psychological adjustment of children in special education. *Journal of Emotional and Behavioral Disorders* 12:66–78.

Kusché, C.A., and M.T. Greenberg. 1994. *The PATHS curriculum.* Seattle, WA: Developmental Research and Programs.

Lemerise, E.A., and W.F. Arsenio.. 2000. An integrated model of emotion processes and cognition in social information processing. *Child Development* 71:107–18.

Lewis, C., E. Schaps, and M. Watson. 1996. The caring classroom's academic edge. *Educational Leadership* 54:15–21.

Matthews, G., M. Zeidner, and R. Roberts. 2003. *Emotional intelligence: Science & myth.* Cambridge, MA: The MIT Press.

Mayer, J.D., and P. Salovey. 1997. What is emotional intelligence? In *Emotional development and emotional intelligence: Educational implications.* Ed. P. Salovey and D.J. Sluyter. New York: Basic Books.

McMahon, S.D., J. .Washburn, E.D. Felix, J. Yakin, and G. Children. 2000. Violence prevention: Program effects on urban preschool and kindergarten children. *Applied and Preventive Psychology* 9:271–81.

O'Donnell, J., J.D. Hawkins, and R.D. Abbott. 1995. Predicting serious delinquency and substance use among aggressive boys. *Journal of Consulting and Clinical Psychology* 63(4): 529–37.

O'Donnell, J., J.D. Hawkins, R.F. Catalano, R.D. Abbott, and L.E. Day. 1995. Preventing school failure, drug use, and delinquency among low-income children: Long-term intervention in elementary schools. *American Journal of Orthopsychiatry* 65:87–100.

Perry, C.L., and R. Jessor. 1985. The concept of health promotion and the prevention of adolescent drug abuse. *Health Education Quarterly* 12:169–84.

Weissberg, R.P. 2005. Social and emotional learning for school and life success. Paper presented at the Annual Convention of the American Psychological Association. Chicago, Illinois, August, 2005. Available on the internet at http:/www.casel.org/downloads/apa008.20.05.ppt (accessed 6 June 2006).

Weissberg, R.P, M.Z. Caplan, and P.J. Sivo. 1989. A new conceptual framework for establishing school-based social competence promotion programs. In *Primary prevention and promotion in the schools.* Ed. L.A. Bond and B.E. Compas, pp. 158–73. Newbury Park, CA: Sage.

Wilson, D.B, D.C. Gottfredson, and S.S. Najaka. 2001. School-based prevention of problem behaviors: A meta-analysis. *Journal of Quantitative Criminology* 17:247–72.

Zins, J.E. 2001. Examining opportunities and challenges for school-based prevention and promotion: Social and emotional learning as an exemplar. *The Journal of Primary Prevention* 21(4): 441–46.

Zins, J.E., M.R. Bloodworth, R.P. Weissberg, and H.J. Walberg. 2004. The scientific base linking social and emotional learning to school success. In Zins, Weissberg, Wang, and Walberg.

Zins, J.E., R.P. Weissberg, M.C. Wang, and H.J. Walberg. Eds. 2004. *Building academic success on social and emotional learning: What does the research say?* New York: Teachers College Press.

Zins, J.E., R.P. Weissberg, and M. Utne O'Brien. in press. Building success in school and life on social and emotional learning. In *Emotional intelligence: Knows and unknowns.* Ed. G. Matthews, M. Zeidner, and R.D. Roberts. New York: Oxford University Press.

7

The Comer School Development Program: A Pioneering Approach to Improving Social, Emotional and Academic Competence

Norris M. Haynes

Introduction

Low academic achievement is often viewed from a purely cognitive perspective as evidence of low academic ability, or from a socio-cultural perspective as the internalization of value systems that impede intellectual development. However, the complex social and emotional factors, including interpersonal interactions that occur within schools and significantly influence students' adjustment and performance, cannot be ignored or denied. Among these interactions is the nature and level of expectations that teachers have of students and the ways in which these expectations are expressed in schools and classrooms. Schools that promote positive self-esteem, confidence and high self-expectations among students are more likely to engender academic success and positive personal growth among students compared to schools that do not expect and support high achievement.

The need for schools to create a climate of high expectations for students in general, and for students from difficult backgrounds in particular, is of considerable importance. Many students come from severely stressful social conditions. Their existence is often marginal to the mainstream of society, and they tend to see little hope for a bright future.

Despite the social isolation and economic deprivation that they face, many of these children come to school with as much potential, eagerness to learn and willingness to please adults as other children. They are no less intelligent, no less capable and no less malleable than their more privileged counterparts. Frequently, the problem is that these students, fuelled in part by messages that they receive from teachers and other staff, may perceive themselves as being less able than they really are.

There is strong evidence to show that children from extremely poor backgrounds can, and do, succeed when school environments are responsive to their needs (Comer 1980; Comer, Haynes, Joyner & Ben-Avie 1996; 1999). Entering its third decade, the Yale Child Study Center School Development Program has sought to specify the aspects of the school environment that are most important as well as the ways in which to organize, develop and implement strategies that address the psychoeducational needs of urban students and their families. In this chapter, I describe this pioneering project in social and emotional learning.

History, Philosophy and Evolution of the School Development Program

The School Development Program (SDP) model was established in 1968 in two elementary schools as a collaborative effort between the Yale University Child Study Center and the New Haven School System. The two schools involved were the lowest achieving in the city; they had poor attendance and serious relationship problems among and between students, staff and parents. Furthermore, staff morale was low. Parents were angry and distrustful of the schools. Despair was pervasive.

The Yale Child Study Center staff social worker, psychologist, special education teacher and child psychiatrist provided the traditional support services from these disciplines. But we focused more on trying to understand the *underlying* problems and how to correct them or, whenever possible, to prevent them from manifesting than we focused on the treatment of individual children, or on finding deficiencies among staff and parents. Eventually, we identified underlying problems on both sides: family stress and student underdevelopment in areas needed for school success, and organizational, management and child development knowledge and skill needs on the part of school staff.

Because of pre-school experiences in families under stress, a disproportionate number of low-income children presented themselves to the schools in ways that were understood as 'bad', under-motivated and of low academic potential. More accurately, these behaviors reflected underdevelopment or simply development that was appropriate on the playground, at home or other places *outside* of school, but inappropriate *in* school. The school staff lacked training in child development and behavior, and understood school achievement as a function of genetically determined intellectual ability and individual motivation only. Thus, the schools were ill prepared to modify behavior or close the developmental gaps of their students. The staff usually responded with punishment and low expectations. Such responses were understandable under the circumstances, but they usually led to more difficult staff-student interactions, and, in turn, difficult staff-parent and community interactions, staff frustration and a lower level of performance by students, parents and staff alike.

Even when there was a desire to work differently, there was no mechanism at the building level to allow parents, teachers and administrators first to understand the needs, and then to collaborate with and help each other to address them in an integrated, coordinated way. This led to laying of blame, fragmentation, duplication of effort and frustration. There was no sense of ownership and pride in the school. The kind of synergy that develops when people work together to address problems and opportunities could not exist. This resulted in frequent and severe behavior problems and a sense of powerlessness on the part of everyone involved.

Thus the SDP was strongly influenced by careful and deep understanding of education as experienced by disadvantaged urban youth. Its guiding conceptualization was not derived from a specific theory or model. However, it contains critical elements of several theoretical frameworks that were articulated in conjunction with or after its inception. These include the social action model, the ecological model and a child development model. The SDP resembles a social action model in that it attempts to serve children through social change (Kelly 1966; Weinstein & Frankel 1974). More specifically, it seeks to open social structures to a variety of inputs, build parent involvement and empower a community. However, the intervention is best conceptualized as an example of the ecological approach to prevention.

In the broadest sense, the ecological approach to intervention may be seen as a restatement of Lewin's (1936) model of social psychology, which articulated that behavior is a product of the interaction of person and environment. The refinement of the statement for use among clinical psychologists and psychiatrists with an early intervention orientation has resulted in a set of concrete principles of 'the environment'. The adoption of the ecological approach in intervention and research programs is being supported and promoted by a growing number of mental health professionals (Adelman & Taylor 2006).

Essential to the conceptualization of the ecology is the incorporation of a developmental perspective. Comer (1980) proposes that to be successful in school and in life, children must experience optimal development along six critical interconnected developmental pathways. Table 7.1 presents and describes each pathway.

Another important set of conceptualizations relates to how schools must be organized to nurture growth along these pathways, especially children's emotional and social competence. To be effective, schools must practice the 'ABCs of educational responsibility', that is, acceptance, belief and challenge (Haynes 1993). As we mentioned above, when it comes to low academic achievement, we should not ignore complex social and emotional factors, including interpersonal interactions which occur within schools and significantly influence students' adjustment and performance.

Table 7.1   Pathways to good child development and success in school

Pathways	Important Elements
Physical	• Healthy nutrition • Adequate healthcare • Safe and caring environment.
Language	• Help with holding a good conversation • The ability to read regularly and well • Help with listening, speaking and writing well.
Ethical	• Help with making good and healthy choices and decisions • Knowledge and understanding of consequences of behavior.
Social	• Help with interacting and dealing effectively with other children and adults • Help with solving problems in a socially acceptable way.
Psychological	• Help with controlling and managing anger • Maintaining a positive self-esteem • Help in dealing effectively with disappointment, hurt and pain • Having a positive outlook on life and hope for a bright future.
Cognitive	• Help with homework • Need to do well in schoolwork and to master basic reading, writing, language and math skills • Help with learning to think well and to solve problems well.

(Source: Comer 1980)

The ABCs entail the following:

• **Acceptance:** Acceptance involves the provision of opportunities in schools for the expression of culture, for the exchange of cultural information in an atmosphere of mutual respect, and for individual growth. The school's curriculum, textbooks, social agenda, student population, teachers, staff interactions and evaluation practices reflect the acceptance temperature of that school. When a child from a poor background feels just as comfortable and respected as a child from a middle-income background or vice versa in a school, then the acceptance barometer goes up.

• **Belief:** The literature confirms the fact that expectancy effects are very much alive in schools and classrooms. Expectancy effects often lead to self-fulfilling prophecies in which beliefs about students affect the way they are taught. Because the teaching is premised on beliefs about some students' limited academic abilities, these students tend to respond in ways that confirm these beliefs.

• **Challenge:** Some educators believe that many students come from dysfunctional backgrounds and that these students are deficient in intellectual skills and cannot learn. When educators believe that some students cannot learn, or do not want to learn, and that their presence in a classroom or school impedes the learning of others, the educators adopt policies and procedures which disadvantage these children. Serious efforts to effect positive change and growth among

low-achieving students recognize that the argument of inherent intellectual supe-
riority or inferiority is a false one. Social conditions do not have to be a limiting
factor because strategies can be implemented to change conditions, which
suggests that social status does not have to limit academic ability.

Schools that promote positive self-esteem, confidence and high self-
expectations among students are most likely to generate social-emotional competence as well as academic success among students. Operationalizing ways that
schools can provide the ABCs and nurture the developmental pathways was
one of the greatest challenges that the SDP team faced.

The SDP Process and Components

Comer (1980) proposes that schools adopt three basic mechanisms as guiding
principles for their organization:

1. A **management team** that establishes policy and coordinates school activities.
2. A **support team** that is concerned with preventive and proactive psychosocial
   strategies.
3. A program for involving **parents and the community** in the school and for
   involving **the school** in the community.

The need for an organizational and management system based on knowledge
of child development and relationship issues was clear. It was also evident that
a comprehensive approach would be best, rather than one that addressed any
particular area of need. Several realities about the US educational system became
apparent to Comer during the early years of his program. And many of these
realities are still true today. The organization and management of the vast
majority of US schools is deeply entrenched in the attitudes, values and ways
of the larger society, and maintained by traditional training and practice. Most
individuals and systems generally resist change. Thus, research findings,
mandates from outsiders, administrators, in-service education and the like rarely
bring about significant or sustained change.

To his credit, Comer realized and continues to maintain that in order for such
change to be promoted, mechanisms had to be created that allow parents and
staff to engage in a process in which they gain and apply child development,
systems and individual behavior knowledge and skills to every aspect of a school
program in a way and at a rate that is understandable and not threatening. Each
successful activity outcome for staff, students and parents encourages the staff
to use these ways of working again, until the new eventually replaces the old.

These guiding principles became the cornerstone of a model that is now
comprised of nine components: three mechanisms, three operations and three
guidelines. Let us briefly explore them.

The **three mechanisms** have been organized into three specific program
areas:

1. A *school planning and management team* representative of the parents, and teachers, administrators and support staff.
2. A *student support staff team.*
3. A *parents' program.*

The **school planning and management team** carries out three critical operations:

1. The development of a *comprehensive school plan* with specific goals in the social climate and academic areas.
2. *Staff development activities* based on building level goals in these areas.
3. *Periodic assessment* which allows the staff to adjust the program to meet identified needs and opportunities.

Several important **guidelines** and **agreements** are needed:

1. Participants on the governance and management team *cannot paralyze the leader.* Moreover, the leader cannot use the group as a 'rubber stamp', that is, a source of automatic approval and support without debate.
2. While the school principal usually provides leadership to the governance and management group, *decisions are made by consensus* to avoid 'winner-loser' feelings and behavior.
3. A *'no fault', problem-solving approach is used by all of the working groups in the school,* and eventually these attitudes permeate the thinking of most individuals.

We now examine the structures through which the three key mechanisms work.

School planning and management team

The school planning and management team (SPMT) is the most important component in this educational process. Made up of representatives of all the adult stakeholders, and including students in middle and high school, it contains the 'seeds' of a sense of community that flourishes throughout the school when the process is carried out properly. Working collaboratively, members of the SPMT give a school a sense of direction; they prioritize and coordinate activities, they provide communication and, most importantly, they allow everyone to have a sense of ownership and a stake in the outcome of the program. This motivates desirable behavior among parents, staff and students, and helps the school to effectively address the academic, social and emotional needs of all its students.

In some cases, often after everyone involved has become comfortable with the process, a staff member rather than the principal serves as the leader of the SPMT. This works when it is a genuine arrangement to promote leadership from within the staff and not an act of disengagement. With this arrangement, it is important for the principal to continue to be present and fully involved in meetings and in facilitating the process.

Student and staff support team

A support or mental health staff member serving on the SPMT helps to apply child development and relationship knowledge to all of the activities. The mental health team, meeting separately, addresses individual student behavior problems, but focuses also on trying to prevent the problems. This is done by recommending and facilitating changes in school procedures and practices found to be harmful to students, staff and parents.

Parent programs

Parents participate in three major ways in the SPMT:

1. Through the representatives they select.
2. As a parent group or team working with the staff to plan and support social and academic activities.
3. As they attend various school events.

With staff, parents sponsor projects designed to create a good social climate in the schools. They also work as assistants in classrooms, the cafeteria and the library, and participate in other school functions. A teacher or other staff member serves as a liaison to facilitate parental involvement. What is not conveyed adequately is the pervasive philosophy of engaging and involving parents as fully as possible.

As the SPMT addresses the problems and opportunities in a school in a systematic way, the functioning of students, staff and parents improves, and the hope and energy levels of the staff rise. This increases time for planning and leads to improved curriculum development. Eventually, the curriculum—and indeed the entire school experience—begins to promote overall development among students. The SDP helps teachers to gain the skills necessary to promote personal, social and academic growth among students. Significant academic and social behavior gains often result.

Student social and emotional competence has also been affected directly by the Social Skills Curriculum for Inner City Children. Through this program, Comer (1988) integrated the teaching of basic social, emotional and academic skills. Many of these skills are similar to what we now refer to as 'emotional intelligence' (Goleman 1995). Additionally, Comer emphasized an appreciation of the arts in a way that channelled the aggressive energy of the students into the energy of learning and/or work. This effort has been expanded into an SDP, applying to pre-school children through to Grade 12, that is designed to give students the mainstream skills gained by middle-income children from better-educated families simply by living with their parents. In the upper grades the program intends to relate the students to the mainstream economy. Student improvement ultimately derives from creating caring climates and fostering growth in social-emotional competence on the part of the entire school ecology: staff, parents and students alike.

National Dissemination of the SDP

The SDP is now being utilized in hundreds, if not thousands, of elementary, middle and high schools in numerous school districts in the US. A current major thrust of the SDP is the training of school personnel from various school districts to implement the program in their own schools, thus developing internal capacity for SDP implementation and integration, with less reliance on the core SDP staff at Yale. Change agents or facilitators are selected and trained to implement the program under the direction of their local school superintendent, with minimal direct support from the Yale Child Study Center. In addition, small representative groups of parents, teachers, administrators and district office staff participate in orientation workshops. This exposure enables the change agent, with others, to implement the process in their home districts.

The SDP has developed partnerships with schools of education, state departments of education and other institutions, and school districts within the US, which will eventually enable the former to support the efforts of local and neighboring school districts independent of the Child Study Center and work with other school districts of their choosing. For example, many years ago, the SDP developed a consortium in which the SDP staff worked with the New Haven School System and Southern Connecticut State University to develop a curriculum at the University to better prepare their students for work in urban areas. The SDP staff developed 'how to . . .' videotapes of commercial quality and manuals to complement its work in school districts where the program was directly implemented. The videos enabled other school districts to implement the program with minimal hands-on involvement of the SDP core staff at Yale.

Differences Between the SDP and Other School Reform Efforts

Many school improvement approaches have emerged in recent years. They tend to differ from our approach in at least three significant ways:

1. Most programs give specific attention to one major group within a school setting: the students, the teachers or the parents; or to one program area: curriculum, social skills or artistic expression, for example. By contrast, the SDP uses a comprehensive approach in which all groups work in a collaborative way and resources and programs are coordinated to establish and achieve school objectives and goals.

2. They are not driven by child development and relationship concepts, or at most utilize such concepts only in regard to the students. By contrast, *every aspect*

of the SDP's work is driven by relationship and child development imperatives, and focuses on institutional arrangements that hinder adequate functioning.

3. Many programs pay attention exclusively to academic achievement. While the SDP focuses on academic achievement, more importantly it also attempts to create a school climate in which parents and staff support the overall development of students in a way that makes academic achievement and desirable social behavior possible and expected. Comer and colleagues (1996) believe that this approach has a much greater potential for improving students' chances of achieving school success, for decreasing the likelihood of their involvement in problem behaviors and, in turn, for increasing their chances for life success.

Comer understood from the beginning that his program must help to create the social infrastructure that makes improved teaching and learning possible. The SDP process is a critical link that is too often missing in education reform. It permits many schools to transform and improve their programs, but could permit many more with adequately trained staff and appropriate teaching and curriculum approaches.

Effects of the SDP

The evidence suggests that Comer's SDP has a significant effect on measures of students' academic performance, on their social and emotional adjustment in school and on the school climate. We now briefly look at this evidence (see Cook, Habib, Philips et al. (1999); Cook, Murphy and Hunt (2000); and Haynes (1998) for more details).

Academic effects

School-level aggregated data analyses provide evidence of significant SDP effects on achievement. In 1986, an analysis of achievement data in the Benton Harbor, Michigan area schools showed significant average four-year gains, between 7.5 and 11.0 percentile points, in reading and math, at the second, fourth, fifth and sixth grades for SDP schools, exceeding gains reported for the school district as a whole. Program schools also registered higher gains in math and reading than the district as a whole, with regard to the percentage of students obtaining 75% and above of the objectives on the Michigan Educational Assessment Program.

An assessment of SDP effects conducted by the research office of the Prince George's County Public Schools in 1987 revealed that average percentile gains on the California Achievement Test between 1985 and 1987 were significantly greater for SDP schools than for the district as a whole. At the third-grade level, SDP schools gained about 18 percentile points in math, 9 percentile points in reading and 17 percentile points in language. The district, as a whole, registered gains of 11, 4 and 9 percentile points respectively in math, reading and language. At the fifth grade, program schools recorded gains of 21, 7 and 12 percentile points in math, reading and language compared to gains of 11, 4 and 7 percentile points for the district as a whole. Further analysis also revealed that academic gains were linked to the degree and quality of implementation of the SDP.

A trend analysis of achievement data among fourth graders in the two pioneer SDP schools in New Haven conducted by our SDP research team indicated steady gains in math and reading between 1969 and 1984. The grade equivalent scores for the two schools increased from about 3.0 in reading and math in 1969 to 6.0 in reading and 5.0 in math in 1984.

Several experimental control group studies involving randomly selected students in carefully matched schools reported significant differences in academic achievement between students in SDP schools and students in non-SDP control schools. A study by Cauce, Comer and Schwartz reported that seventh-grade students in SDP schools had significantly higher averages in math and overall grade point average than students in non-SDP schools (Haynes 1998). Studies by Haynes, Comer and Hamilton-Lee reported that elementary school students in SDP schools showed significantly greater one-year positive changes in grade equivalent scores in reading, math and language on the California Achievement Test when compared to students in non-SDP schools. SDP students also had significantly greater positive changes in classroom grades than non-SDP students.

In a retrospective follow-up study, 92 sixth- and eighth-grade students were studied. Fifty-seven (62%) were from a non-SDP elementary school and 45 (38%) were from a program school. The academic achievement of these students was measured by report-card grades and by percentile scores on the Metropolitan Achievement Test. Significant differences in favor of the SDP students were found for sixth graders in math, language and total battery on the Metropolitan Achievement Test. SDP students obtain consistently higher scores on all other achievement measures, but these differences were not significant. At the eighth-grade level, no difference was significant, but again SDP students consistently scored higher than non-SDP students.

Behavior and school adjustment effects

Measures of attendance, suspensions, classroom behavior, group participation and attitude toward authority were used to assess students' school adjustment. Aggregated data analysis conducted in Benton Harbor, Michigan indicated that between 1,982 and 1,985 SDP schools experienced significantly greater declines in suspension days, absent days and number of corporal punishments recorded, when compared to the district as a whole. For example, SDP schools recorded a 19% decline in suspension days compared to a 34% increase in suspension days for the district as a whole. Similarly, for corporal punishments, SDP schools recorded a 100% decline compared to a 36% decline for the district as a whole. Corporal punishment is no longer legal in the Benton Harbor area schools.

The above mentioned study by Haynes, Comer and Hamilton-Lee indicated that SDP students experienced significantly greater positive changes in attendance, as well as teacher ratings of classroom behavior, attitude toward authority and group participation, when compared to non-SDP students. Cauce, Comer and Schwartz also found that SDP students reported significantly better perceived school competence and self-competence compared to a control group of non-SDP students.Self-concept

SDP students in the fourth and sixth grades were compared with non-SDP students on six self-concept dimensions on the Piers Harris Self-Concept Scale. Both groups of students were also compared with the national normative sample on total self-concept. Analysis of covariance was used to control for pre-test differences that existed between SDP and non-SDP students. On the post-assessment measures, SDP students scored significantly higher than the control group of non-SDP students on all six self-concept dimensions, and also significantly higher than the normative group on total self-concept. Other studies furthermore indicated that SDP students showed significantly greater positive changes in self-concept when compared to non-SDP students.

Classroom and school climate

In a study involving 288 students, students in SDP schools reported significantly more positive assessments of their classroom climate than did students in non-SDP schools. One hundred and fifty-five parents and 147 teachers completed a school climate questionnaire designed by the researchers. Parents and teachers of students in SDP schools reported significantly more positive assessments of their schools' climate when compared to parents and teachers of children in non-SDP schools.

Implications of Educational Practice

Effective schooling must address students' academic, social and emotional needs by providing qualitatively relevant and meaningful curricula and adequate contextual support for them all. The socially and emotionally responsive learning environment becomes evident in a school ecology that is supported by an educational philosophy which fosters respect and caring and a climate of challenge that reaffirms the dignity and capability of each child at developmentally appropriate levels.

In order for students to be effectively challenged, several conditions must exist. School staff should:

- understand students' socio-cultural frames of reference
- include elements of these frames of reference in pedagogy
- create a climate that provides acceptance and positive belief
- set high standards of performance consistent with developmental capabilities
- recognize and appreciate achievement and remediate deficiencies

- provide hope for a better life
- help students to set and achieve reachable goals
- engage the interest and involvement of parents and other caregivers
- use fair and helpful assessment techniques
- obtain adequate resources needed to serve students effectively.

These considerations have value independent of the SDP, but the SDP exists to make sure they are operationalized within schools in an integrative, powerful way. This is essential for having a sustained, positive impact on the most disadvantaged students.

Conclusion

The SDP is not a 'quick fix', and it is not an 'add on'. It is not just another new activity to be carried out in a school. It is a nine-component process model that takes significant time, commitment and energy to implement. It is a different way of conceptualizing and working in schools, and it completely replaces traditional organization and management. All of the activities in a school are managed through the SDP process, which promotes six developmental, intertwined pathways. Most importantly, the SDP can produce desirable outcomes only once a cooperative and collaborative spirit throughout a school has come into being, and only when there is faithful replication of the process.

References

Adelman, H.S., and L. Taylor. 2006. *The implementation guide to student learning supports in the classroom and schoolwide.* San Francisco: Jossey-Bass.

Comer J.P. 1980. *School power.* New York: Free Press.

Comer, J.P., N.M. Haynes, E. Joyner, and M. Ben-Avie. 1996. *Rallying the whole village: The Comer process for reforming education.* Teachers College Press, Columbia University.

———. 1999. *Child by child: The Comer process for change in education.* New York: Columbia University Teachers College Press.

Cook, T. D., F. Habib, M. Phillips, R.A. Settersten, S. Shagle, and M. Degirmencioglu. 1999. Comer's school development program in Prince George's County, Maryland: A theory-based evaluation. *American Educational Research Journal* 36(3): 543–97.

Cook, T., R.F. Murphy, and H.D. Hunt. 2000. Comer's school development program in Chicago: A theory-based evaluation. *American Educational Research Journal* 37(2): 543–97.

Goleman, D. 1995. *Emotional intelligence.* New York: Bantam Books.

Haynes, N.M. 1993. *Critical issues in educating African-American children.* Langley Park, MD: IAAS Publishers, Inc.

———. 1998. *Changing schools for changing times: The Comer School Development Program.* Mahwah NJ: Lawrence Erlbaum Associates, Publishers.

Kelly, J.G. 1966. Ecological constraints on mental health services. *American Psychologist* 21:535–39.

Lewin, K. 1936. *Principles of topological psychology.* New York: McGraw Hill.

Weinstein, M. and M. Frankel. 1974. Ecological and Psychological Approaches to Community Psychology. *American Journal of Community Psychology* 2:43–52.

—— 8 ——

The Self-Science Approach to Social-Emotional Learning

Karen McCown, Anabel L. Jensen and Joshua Freedman

Introduction

What can we gain by sailing to the moon, if we are not able to cross the abyss that separates us from ourselves? This is the most important of all voyages of discovery, and without it, all the rest are not only useless, but disastrous.

Thomas Merton ('The wisdom of the present' quoted by Soygal Rinpoche
Tibetan book of living and dying)

Set your imagination free for a moment to envisage the 'ideal school': a place where learning is both joyful and disciplined; where students become smarter, more conscious, more aware; where they achieve while finding wisdom and confidence and strength. Imagine also that the students, teachers and parents work together to learn, grow and succeed as partners.

What skills would students need to develop in order to take ownership of their learning and responsibility for their lives? How would people in the community treat one another, and how would they learn to do that? What kinds of questions would people in this community ask each other? What kinds of behaviors would the teachers and parents demonstrate?

Academic achievement is an essential goal of education; learning is the 'silver bullet' that gives young people the tools for lifelong success—that transforms struggle into hope. To meet this promise, it is equally essential that children develop mastery of the 'human side' of learning: to know themselves, to communicate effectively and to solve problems. Self-Science is a curriculum designed to teach these important skills.

For the last 38 years, we have taught teachers, students, parents, community members, administrators and policy-makers, as well as managers and executives, how to develop EI. In this chapter, we attempt to answer the following practical questions about the process:

- How did the Self-Science curriculum develop?
- What are some benefits of SEE?
- What are the keys to making SEE effective based on the Self-Science approach?
- What is the history of Self-Science?

In the mid-1960s, inspired by the human potential movement and her own children, Karen McCown began developing an innovative school. She gathered advice from teachers, scholars, business and civic leaders, and children themselves. Her vision was crystallized by a panel of Nobel laureates. When asked, 'What would you have wanted in a school?', they responded with a plea for a learning environment that blended academic excellence with the teaching of social-emotional skills.

To meet this challenge, McCown developed a curriculum called 'Self-Science', named to emphasize the importance of objective self-observation. The curriculum looks at social interactions and patterns in the same way a scientist makes observations in a laboratory. The difference is that the laboratory for this class is the student's daily life. Self-Science classes go beyond 'exploring emotions' to help students to develop practical strategies and tools. The goal is to help children understand themselves, express themselves, form healthy relationships, manage conflict, and live with respect, responsibility and resiliency.

By the 1990s, over 2,000 visitors were coming to the Nueva School in California each year to learn about this approach. The school became one of only a few schools ever to win two Federal Blue Ribbon Awards for Excellence in Education. In both instances, the award noted the power of integrating the social-emotional curriculum into the classroom and into the total school culture. Social-emotional learning was part of the fabric of the school, and the norms and practices of Self-Science were apparent not only in every class— from physical education to music, from math to history, from reading to art —but also during break and in the hallways.

Perhaps more important than national awards are the individual stories of students and families. One that stands out was from Grade 8 learner Brad Livermore, after he and his two sisters lost their mother to a virulent, accelerating breast cancer in 1997.

He stated:

My mother was my anchor, my support system. I confided everything to her: my fears, my anxieties and my uncertainties. Without her, I felt totally adrift. As a result,

I often acted out: misbehaved in the classroom, or picked on classmates. It was in Self-Science that I heard her messages repeated and reinforced. It was there that I recalled her generosity and kindness. It was there that I was reminded of what she wanted me to become. It was there that I promised to do so.

In 1993, school trustee Eileen Rockefeller Growald invited Daniel Goleman to observe Self-Science. Impressed by the way students were able to recognize, articulate and manage feelings, Goleman wrote glowingly about Self-Science in his book *Emotional intelligence: Why it can matter more than IQ* (1995).

His book brought the concept of EI fully into the mainstream, and more people began asking for practical programs and tools for teaching these skills. To meet the demand, McCown brought together former Nueva School administrators and teachers Anabel Jensen, Joshua Freedman and Marsha Rideout to become the core staff of a new non-profit organization: the Six Seconds EQ Network. The organization was created to disseminate the tools and strategies of Self-Science into other schools as well as into organizations, families and communities. In 1998, the second edition of *Self-Science* was published (McCown, Jensen, Freedman & Rideout 1998).

The Purpose of Self-Science

Self-Science students participate in activities, discussions and assignments that lead them through a sequence of developmental goals. The exercises and discussions encourage them to:

- increase their self-awareness and awareness of others
- evaluate the consequences of choices
- develop healthy and effective coping strategies.

Originally designed for elementary-school students, the Self-Science approach is being used from pre-school through college and beyond. As Remy Franklin, age 13, Self-Science student, describes it:

Well, it's like science about yourself. You just learn about emotions, and about why you act the way you do, and you get to be more conscious about your choices.

Self-Science is a comprehensive, developmental and research-based curriculum for creating a school-wide culture of EI. The curriculum teaches specific skills related to self-awareness, self-management and self-direction. These skills include recognizing patterns of behavior in ourselves and others, becoming more aware of multiple and complex feelings, accepting responsibility and using optimistic thinking. Structured to help students to integrate thinking, feeling and behavior, the classes typically include an individual or group activity, a discussion and analysis of the activity, and application of the lessons from the class to daily life.

The primary purpose of Self-Science is *to make conscious choices about thoughts, feelings and actions.* People often seem to react 'on autopilot', which leads to thoughts, feelings and actions that they would not have if they were paying closer attention. We hope they can learn to be more careful about their choices, thus leading them to have a more appropriate set of thoughts, feelings and actions.

The program blends the development of key EI skills, such as emotional literacy and emotional management, with a structure that enables students to practice the skills with each other in 'social problem-solving situations' that lead them to managing and resolving their social concerns.

Rather than telling children what not to do, Self-Science provides multiple options of what to do. It helps children to become more aware of themselves and make decisions with more consideration. We believe the feeling that the student *has a choice* is key to the student developing both independence and interdependence. As students learn about the range of responses they have available, they can increase both accountability, which is the ownership of their choices, and personal power, the self-direction to pursue those choices.

While some CE programs focus on obedience to rules, Self-Science works to build children's capacity to make their own decisions. As children grow up today, they will almost certainly face decisions for which we have no rules, such as how to distribute scarce financial resources, how to use our time, and which relationships and causes deserve the most of our time and energy. So we would like to guide them in developing the competencies that will help them to make decisions carefully and thoughtfully. We believe that attending to both feelings and thoughts will help them to do this.

This empowering approach has been highly valued by students, teachers and parents alike. In 1995, Nueva School Alumni Director Anne Bennett interviewed approximately 1,000 Nueva graduates and their parents and teachers from the previous 28 years. Exploring their elementary school experience and how it supported them in their lives, Bennett found an overwhelming appreciation of Self-Science:

- Seventy per cent of the students reported Self-Science as the class that had the most significant impact on their lives.

- Alumni parents conveyed that Self-Science helped their children to develop many vital skills, including self-awareness, empathy, altruism, consequential thinking and self-advocacy.

- Educators indicated that Self-Science was a significant factor in developing leadership skills, building community ties and positive emotional risk-taking.

Based on these anecdotal data, students continue to use the Self-Science tools long after they have graduated. For example, we interviewed Lauren Keane in her final year at Yale University. She had participated in Self-Science for six years, starting when she was eight years old. When asked what Self-Science lessons she was continuing to use, Lauren replied, 'The biggest one is just learning to be a good listener, and that was always step one in the Self-Science process.'

To expand on the anecdotal data, Six Seconds conducted two pilot studies of the curriculum, with a third currently in process. The 2001 study included 311 students in 13 classrooms. The students were aged 7–16, 29% minority, 9% special needs. The schools cover a wide range—public and private, special needs and mainstream—from three US states plus the Virgin Islands. A detailed report of this study is available on the Self-Science website at www.self-science.com.

In the study, 100% of the teachers reported that the program increases co-operation and improves classroom relationships (Jensen, Freedman & Rideout 2001). Teachers also agreed, at 92%, that the program helped to:

- increase student focus and attention
- improve teacher-student relationships.

They also agreed, at 77–85%, that it worked to:

- improve student learning
- enhance collaborative work
- increase positive verbal statements
- decrease 'put downs', which are negative verbal messages, between students.

In other words, teachers indicated that the program helps to create a more positive learning environment. In turn, this environment engenders improved learning (this is well documented; see, for example, CASEL (2003); Murdock (1999); and Wentzel (1993)).

The 2002 Self-Science Pilot Study used the youth version of the EQ-i, namely, the EQ-i:YV, for examining the children's EI behavior before and after they were exposed to this curriculum. One of the most successful examples was a Grade 7 classroom of 26 students: a comparison of their pre- and post-assessments revealed significant improvement in self-awareness and self-expression, social awareness and interaction, and emotional management (Bar-On 2003; Freedman 2003).

The Process of Self-Science

Self-Science classes begin with a 'rating scale' with which participants check in on a daily basis. Each student and teacher describes how they are feeling by sharing a feeling word, expressing their feelings with a metaphor, or rating themselves on a scale of 1–10. This serves as a 'hook' into the class and indicates whether there are pressing emotional or social issues that need to be addressed. Typically, the class then progresses to a hands-on activity, called an 'experiment', which is followed by discussion and action planning.

The lessons follow a simple process:

1. **Rating scale**—to check in with students.
2. **Introduction**—to focus attention on a particular topic.
3. **Experiment**—an exercise, simulation or role-play that lets students experience the topic under discussion.
4. **Debriefing**—a discussion of the feelings, thoughts and actions that appeared during the experiment.
5. **Closure**—a wrap-up of key concepts and an invitation for future practice.

Self-Science is built on ten developmental goals, each having cognitive and emotional components. The cognitive, 'thinking' components are important because they increase students' ability to apply the emotional, 'feeling' skills outside the class. Successfully meeting the goals means building a bridge between thinking, feeling and acting.

Students consider their emotional responses and what they are telling themselves, and how they turn that into action or how they do not take action. When students become clear that their thinking, feeling and acting are inexorably linked, they dramatically improve their self-efficacy—they become better able to make small and large choices (Prochaska, Norcross & Diclemente 1995).

While there are research findings that show a link between self-awareness of choices and the ability to make good choices (Ajzen & Fishbein 1980; Brown 1993), further research needs to be conducted to examine this link in depth.

The Differences of Self-Science

While all SEL programs invite students to think about behavior and choices, Self-Science is unique in three ways:

1. *Lessons are experiential.* While it is certainly possible to talk about feelings in the abstract, we believe that students learn better when the lesson comes to life. This is why Self-Science has 'experiments' which students actually carry out. They think, they feel and they act. As in a science laboratory, the experiment provides a powerful source for dialogue and reflection based on the real-life study of thoughts, feelings and actions. This approach is consonant with the principles of brain-based learning (see, for example, Jensen (1998)). Moreover, it ensures an exciting, positive experience for the students.

2. *Students find their own solutions.* While Self-Science classes form agreements about how they will work together, there is no arbitrary 'code of conduct' espoused by Self-Science. The program encourages students to develop their own solutions through respectful, honest dialogue. The process helps them to evaluate their choices and the consequences thereof, and then to act intentionally, as opposed to react impulsively. The facilitator's job is to help clarify interactions on both cognitive and emotional levels, so students understand it as well as 'get it'. They become conscious of their choices and the consequences of those

choices. Rather than teaching children to be rule followers, Self-Science seeks to teach them to make good decisions.

3. *Facilitators set the context and push the process forward.* One of the axioms of Self-Science is that the students bring the content; the facilitator creates the context in which the students learn. This is one of the reasons why the program works with all kinds of people in all kinds of cultures—the curriculum is a process in which the content comes from the participants. Therefore, Self-Science teachers have to be flexible; they must be ready to toss out their lesson plans and discuss what students are preoccupied with at the time. 'Student-centered' also means that the Self-Science teacher is a facilitator, not the 'boss' or expert. The students are the experts—each of us is the only real expert on what is going on inside us! This approach is consonant with research on how people learn about themselves (Bruning, Shaw & Ronning 1995).

Along with skilled facilitation and thoughtfully designed lessons, these three factors come together to meet the essential need of absolute emotional safety. Students must feel safe; they must feel that they will not be judged, humiliated or shamed, and that there will be no recrimination as a result of being honest. Whatever SEL curriculum is employed, the first concern should be forming a trusting and trustworthy learning environment. An SEL class requires a special kind of risk-taking; it works when students are able to be open and honest with themselves and with each other. This happens only when trust levels are high.

The importance of safety is illustrated by this email from Katie Jinkerson, 29, about her experience with Self-Science as a Grade 6 learner:

> I remember a Self-Science class in which fears were the major topic. At the time my grandfather was about to die. As the group discussed old age, death and dying, I realized others share my fears. I was relieved and felt comforted. Because of this experience, I shared in Self-Science that my parents were getting divorced. It was here in Self-Science that I learned to process my feelings and to find appropriate outlets for my anger and frustration through such practices as journaling.

Creating a trustworthy and trusting environment requires special care on the part of the teacher. Good Self-Science teachers are honest, tactful, respectful and direct. Perhaps that is why many Self-Science teachers report that this kind of teaching affects their entire approach to education; they find themselves forming more collaborative relationships with students and parents, and building truly respectful learning communities.

The Success of SEL

We have identified three factors that help people to succeed with SEE. The first and foremost is the attitude of the teacher. The second relates to the way students are engaged in the process. The third comes from the way the parents and community are brought in.

We now explore some tips that relate to each of these factors.

Tip 1: Trust in role modelling

Self-Science facilitators do not exercise absolute authority. They are real humans in dialogue with other—younger—real humans. Together, they learn more effectively how to recognize, understand and manage emotions, how to solve problems, and how to set and meet goals. In Self-Science, teaching entails asking rather than telling; facilitators encourage curiosity, exploration, redefinition, reframing, questioning and multiple solutions rather than one right answer.

The traditional classroom teacher's role often approaches that of a manager, that is, the teacher is primarily concerned with controlling and directing students—if not policing them. In Self-Science, while teachers must certainly maintain order and set limits, their primary role as facilitator is of leading, pulling, tugging and demonstrating how to negotiate and keep the process going. Traditional curricula center around *what* is taught, that is, the **content** of the lesson. In Self-Science, the focus is almost reversed; the most powerful lesson is *how* the program is taught and what is role-modelled, that is, the **process** of the lesson. We believe this is true of EI in general: if you want people to practice the skills of EI, model those skills.

Students can be remarkably perceptive. They observe, consciously and unconsciously, and experiment with behaviors that they see. The facilitator is part of the Self-Science group and curriculum. An honest emotional expression, care in dealing with others' feelings, careful choice of words and follow-through on commitments are all integral ingredients of the students' learning. While we all make mistakes, students have little tolerance for hypocrisy. Thus, whatever is asked of them, they (and we) expect even more of adults.

Before teachers or administrators consider initiating a Self-Science program, they should explore and clarify their own responses to these major questions:

- Are the goals of Self-Science consistent with our personal values?
- Are the goals of Self-Science philosophically consistent with the values of the school in which we teach?
- Do we have the leadership qualifications for Self-Science?

Self-Science teachers should endeavor to meet the following goals:

- Foster EI for the long term.
- Create commitment to experiment with Self-Science strategies.
- Motivate participants to set new goals and priorities; include the choice to build intrinsic motivation.
- Make this learning positive, stimulating and enjoyable by emphasizing humor and high-order thinking, that is, analysis and synthesis as opposed to rote learning.
- Engage multiple learning styles through visual aids, sound, activities, discussion, introspection and other multimedia pedagogies.
- Help students to transfer key ideas and practices from the class to their lives.
- Expand their vocabulary related to emotions and feelings.

- Create alliance, a feeling of community and trust in the group, including making yourselves available as resource and support persons.
- Model excellent communication and instruction.
- Illustrate that people follow patterns of behavior which they can redirect in many instances.
- Provide current research in a practical manner.
- Use the power of optimism.

The more the students understand the process, the safer the group will feel. Teachers can model trust by expressing their feelings openly, labelling actions clearly but *not* labelling people, and by giving feedback and reassurance so that there are no hidden surprises. Teachers build trust by participating in experiments as a member of the group.

Facilitators should note that providing a role model is not a magical process. It simply means being yourselves, while perhaps changing the emphasis on certain skills that you already have. Your hardest job may be to examine the conditioning behind your own (possible) tendencies to take control, wield authority and moralize. While you will never 'let go' completely—you are still operating within a classroom, after all—your efforts should be toward working for greater initiative from the group and less direction from yourselves as time goes on.

Tip 2: Respect the students

There are many programs that claim to teach character, values or social skills, while they actually teach compliance (Kohn 1999). In a behaviorist model, people will act only to avoid pain and seek pleasure. We believe that there is an innate quality in humans that leads them to seek accord, belonging and connection (Doyle 1983). Self-Science nurtures that quality and offers students a chance to develop inner strength. Self-Science leads students to follow their own values 'even when no one is looking'. Sometimes, students experiment with choices, even values, that are anti-social; rather than judging them as wrong or bad, Self-Science facilitators will help the student to explore the benefits and costs of the choices. We believe that when this is done effectively, students develop pro-social values—because people are essentially social creatures. But it takes time.

Self-Science is rooted in the philosophy of humanistic education. A specific example comes from the way this approach uses rules. Self-Science is intended to be part of the fabric of a school committed to learning. In a learning environment, the goal is learning, not obedience. When students break rules, they have created an opportunity for learning. Consequences can be part of the learning, but the purpose is to build insight rather than to show who has power.

For example, one agreement that is a part of most Self-Science classes is confidentiality. This means that students can talk about what happened in Self-Science, which we encourage, and about what they said and did, but they should not identify individuals' words or actions. Put differently, students are encouraged to talk about the content of the class while protecting the anonymity of the other participants. Failing to do this would reduce trust in the group.

One teacher wrote to us in frustration about a 12-year-old student, Joey, who would not respect the confidentiality agreement. When confronted, he appeared intransigent—he insisted that he obtained power and popularity from sharing secrets. We recommended that the teacher bring this issue into the Self-Science class and use it as the basis of a lesson, or several lessons. The teacher asked Joey if they could discuss this issue in Self-Science, and he agreed. 'Confidentiality' became a topic of several classes. The students were able to use the Self-Science process to look at their choices about confidentiality and the costs and benefits of those choices. Moreover, they were able to identify and try out alternatives. Joey came to see that he was not getting the kind of power and popularity he wanted, and that he could get what he most wanted—which was a sense of belonging—in another, more productive way. In other words, no externally driven punishment or reward was needed to elicit a profound change in the child's behavior; all that was needed was a process of clarifying the choices and analyzing the costs and benefits thereof.

Tip 3: See parents as partners

One of the major hurdles of a successful SEL program is engaging parents in the process (Elias, Zins, Weissberg et al. 1997). Parents are not usually opposed or unwilling, but schools often do not have the time and resources to include families as part of their core mission. Perhaps it is time for schools to re-evaluate how they define their 'client' and move toward educating families, not just children.

We are frequently invited to present at parent meetings, and schools are usually surprised by the large attendance—often, two or three times as many parents attend compared to the average. Many parents seem to be interested in and concerned about how children can develop emotional and social skills.

Involving parents in Self-Science is much like involving them anywhere else in schools: if the school wants meaningful involvement, they need to give the parents a meaningful role. As parents realize the importance of the role they play, they become increasingly committed to participating. Parents can be trained as co-facilitators, although not in their own child's classroom, and every parent volunteer should learn about the Self-Science approach and process so they can use these tools in their daily interactions at school and at home.

Schools can offer Self-Science classes for parents, using the same process and curriculum that the students experience. Parents have been enthusiastic about the opportunity to learn what students are doing—and grateful for a chance to discuss the emotional and social issues they face as parents.

In the above mentioned 2001 pilot study, we also asked teachers if they had support from parents and administrators. Teachers who indicated that they did were more successful with the program.

The Use of Self-Science

In order to be effective, Self-Science needs to be implemented in three areas. A full program includes:

1. the class itself
2. integrating Self-Science norms and tools into classes
3. integrating Self-Science norms and tools into the school community.

We now discuss these in more detail.

The Self-Science class

Self-Science is held 30–60 minutes per week, with shorter periods for children under eight, and ideally with a consistent group membership and facilitator. Many schools have used the program in various configurations. In some instances, Self-Science has been the focus of the school's entire design and, in other cases, it has been used as a supplement or enrichment program.

Elementary schools with circle time or class meeting, which are two kinds of daily student-teacher meetings, often use Self-Science once or twice a week in an extended class meeting. Middle schools with homeroom or advisory use the program in those sessions. Teachers tell us that they have added Self-Science to math, science, language arts, history, health, psychology, religion and fitness classes. Some high-school teachers have dedicated a full period of scholastic instruction a week in order to deliver Self-Science because they find that doing so lets them accomplish more curriculum in the rest of the week.

Integration into classes

Teachers can use many of the principles and processes of Self-Science in their other classes. Using a rating scale to check in on feelings can help to focus students before math class, for example. Asking social problem-solving questions in humanities, like, 'What are some alternate ways for the character to express his feelings?', can reinforce the lessons of Self-Science while enhancing the depth of literature discussions.

Integration into the community

Just as Self-Science facilitators assist their class to develop a trusting and trustworthy climate, leaders can do the same school-wide and even system-wide. For example, students, teachers, parents and administrators can come together to look at the ways in which they communicate and the impact of those patterns. They should continuously discuss how the school can turn values into action, and how it can build partnerships in support of learning. Schools can create themes, develop school-wide agreements, move away from extrinsic rewards and punishments, and increase the amount of open dialogue.

Conclusion

What are your goals for education: Lifelong learning? Positive citizenship? Continuing to the next stage of schooling? However we define educational success, helping students to make positive, careful choices is an essential ingredient. In an era where educational policy is acutely focused on 'back to basics' and 'reach those standards', it is worth remembering that the interpersonal dynamics of our schools and classrooms are *the* basic and fundamental building blocks for all learning. Thirty-eight years of implementing Self-Science has convinced our team and others that this program is an essential component of meeting the vision of successful education. Fortunately, there are now many organizations that are promoting the implementation of social-emotional education worldwide—such as the Six Seconds EQ Network, CSEE and CASEL in the US. What matters most is that we create a school in which students are safe, self-reflective and, therefore, best able to learn. The foundation for this innovative approach in education is a combination of self-knowledge and trusting relationships.

The evening news provides enough reason for SEE to be implemented around the world. We have not yet succeeded in helping our youth to build emotionally intelligent lives. Obviously, thinking by itself is insufficient. Instead, wisdom is forged through the fusion of the intellect with emotions in order to generate creative and compassionate actions. It is fortunate that some seeds have been planted. The students, parents and teachers to whom we have referred in this chapter are representative of the many who are working diligently to spread the lessons they learned in Self-Science and similar programs at school, in business and in their families.

References

Ajzen, I., and M. Fishbein. 1980. *Understanding attitudes and predicting social behavior.* New Jersey: Prentice Hall.

Bar-On, R. 2003. How important is it to educate people to be emotionally and socially intelligent, and can it be done? *Perspectives in Education* 21(4): 3–13.

Brown, B.B. 1993. *School culture, social politics, and the academic motivation of US students*, in *Motivating Students to Learn: Overcoming Barriers to High Achievement.* Ed. T.M. Tomlinson. California: McCutchan.

Bruning, R.H., G.J. Shaw, and R.R. Ronning. 1995. *Cognitive psychology and instruction* 2nd ed. New Jersey: Merrill/Prentice Hall.

Collaborative for Academic, Social and Emotional Learning (CASEL). 2003. "SEL & Academic Performance." *Safe and sound: An educational leader's guide to evidence-based social and emotional learning programs.* Chicago: Collaborative for Academic, Social, and Emotional Learning.

Doyle, W. 1983. Academic Work. *Review of Educational Research* 53(2): 159–99.

Elias, M.J., J.E. Zins, R.P. Weissberg, K.S. Frey, M.T. Greenberg, N.M. Haynes, R. Kessler, M.E. Schwab-Stone, and P. Shriver. 1997. *Promoting social and emotional learning: Guidelines for educators.* Virginia: ASCD.

Freedman, J. 2003. Key lessons from 35 years of social-emotional education: How Self-Science builds self-awareness, positive relationships, and healthy decision-making. *Perspectives in Education* 21(4): 69–80.

Goleman, D. 1995. *Emotional intelligence.* New York: Bantam Books.

Jensen, A., J. Freedman, and M. Rideout. 2001. *Self-Science 2001 pilot report.* San Francisco: Six Seconds.

Jensen, E. 1998. *Teaching with the brain in mind.* Virginia: ASCD.

Kohn, Alfie. 1999. *Punished by rewards: The trouble with gold stars, incentive plans, A's, praise, and other bribes.* New York: Mariner Books.

McCown, K, A. Jensen, J. Freedman, and M. Rideout. 1998. *Self-Science: The emotional intelligence curriculum.* San Francisco: Six Seconds.

Murdock, T.B. 1999. The social context of risk: Status and motivational predictors of alienation in middle school. *Journal of Educational Psychology* 91:62–75.

Prochaska, J., J. Norcross., and C. Diclemente. 1995. *Changing for Good.* New York: Avon.

Wentzel, K.R. 1993. Does being good make the grade? Social behavior and academic competance in middle school. *Journal of Educational Psychology* 85:357–64.

Creating an Emotionally Intelligent School District: A Skills-Based Approach

*Marc A. Brackett, Bruce Alster, Charles J. Wolfe,
Nicole A. Katulak and Edward Fale*

Introduction

School personnel have long understood the importance of programs to simultaneously enhance social, emotional and academic learning (Elias, Zins, Weissberg et al. 1997; Greenberg, Weissberg, O'Brien et al. 2003). Links between these areas of learning have been unclear. However, a recent meta-analysis of over 300 studies has shown that SEL programs significantly improve social-emotional skills as well as academic performance (Durlak & Weissberg 2005). Although these findings are promising and the importance of such programs is evident, actually incorporating the programs into districts can be challenging, as they require school-wide support (Elias et al. 1997; Zins, Weissberg, Wang & Walberg 2004). For example, according to CASEL (2003), initiatives to integrate SEL programs into schools should provide training in these skills to both teachers and administrators in addition to students, and should have support at all levels of the district. Moreover, the programs should be field-tested, evidenced-based, and rooted in sound psychological or educational theory (Elias et al. 1997; Matthews, Zeidner & Roberts 2002; Zins et al. 2004). CASEL's (2003) recommendations also emphasize:

- teaching children to apply social-emotional skills both in and out of school
- building connections to schools by creating a caring and engaging learning environment

- providing developmentally and culturally appropriate instruction
- enhancing school performance by addressing the cognitive, affective and social dimensions of learning
- encouraging school-family partnerships
- including continuous evaluation and improvement.

In this chapter, we describe a model developed to address these needs, which was employed to create an Emotionally Intelligent School District in Valley Stream, New York. Our work in the district began after the second author, a former school principal, had attended an EI workshop developed by the third author and psychologist David Caruso (Wolfe & Caruso 2000). The principal believed that infusing programs that are designed to develop the social-emotional skills of administrators, teachers and students would help to create a nurturing school environment and prevent increasingly prevalent problem behaviors such as substance use and abuse, and teenage pregnancy. Furthermore, these types of programs were compatible with mandates set by the No Child Left Behind Act (NCLB) of 2001, and the New York State Education Department's (NYSED) Project SAVE—the Safe Schools Against Violence in Education Act of 2001—which required instruction in civility, citizenship and CE.

The process we describe is rooted in the model of EI promoted by Mayer and Salovey (1997), which involves four fundamental emotion-related skills:

1. Identification and expression of emotion.
2. Use of emotion to facilitate thinking.
3. Understanding of emotion.
4. Management of emotion in ourselves and others.

In this tradition, EI relates to a person's capacity to reason about emotions and to process emotional information in order to enhance cognitive processes and regulate behavior. Importantly, this model focuses on the four skills and does not incorporate other variables such as personality characteristics, like optimism and empathy, that might accompany EI but are better addressed as *distinct* from EI (Brackett & Mayer 2003). In our view, restricting EI to a skills-based approach enables the assessment of the degree to which EI skills specifically contribute to a person's behavior; it also provides a firm foundation for developing programs to increase these skills and for evaluating the efficacy of the program (Brackett & Geher in press).

Table 9.1 gives an overview of Mayer and Salovey's (1997) four-domain EI model. The skills are expected to influence a person's ability to communicate effectively with others, handle stress and conflict, and create a positive work environment. For example, the teacher who is sensitive to subtle changes in emotions may notice sooner when a student begins to get bored or irritated, and

Table 9.1   The Mayer and Salovey model of emotional intelligence

Domain	Skills
Identification of emotion	Ability to perceive emotions in oneself and others, as well as in other stimuli, including objects, art, stories, and music.
Use of emotion to facilitate thinking	Ability to use or generate emotions as necessary: • to focus attention • to communicate feelings • in other cognitive processes such as reasoning, problem-solving, and decision-making.
Understanding of emotion	Ability to understand emotional information, communicate feelings effectively, and understand how emotions combine, progress, and transition from one to another.
Management of emotion	Ability to be open to feelings and to employ effective strategies so as to promote personal understanding and growth.

(Source: Mayer and Salovey 1997.)

perhaps empathize better with the student, depending on the situation. In this way, the teacher has demonstrated good *identification* of emotion and good *use* of emotion respectively. Moreover, if the teacher knows what caused the student's reaction, thus showing good *understanding* of emotion, they may be able help the student to effectively handle the emotion, thereby showing good *management* of emotion.

There are certain performance tests that map onto the Mayer and Salovey (1997) model, including the Mayer-Salovey-Caruso Emotional Intelligence Tests for both adults (MSCEIT) (Mayer, Salovey & Caruso 2002a) and children (MSCEIT-Youth Version) (Mayer, Salovey & Caruso 2005). Research now shows that EI, as measured with these tests, is associated with a wide range of important outcomes at home (Brackett, Warner & Bosco 2005), at school (Gil-Olarte Márquez, Palomera Martín & Brackett in press) and in the workplace (Lopes, Côté, Grewal et al. under review). For example, in a recent study involving approximately 250 Grade 5 and 6 learners, EI scores as assessed by the MSCEIT-YV were associated significantly with teacher-rated outcomes, including adaptability, leadership, study skills, aggression, anxiety, conduct problems, hyperactivity, and attention and learning problems, as well as self-reported smoking behavior, all in the expected directions (*r*s in the |.20 to .50| range) (Brackett, Rivers & Salovey 2005). These findings remained statistically significant after controlling for verbal intelligence, ethnicity and grades. Moreover, the findings support and extend prior research on EI with adolescents (see, for example, Trinidad and Johnson (2001)) and are consistent with several studies conducted on college students (see, for example, Brackett, Mayer and Warner (2004); and Lopes et al. (2004); as well as Brackett and Salovey (2004); and Mayer, Salovey and Caruso (2004)).

We believe that our work in Valley Stream District number 24, which is now being replicated in other districts, provides a useful model of how to implement successfully district-wide SEL programs. Our approach entails two full-day workshops for teachers and administrators. In the first, EI Critical Skills Training, participants learn innovative strategies, tools and techniques to:

- increase their awareness of the importance of EI skills
- enhance their ability to employ these skills in their personal and professional relationships.

In the second workshop, teachers learn how to easily integrate an emotional literacy program into history and language arts curricula, as well as district initiatives such as CE.

We now explore the two workshops in more detail.

Stage 1: EI Critical Skills Training for School Leaders and Teachers

Overview

This workshop is highly interactive and provides participants with:

- in-depth information about the Mayer and Salovey (1997) model
- knowledge of how EI skills can be applied to professional practice
- a powerful tool, the emotional *Blueprint,* which helps them to apply EI skills in their personal lives and work environments
- an opportunity to provide us with their feedback on the program.

There is also the option of an additional half-day, which includes a personal assessment of the four EI skills with feedback. Time constraints and district-specific objectives need to be considered in the determination of the suitability of the one- versus two-day option.

The repertoire of tools offered in the workshop is designed to serve as a set of coping mechanisms for stress, which continually ranks as the top reason for teachers leaving their jobs (Darling-Hammond 2001). Furthermore, the workshop focuses on the improvement of relationships among all the various stakeholders in the school community, as interpersonal relationships have been shown to be a prominent determinant of school efficacy (Teddlie & Reynolds 2000). Topics include classroom management and healthy interactions with parents and administrators, with an emphasis on creating a productive, safer, satisfying and caring school environment. The workshop also pays attention to leadership and professional development, and provides guidance to enhance EI skills.

Each EI skill is presented with group activities, simulations, discussions and ideas for applying the skills in school. For example, to learn about the value of using the emotion-based planning and problem-solving model taught in the workshop, small group discussions are formed using several real case studies pertaining to classroom management, bullying and parent interactions, among others. The case studies demonstrate how the *Blueprint* can be useful in every aspect of intrapersonal and interpersonal relationships.

Personal EI assessment and feedback

Participants in the extended workshop complete the MSCEIT. The MSCEIT is administered online and takes approximately 40 minutes to complete. The test assesses the four-domain model of EI—identifying, using, understanding and managing emotions—with items that are divided between eight tasks, two for each domain. An individual's score is computed by comparing their responses either:

1. to those of the normative sample, comprising over 5,000 people from the US and Canada

2. or to a group of 21 emotions experts who have spent much of their careers investigating how emotions are conveyed in facial expressions, emotional language and emotion regulation.

You can find more information on the MSCEIT in Brackett and Salovey (2004); and Mayer, Salovey and Caruso (2002b).

Participants receive one of the following five types of feedback on their MSCEIT scores, with a brief description:

1. Develop.
2. Consider developing.
3. Competent.
4. Skilled.
5. Expert.

Participants are informed that the MSCEIT is just one way of estimating EI skills, and that low or high scores may not necessarily reflect actual performance, but may have an impact on performance. Also, considerable time is spent on discussing how individuals may be able to develop their emotion-related skills with proper training and effort, and how individuals with high EI can potentially leverage their skills more effectively using the *Blueprint.*

The emotional *Blueprint*

The *Blueprint* (Caruso & Salovey 2004; Wolfe & Caruso 2004) integrates scientific theory on EI with its practical applications. The *Blueprint* helps participants to deal effectively with their own and others' emotional experiences in order to enhance interpersonal interactions.

To learn how to apply the *Blueprint,* individuals analyze a situation that elicited an emotional response. They ask themselves: Who was involved? What were the circumstances? Then they work through the EI model, skill by skill. The steps of the *Blueprint* are hierarchical, beginning with identifying emotions and ending with managing emotions or using the specific strategies that people need to handle their own emotions and those of others. In Table 9.2, the four skills in the first column represent each EI domain. The questions in the second column provide a template for selecting tactics or strategies for dealing with the emotional content of situations based on the skills. The statements in the third column represent scientific principles embedded in the EI model that support the selection of these questions.

We now explore how a school principal applied the *Blueprint* to dealing with an extremely challenging parent. The parent was adamant about having her child's class changed, even though the principal and faculty did not believe it was in the best interest of the child. Based on dealings with the parent, the principal knew that the situation could escalate until he was forced to accommodate her request.

The example has been broken down into the four steps:

- **Step 1: Identifying emotion.** The principal identified how he was feeling, for example concern for the child, irritation with the parent's reaction, worry that his advice would be ignored. Then he imagined the various emotions that the parent may be experiencing, such as concern, worry and a need to be combative.

- **Step 2: Using emotion to facilitate thinking.** He determined how he wanted the parent to feel about the situation, for example be open to various potential solutions and secure that the child's best interest was considered, and how he wanted to feel himself, such as satisfied with the solution and optimistic about his relationship with the parent.

Table 9.2   The emotional *Blueprint*

EI skill	Questions	Scientific basis
Identify	How do we both feel?	Emotions contain data about people and the environment.
Use	How do I want each of us to feel?	Feelings influence how we think and what we think about.
Understand	Why are we feeling the way we do and how might the feelings change?	Emotions have underlying causes, and they follow certain rules.
Manage	What are we able to do—and what are we willing to do—to keep or change these feelings?	Optimal decisions and actions need to blend thinking with the wisdom in feelings.

(Source: Wolfe and Caruso 2004.)

- **Step 3: Understanding emotion.** Now he needed to understand his and the parent's feelings and how the feelings could change to lead to the best possible outcome. For example, he decided that in order to shift the parent's state of mind from combative to open and trusting, he should demonstrate empathy for the parent, compassion for the child, and commitment to making a decision that would be supported by the school and the parent.

- **Step 4: Managing emotion.** The principal needed to determine what he was willing and able to do about the situation. He decided first to inform the parent in a caring tone that he was willing to place the child in the classroom that she had requested. After watching the parent's demeanor change from combative to satisfied, the principal then asked the parent if he could share why he and the faculty felt the change was not in the child's best interest. The parent agreed. The principal gave his explanation in a compassionate way. The parent then asked for time to reflect, and eventually decided to allow her child to remain in the current classroom placement. Finally, a better relationship was developed between the parent and principal.

Evaluation of the workshop

The final element of this first workshop is an evaluation of the training program. Thus far, evaluations have relied primarily on written feedback in the form of a questionnaire distributed at the end of the workshop as well as anecdotes from teachers and administrators who have either used the *Blueprint* themselves or received feedback from colleagues. In Valley Stream, a core group of 14 people participated in the training, including the superintendent, assistant superintendent, three principals, the author of the district's CE curriculum and eight faculty members.

In a series of interviews conducted six months after the training, the authors discovered a variety of improvements that the core group attributed to what they had learned in the workshop. Administrators felt that they had improved the way they conducted performance evaluations by understanding how emotions change at the beginning, middle and end of emotionally charged discussions. Classroom teachers recognized the need to be sensitive to the emotions that students brought with them from home and the playground. For example, instead of rushing directly into schoolwork, one teacher now allows a few minutes first thing in the morning for students to share their feelings. He claimed that spending just 5–10 minutes on this topic made students comfortable and resulted in a better mental state for starting the day's agenda. A special education teacher noted that she had benefited by learning to control her own emotions and becoming more sensitive to the classroom teachers' feelings and needs regarding the mainstreaming of the students for whom she provided services. Finally, one teacher discussed how she used the *Blueprint* to handle her own and other teachers' feelings of sadness and anger regarding the retirement of a well-liked principal. The teachers were struggling to deal with both losing the retired principal and accepting the new one.

We are in the process of designing studies to examine whether the EI training provided in this workshop results in quantifiable changes in EI, work-related stress, and other important outcomes evaluated by teachers, other faculties and administrators.

Summary

In this section we discussed the EI Critical Skills Workshop, which is the first stage in our process of creating an Emotionally Intelligent School District. Our overarching goals are to provide school leaders and teachers with an overview of EI theory, an optional assessment and feedback session, and innovative strategies and techniques such as the emotional *Blueprint* to enhance their own and others' EI skills. The workshop provides participants with an emotional education so that they may see first-hand how emotions play an integral role in decision-making, healthy interpersonal relationships, team-building, managing change and the overall quality of life. Lastly, the workshop provides a framework for teachers and administrators to recognize the importance of incorporating EI skills into the school culture and the standard classroom curriculum, which leads to the second stage in our process.

Stage 2: Emotional Literacy in the Classroom

Overview

The second stage of becoming an Emotionally Intelligent School District is for administrators to select teachers for training in the implementation of a theoretically and evidence-based SEL program that is developmentally appropriate. In Valley Stream, we implemented *Emotional Literacy in the Middle School: A Six Step Program to Promote Social, Emotional, and Academic Learning (ELMS)* (Maurer & Brackett 2004), which is rooted in EI theory. In accordance with CASEL's stance that EI skills should be introduced as early in life as possible and reinforced continuously throughout development (Elias et al. 1997), our ultimate goal is a district-wide initiative with programs for pre-school through Grade 12. We are finalizing a program called 'Emotional literacy in the elementary school', which will be published in spring 2006 (Brackett, Kremenitzer, Maurer & Carpenter in press).

ELMS was designed specifically for children between the ages of 10 and 13 who have either begun middle school or are preparing to transition to a middle-school environment. This is a time when children become more self-aware they establish their sense of identity, and their emotional and social abilities become increasingly important (Eccles 1999). The transition to middle school is also associated with an increase in depression and other problems for many adolescents (Robinson, Garber & Hilsman 1995; Seidman, Allen, Aber et al. 1994). *ELMS* serves as an appropriate starting point for similar programs designed for other age groups, as it is targeted at a population during a developmental period in which cognitive, social and academic pressures converge to increase risk of psychopathology and poor social and academic functioning.

Furthermore, *ELMS* was designed to provide children with social-emotional skills that are vital to their healthy development. The goal of the program is to encourage students to become emotionally literate by gaining a holistic understanding of 'feeling' words—words that characterize the extent of human experience such as elation, guilt, alienation and commitment. The program fosters social skills by teaching students self- and social awareness, empathy and healthy communication. It is also geared toward developing emotion-related skills as students are taught to recognize, label, understand and express feelings. Finally, it aims to promote overall academic learning by enhancing vocabulary, comprehension, abstract reasoning, creative writing, critical thinking and problem-solving skills.

ELMS integrates directly into traditional school subjects such as language arts and history. Given the current environment in schools, language arts and literacy curricula are the most practical vehicles with which to teach social-emotional skills (Bucuvalas 2003). Lessons in both history and literature invariably involve characters who have a wide range of emotional experiences that need to be expressed, understood and regulated. These characters provide 'real-world' examples of how emotions play an integral role in human development. The program is also organized to help teachers to differentiate instruction, thereby supporting the unique and full development of every student.

At a practical level, *ELMS* provides teachers with six 'how to...' steps for quick and easy implementation. Table 9.3 elaborates on these steps.

In addition to the weekly introduction of feeling words through the six steps, there are student projects which are designed to have students work intensively on certain emotional literacy skills, including the identification and regulation of emotion. For example, one project requires students to collect pictures from newspapers and magazines and use them to create collages or mobiles depicting various emotions. In another project students are asked to pick a song and, among other tasks, think and write about the emotional content of its lyrics and the feelings that it evokes.

Training

In Valley Stream, teachers were mailed the curriculum during the summer so that they could prepare for the training workshop that preceded the implementation of the program. Two individuals trained extensively in EI theory and the *ELMS* program led the training, which consisted of an overview of EI theory, a detailed description of the six steps of the emotional literacy program, and sample lessons. Teachers were also provided with information for parents and tips for getting parents involved in the program (see Maurer and Brackett (2004) for more information). Finally, six quality-assurance visits were made to the schools

Table 9.3 The six steps to implementing ELMS

Step	Description	Example	Significance
Step 1: Introduction of Feeling Words	Learning emotion-related vocabulary words by relating their meanings to student experiences	For the word "elated," students talk about a situation in which they felt very excited and happy	Words introduced within the context of their own personal experiences may enhance the understanding and recall of the words and their meanings
Step 2: Designs and Personified Explanations	Interpreting and explaining abstract designs in terms of their possible symbolic representations of feeling words	Students explain how a design consisting of several circles connected by lines looks like the word elated	Encourages divergent thinking and the visualization of the elements and actions that represent meanings of feeling words
Step 3: Academic and Real World Associations	Relating feeling words to social and academic issues	Students are asked to link the word elated to the 2004 Tsunami disaster	Teaches students to evaluate how people of different societies and time periods experience, express, and manage emotions
Step 4: Personal Family Association	Discussing feeling words with family members at home	Students ask parents about a time when they felt elated	Parents are involved in students' academic work; Students have increased self-understanding by relating to parents
Step 5: Classroom Discussions	Initiating class discussions based on sharing of Real World Associations and Personal Family Associations with Class	When a student says refugees in Thailand were elated after receiving help and food, the teacher asks the class how they feel when they help others	Students expand each other's knowledge and are exposed to others' viewpoints
Step 6: Creative Writing Assignments	Writing essays using the feeling word of the week	Students are asked to tell a story with a beginning, middle, and end about a person who went from feeling forlorn to elated	Students incorporate their own ideas and personal experiences into writing and think critically about how emotions progress and transform life experiences

(Source: Maurer and Brackett 2004.)

during the curriculum implementation to provide ongoing support and training to the teachers.

Evaluation of the workshop

A comprehensive multi-method system was implemented to evaluate *ELMS*. Anecdotal feedback was collected in monthly meetings with faculty members. In the meetings, the researchers, superintendent, school principals and teachers discussed several topics ranging from the students' work to the teachers' concerns to anecdotes about the progress of the program. For example, teachers often shared their students' worksheets and essays, and discussed what had occurred during the classroom discussions.

Teachers and students are exhibiting strong, positive reactions to *ELMS*. According to the teachers, their students:

- report feeling more comfortable expressing themselves in class without fear of being judged or ridiculed
- are gaining a better understanding of their peers and family members
- are interacting more effectively; for example, one teacher reported better-quality relationships among groups of students who had previously been unable to interact positively with each other, whereas another reported a decrease in problem behavior and an increase in pro-social behavior
- are writing better and incorporating feeling words into curriculum areas.

Teachers also report:

- more positive relationships between themselves and other students
- seeing changes in themselves; for example, they report being:
- more comfortable with sharing their own experiences
- better at recognizing and responding constructively to their students' social-emotional needs
- keenly aware of their own emotions and how these contribute to maintaining a healthy climate in the classroom. This is particularly important because research indicates that teachers' emotions influence both their own and their students' cognitions, motivations and behaviors.

(Sutton & Wheatley 2003)

Moreover, a grant-funded randomized field experiment is currently being conducted in Valley Stream to test the efficacy of *ELMS*. The study examines the program's impact on students':

- emotion skills, for example understanding of emotion and emotion management
- attitudes toward health-risk behaviors, deviance and school
- social competence, for example pro-social and aggressive behavior, measured with self- and teacher ratings
- mental health, for example anxiety and depression

- academic achievement, including the students' writing, problem-solving skills and standardized test scores.

In the study, Grade 5 and 6 learners in the randomly assigned intervention and control groups are being compared at baseline, that is, one week before program implementation; after four months; and one week after the program is finished, that is, seven months later. There will be two additional post-tests, six months and one year after the first one, to examine the long-term effects of the program. Preliminary analyses of these data suggest that students who received *ELMS,* as compared to the control group, were perceived by teachers to be more adaptable and to possess stronger leadership, social and study skills as well as to be less anxious, depressed, hyperactive, avoidant and negative toward school after four months of experiencing the *ELMS* program (Brackett, Rivers & Salovey 2005). Significantly, the students in the *ELMS* group as compared to the control group had higher year-end grades, particularly in writing.

Summary

A main objective of the *ELMS* program is for emotions and feeling words to become concepts that help students to govern their lives in a purposeful and pro-ductive manner. Among the many potential benefits, students may gain these abilities:

- Identify, compare and evaluate their own and others' thoughts, feelings and actions.
- Understand the main idea of stories.
- Describe real-life events and problems.
- Discuss and write articulately about social and personal experiences.

The program furthermore encourages children to make intelligent decisions that are informed by feelings. This may help them to deal effectively with the increasing dangers that they face, such as substance abuse and dysfunctional relationships with friends and family members. Thus far, both the anecdotal and empirical findings support these goals.

Conclusion

In this chapter, we described a two-stage process that was used to infuse social-emotional skills into a school district. The first stage is the EI Critical Skills Workshop for key members of the administration and faculty. The work-shop provides participants with an overview and personal assessment of EI and the emotional *Blueprint* to help them to infuse EI skills into their personal and professional lives. In the second stage, we trained language arts and social studies teachers to implement *ELMS* into their classes.

These programs are currently being evaluated. Thus far, the anecdotal feedback from both teachers and students indicates that the two workshops are well received and enjoyable, and produce consequential results. Teachers and principals report having improved relationships with colleagues, parents and students. In turn, students report fostering better quality relationships with their peers, teachers and parents. The anecdotal feedback and results also demonstrate that *ELMS* has a positive impact on psychosocial and academic outcomes. Our next steps involve replicating the program in other school districts and following teachers and students in a longitudinal effort to determine the lasting impact of social-emotional skills training.

There is now substantial evidence demonstrating that social-emotional skills play an integral role in people's daily lives (Durlak & Weissberg 2005; Mayer, Salovey & Caruso 2004). Consistent with the views of CASEL (2003), we assert that integrating social-emotional skills training into a school district will result in a number of benefits for students, teachers and administrators. Thus, creating an Emotionally Intelligent School District acknowledges that emotions are an important topic for discussion and that none of us can be fully intelligent if we do not value and work with emotion.

Acknowledgments

This research was supported in part by a grant awarded to Marc A. Brackett and Peter Salovey from the Institution for Social and Policy Studies at Yale University. We would like to thank Marvin Maurer, Marilyn Carpenter, Susan Rivers and Amy Latimer for their input and invaluable feedback on earlier drafts of this chapter.

References

Brackett, M.A., and G. Geher. in press. Measuring emotional intelligence: Paradigmatic shifts and common ground. In *Emotional intelligence and everyday life* 2nd ed. Ed. J. Ciarrochi, J.P. Forgas, and J.D. Mayer. New York: Psychology Press.

Brackett, M.A., and J.D. Mayer. 2003. Convergent, discriminant, and incremental validity of competing measures of emotional intelligence. *Personality and Social Psychology Bulletin* 29:1147–58.

Brackett, M.A., J.D. Mayer, and R.M. Warner. 2004. Emotional intelligence and its relation to everyday behaviour. *Personality and Individual Differences* 36:1387–1402.

Brackett, M.A., S. Rivers. and P. Salovey. 2005. Emotional Intelligence and its relation to social, emotional, and academic outcomes among adolescents. Unpublished data, Yale University.

Brackett, M.A., and P. Salovey. 2004. Measuring emotional intelligence as a mental ability with the Mayer-Salovey-Caruso Emotional Intelligence Test. In *Measurement of Emotional Intelligence*. Ed. G. Geher, pp. 179–94. Hauppauge, NY: Nova Science Publishers.

Brackett, M.A., R.M. Warner, and J. Bosco. 2005. Emotional intelligence and relationship quality among couples. *Personal Relationships* 12:197–212.

Bucuvalas, A. 2003, February 1. Teaching social awareness. An interview with Larsen Professor Robert Selman. Retrieved April 21, 2005 from http:/www.gse.harvard.edu/news/features/selman02012003.html.

Caruso, D., and P. Salovey. 2004. *The emotionally intelligent manager.* New York: Jossey Bass.

Collaborative for Academic, Social, & Emotional Learning (CASEL). 2003. *Safe and sound: An educational leader's guide to evidence-based social and emotional learning programs.* Chicago: Author.

Darling-Hammond, L. 2001. The Challenge of Staffing Our Schools. *Educational Leadership* 58:12–17.

Durlak, J.A., and R.P. Weissberg. 2005, August *A major meta-analysis of positive youth development programs.* Invited presentation at the Annual Meeting of the American Psychological Association. Washington, DC.

Eccles, J.S. 1999. The development of children ages 6–14. *The Future of Children* 9:30–44.

Elias, M., J. Zins, R. Weissberg, K. Frey, T. Greenberg, N. Haynes, R. Kessler, M. Schwab-Stone, and T. Shriver. 1997. *Promoting social and emotional learning: Guidelines for educators.* Alexandria, VA: Association for Supervision and Curriculum Development.

Gil-Olarte Márquez, P., R. Palomera Martín, and M.A. Brackett. in press. Relating emotional intelligence to social competence, and academic achievement among high school students. *Psicothema.*

Greenberg, M.T, R.P. Weissberg, M.U. O'Brien, J. Zins, L. Fredericks, H. Resnik, and M.J. Elias. 2003. Enhancing school-based prevention and youth development through coordinated social, emotional, and academic learning. *American Psychologist* 58:466–74.

Kremenitzer, J.P., and M.A. Brackett, with M. Maurer., M. Carpenter, S.E. Rivers, and N. Katulak. 2007. *Emotional literacy in the elementary school.* Portchester, NY: National Professional Resources.

Lopes, P.N., S. Côté, D. Grewal, J. Kadis, M. Gall, and P. Salovey. under review. Emotional intelligence and positive work outcomes.

Lopes, P.N., M.A. Brackett, J.B. Nezlek, A. Schütz, and I. Sellin, and P. Salovey. 2004. Emotional intelligence and social interaction. *Personality and Social Psychology Bulletin* 30:1018–34.

Matthews, G., M. Zeidner, and R.D. Roberts. 2002. *Emotional intelligence: Science and myth.* Cambridge, MA: The MIT Press.

Maurer, M., and M.A. Brackett. 2004. *Emotional literacy in the middle school: A six-step program to promote social, emotional, and academic learning.* Portchester, NY: National Professional Resources.

Mayer, J.D., and P. Salovey. 1997. What is emotional intelligence? In *Emotional development and emotional intelligence: Implications for educators.* Ed. P. Salovey & D. Sluyter, pp. 3–31. New York: Basic Books.

Mayer, J.D., P. Salovey, and D. Caruso. 2002a. *The Mayer-Salovey-Caruso Emotional Intelligence Test (MSCEIT),* Version 2.0. Toronto, Canada: Multi Health Systems.

———. 2002b. *MSCEIT technical manual.* Toronto, Canada: Multi Health Systems.

———. 2004. Emotional intelligence: Theory, findings, and implications. *Psychological Inquiry* 15:197–215.

————. 2005. *The Mayer-Salovey-Caruso Emotional Intelligence Test—Youth Version (MSCEIT-YV)*, Research Version 1.0. Toronto, Canada: Multi Health Systems.

No Child Left Behind Act, PL 107-110. 2001.

Project SAVE: *Safe Schools Against Violence in Education*, New York State Education Department (2001).

Robinson, N.S., J. Garber, and R. Hilsman. 1995. Cognitions and stress: Direct and moderating effects on depressive versus externalizing symptoms during the junior high school transition. *Journal of Abnormal Psychology* 104:453–63.

Seidman, E., L. Allen, J.L. Aber, C. Mitchell, and J. Feinman. 1994. The impact of school transitions in early adolescence on the self-system and perceived social context of poor urban youth. *Child Development* 65:507–22.

Shriver, T.P., and R.P. Weissberg. 2005, August 16. No emotion left behind. *The New York Times* 13.

Sutton, R.E., and K.F. Wheatley. 2003. Teachers' emotions and teaching: A review of the literature and directions for future research. *Educational Psychology Review* 15:327–58.

Teddlie, C., and D. Reynolds. 2000. The international handbook of school effectiveness research. London: Falmer.

Trinidad, D.R., and C.A. Johnson. 2001. The association between emotional intelligence and early adolescent tobacco and alcohol use. *Personality and individual differences* 32:95–105.

Wolfe, C., and D. Caruso. 2000. Emotionally intelligent MSCEIT Certification Workshop. Simsbury, CT: Charles J Wolfe.

Wolfe, C., and D. Caruso. 2004. *Emotional intelligence critical skills for success participant manual* 1st ed. Shelton, CT: New Haven Consulting Group, Inc.

Zins, J.E., R.P. Weissberg, M.C. Wang, and H.J. Walberg, eds. 2004. *Building academic success on social and emotional learning.* New York: Teachers College Press.

— 10 —

First Steps in Developing a Community-Based Teacher Training Program Designed to Educate Children to Be Emotionally Intelligent

Jacobus G. Maree and Queen Esther M. Mokhuane

Introduction

During Youth Day celebrations in South Africa, speaker after speaker regularly emphasizes the need for young people to 'abstain from sexual intercourse, stay away from drugs, refrain from considering taking their own lives and from becoming involved in criminal activities', stressing that young people's futures lie in their own hands. Curiously, however, not a single person refers to the crucial concept of EI. Yet research findings consistently demonstrate that SEL represents a highly successful approach to dealing with the increasing problems afflicting youth in South Africa and around the world.

A growing body of research findings indicating that well-designed and well-implemented SEL programming can positively influence a diverse array of academic, social and health outcomes is highly relevant for education in South Africa (Zins, Elias & Greenberg 2003). Furthermore, Bar-On stresses the need to recruit emotionally and socially intelligent individuals to educate others in becoming more emotionally and socially intelligent: 'It is logical to assume that these people will be the best teachers...[and] if we succeed in raising and educating more emotionally and socially intelligent children, we will contribute to building more effective and productive organizations, communities and societies' (Bar-On 2003:13).

EI is much more than a program that preaches about morality, behavior, responsibilities, self-awareness and maximizing our potential. It is crucial for individuals to recognize their own and other people's emotions, to understand these emotions and to express them in a non-destructive way. Indeed, emotions can and should be used as sources of 'creativity, problem-solving, decision-making, and motivation [and] should be encouraged by schools and families' (Salovey 2003:96). It has been established that being emotionally and socially intelligent can help people to become more successful in both their work (Druskat, Sala & Mount 2005) and in their personal lives (Bar-On personal communication 2005).

In light of this, we need to ask ourselves these questions:

- Should skills related to EI find their way into school curricula in South Africa?
- Given the current educational paradigm, can such skills be effectively developed in our schools?
- Would the introduction of skills related to EI radically modify schools or would schools mock such skills?

In this chapter, we will attempt to address these questions. We will outline the challenges that face South African educators as they contemplate the implementation of EI programs in schools and will hopefully provide one of the essential building blocks in the development of such programs. We will also describe the first steps in the development of a community-based teacher training EI program in South Africa, which may provide a general outline for such planning in other countries.

Challenges Facing South African Educators

South Africa (SA) is at a highly critical stage with regard to education. Years of turmoil in the country have taken their toll, and unless decisive and drastic steps are taken, the problems will continue to plague the educational system. The consequences may not be immediately visible, but the long-term implications can prove to be disastrous for a nation struggling to find its feet. The challenges facing South African educators are numerous and affect the educational system at every level. Furthermore, South Africa provides 'a context where unemployment stands at 36% [some say 40+%] and where child poverty is estimated at 40%' (Folscher, in Motala & Perry 2001:12). Southern Africa is 'the site of the worst humanitarian crisis in the world today', according to James Morris, UN Special Envoy for Humanitarian Needs in Southern Africa (in Tromp 2004:2). Kriegler (1993:64) stresses the fact that 'the vast educational, psychological, and social needs of the non-privileged majority are minimally provided for.... The average ratio [educational psychologist:number of students] for black education is 1:30,000, whereas for whites it is 1:2,750'. There is every reason to believe that this situation has not changed significantly since 1994.

According to Pillay, Naidoo and Lockhat (1999), epidemiological data are by and large absent in South Africa. Nonetheless, it is roughly estimated that 15% of SA's adolescent population are experiencing mental health problems, which translates into approximately two million adolescents, the majority of whom have grown up in varying degrees of being disadvantaged.

McLoyd (in Grieve 2001:333) argues conclusively that poverty increases developmental risk in children, since 'economic adversity and negative life events have an impact on parenting ability that leads to a diminished expression of affection, lessened responsiveness to children's expressed needs, a tendency to issue commands without explanation...and less likelihood of rewarding a child verbally'. Clearly, these matters have a significant negative impact on children's acquisition of EI, as well as on their intellectual growth in general.

We must also view the above mentioned against the frame of reference of a serious poverty cycle, which is resulting in escalating socio-economic deprivation, lack of education, joblessness—a large percentage of society being forced to rely on government grants for survival—and high crime levels. Furthermore, the fact that millions of people in SA are undernourished and that this figure is rising by many thousands per year prompts us to ask the following question: How can we better show EI and wisdom, in the Sternbergian sense of promoting the idea of the common good (Sternberg 2001), in SA?

Over ten years after the demise of the apartheid system in this country, our society is threatened by high crime levels, unacceptable teenage suicide rates, and the continued use of corporal punishment and other forms of child abuse in schools, despite the latter being outlawed in 1997. As is the case in the US (Van Tassel & Wills, in Begoray & Slovinsky 1997), far too many parents are often absent, engaged in long hours of work in low-paying jobs, and lack even the most basic educational skills, the result being little interest in emotional, social, academic or intellectual pursuits. Thus, a vicious cycle is created. The situation is at its worst in the rural areas of SA.

Professionals agree that it is crucial for individuals to recognize their own and other people's emotions, to understand these emotions and to express them in a non-destructive way (Maree & Molepo 2004). However, this is not happening in South Africa. Far too often, we observe:

- a marked discrepancy between expected and actual performance
- inconsistency in accomplishing goals
- impaired levels of self-confidence
- feelings of inferiority
- blaming others for our own troubles
- evidence of withdrawal and alienation.

This checklist suggests that a high IQ alone does not 'guarantee' satisfactory achievement, and other factors have to be taken into account in the attempt to explain the great variance in human achievement.

Goleman (2003:1) argues that 'we have been inadvertently short-changing our children because of this split between thought and feeling'. In order to facilitate a 'fairer deal' for youth in SA, intelligence should be redefined in order to include a person's capacity to monitor their own and others' emotions, to discriminate among these emotions and to use this information to guide their thinking and actions (Salovey & Mayer 1990). In this chapter, we will focus on the application, or generalization, of learning to show evidence of a move toward a more inclusive definition of intellectual functioning and intelligent behavior. After all, research has conclusively exposed the 'extremely limited predictability of cognitive potential in determining success in life' (Brady 1998:3).

EI Programs in South African Schools

Modelling emotionally intelligent behavior at home is the first step in nurturing emotionally intelligent children (Elias, Tobias & Friedlander 2000; Stern & Elias 2005). At school, parents can continue to work with educators and other members of their community to create a climate that supports SEL in and out of the classroom. And it is increasingly evident that a high degree of EI is required in order for the workplace of the 21st century to be maximally creative, productive and company-centered (Druskat et al. 2005). There are indications that EI skills may not only be playing a more important role in microeconomics (Bar-On 2004), they could also impact on the economics of nations as diverse as SA, and possibly the global economy, at least to some extent.

To moderate the acquisition of the above mentioned EI skills, we need dedicated parents, teachers, counsellors and administrators who will play a crucial role in the program described in this chapter. We wish to emphasize the point that this is a work in progress. During the next phase of our project, we will focus on the respective roles of counsellors, administrators and policy makers.

The Role of Teachers and Parents

There is evidently a need for an EI training program in SA schools. In this section, we will highlight this need and the apparent shortcomings in the current methods of preparation in SA.

In our country, teachers are trained predominantly at universities, where they typically complete a three-year degree, followed by a postgraduate certificate in education (PGCE). Conversely, they may wish to enroll for a four-year teaching degree, a Bachelor of Education (BEd). Regardless of the training mode, it is possible but in no way guaranteed that these teachers will encounter the concept of EI during training. However, even when EI is introduced into training programs, teachers receive at best a superficial overview of the concept, with little or no practical training. To understand this situation better, we need to read this against the backdrop of the following scenario.

Children's well-being and development depend very much on the security of family relationships and a predictable environment, including a stable and adequate educational environment. If children lose the protection of their family, if the family is seriously weakened or if the educational system fails them, they are immediately vulnerable to various distressing situations and experiences. In SA, a large percentage of children—especially those in the rural areas—live with caregivers other than their parents, for instance their grandmother, or *mak-golo*. An example of secondary distress that is encountered is the unnecessary separation of children from their widowed mothers or siblings when placed in institutions or foster families, where the risk of neglect and abuse is greater, sometimes posed by those who should be caring for them. Caregivers cannot always protect children from secondary distress, which is all too evident (Millwood 2002).

As far as the educational support system in SA is concerned, it is not uncommon to see 70+ learners crammed into a single classroom. Learner support material is often non-existent. In other studies, related to the project described here, we conducted in-depth interviews with principals, and we often sensed their 'thick', that is, abundant, **demotivation** or lack of motivation. We saw hungry children faint while we were addressing schools. We saw children walking to school 12 km from their homes. We were informed that the norm in many of the rural areas is a travelling distance of 7–12 km to and from school. According to teachers, moreover, children are regularly dropping out of school to assume household duties, often to look after siblings.

We witnessed degrading sanitation conditions, we saw inhumane living conditions, and we heard heart-rending tales about children prepared to do anything for money to buy the most basic foods. Frequently, we could not find a trace of recreational facilities. Running water is often a luxury; and even when it is available, many children have to share a single water tap. Telecommunication links and electricity tend to be rare. The number of teachers taking lengthy periods of leave or falling ill and becoming unable to fulfil their teaching duties is an ever-increasing phenomenon. Feelings of despair, hunger and isolation leading to an external locus of control are often experienced by the learners we have encountered. We could not help wondering: How do we reconcile these circumstances with the spirit and letter of the Convention on the Rights of the Child and with the Constitution of South Africa, specifically the section that refers to the rights of children?

Our crucial question has become this: How can life skills acquisition be facilitated in these circumstances? Looking at the contents of the Life Orientation curriculum developed for South African schools, we realize the potential contradictions in trying to seriously emphasize human dignity—*ubuntu*—when 10 million people are living in squatter camps. For example, how do we teach these children about the need to wash their hands after visiting the toilet and before a meal when they do not have a toilet or a meal, nor running water, nor a bar of soap? How do we teach them about stress management, or about banks? How do we facilitate their acquisition of a healthy self-image and adequate self-realization when they do not have clothes to wear, and when it appears that no one cares? How exactly should students deal with their strong emotions, emotions that many have learned to ignore or repress, perhaps adaptively? It seems that many teachers do not have the ability or, understandably, the motivation to deal with life skills issues. As one teacher bluntly put it: *'Ga re na tshepo'* ('We do not have any hope'), let alone the motivation to teach basic life skills.

Clearly, the lives of children in SA are rife with interpersonal challenges, requiring them to be adept at recognizing emotions in themselves and others; being able to establish caring relationships; knowing when, where and how to extend trust; knowing how to work together with others, and to put off the mantle of isolationism and individualized desperation that serves to maintain those in greatest need in the most dire situations. We believe that children deserve to be prepared with skills to address the challenges of life. We believe they have an absolute right to it, a development right. EI programs need to be implemented in all schools and institutions in SA, and must involve every learner, student, educator and other staff member. Indeed, when it comes to equipping children with life skills, *failure is not an option,* as Alan Blankstein (2004) argues so well in his book of the same name.

The South African government has identified the implementation of a Life Orientation program at primary and secondary schools as a key element in its fight against the HIV/Aids pandemic. However, Millwood (2002) emphasizes the fact that a long-term perspective that incorporates the psychosocial well-being of children will have to be adopted if Aids is to be combated effectively. Although this includes supplying material aid such as water and sanitation facilities, food, shelter and health care, non-material factors—including enhancing EI—are central to increasing such well-being. Millwood (2002) aptly states that it is essential to ensure that the help that is provided does not create passive receivers—people must be helped to help themselves. Moreover, he refers to the importance of career-counselling skills training for young people being enhanced, not only to help augment income-earning ability and economic independence, but also serving to increase a feeling of identity and self-worth that enables psychological healing.

Van der Linde (2005) stresses the fact that South African teachers appear to be poorly equipped to deal with EI issues. This is clear from, inter alia, the following: only 52% of all South African teachers have attended a workshop on life skills, while 55% of teachers have already considered leaving the profession. Furthermore, these teachers cite the following reasons for wanting to leave the education profession:

- Lack of career development.
- Increased workload, which precipitates increased stress levels.
- Job insecurity.

Teachers' health also, and interestingly, appears to be poorer than that of the rest of the population. Van der Linde (2005:4) recommends that the National Department of Education 'set up a comprehensive workplace healthcare programme', which should clearly include an EI program.

A Community-Based Teacher Training Program in SA

According to CASEL's SEL guidelines (in Elias, Zins, Weissberg et al. 1997), researchers must begin from a known starting point such as an established, evidence-based program; then, through action research, refine the approach. We uphold this view and intend to tailor the approach to the unique circumstances that we are facing in SA.

Training teachers is the first stage in implementing SEL programs. We must provide teachers with the relevant EI/SEL background so that they can teach learners to be emotionally intelligent. The best teachers are themselves more emotionally intelligent, based on a recent study conducted in the US (Haskett 2002). This may have implications for admitting students to undergraduate programs in education, or at least selecting them to deliver EI/SEL programs. Even though the specific empirical base connecting EI (as measured by the EQ-i, for example), teachers and teaching is still in its infancy, the EI construct's relationship to teachers and teaching is well supported (Elias 2003). In fact, there is ample evidence across studies of teacher selection and preparation to suggest that EI is a valuable quality for teachers to have, although these studies may never mention the words 'EI' or 'SEL' (Bar-On personal communication 2005).

In order to facilitate the implementation of the community-based program described here, teachers and parents are trained in four South African provinces: Gauteng, Limpopo, Mpumalanga and North-West. A number of schools in these provinces will hear about the concept of EI for the first time. Parents will simultaneously be involved in EI training. Through a series of workshops, teachers will be provided with guidelines regarding ways to optimize the EI skills of learners.

This is a pilot study in every sense of the word, especially in a context like SA. Therefore, it is premature to contemplate replication based on our work to date. But we would like to emphasize the process, the meticulous preparation and thoughtfulness, and the responsiveness of investigators to what we are witnessing. These teachers and parents will facilitate EI skills acquisition for many others, including learners, other teachers and parents, via the process of peer-teacher learning, thereby potentially empowering many other colleagues. Moreover, thousands of learners will benefit greatly from the proposed intervention. Networking between schools and communities will be enhanced, which in turn will activate community-based support structures representing assets for children in our traumatized society.

Objectives

According to our initial planning, after the successful implementation of this project, the following objectives will have been attained:

- Four teachers in six schools, that is, 24 teachers, will have been directly involved in each of the four provinces, with a focus on traditionally disadvantaged regions. They will have become familiar with the concept of EI for the first time.

- Thirty learners in six schools, that is, 180 learners, will be assessed with the 60-item EQ-i:YV (Bar-On & Parker 2000). This will be done to evaluate changes in their EI based on pre- and post-intervention assessments. Since eight schools have subsequently opted to take part in our study, 32 teachers—4 x 8—and 320 learners—8 x 40—are currently involved in the program.

- Thousands of learners will have benefited from the proposed intervention. Most of them will have benefited from developing EI skills for the first time.

- Many parents will have been reached through this intervention, potentially empowering thousands of others.

- Networking between schools and communities will have been enhanced, thereby activating community-based support structures.

- Since, in our view, and in the above mentioned context, EI forms an integral part of the counselling process in schools, our theory base in social-emotional counselling will have been broadened to include one that is to make it 'holistic, contextual, and multicultural' (Savickas 2003:89).

Rationale

The following four key factors prompted the implementation of the proposed SEL program described in this chapter:

1. A growing realization of the importance of the EI concept globally:

The importance of EI in the 21st century is extremely popular, especially in education and in the workplace. Although for many years SEL was regarded as a 'soft' concept and dismissed as unimportant and not scientifically based, over the past five years 'the inter-linkage of cognitive and emotional skills and behavioral functioning' has received due recognition (Cohen & Sandy 2003:44).

As early as 1979, Madge (1979:55) was at pains to point out that 'no one has ever suggested that a measurement of intelligence or IQ can estimate an individual's chance of becoming an active, responsible member of society, his role as a community leader, his contributions to mankind, or his ability to get along with people. There are many human qualities such as warmheartedness, cheerfulness, unpretentiousness, courage and empathy which have no relationship whatsoever with IQ...[which is] certainly not intended to tell everything about a child'.

Clearly, she was referring intuitively to factors that are currently assessed by EQ tests. In fact, part of her assumption has been already confirmed by a growing body of research findings demonstrating that EQ is a better predictor of success in life than IQ, which in turn is strengthened by Richer Wagner's 1997 meta-analytic study demonstrating that cognitive intelligence predicts little in life other than academic performance (Bar-On personal communication 2005).

2. The erroneous view that IQ, on its own, predicts life success and happiness.

Even early in the 21st century, many parents, children and researchers still consider cognitive intelligence to be the most important predictor of success in life. Learners hearing from their parents and teachers that they have a low or high IQ tend to perform in accordance with the expectations that are associated with this, thereby enacting a self-fulfilling prophecy. For example, if teachers believe that certain children have a relatively low IQ, the marks given to these children quite often agree with their low expectation. However, it is unclear if the low marks are based primarily on the low expectations of the teachers and/or of the learners, because IQ truly impacts academic performance with correlation coefficients traditionally ranging between the .60s and the .80s. It is most likely the combination of factors that impacts on their marks (Bar-On personal communication 2005).

Inversely, teachers often tend to allocate higher marks to children whom they believe to have a high intelligence. It is therefore feasible that if the expectations that parents and teachers have of children become more positive, these learners should begin to actualize their true potential to a greater extent.

3. The importance of realizing that other factors explain the great variance in life success:

Cognitive intelligence is only *one* aspect of intelligence. David Wechsler (1940; 1943) pointed this out more than half a century ago when he discussed 'intelligent behavior'. He was one of the first to discuss the impact of 'conative' and 'non-intellective', or non-cognitive, factors on 'intelligent behavior' in addition to cognitive intelligence. However, even in 2006, both laypeople and professionals still confuse cognitive intelligence with general intelligence, as if these concepts are the same—rather than the former being a component of the latter. This mistake impacts on educational goals (Bar-On personal communication 2005).

Bar-On (2004; personal communication 2005) has demonstrated that EI impacts on a wide range of human behavior, such as scholastic performance, occupational performance, interpersonal relations, and self-actualization, as well as overall subjective well-being. In other words, factors other than IQ appear to explain most of the variance in success in different areas of life. The degree of variance in occupational performance represented by cognitive intelligence, for example, ranges between 4% and 9%, based on Wagner's findings (averaged correlation coefficients ranged from .20 to .30).

Conclusions regarding types of performance other than academic and occupational performance are even more problematic to evaluate. Clearly, the contributions of EI to success in school, family and community life, and in the workplace, have been under-appreciated traditionally, while the importance of IQ to those successes has been extolled to a degree far greater than data can support. Kapp (2000:151) rightly notes that the concept of EI has taken the world by storm.

4. The realization that EI addresses dimensions of intelligence that are vital to daily functioning:

Internationally, there is a growing realization that EI addresses the emotional, personal, social and survival dimensions of intelligence. EI is concerned with understanding ourselves and others, relating to people, and adapting to and coping with our immediate surroundings. These factors increase our ability to be more successful in dealing with daily demands as they arise. This construct is tactical and immediate in nature; as such, it reflects our 'common sense' and our ability to 'get along' in the world (Bar-On 1997; Elias 2003).

Proposed intervention

Our intervention is based on the following guidelines (Dalton, Elias & Wandersman in press):

1. Carry out environmental reconnaissance to understand the context within which the intervention will take place.
2. Ensure strong agreement on program goals among all stakeholders.
3. Ensure connection of program goals to the core mission of the host setting.
4. Consider a coalition with related local settings.
5. Develop strong, clear leadership among teachers.
6. Describe the innovation in simple terms, especially in the beginning.
7. When the program begins, ensure implementation of its core principles and elements.
8. Measure program implementation and attainment of program objectives throughout the operation of the program and continuously refine based on qualitative and quantitative action research data.
9. Search for unintended effects of the program.
10. Plan for institutionalization of the program in the host setting.
11. Establish external linkages with similar programs in other settings.

Learners are at the center of the intervention. However, teachers, parents, psychologists and other health care professionals are involved to facilitate a joint strategy. The basic plan has been to select certain schools, carry out pre-intervention EI assessments of a number of learners and teachers in these schools, and then introduce the EI program at these schools. We will conclude by conducting a post-intervention EI assessment to help to evaluate the success of the program. In addition to comparing pre- and post-intervention assessments for increases in emotionally and socially intelligent behavior, a follow-up investigation will comprise a combination of qualitative and quantitative research strategies to facilitate triangulation of our findings. The following steps will be undertaken with a reasonable degree of flexibility.

We have begun making **introductory visits to purposefully selected schools** to assess their primary needs as these relate to the children's EI level and general behavior as it relates to the above mentioned parameters. Our training is imparting basic understanding about EI and SEL and what we consider key pedagogical guidelines, after which we will engage in a process of selecting a specific intervention.

During training, we would like to inculcate the following beliefs in teachers:

- Non-judgemental acceptance and respect, which is central to the process of individual growth.
- Appropriate, non-manipulative disclosure of thoughts and feelings about self and others is valued and facilitates personal growth.
- Experiencing of the present moment, the 'here and now' of learners and teachers.
- Learning words for their emotions, in addition to conveying it to their students.

With regard to **follow-up visits to schools,** once formal training is over, schools will be visited at least once a month for the duration of eight months. Teachers' interactions will be observed and noted *in situ* on an observation schedule.

The importance of networking with professionals from all walks of life is stressed consistently in the SEL literature, the main idea being to facilitate a supportive, non-threatening and encouraging environment. The isolation and extremely impoverished nature of the regions in which our work is done necessitates this. Networking is occurring during the visitations, and through our collaboration with Department of Education officials we are hoping to establish a mechanism whereby this will move beyond a recommendation of something that teachers do on their own to a systematic and structured part of our plan.

Accomplishments to Date, and the Way Forward

We have had to alter some of our original plans. After our initial workshop, on-site visits to schools began immediately. Every learner in the sample has completed the pre-intervention EI assessment. Teachers in each of the schools have completed the EQ-i as well and have been introduced to the EI concept.

However, the program has not proceeded without technical setbacks, including the following:

- In a number of schools, principals have proved to be unwilling to allow teachers to take part in EI training during school hours, which meant that we had to try to collaborate with staff after hours. However, colleagues were not always willing to do this.

- The over-emphasis on achievement in subjects such as math and physical science makes it difficult for us to convince principals and teachers of the need to introduce our EI program.

- Negotiating with principals for sufficient time to carry out our intervention is a significant predicament. Furthermore, the fact that schools are geographically far apart makes it virtually impossible to involve more than two schools, at most, at a time in EI training.

- English is not the first language for most learners, which slows down the entire process.

- There are insufficient facilities. Usually, we must conduct research under less than optimal conditions, for example there being few or no desks at which learners can work.

- At present, teacher morale is particularly low. Discussions about EI often drift into the realm of complaints about matters such as salaries, working conditions and lack of support from various stakeholders.

- Involving communities is a major challenge, in the sense that few members of the student governing bodies (SGBs) are willing to become involved in EI training programs, opting instead to involve themselves in what they perceive to be more strategic matters, such as facilitating more adequate achievement in gateway subjects, than tertiary training.

On the positive side, despite these setbacks, the program is running fairly smoothly. We are behind schedule, but we have negotiated extra time for the completion of our pilot program. The teachers and principals taking part in the study are extremely positive about the possible significance of our study and, indeed, of introducing EI into schools throughout the country.

In the next part of our program, we will investigate a narrative for EI facilitation in other South African schools and develop programs that can be used countrywide, since this narrative may have larger ramifications, including for the counselling field. Policy-makers will hopefully adopt these as well; after all, our aim is to facilitate sustainability and policy intervention in order to engage in the larger discourse of societal problems endemic to the context of a developing country.

As is always the case with action research, the action dictates the research. Thus it is not until we know about the next steps in the project—which we are unlikely to be able to speculate about in detail until we know what happened in the pilot—that we will be able to elaborate in detail the research that we will undertake. However, the caveat for success is the following: evaluating our project cannot merely be another exercise in experimental psychology; it needs to be an attempt to find out which programs work best with whom, as well as where to improve or replace weaker components of the program. We aim to focus on implementation and formative evaluation, especially during this early part of the process, and not merely to look for definitive outcomes before the program is clearly established and running smoothly.

We would also like to reiterate that the South African context is not the typical context in which SEL has been applied in schools elsewhere in the world. Hence, SEL's application in SA is an open and legitimate question, which lies at the heart of our current investigation. After all, clearly the dearth of EI programs in our schools is a hiatus in our education system.

Acknowledgments

The authors wish to thank Reuven Bar-On and Maurice Elias sincerely for their invaluable comments on earlier drafts of this chapter. Thank you, colleagues, for explaining what the concept of EI entails and for providing precious guidance in developing an SEL curriculum in South Africa. You have done this in a truly emotionally intelligent style.

References

Bar-On, R. 1997. *Bar-On EQ Inventory: Technical Manual.* Toronto: Multi-Health Systems.

————. 2003. How important is it to educate people to be emotionally and socially intelligent, and can it be done? *Perspectives in Education* 21(4): 3–16.

————. 2005. Information given to J.G. Maree during a personal communication in 2005.

Bar-On, R. and J.D.A. Parker. 2000. *Bar-On Emotional Quotient Inventory: Youth version. Technical manual.* Toronto: Multi-Health Systems.

Bar-On, Z. 2004. A broad view of productive human capital. Unpublished doctoral dissertation, the University of California at Berkeley.

Begoray, D. and K. Slovinsky. 1997. Pearls in shells. *Roeper Review* 20(1): 45–49. [Online serial]. URL http:/search.epnet.com/direct.asp?an=9710254863 anddb=aph.

Blankstein, A. 2004. *Failure is not an option.* Thousand Oaks, CA: Corwin Press.

Brady, C.G. 1998. *The relationship between emotional intelligence and underachievement in adolescence.* Unpublished MA dissertation.Pretoria: University of Pretoria.

Cohen, J. and S. Sandy. 2003. Perspectives in social-emotional education: Theoretical foundations and new evidence-based development in current practice. *Perspectives in Education* 21(4): 41–54.

Dalton, J., M.J. Elias, and A. Wandersman. in press. *Community psychology: Linking individuals and communities* 2nd ed. Belmont, CA: Wadsworth.

Druskat, V., F. Sala, and G. Mount, eds. 2005. *Linking emotional intelligence and performance at work: Current research evidence.* Mahwah, NJ: Lawrence Erlbaum.

Elias, M.J. 2003. *Academic and social-emotional learning: Educational Practices Series, Booklet #11*. Geneva, Switzerland:International Academy of Education (IAE) and the International Bureau of Education (IBE), UNESCO. http://www.ibe.unesco.org.

Elias, M.J., S.T. Tobias, and B.S. Friedlander. 2002. *Raising emotionally intelligent teenagers*. New York: Three Rivers Press.

Elias, M.J., J.E. Zins, R.P. Weissberg, K.S. Frey, M.T. Greenberg, N.M. Haynes, R. Kessler, M.E. Schwab-Stone, and T.P. Shriver. 1997. *Promoting social and emotional learning: Guidelines for educators*. Alexandria, VA: Association for Supervision and Curriculum Development.

Goleman, D. 2003. Educating people to be emotionally and socially intelligent. *Perspectives in Education* 21(4): 1–2.

Grieve, K.W. 2001. Factors affecting assessment results. In *An introduction to psychological assessment*. Ed. C. Foxcroft and G. Roodt, pp. 315–43. Oxford: University Press.

Haskett, R.A. 2002. Emotional intelligence and teaching success in higher education. Unpublished doctoral dissertation, Indiana University.

Kapp, C.A. 2000. Emotional intelligence (EQ) and success in post-graduate studies: A pilot study. *SA Journal of Higher Education* 14(3): 151–60.

Kriegler, S. 1993. Options and directions for psychology within a framework for mental health services in South Africa. *South African Journal of Psychology* 23(2): 64–70.

Madge, E.M. 1979. The intelligent use of intelligence tests. *Education Bulletin* 23(2): 54–62.

Maree, J.G., and J.M. Molepo. 2004. Facilitating postmodern career counselling in the Limpopo Province of South Africa: A rocky ride to hope. *Australian Journal of Career Development* 13(3): 47–54.

Millwood, D. 2002. Working Paper No. 1 Working group on children affected by armed conflict and displacement. Promoting psychosocial well-being among children affected by armed conflict and displacement: Principles and approaches.

Motala, S. and H. Perry. 2001. The 2000 senior certificate examination. *Quarterly Review of Education and Training in South Africa* 8(1): 1–12.

Pillay, A.L., P. Naidoo, and M.R. Lockhat. 1999. Psychopathology in urban and rural/peri-urban children seeking mental health care. *South African Journal of Psychology* 29(4): 179–83.

Salovey, P. 2003. Educating people to be emotionally and socially intelligent. *Perspectives in Education* 21(4): 95–97.

Salovey, P., and J.D. Mayer. 1990. Emotional intelligence. *Imagination, Cognition and Personality* 9:185–211.

Savickas, M.L. 2003. Advancing the career counseling profession: Objectives and strategies for the next decade. *The Career Development Quarterly* 52: 87–95.

Sharp, P. 2001. *Nurturing emotional literacy: a practical guide for teachers, parents and those in the caring professions*. U.K.: David Fulton Publishers.

Stern, R., and M.J. Elias. 2005. Emotionally intelligent parenting. In *Educating children and adults to be emotionally intelligent*. Ed. R. Bar-On, J.G. Maree, and M.J. Elias. New York: Heinemann.

Sternberg, R.J. 2001. Wisdom and education. *Perspectives in Education* 19(4): 1–16.

Stone, V.E., S. Baren-Cohen, and R.T. Knight. 1998. Frontal lobe contributions to theory of mind. *Journal of Cognitive Neuroscience* 10:640-656.

Tromp, B. Centre of crisis is in Southern Africa. *Pretoria News* June 23, 2004, 2.

Van der Linde, I. 2005. Results of a comprehensive survey of factors determining educator supply and demand in South African public schools. Pretoria: Human Sciences Research Council.

Zins, J., M.J. Elias, and M. Greenberg. 2003. Facilitating success in school and in life through social and emotional learning. *Perspectives in Education* 21(4): 55–67.

—— 11 ——

Developing Emotional Intelligence Through Coaching for Leadership, Professional and Occupational Excellence

Richard E. Boyatzis

Introduction

In the following example I use a pseudonym for a real person who prefers not to be identified. Elena, the chief financial officer (CFO) of a large corporation in Moscow, was upset. She was snapping at people and felt out of sorts. She had not slept well the night before, and something in the previous day's seminar had bothered her. She had been considering how to improve her leadership style through enhancing her EI. The instructor had explained that such efforts were short-lived if not anchored in a personal vision. Just after lunch, it dawned on Elena what was so troubling: she did not know what she wanted out of life. She does not think or dream about the future and thus found it difficult, if not impossible, to conceive of a personal vision.

It certainly was not because she did not have a bright future. She was among the elite in her country. But she had trained and entered corporate life in Russia 20 years earlier, under a regime which had different assumptions about possibilities in life and a career. Her subordinates were also frustrated. Elena had trouble eliciting excitement among them about a future for the organization. She had learned not to dream about the future, but to react to things as they occurred. It had shaped her approach to leadership into a reactive style—one that was not working well.

There are millions of 'Elenas' working in organizations throughout the world. They want to be better managers and leaders, but are puzzled as to how to reach this elusive goal. With the best of intentions, they attend training programs, get Master of Business Administration degrees (MBAs), and hire consultants and coaches to help. And yet the degree of change is often minimal. The people feel compelled to throw more resources into training, or slowly develop a belief that great managers and leaders are born and not made. While management of organizations seems better than it was decades ago, it is a sobering thought that the return on this massive investment in management and leadership development is so small (Spencer 1988; 2001). If the outcomes were subjected to a rigorous utility analysis, a prudent businessperson would liquidate or divest the effort.

The most common mistake is to think that acquiring more knowledge will make us better managers or leaders. To be effective managers or leaders, we need the ability to use our knowledge and to make things happen. We can call these **'competencies'**, which I define as the underlying characteristics of a person that lead to effective and outstanding performance (Boyatzis 1982). Whether direct empirical research is reviewed (Boyatzis 1982; 2005; Howard & Bray 1988; Kotter 1982; Luthans, Hodgetts & Rosenkrantz 1988; Thornton & Byham 1982) or meta-analytic syntheses are used (Goleman 1998; Spencer & Spencer 1993), there is a specific set of competencies that have been shown to predict outstanding managerial or leadership performance. Regardless of author or study, they tend to include abilities from these three clusters:

1. Cognitive or cognitive-intellectual ability, such as systems thinking.
2. Self-management or intrapersonal abilities, such as adaptability.
3. Relationship management or interpersonal abilities, such as networking.

The latter two clusters make up the key components of what we call 'EI competencies' (Bar-On 2005; Boyatzis & Sala 2004; Goleman, Boyatzis & McKee 2002).

Beyond knowledge and competencies, an additional ingredient necessary to outstanding performance appears to be the desire to use our talent. This seems driven by our values, philosophy, sense of calling or mission, unconscious motives and traits. These domains of capability help us to understand:

- *what* we need to do—knowledge
- *how* we need to do it—competencies
- *why* we will do it—motivational drives, motives, values and unconscious dispositions.

For too long, the assumption has been that these abilities or competencies are characteristics with which we are born. This deterministic view has led to a focus on selection and placement rather than development. While it might seem more intelligent to focus on certain factors that are empirically known to impact performance in recruitment, hiring and succession planning, and then to refocus on the same factors in training and coaching to maximize smart selection decisions, it is equally likely that 'placement' focuses on a different set of competencies than 'development'. For example, in placement, we are concerned with corporate compatibility and threshold abilities like relevant experience, whereas in development we would focus on capability, both latent and manifest, and on dreams and aspirations. But these competencies, and in particular EI competencies, can be developed. Other chapters in this book, and Cherniss and Adler (2000), explore and explain this distinction in more detail.

A growing body of research has helped us to discover a process that yields sustained behavioral change (references will appear in paragraphs to follow). These long-term improvements provide hope and evidence that people can develop as managers, leaders and advanced professionals, and in various occupations. Although the process appears to be common sense, it is not common practice. The necessary elements in an effective process of change, as well as those elements sufficient to yield sustainable change, have not been conceptualized well. The result is confusion about change and its feasibility. The work I describe in this chapter, which has been developing since the latter half of the 1960s, should provide both insight into and hope about change. People *can* develop the competencies that matter the most when it comes to outstanding performance: the ones we call EI.

Sustained Talent Growth and Development

Decades of research on the effects of psychotherapy (Hubble, Duncan & Miller 1999), self-help programs (Kanfer & Goldstein 1991), cognitive behavior therapy (Barlow 1988), training programs (Morrow, Jarrett & Rupinski 1997) and education (Pascarella & Terenzini 1991) have shown that people can change their behavior and moods, and even their self-image. But most of the studies focused on a single characteristic, like maintenance of sobriety or reduction of a specific anxiety, or on a set of characteristics often determined by the assessment instrument, such as the scales on the Minnesota Multiphasic Personality Inventory (MMPI). For example, Achievement Motivation Training (AMT) has demonstrated a dramatic impact on small business success, with people creating more new jobs, starting more new businesses and paying more taxes than comparison groups (Miron & McClelland 1979). The impact of Power Motivation Training (PMT) was improved maintenance of sobriety (Cutter, Boyatzis & Clancy 1977). But there are few studies showing sustained improvements in the sets of desirable behavior that lead to outstanding performance.

The 'honeymoon effect' of typical training programs often starts with improvement immediately following the program; but within a few months it drops sharply (Campbell, Dunnette, Lawler & Weick 1970). In a global search of the literature by the Consortium on Research on Emotional Intelligence in

Organizations (CREIO), only 15 programs were found to be designed to improve EI. Most of these showed impact on job outcomes, such as number of new businesses started, or life outcomes, such as finding a job or satisfaction (Cherniss & Adler 2000), which were described as the ultimate purpose of the development efforts. But showing an impact on outcomes, while desired, may also blur how the change actually occurs. Furthermore, when a change has been noted, a question about the sustainability of the changes is raised because of the relatively short time periods studied. (The same question can and should be asked regarding the positive effects of education and psychotherapy, but this is beyond the scope of this chapter.)

The few published studies examining improvement of more than one of these competencies show an overall improvement of about 10% in EI abilities 3–18 months after training (Hand, Richards & Slocum 1973; Latham & Saari 1979; Noe & Schmitt 1986; Wexley & Memeroff 1975; Young & Dixon 1996). This was calculated by dividing the post minus pre-scores by the pre-scores on coded behaviors from videos or live assessment centers, or through questionnaires that asked informants about a person's behavior (not self-assessment). The EI competencies addressed included empathy, communications, developing others, emotional self-control, and so on (see Spencer and Spencer (1993) for a later conceptualization of the longer list from which they were drawn). Meta-analytic studies and utility analyses confirm that significant changes can and do occur, but not with the impact that the typically high level of investment would lead us to expect (Baldwin & Ford 1988; Burke & Day 1986; Morrow et al. 1997).

The results from standard MBA programs do not appear better, even where there is no attempt to enhance EI abilities. A major research project by the American Assembly of Collegiate Schools of Business found that the behavior of graduating students from two highly ranked business schools compared to their behavior when they began their MBA training showed improvements of only 2% in EI skills (Development Dimensions International 1985). Indeed, when students from four other high ranking MBA programs were assessed with a wide range of tests and direct behavioral measures, they showed a gain of 4% in self-awareness and self-management abilities, but a decrease of 3% in social awareness and relationship management (Boyatzis, Renio-McKee & Thompson 1995; Boyatzis & Sokol 1982). Again, the results were computed from graduating minus entering students' scores, then dividing by the entering scores on behavioral coding, assessment center ratings and tests. EI competencies addressed included empathy, communications, developing others, emotional self-control, and so forth.

A series of longitudinal studies currently underway at the Weatherhead School of Management (WSOM) of Case Western Reserve University have shown that people can change with respect to their EI and the cognitive competencies that distinguish outstanding performers in management and in various professions. In research studies to date, the improvement has lasted for up to seven years.

Figure 11.1 shows the percentage improvement of EI from the behavioral measurement of competencies of various MBA graduates taking LEAD. (With regard to the figure, for '*n*' and a description of the measures, see Boyatzis, Stubbs and Taylor (2002); and for a list of comparison references see Goleman et al. (2002).)

MBA students, averaging 27 years of age at entry into their academic program, exhibited dramatic changes in EI and cognitive competencies, such as empathy, initiative, developing others and communications. They were assessed with videotaped and audiotaped behavioral samples and questionnaires. This was conducted as part of a competency-based, outcome-oriented MBA program implemented in 1990 (Boyatzis, Stubbs & Taylor 2002). The studies were done with four sets of full-time MBA students graduating from 1992 to 1995, and three sets of part-time MBA students graduating from 1994 to 1996.

Perhaps the most impressive results came from Jane Wheeler (1999), who tracked two sets of part-time MBAs for two years after they had graduated. They showed improvements of 63% on the self-awareness and self-management competencies, and 45% on the social awareness and relationship management competencies. This is in contrast to the WSOM MBA graduates of the 1988 and 1989 traditional full-time and part-time program, who showed improvement in substantially fewer of these competencies.

The positive effects of this program were not limited to the MBAs. There is a longitudinal study of four classes completing the Professional Fellows Program, that is, an executive education program at the Weatherhead School of Management. Ballou, Bowers, Boyatzis and Kolb (1999) revealed that these 45–65-year-old professionals and executives improved in self-confidence, leadership, helping, goal setting and action skills. These were 67% of the EI competencies assessed in this study.

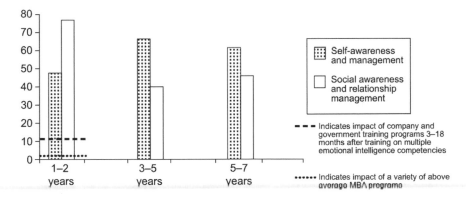

Figure 11.1   EI improvement in certain MBA graduates

(Source: Boyatzis and Renio 1990; Boyatzis, Baker, Leonard and Rhee 1996; Boyatzis, Cowen and Kolb 1995; Boyatzis, Stubbs and Taylor 2002.)

Intentional Change Through Coaching

The above mentioned studies have shown that adults learn *what they want to learn*. Other things, even if acquired temporarily such as for a test, are soon forgotten (Specht & Sandlin 1991). Students, children, patients, clients and subordinates may act as if they care about learning something and go through the motions, but they proceed to disregard it or forget it unless it is something which they want to know.

The idea supports the motivational component that facilitates emotionally intelligent behavior, individual performance and organizational productivity. This is what David Wechsler (1940; 1943) described, over 60 years ago, as 'conative non-intellective factors' which strongly contribute to 'intelligent behavior' (Wechsler 1958). Now, we should weave the factors into the coaching procedure and see their impact on coaching outcomes. The factors do not include changes induced, willingly or unwillingly, by chemical or hormonal changes in a person's body. But even in such situations, the interpretation of the changes and behavioral comportment following it will be affected by the person's will, values and motivations.

From all of the change studies reviewed and referenced to date, and the deplorably small changes resulting from some, it appears that most, if not all, sustainable behavioral change is intentional and must be self-motivated. Coaching involves helping individuals along their intentional change process. **Intentional change** is a desired change in an aspect of who a person is: the Real, or who they might want to be: the Ideal, or both.

Figure 11.2 shows the process of intentional change. This representation is an enhancement of earlier models called the 'Self-Directed Learning and Change' model developed by David Kolb, Richard Boyatzis and colleagues (Kolb & Boyatzis 1970).

We organize our description and explanation of the process around five points of discontinuity. The theory starts from a complexity perspective drawing on the observation that much behavioral change appears to be discontinuous (Boyatzis in press). In other words, we do not make behavioral changes, or changes to our habits, in incremental steps at even intervals of time or effort; instead, we change in what appears to be 'fits and starts'. These are **discontinuities,** which might be experienced as epiphanies or sudden realizations. For ease of description, we have called them 'discoveries' (Goleman et al. 2002).

When we review the research results from longitudinal studies and clinical studies, it appears that five of these discoveries seem always to be needed to make the change sustainable. They are as follows:

1. A person discovering their Ideal Self, or personal vision—what they want out of life or what kind of person they want to be.

2. A person discovering their Real Self—how they come across to others. This leads directly to a sense of strengths and weaknesses—how their actions compare to their Ideal Self.

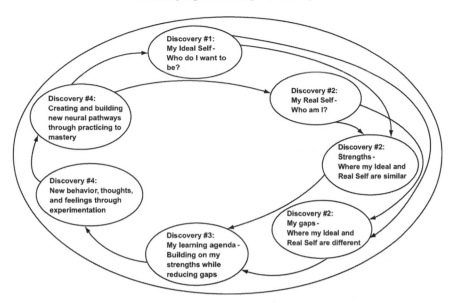

Figure 11.2   Boyatzis's intentional change theory

(Source: Boyatzis 2001; Boyatzis in press; Boyatzis and McKee 2005; Goleman, Boyatzis, & McKee 2002.)

3. A person discovering their agenda for the coming time periods.

4. A person discovering ways to experiment and practice moving toward their Ideal Self.

5. A person discovering trusting, supportive relationships that help them along the process.

Each of these tends to come to the person's conscious realization as a moment of awareness.

This model describes the process which was designed for a required course in the MBA and executive programs, and first implemented in 1990, at the Weatherhead School of Management (Boyatzis 1994). Although the course was subsequently modified in a continuous improvement process, the architecture and basic design, as described here, was determined before the course was first implemented. Experimentation and research into the various components of this model have resulted in the refinement of the factorial components, as discussed in this chapter. For a detailed description of the course, you can refer to Boyatzis (1994; 1995). Significantly, a key element of this model is the one-to-one coaching of each MBA student, advanced PhD student or executive specially trained as coaches.

Let us examine the five discoveries that appear necessary for change.

The first discontinuity: Catching our dreams, engaging our passion

The potential starting point for the process of intentional change is the discovery of who we want to be. Our Ideal Self is an image of the person we want to be (Boyatzis & Akrivou-Napersky 2005). It emerges from our ego ideal, dreams and aspirations. The literature of the last 20 years supports the power of positive imaging or visioning in sports psychology, meditation, biofeedback research and other psycho-physiological research. It is believed that the potency of focusing our thoughts on the desired end-state of condition is driven by the emotional components of the brain (Goleman 1995).

The findings of this research indicate that we can access and engage people deeply if we engage our passions and conceptually 'catch' our dreams in our Ideal Self-image. It is an anomaly that we know the importance of consideration of the Ideal Self and yet often, when engaged in a change or learning process, we overlook the clear formulation or articulation of our Ideal Self-image. If a parent, spouse, boss or teacher tells us that something about us should be different, they are telling us about the person they want us to be. As adults, we often allow ourselves to be anesthetized to our dreams and to lose sight of our deeply felt Ideal Self.

However, there are also times when a 'wake-up call' shocks us into the realization that we should consider change (Goleman et al. 2002). Such instances may be negative or positive. But for the change to proceed and sustain itself, the experience and drive must be changed from a negative or stressful aspect of the wake-up call to the positive drive from the Ideal Self.

The second discontinuity: Am I a boiling frog?

After building a sense of the Ideal Self, we turn to our awareness of the current self, the person that others see and with whom they interact. This self is elusive—our mind protects us from potentially threatening input to our conscious realizations about ourselves through the unconscious use of ego-defence mechanisms. These mechanisms also conspire to delude us into an image of who we are that feeds on itself, becomes self-perpetuating and eventually may become dysfunctional (Goleman 1985).

The greatest challenge to an accurate current self-image—that is, to seeing ourselves as others see us and consistent with other internal states, beliefs and emotions—is the 'boiling frog syndrome'. If a frog is dropped into a pot of boiling water, it will immediately jump out of the pot. But if the frog is placed in a pot of cool water, which is gradually brought to a boil, then the frog will remain in the water until cooked.

Several factors contribute to our becoming boiling frogs. People around us may not let us see a change. They may not give us feedback or information about how they see it. Moreover, they may be victims of the boiling frog syndrome themselves, as they adjust their perception on a daily basis. Enablers, that is, those forgiving the change, being frightened of it or not caring about it, may allow it to pass unnoticed.

To truly consider changing, we must have a sense of what we value and want to keep about ourselves. The areas in which our Real Self and Ideal Self are congruent can be considered strengths. Likewise, to consider what we want to preserve about ourselves involves admitting aspects that we wish to change or adapt in some manner. Areas in which our Real Self and Ideal Self are not consistent can be considered gaps.

All too often, we explore growth or development by focusing on the gaps, or deficiencies. Organizational training programs and managers conducting annual reviews often make this mistake. There is an assumption that we can 'leave well enough alone' and pay attention to the areas that need work. It is no wonder that people feel battered, bruised and misguided by many of the programs or procedures intended to help them to develop.

The third discontinuity: Mindfulness through a learning agenda

Once we have developed our Ideal Self and identified our strengths and weaknesses, we need to compile an agenda and focus on the future we desire. While our performance at work or happiness in life may be the eventual consequence of our efforts, a learning agenda focuses on development. A learning orientation arouses a positive belief in our capability and the hope of improvement. This leads us to set personal standards of performance rather than 'normative' standards that merely mimic what others have done (Beaubien & Payne 1999). By contrast, a performance orientation evokes anxiety and doubts about whether or not we can change (Chen, Gully, Whiteman & Kilcullen 2000).

As part of one of the longitudinal studies conducted at the Weatherhead School of Management, Leonard (1996) showed that MBAs who set goals desiring to change certain competencies changed significantly in those competencies as compared to other MBAs. Other goal-setting literature has shown how goals affect certain changes in specific competencies (Locke & Latham 1990), but has failed to provide evidence of behavioral change in the comprehensive set of competencies that constitute EI.

A major threat to effective goal setting and planning is the fact that many of us are busy and cannot add anything else to our lives. In this case, success with self-directed change and learning will occur only if we can determine what to say 'no' to; in other words, if we can remove certain current activities from our lives to make room for new ones.

Another potential challenge is the development of a plan that calls for us to engage in activities that are different from our preferred learning style or learning flexibility (Boyatzis 1994; Kolb 1984). When we do this, we become demotivated and often stop the activities, or we become impatient and decide that the goals are not worth the effort.

The fourth discontinuity: Metamorphosis

This discontinuity entails experimentation and practice of the desired changes. Acting on the plan, and toward the goals, involves many activities, often carried out in the context of experimenting with new behavior. Typically, following a period of experimentation, we practice the new behavior in actual settings within which we wish to use them, such as at work or at home. Here, intentional change begins to look like a 'continuous improvement' process.

To develop or learn new behavior, we must find ways of learning more from current or ongoing experiences—the experimentation and practice does not always require us to attend courses or engage in new activities. We could try something different in a current setting, reflect on what occurs and experiment further in this setting. Sometimes, this part of the process entails finding and using opportunities to learn and change. We may not think we have changed until we have tried new behavior in a work or 'real world' setting.

Dreyfus (1990) has studied managers of scientists and engineers who were considered superior performers. She has documented that they used considerably more abilities than their less effective counterparts, and she pursued the way in which they did this. A distinguishing ability was group management, or team-building. Dreyfus (1990) found that many of the middle-aged managers had first experimented with team-building skills in high school and college, in sports, clubs and living groups. Later, when they became 'bench scientists and engineers' working on problems in relative isolation, they continued to practice this ability in activities outside of work, that is, in social and community organizations.

The experimentation and practice are most effective when they occur in conditions in which we feel safe (Kolb & Boyatzis 1970). The sense of psychological safety creates an atmosphere in which we can try new behavior, perceptions and thoughts with relatively less risk of shame, embarrassment or serious consequences of failure. The challenge is to practice to the point of mastery, and not merely the point of comfort.

The fifth discontinuity: Relationships that enable us to learn

The above mentioned experimentation and practice allows for development of new relationships, or for strengthening existing ones. However, in reality, this fifth discovery may be the first one, and it may enable the others. Our relationships are an essential part of our environment. The crucial relationships are often a part of groups that have particular importance to us. These relationships and groups give us a sense of identity, guide us as to what is appropriate and 'good' behavior, and provide feedback on our behavior. In sociology, they are called 'reference groups'. The relationships create a 'context' within which we interpret our progress on desired changes and on the utility of new learning, and which contribute significant input to formulation of the Ideal (Kram 1996).

In this sense, our relationships are with mediators, moderators, interpreters, sources of feedback, and sources of support and permission of change and learning. They may also be the most important source of protection from relapses or return to our earlier forms of behavior. Wheeler (1999) analyzed the extent to which MBA graduates worked on their goals in multiple 'life spheres', that is, work, family, recreational groups, and so on. In a two-year follow-up study of two of the graduating classes of part-time MBA students, she found that those who worked on their goals and plans in multiple sets of relationships improved the most—more than those working on goals in only one setting, such as work, or within one relationship (Wheeler 1999).

In the studies that examined the impact of the above mentioned year-long executive development program for doctors, lawyers, professors, engineers and other professionals, Ballou et al. (1999) found that participants gained self-confidence during the program. However, even at the beginning, others would describe these participants as being high in self-confidence. It was a curious finding. The best explanation came from follow-up questions answered by the graduates of the program. The results indicated that the greater self-confidence arose from an increase in the confidence to change. The graduates' existing reference groups—family, groups at work, professional groups, community groups—all had an investment in them staying the same, whereas they themselves wanted to change. The Professional Fellows Program allowed them to develop a new reference group, which encouraged change.

Based on social identity, reference group and related theories, our relationships both mediate and moderate our sense of who we are and who we want to be. Within these contexts:

- we develop or elaborate our Ideal Self
- we label and interpret our Real Self
- we interpret and value strengths
- we interpret and value gaps.

Conclusion

In the example at the start of this chapter, Elena realized that she did not know what she wanted out of life. Her subsequent awareness of her need to dream of a desired future was not a gentle moment of clarity—it was a shocking revelation. The instructor, her colleagues and a coach helped her to transform that wake-up call into a personal vision. They then coaxed her through the further discoveries. At that point, she embarked on her journey through intentional development and being a more effective executive.

Almost every adult can develop leadership and EI. Through intentional change theory and process, coaches can help us to make our dreams come true and drive our performance. Through the process, we have the opportunity of making a genuine difference, as happened with Elena. Whether applied in universities or companies, government agencies or NGOs, this process can help us to coach others and create the social environments that are so conducive to making a difference in our lives.

References

Ballou, R., D. Bowers, R.E. Boyatzis, D.A. and Kolb. 1999. Fellowship in lifelong learning: An executive development program for advanced professionals *Journal of Management Education* 23(4): 338–54.

Baldwin, T., and J.K. Ford. 1988. Transfer of Training: A Review and Directions for Future Research. *Personnel Psychology* 41:63–105.

Barlow, D.H. 1988. *Anxiety and disorders: The nature and treatment of anxiety and panic.* New York: The Guilford Press.

Bar-On, R. 2006. The Bar-On model of emotional-social intelligence (ESI). *Psicothema* 18.

Beaubien, J.M. and S.C. Payne. 1999, April. Individual goal orientation as a predictor of job and academic performance: A meta-analytic review and integration. Paper presented at the meeting of the Society for Industrial and Organizational Psychology, Atlanta, GA.

Boyatzis, R.E. 1982. *The competent manager: A model for effective performance.* New York: John Wiley & Sons.

———. 1994. Stimulating self-directed change: A required MBA course called Managerial Assessment and Development. *Journal of Management Education* 18(3): 304–23.

———. 1995. Cornerstones of change: Building a path for self-directed learning. In *Innovation in Professional Education: Steps on a Journey from Teaching to Learning.* Ed. R.E. Boyatzis, S.C. Cowen, and D.A. Kolb, 50–94. San Francisco: Jossey-Bass.

———. 2001. How and why individuals are able to develop emotional intelligence. In *The emotionally intelligent workplace: How to select for, measure, and improve emotional intelligence in individuals, groups, and organizations.* Ed. C. Cherniss and D. Goleman. San Francisco: Jossey-Bass.

———. 2005. Using tipping points of emotional intelligence and cognitive competencies to predict financial performance of leaders. *Psicothemia* 17.

———. 2006. Core competencies in coaching others to overcome dysfunctional behavior. to appear in *Emotional Intelligence and Work Performance.* Ed. Druskat, V., Mount, G., and Sala, F. Mahwah, NJ: Lawrence Erlbaum.

———. in press. Intentional change theory from a complexity perspective. *Journal of Management Development.*

Boyatzis, R.E., and K. Akrivou-Napersky. in press. The Ideal Self as a Driver of Change *Journal of Management Development.*

Boyatzis, R.E., A. Howard, B. Rapisarda, and S. Taylor. 2004, March 11. Coaching can work, but doesn't always. *People Management.*

Boyatzis, R.E., D. Leonard, K. Rhee, and J.V. Wheeler. 1996. Competencies can be developed, but not the way we thought. *Capability* 2(2): pp. 25-41.

Boyatzis, R., and A. McKee. 2005. *Resonant leadership: Renewing yourself and connecting with others through mindfulness, hope and compassion.* Boston: Harvard Business School Press.

Boyatzis, R.E., and A. Renio. 1989. The impact of an MBA program on managerial abilities. *Journal of Management Development*, 8(5).

Boyatzis, R.E., A. Renio-McKee, and L. Thompson. 1995. Past accomplishments: Establishing the impact and baseline of earlier programs. In *Innovation in professional education: Steps on a Journey from teaching to learning*. Ed. R.E. Boyatzis, S.S. Cowen, D.A. and Kolb. San Francisco: Jossey-Bass.

Boyatzis, R.E., and F. Sala. 2004. Assessing emotional intelligence competencies. In *The Measurement of Emotional Intelligence*. Ed. Glenn Geher. Hauppauge, NY: Novas Science Publishers.

Boyatzis, R.E., M. and Sokol. 1982. *A pilot project to assess the feasibility of assessing skills and personal characteristics of students in collegiate business programs*. Report to the AACSB (St. Louis, MO).

Boyatzis, R.E.; E.C. Stubbs, and S.N. Taylor. 2002. Learning cognitive and emotional intelligence competencies through graduate management education. *Academy of Management Journal on Learning and Education* 1,2:150–62

Burke, M.J., and R.R. Day. 1986. A Cumulative Study of the Effectiveness of Managerial Training. *Journal of Applied Psychology* 71(2): 232–45.

Campbell, J.P., M.D. Dunnette, E.E. Lawler III, and K.E. Weick. 1970. *Managerial behavior, performance, and effectiveness*. NY: McGraw Hill.

Chen, G., S.M. Gully, J.A. Whiteman, and R.N. Kilcullen. 2000. Examination of relationships among trait-like individual differences, state-like individual differences, and learning performance. *Journal of Applied Psychology* 85(6): pp. 835–47.

Cherniss, C., and M. Adler. 2000. *Promoting emotional intelligence inorganizations: Make training in emotional intelligence effective*. Washington D.C.: American Society of Training and Development.

Cutter, H., R.E. Boyatzis, and D. Clancy. 1977. The effectiveness of power motivation training for rehabilitating alcoholics. *Journal of Studies on Alcohol* 38(1).

Development Dimensions International (DDI). 1985. *Final Report: Phase III*. Report to the AACSB (St. Louis, MO).

Dreyfus, C. 1990. The characteristics of high performing managers of scientists and engineers. An Unpublished Doctoral Dissertation, Case Western Reserve University.

Goleman, D. 1985. *Vital lies, simple truths: The psychology of self-deception*. New York: Simon and Schuster.

———. 1995. *Emotional intelligence*. New York: Bantam Books.

———. 1998. *Working with emotional intelligence*. New York: Bantam.

Goleman, D., R.E. Boyatzis, and A. McKee. 2002. *Primal leadership: Realizing the power of emotional intelligence*. Boston: Harvard Business School Press.

Hand, H.H., M.D. Richards, and J.W. Slocum Jr. 1973. Organizational climate and the effectiveness of a human relations training program. *Academy of Management Journal* 16(2): 185–246.

Howard, A., and D. Bray. 1988. *Managerial lives in transition: Advancing age and changing times*. New York: Guilford Press.

Hubble, M.A., B.L. Duncan, and S.D Miller, Eds. 1999. *The heart and soul of change: What works in therapy*. Washington, D.C.: American Psychological Association.

Kanfer, F.H., and A.P. Goldstein, Eds. 1991. *Helping people change: A textbook of methods* 4th ed. Boston: Allyn and Bacon.

Kolb, D.A. 1984. *Experiential learning: Experience as the source of learning and development*. Englewood Cliffs, NJ: Prentice-Hall.

Kolb, D.A., and R.E. Boyatzis. 1970. Goal-setting and self-directed behavior change. *Human Relations* 23(5): 439–57.

Kotter, J.P. 1982. *The general managers.* New York: Free Press.

Kram, K.E. 1996. A relational approach to careers. In *The Career is Dead: Long Live the Career.* Ed. D.T. Hall, pp. 132–57. San Francisco, CA: Jossey-Bass Publishers.

Latham, G.P. and L.M. Saari. (1979). Application of Social-learning Theory to Training Supervisors through Behavioral Modeling. *Journal of Applied Psychology* 64(3): 239–46.

Leonard, D. 1996. *The impact of learning goals on self-directed change in management development and education.* Doctoral dissertation, Case Western Reserve University.

Locke, E.A., and G.P. Latham. 1990. *A theory of goal setting and task performance.* Englewood Cliffs, NJ: Prentice Hall.

Luthans, F., R.M. Hodgetts, and S.A. Rosenkrantz. 1988. *Real managers.* Cambridge, MA: Ballinger Press.

Miron, D., and D.C. McClelland. 1979. The impact of achievement motivation training on small business. *California Management Review* 21(4): 13–28.

Morrow, C.C., M.Q. Jarrett, and M.T. Rupinski. 1997. An investigation of the effect and economic utility of corporate-wide training. *Personnel Psychology* 50:91–119.

Noe, R.A., and N. Schmitt. 1986. The influence of trainee attitudes on training effectiveness: Test of a model. *Personnel Psychology* 39:497–523.

Pascarella, E.T., and P.T. Terenzini. 1991. *How college affects students: Findings and insights from twenty years of research.* San Francisco: Jossey-Bass.

Specht, L., and P. Sandlin. 1991. The differential effects of experiential learning activities and traditional lecture classes in accounting. *Simulations and Gaming* 22(2): 196–210.

Spencer, L.M. Jr., and S.M. Spencer. 1993. *Competence at work: Models for superior performance.* New York: John Wiley & Sons.

Thornton, G.C. III, and W.C. Byham. 1982. *Assessment centers and managerial performance.* New York: Academic Press.

Wexley, K.N., and W.F. Memeroff. 1975. Effectiveness of positive reinforcement and goal setting as methods of management development. *Journal of Applied Psychology* 60(4): 446–50.

Wheeler, J.V. 1999. The impact of social environments on self-directed change and learning. An unpublished doctoral dissertation. Case Western Reserve University.

Young, D.P., and N.M. Dixon. 1996. *Helping Leaders Take Effective Action: A Program Evaluation.* Greensboro, NC: Center for Creative Leadership.

12

The Practice of Emotional Intelligence Coaching in Organizations: A Hands-On Guide to Successful Outcomes

Charles J. Wolfe

Introduction

In this chapter, we take a practical, innovative approach to coaching individuals, teams and organizations by applying an emotion-based planning and problem-solving process that I adapted from the Mayer and Salovey (1997) model of EI.

We begin by reviewing a documented case study of cultural transformation at Dell Computer. The case is not my own. Dell is a company that is widely discussed in the public domain. In this instance, the company faced a complex situation involving strong emotions, and it produced a successful outcome which can be explained, at least in part, by the emotion-based process I have created. Following the Dell case are three examples from my coaching in which I applied this process to:

1. A talented executive who was demoted and demoralized.
2. The re-organization of an information technology (IT) department.
3. A negotiation between a landlord and lessee.

Other than in the Dell case, all names in this chapter are fictional. By the end of this chapter, you should understand how to use my hands-on approach to EI coaching to produce successful outcomes.

Gosling and Mintzberg (2003:60–61) suggest the following: Imagine your organization as a chariot pulled by wild horses...These horses represent the emotions, aspirations, and motives of all the people in the organization. Holding a steady course requires just as much skill as steering to a new direction.

Philosophers have used this metaphor to describe the need to harness emotional energy; it works well for management, too. An action mind-set at senior levels is not about whipping the horses into a frenzy...it is about developing a sensitive awareness of the terrain and of what the team is capable of...helping to set and maintain direction, coaxing everyone along.

In this chapter, I answer these questions:

- What is the ability-based model of EI and the corresponding emotion-based planning and problem-solving process?

- How can using this process help to produce more successful organizational outcomes by harnessing and leveraging emotional energy?

Mayer and Salovey first presented their EI model in 1990 (Salovey & Mayer 1990), and updated it in 1997 (Mayer & Salovey 1997). The following most recent definition is taken from John Mayer's website (see www.unh.edu/emotional_intelligence/eiemotint2.htm).

The Four-Branch Ability Model of Emotional Intelligence

This model is a refinement of the first formal models and measures of EI (Mayer n.d.) The model proposes four ability areas that collectively describe EI:

1. Accurately perceive emotions in ourselves and others.
2. Use emotions to facilitate thinking.
3. Understand emotional meanings.
4. Manage emotions.

In order to apply the model in the workplace, I generated a set of questions to help individuals logically think through how best to handle any emotional situation that has high stakes. The model includes each of the abilities with specific questions that guide the coaching process, as shown in Table 12.1.

We can describe the four actions in the process as follows:

1. **Identify**—what is real regarding existing feelings.
2. **Use**—a vision of what would be ideal feelings for all key people involved.
3. **Understand**—requires having vocabulary to discuss feelings, and knowing how feelings originate and what makes them change. Since there is often a gap between what people feel and what is ideal, the next step involves generating possible alternatives to close the gap.

Table 12.1   Emotion Roadmap™
The emotion-based planning and problem-solving process

Abilities	Questions (Template)
Identify What is the situation and what are the current feelings?	• Who are the key people involved? • How is each key person feeling?

Use
What feelings will most likely
facilitate a successful outcome?
	• Based on what we want to have happen,
	  what feelings would be ideal for each key
	  person?

Understand Are the current feelings the ones we want or is there a gap?	• Why are people feeling the way they do? • How can we create the feelings we want?
Manage Execute a plan and modify as necessary	• What are we able to do? • What are we willing to do to keep or change these feelings?

(The Emotion Roadmap™ is a registered trademark of Charles J. Wolfe Associates.)

4. **Manage**—based on the analysis of current and ideal feelings, on the selection of one or more alternatives to close the gap, and on execution and modification as needed.

To explore the process, we consider the case of Dell Computer prominently featured in the *Harvard Business Review* (Ludeman & Erlandson 2004; Stewart & O'Brien 2005). This case demonstrates how a complex business situation involving strong emotions can benefit from a thoughtful approach to the feelings of key leaders and employees. Reviewing the case through the lens of emotion-based planning and problem-solving will help you to understand how to use the process to review past or current situations that elicit strong emotions.

Step 1 Identify: Assess the situation and the feelings of key people

Dell has been financially successful. In March 2005, the company was reported to be worth US$100 billion. The tough culture built by chief executive officer (CEO) Michael Dell and president Kevin Rollins needed to change once the company began to mature and the tech industry went through a major turndown in 2000–01. These leaders realized that they had to address the emerging gaps in their culture. Through a survey conducted in 2001, the leaders learned that many people no longer felt loyal to Dell. Employees expressed ambivalence about staying at Dell and disappointment in the stock market and the industry. The leaders were concerned by the survey results.

Step 2 Use: Decide what feelings would be ideal

The leaders wanted to feel accountable; they accepted that they needed to change and were determined to improve the situation. With regard to the workforce, they wanted passion and loyalty to replace ambivalence and disappointment. They also wanted their employees to feel appreciated by the company and proud to be part of it.

Step 3 Understand: Consider how to change the feelings

To close the gap, Dell needed to begin by understanding current feelings. The company had created a wealthy workforce with a culture tied to stock price. Many employees felt disappointed in the stock price and wondered if opportunities for growth would disappear. The apparent lack of opportunities contributed to their ambivalence about staying at Dell.

Rollins commented: 'We want the world to see not just a great financial record and operational performance, but a great company...We want to be such a great place to work that no one wants to leave.' A Dell representative explained: 'We care about our people, but we don't exist to make people feel good. We want to win and have fun at the same time.' Rollins further stated: 'If a company with great financials and a great culture sees results start to slide, the culture will die real fast. So we've told our people that we're building a winning culture on top of great financial results. If we stop delivering results, the culture will slide into the ditch. We have to keep them both going' (Stewart & O'Brien 2005:111).

Success in leading others requires the cognitive intelligence to produce the infrastructure that drives success, at which Dell has excelled, and the emotional intelligence to create a culture that generates employee and customer loyalty. Dell and Rollins knew that in order to create this winning culture they needed to improve their behaviors with each other and with their executive team. They also realized that they needed to reach the 53,000 people who worked for Dell in 80 countries around the world.

Step 4 Manage: Decide what to do to create the desired changes

With coaching support, Dell and Rollins decided to create open, honest dialogue with employees in order to understand how they viewed the current social contract (Ludeman & Erlandson 2004). They created the Soul of Dell initiative and the Tell Dell survey to measure their ability to create a winning culture. As a result of the survey, they found that people had tremendous desire for more professional development. They also learned that they should provide greater recognition, and develop more meaningful relationships with people on their executive teams. They realized that their employees worldwide might be slow to change their feelings and they would need to persevere to make these people feel they were serious about developing a winning culture (Stewart & O'Brien 2005).

Initially, the Tell Dell surveys were flat and showed little improvement. However, the leaders stayed committed and eventually the survey results improved. The leaders felt that the keys to improvement included senior executives travelling to meet with high potential managers, intense leadership training and built-in accountability. Managers could not get promoted if they did not take the Tell Dell metrics and the winning culture initiative seriously.

At every organizational level, accountability is critical to success. Each manager is expected to share their Tell Dell results with the next level up and with their employees. Even Dell and Rollins share their results with the board and their team.

Initial employee scepticism gave way to enthusiasm and pride. The Soul of Dell initiative, with its Tell Dell survey, is an excellent example of emotion-based planning and problem-solving. Through executive meetings with high potential managers and Tell Dell surveys, employee's feelings are constantly monitored and managers are held accountable (Stewart & O'Brien 2005).

The above mentioned Dell case is an example of applying the emotion-based planning and problem-solving process retrospectively. The following examples show the process being used specifically in coaching to produce successful outcomes.

These brief sketches, and the step-by-step template that follows, demonstrate how coaching works directly with the emotion-based planning and problem-solving process. The examples comprise:

1. a hard-charging, highly aggressive manager who is rewarded for learning to manage her emotions
2. a director who focuses on the feelings of regional staff experiencing an unwelcome change in organization structure
3. a business owner who leases part of his facility to another businessman.

Example 1: EI and Individual Behavior Change

The manager, Margaret: So during the meeting with my new manager, what I heard was 'Charge!' I felt he was telling me to aggressively go after the outcomes we discussed.

Coach: Yes, but you always hear 'charge' and think you need to be aggressive. Are you *sure* that was what was meant, or is it just what you want to do?

Margaret (laughing):   You're right. He simply said 'Get the job done', but I insinuated he meant for me to be aggressive. In fact, he may have been telling me to slow down, but the organization does desperately need a new product development strategy.

This conversation is based on a coaching experience with a manager who had been demoted in a recent organizational restructuring. Margaret had been demoted one level and now reports to someone she viewed as inferior.

When we first began the coaching process, she told me she had some 'rough edges' that needed work. An internal consultant had been working with her and recommended that she work with me on EI.

One week after my first session with her, her company's reorganization was announced. Two weeks later she learned about her new position.

At our next meeting, she expressed her anger and disappointment, and said she was thinking about leaving but first wanted to find out why she had been demoted. Although unhappy with what she heard, the comments reinforced what the internal consultant had been telling her and emphasized why EI coaching might benefit her.

She had learned that colleagues viewed her as brilliant regarding product strategy, but extremely difficult to deal with. Some executives had recommended that she be terminated. However, her expertise and results orientation were too highly valued by a few key leaders who wanted to retain her. Margaret made the decision to stay and to see if she could learn to be more emotionally intelligent.

In our sessions, I would often listen and then go through the emotions-based process with her, as follows.

Step 1 Identify: Assess the situation and the feelings of key people

Margaret felt anger and disappointment, while I felt confident that I could help her. We discussed her feelings about the demotion and the feedback she had received and acknowledged her disappointment, anger and overall sense of injustice. I asked if she had ever received feedback like this before, and she sheepishly admitted that she had.

Step 2 Use: Decide what feelings would be ideal

To maintain confidence, I needed Margaret to feel excited and energized about the challenge of becoming more team-oriented and less aggressive.

Step 3 Understand: Consider how to change the feelings

Margaret was driven to achieve results and prided herself on her intellect and her ability to meet challenges. She could be volatile, and often had difficulty managing her emotions when she disagreed with someone. I decided that the best way to create excitement about her becoming more emotionally intelligent would be to position this as another challenge, another result to be achieved. Moreover, it was important that she understood that if she left the company without making these changes she would probably get similar feedback elsewhere. Initially, to be successful, I needed to help her to move from defensiveness and anxiety to calm and reflectiveness before she would consider this a worthwhile challenge.

Step 4 Manage: Decide what to do to create the desired changes

I told Margaret that I would support her for the duration of the contract whether she stayed or left the organization, and that I thought I could help her in the areas that people had criticized. She reflected momentarily and then made a quick decision to 'get right to it!' And so our conversations began in earnest.

As she thought about her circumstances, she resolved to stay in her current role and prove that she was capable of handling the situation. Over a series of conversations, she began to accept that her aggressive, hard-charging behavior had been the main reason for her demotion. Although intellectually she quickly accepted this, it was difficult for her to accept it emotionally.

Once we had formed a bond of trust, I helped her to understand that she no longer had to prove she was an achiever. She understood that everyone already acknowledged her high level of achievement. Next, I helped her to channel her high energy and drive in the direction of her new challenge, that is, to get others to view her as a team player. She needed to alter people's perceptions of her as a hard-driving individual; brilliant, but uncaring about others. She needed to accept that the change process began with managing her own emotions. She needed to recognize that she derived emotional energy from achievement, but that achievement could come in different forms. It could be subtle and come through cooperation, rather than through driving others and demonstrating behavior that was often viewed as adversarial.

The process we used to help her emotionally accept what she needed to do in order to advance was to help her to learn how to work effectively as a team member. Our interactions mirrored the way in which she needed to act with peers and other senior managers. In our meetings, we consistently revisited and modified my questions related to the ability-based model of EI:

1. **Identify:**

   a. How was she feeling?

   b. How did she think others were feeling about her?

2. **Uses:** Was she able to generate feelings of trust with her new manager, peers and other senior managers?

3. **Understand:** How was she progressing in understanding how to deal with her own and others' feelings?

4. **Manage:** Has she been managing those flash points in which the urge to plough through barriers was no longer an automatic response so that instead she considered whether, indeed, the response was suitable to the context of the situation?

The coaching has ended, but the relationship continues. Recently Margaret told me that she had been promoted to the senior team and was in charge of product strategy. She sounded gracious and excited when she proudly exclaimed, 'Cooperation really works! We just received approval for the strategy we began engineering two years ago, and everyone was pleased with the way it had got done! Who would have believed it? Not only that, but the chairman of our parent company came from Europe the other day, and I was introduced as one of the key people running our American company! A senior manager told me people were quite pleased with the way I interacted with others over the last 14 months. I really want to thank you for all your help, and I also have someone else for you to coach.' This case demonstrates how the use of the emotion-based planning and problem-solving process to coach people enables us to help ourselves in the future. When clients successfully internalize the four steps, they rarely need additional assistance.

Example 2: EI and Team Building

Roger was vice-president of IT for a large health care maintenance organization (HMO). His responsibilities focused on overseeing clinical, financial and administrative information systems development. One of Roger's direct reports, Ahmed, had recently been given added responsibility for the entire financial and administrative systems group. I had coached several executives on Roger's team successfully, and Ahmed had told Roger he was interested in working with me. He was impressed with the practical approach I brought to the coaching experience. He liked that the coaching began with an assessment of his EI abilities and then focused on leveraging his abilities and the emotion-based process to address critical organizational issues. Roger approved the coaching process for Ahmed.

A major reorganization took place in the HMO's IT group when I began coaching Ahmed. After discussing Ahmed's assessment, we explored possibilities regarding how the learning and coaching could be meaningfully applied. Together, we determined that we would use the coaching process to focus on the feelings of regional staff affected by the change in organizational structure. These were staff who no longer reported to the local, regional level. Instead, they were now part of a national organization with reporting relationships far from their offices.

My guidance and counsel were to use the EI process to do the following:

- **Step 1 Identify:** Help Ahmed to determine the morale in the regional offices.
- **Step 2 Use:** Determine the feelings that we wanted people to experience during and after the transition to the new reporting structure.
- **Step 3 Understand:** Identify the problems that were developing as a result of the change, and what we could do to minimize them.
- **Step 4 Manage:** Construct and implement a plan that would identify and deal with problems, raise morale and retain key staff.

We discovered that many people were upset not to be reporting to local management. We began planning how to ensure that there would be no immediate loss in productivity and how to retain key staff. We felt that it was important to address these tactical issues so that the more long-term goal of increasing organizational performance would not be affected by any negative fallout caused by the lowered morale.

At this time Ahmed shared responsibility for managing regional staff. The responsibility for each of the five regional offices had been assigned to five corporate managers, of which Ahmed was one. In this situation, the idea of partnering with another senior manager emerged. The other manager was Mike, senior manager for Medical Billing and Revenue Applications, whom I was also coaching at the time. Since Roger encouraged his senior managers to work as a team, this project offered the opportunity to Ahmed and Mike to partner on solving a potentially difficult organizational problem. Together, Ahmed, Mike and I began planning.

Step 1 Identify: Assess the situation and the feelings of key people

The first thing we did was to identify the feelings of regional staff. We had heard some informal complaints that regional staff members, as a group, were upset and nervous. Ahmed and his peers, at headquarters, were pleased with the centralized control they had been given, but were also concerned about possibly losing talented staff who were upset about the new reporting structure.

Step 2 Use: Decide what feelings would be ideal

Ahmed and his peers wanted to continue feeling pleased with the reorganization and security regarding retention of key staff. They wanted regional employees to feel supported, confident in their employer, and excited about the opportunities presented by the new centralized organization structure.

Step 3 Understand: Consider how to change the feelings

Ahmed, Mike and I discussed the staff's feelings of uncertainty and anxiety, and talked about how to change those feelings. Ahmed and Mike got Roger's approval for me to call and conduct interviews with the managers in the regional offices in order to better understand what people were feeling. Ahmed, Mike and I thought that managers might be reluctant to tell us that they were upset. Thus, we decided on a strategy in which I asked them to tell us how key employees were feeling about the reorganization. Our assumption was that in discussing the feelings and concerns of their staff, they could also include their own concerns and feelings. What we heard confirmed that employees were upset because they no longer reported to the general manager (GM) in the local office. While employees were still expected to do what the GM requested, their priorities would now be set by directors whom they did not know, and who were located far away. They also worried that their jobs would be outsourced to headquarters and sent offshore to India.

Step 4 Manage: Decide what to do to create the desired changes

Ahmed, Mike and I recommended to Roger that we bring Roger's senior leadership team together with the leaders in regional offices who now reported to headquarters to share what we had learned and discuss what we might do to create a positive view of the change in reporting structure. After several conversations Roger approved the expenditure for bringing the people together, and the meeting took place two months later. At the meeting the senior leaders and regional managers determined that it would be important for the following to take place:

- The existing national organization vision would need to be explained to regional staff, and regional staff would have the opportunity to comment on how the vision would need to change to be inspirational to them.
- Professional growth opportunities would be made available and at least some core competency centers would be established in regional offices, away from headquarters. In other words, people needed to believe that they did not have to move to headquarters in order to be considered for exciting career opportunities.
- Senior leaders from headquarters would visit the regions to cement the positive aspects of the change.
- These plans would be implemented, monitored and modified as needed to maintain high levels of performance in regional offices.

All these activities occurred. While senior leaders could not promise that jobs would not be outsourced, they did many things to reinforce the positive aspects of the reorganization. While some turnover was expected, turnover within this group has been lower than the industry average during a period of restructuring. Furthermore, in discussions with regional managers, we heard that people have been surprisingly pleased with the change. Although difficult to quantify, the role of EI coaching is viewed by senior leaders as a key factor contributing to improved morale and the high level of retention.

When asked to comment about the used overall coaching process, Roger had this to say:

Emotional intelligence coaching for the senior leaders and staff had a significant positive impact on their effectiveness. It has improved our relationships with our business customers and our interactions with other internal IT divisions. By understanding the emotional 'landscape', we are much better equipped to understand and manage our own reaction to events in the workplace and to more effectively understand our business and IT partners' frame of reference. As a result, we are more able to use our training in analytical and design skills to produce more effective solutions with our business and IT partners.

And Ahmed commented:

When it came to working with staff during reorganization, I wondered if there was a tool that could help; then I found the emotional intelligence model. It was helpful in understanding and using emotions to make a difficult task successful.

Example 3: EI and Negotiations

In this coaching experience, a small businessman, Ken, had a building available for sale or lease for six months. Ken's business involved computer sales and service. The service end was booming, but sales had been flat. Originally, Ken had another business in his building, but the tenant had moved out. He was left with more space than he needed and less traffic coming into his store. I had coached him in the past, and he approached me to discuss an offer that was made by another small businessman, Sam.

Sam had owned a highly successful coffee-and-sandwich shop for ten years but had been forced to move from his previous location because a Starbucks had come into his area and had attracted a number of his former customers. Ken asked me if we could discuss the offer from Sam. Sam had offered to lease part of the building, but with a number of conditions. He wanted the first month rent free while he would be making the changes necessary to turn the leased part of the building into a restaurant. He then wanted to pay US$3,500 monthly, or US$15 per square foot for six months, which was about US$10 less than the going rate. He had been paying US$4,500 monthly at his previous site, but he knew that, initially, he would not have the clientele to make the business viable, so he was asking for a price break for six months.

Ken had conferred with a few people who advised him that he should not have to give a price break for his prime location. Ken knew that he had a great location, that soon there would be a development built nearby for people over 55 years old, and that a coffee shop would be attractive to this market. He also knew that he had several better offers in the past, but none had worked out for one reason or another. He definitely wanted a deal with someone. However, he did not want to give the lease away for less than it was worth. He also did not want to make it too tough for the other party to make a profit. He felt that when I had coached him before I had always been helpful as a sounding board. Given the amount of money involved, and his pressing desire to make a deal, he felt this would be an appropriate time to have another coaching session. When we discussed the situation, it was clear that Ken wanted to make a deal beneficial to both parties.

Step 1 Identify: Assess the situation and the feelings of key people

I asked Ken how he was feeling and how Sam was feeling. Ken told me he was partially relieved that he had an offer, but he felt also that Sam's conditions were unacceptable. He felt conflicted and needed to talk about how he was feeling. He was uncertain about Sam's emotions, but thought that Sam seemed uncertain and hopeful. Ken also sensed excitement in Sam about being located near the new over-55 housing development.

Step 2 Use: Decide what feelings would be ideal

Ken told me that since Sam would potentially be a tenant he would see every day, he wanted an agreement that both of them would feel good about. He wanted to feel enthusiastic about the business possibilities and confident that he had made a good business decision, which required a fair price for the lease. He was not overly concerned about Sam's feelings, but he knew—from our previous coaching experiences—that it was important to consider them. As we talked, Ken realized that he wanted Sam also to feel enthusiastic about the business possibilities and confident that he was paying a fair price.

Step 3 Understand: Consider how to change the feelings

I asked Ken what it would take for him to feel enthusiastic and confident about the deal. We explored various possibilities and soon realized that the key was taking a long-term perspective. Sam needed time to establish his business. However, once it was established, people coming in for coffee throughout the day would also generate more traffic coming into Ken's computer store. In two years, when the over-55 development property began to fill, Ken felt that people coming to buy coffee were also likely to buy their computers from someone nearby, who could provide IT service as well. As we talked, Sam's conditions became less significant to Ken. Ken found that locking in a long-term lease so that he could capitalize on the potential we were discussing was more important.

Next, I asked what would make Sam confident and enthusiastic. Ken felt that Sam needed him to be supportive. He thought Sam would feel supported if he offered the first month rent free and the next five months at a reduced rate. He also wanted Sam to be committed to staying for three years, as this would provide ample time for him to improve his computer business and to position his building to be sold for at least one-and-a-half times its current worth. He felt that if he reduced the fee for six months, he could have Sam sign a lease for the remainder of the three years at the rate he had been paying at his previous location. By not asking Sam to pay more than before, and by giving him a lower rent initially, Ken felt that Sam would be enthusiastic about the deal.

Step 4 Manage: Decide what to do to create the desired changes

I asked Ken if he was willing and able to settle on this price knowing that he might be able to get more money when others found out about the over-55 housing development. Ken said he felt confident that the coffee shop offered more business traffic on a regular basis than any of the other potential tenants he had met. He felt the price was reasonable if Sam agreed with the three-year plan. He felt hopeful that more people buying his computers would also increase service requests. As he left our last coaching session, he told me he felt uplifted and excited about meeting with Sam that afternoon and sharing the plan we had discussed.

Later that day, Ken called to thank me. He said that Sam had agreed to the deal, and that both of them left their meeting feeling enthusiastic and confident.

Conclusion

In this chapter, we began with a description of EI, of Mayer and Salovey's definition of the concept, and of the way in which I adapted their model to make it easy to apply to coaching. Next, we explored the emotion-based planning and problem-solving process. Specific examples demonstrated how this process can be used in coaching. Using the hands-on approach, I help clients to improve their ability to manage change, hold performance discussions, deal with peers over territorial issues, and manage difficult supervisors and customers.

Most of my clients understand that the way in which a leader, manager, owner or employee feels influences their perceptions, decisions and actions. They learn that to be interpersonally effective requires identifying the feelings of key people, using these or other feelings to assist with the situation, understanding how the feelings arose and what might make the feelings change, and managing to stay open to these feelings in order to make and carry out the right decisions. The ability to combine EI with cognitive intelligence leads to optimal decision-making and enhanced performance.

While there is no quantitative research demonstrating the efficacy of the approach, the emotion-based planning and problem-solving process has nevertheless worked successfully with clients from business, health care, government, the military, universities and schools. It has limitations in the sense that it is based on the client's perceptions of what is real and what others are feeling. The consultant, or coach, requires excellent listening and critical-thinking skills to help generate meaningful alternatives.

People feel more in control of their feelings when they use the emotion-based process. The goals of this process are to teach others to be more intelligent about their own and others' emotions and, as demonstrated particularly in the case of Ken and Sam, to know when to ask for help in dealing with conflicting emotions and high stakes.

References

Bar-On, R. 2006. The Bar-On model of emotional-social intelligence (ESI). *Psicothema* 18.

Caruso, D. 2004, February. Defining the inkblot called emotional intelligence. Retrieved May 03, 2005, from the EI Consortium Web Site http:/www.eiconsortium.org/research/ei_issues_and_common_misunderstandings_caruso_comment.htm.

Caruso, D., and P. Salovey. 2004. *The emotionally intelligent manager.* New York: Jossey Bass.

Caruso, D., and C.J. Wolfe. 2001. Emotional Intelligence at Work. In *Emotional Intelligence in Everyday Life.* Ed. J. Ciarrochi, J.P. Forgas, and J.D. Mayer, pp. 150–67. Philadelphia, PA: Psychology Press.

Caruso, D., and C.J. Wolfe. 2004. Emotional intelligence and leadership development. In *Leader Development for Transforming Organizations.* Ed. D.V. Day, S. Zaccaro, and S. Halpin, pp. 237–63. Hillsdale, NJ: Erlbaum.

Goleman, D. 2005, January. Defining the inkblot called emotional intelligence. Retrieved May 03, 2005, from the EI Consortium Web Site http:/www.eiconsortium.org/research/ei_issues_and_common_misunderstandings_goleman_comment.htm.

Gosling, J., and H. Mintzberg. 2003. The five minds of a manager. *Harvard Business Review* 81(11): 54–63.

Ludeman, K., and E. Erlandson. 2004. Coaching the alpha male. *Harvard Business Review* 82(5): 58–67.

Mayer, J.D. 2005.The four-branch model of emotional intelligence. Retrieved May 03, 2005, from Emotional Intelligence Information Web site: http:/www.unh.edu/emotional_intelligence/eiemotint2.htm.

Mayer, J.D., and P. Salovey. 1997. What is emotional intelligence? In *Emotional development and emotional intelligence: Implications for educators.* Ed. P. Salovey and D. Sluyter, pp. 3–31. New York: Basic Books.

Mayer, J.D., P. Salovey, and D. Caruso. 2002a. *The Mayer-Salovey-Caruso Emotional Intelligence Test (MSCEIT),* Version 2.0. Toronto, Canada: Multi Health Systems.

———. 2002b. *MSCEIT technical manual.* Toronto, Canada: Multi Health Systems.

Salovey, P., and J.D. Mayer. 1990. Emotional intelligence. *Imagination, Cognition, and Personality* 9:185–211.

Stewart, T.A., and L. O'Brien. 2005. Execution without excuses. *Harvard Business Review* 83(3): 102–11.

Wolfe, C.J. 2001. Results of emotionally intelligent actions at Kaiser Permanente. *Competency & Emotional Intelligence* 8(4): 25–26.

Wolfe, C., and D. Caruso. 2004. *Emotional intelligence critical skills for success participant manual.* Shelton, CT: New Haven Consulting Group.

— 13 —

Coaching Executives to Enhance Emotional Intelligence and Increase Productivity

Geetu Bharwaney

Introduction

Executive coaching represents one method of helping adults to increase their EI, their personal performance and their organizational productivity. From an organizational standpoint, coaching can be a risky proposition, because individual executives begin to engage in conversations with a personal coach that could accelerate a desire to leave their 'toxic' work environment. As such risks are inherent in coaching in workplace settings, it is vital that coaching be structured for organizational as well as individual benefit. With respect to this consideration, we view one-to-one coaching in this chapter as a process in which individuals receive assistance from a consultant over a period of time to work through their personal and professional challenges and achieve their goals more easily. In group-based coaching, by contrast, many individuals from within a management team, unit or organization work with a coach or coaches over a period of time in order to achieve their collective goals. The vehicle for group coaching is usually a combination of one-to-one coaching and facilitated group workshops.

We begin this chapter with a definition of coaching and an explanation of its connection to EI. In the following section, we focus on getting started with individual and group coaching. Lastly, we provide a process for setting up coaching to obtain optimal results.

Coaching and EI

Coaching has been described as one of the fastest growing professions in the UK, involving more professionals than doctors and dentists (Gunnell 2004). Gallwey (1986:8) defines coaching as the process of 'unlocking a person's potential to maximize their own performance', and adds that 'it is helping them to learn rather than teaching them'. While in this chapter we look at coaching as a method of increasing EI and productivity, the way in which the application of EI alters the focus of coaching needs to be clarified.

Based on my professional experience, the preferred EI framework to use in coaching is the Bar-On model (1997; 2000; 2005). Taking into account an evolving conceptualization of this construct (Bar-On 1997), Bar-On (2000:385) defines EI as 'a multifactorial array of interrelated emotional, personal and social abilities that influence our overall ability to actively and effectively cope with daily demands and pressures'. I have adapted Bar-On's conceptualization of EI in order to better understand the process of coaching within the organizational context, and to facilitate its application in the workplace, as follows: EI is the essential mix of emotional, personal and social competencies that influences our ability to be personally effective and organizationally productive. This revision of Bar-On's definition recognizes that for an organization to adopt the role of 'paying sponsor' for coaching, a two-fold benefit has to be inherent in this activity:

1. A benefit to the **organization**—receiving more from the employees who are coached in being better able to help the organization to become more productive.
2. A personal benefit to these **employees**—becoming more effective, happier and fulfilled at work as well as in their private lives.

As touched on above, coaching can be either individual- or group-based within the organizational context. Hereafter, I refer to the process as 'EQ coaching'—a process that is designed to help improve EI so that people can be more personally effective and organizationally productive.

Individual- and Group-Based EQ Coaching

The success of EQ coaching depends, in part, on the quality of the initial or set-up phase. It is crucial for coaches to find the right answers to the following questions:

- How do we get started?
- How do we determine a baseline or measured starting point?
- How do we ensure that the methods we use are not limited by our skill?

We will now explore each question in more detail.

Getting started

It is recommended that practitioners start by determining their form of EQ coaching on two spectrums: one spectrum specifying their general form of coaching, and the second specifying the type of intervention. Figure 13.1 illustrates the spectrum of coaching.

The first choice to make is to locate on this spectrum our basic form of coaching within the individual- or group-based EQ coaching that we plan to provide. All successful EQ coaching, if properly implemented, has to be located in the top right-hand quadrant, shown in Figure 13.1, where there is both a high degree of structure in the coaching process and a high degree of willingness on the part of the client to be coached. While this may seem logical, problems can occur if the individual does *not* wish to be coached, which often becomes evident much later in coaching when expected shifts and changes do not occur. Another problem stems from there being insufficient structure within the intervention, and the individual and/or the coach lack motivation to see the intervention to fruition. By clarifying the degree of willingness of the client at the outset, and by agreeing to create the requisite structure, the intervention is more likely to be coherent from the client's perspective and the implementation itself is more likely to be rigorous.

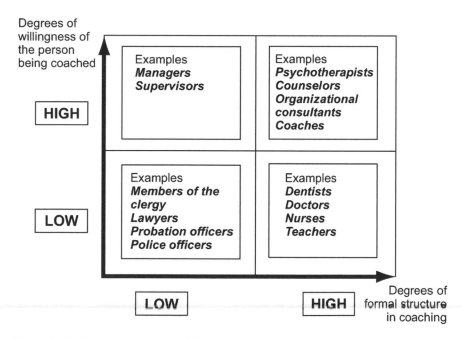

Figure 13.1   The spectrum of coaching

(Source: Bharwaney and Paddock 2003:29.)

Another way of determining the starting point is to map our intervention in relation to the scale of desired impact versus the degree of openness of the organizational client group to be coached, as shown in Figure 13.2. This may be considered an extension of the previous spectrums. In this figure, the word 'impact' is defined as positive value to both the individual and to the organization as a whole.

The matrix in Figure 13.2 encourages us as the coach to consider our specific type of intervention in terms of the desired scale of impact. It has been my experience that EQ coaching can potentially be located anywhere within the four quadrants appearing above. Activities of low impact, where there is also potentially low openness of the group being coached, are likely to include presentations and provide reading material, at the most. Where there is a high degree of openness to being coached, but where low-impact activities are planned, these activities may include EI assessments and short-term workshops, but without any coherent intervention strategy. High-impact activities, where there is a low degree of openness of the group, might include setting up a research project designed to identify the EI components of high productivity, for instance. If EQ coaching is located anywhere other than in the top right-hand quadrant, it is likely to be problematic in its implementation or lose its full potential to make a difference.

Assuming that we decide on our style of coaching and our degree of planning around our specific type of intervention in the top right-hand quadrants of the

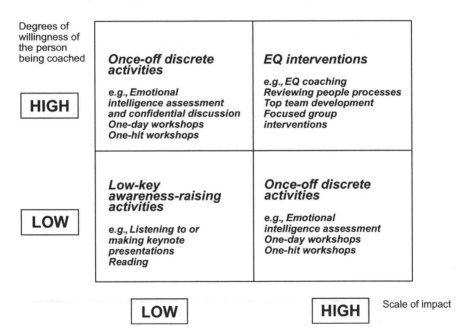

Figure 13.2   The spectrum of interventions

above mentioned spectrums, we are ready to take the next steps in identifying a baseline or measured starting point.

Determining the starting point

One of the key ways in which EI interventions are experienced within organizations is through individual or group coaching. These approaches will involve some form of EI measurement. Without accurate EI measurement, it will not be clear what we are working with, how we are working and what our work is based on. Therefore, an essential early decision must involve how best to measure EI. The Bar-On (1997; 2000; 2005) framework for individual- and group-based EQ coaching is preferable for the following reasons:

1. Bar-On's conceptual and measurement model of EI provides a comprehensive framework that has **high face validity** with executives. It is therefore extremely useful with individual and group coaching. The language of the Bar-On model, together with its associated assessment tool, the EQ-i, generally receives strong support from individuals. Among approximately 4,000 people with whom the EQ-i has been used in my work over the past five years, only one group of 15 individuals had 'reservations' about its use in their organization. Even with highly intelligent and sophisticated individuals, the EQ-i is a tool that has been challenged by relatively few.

2. The framework is **simple to use** and provides a reasonably quick way of assessing EI—it takes about 30 minutes to complete. Its self-report format, with built-in checks and balances to correct for a natural tendency to give an exaggerated impression of ourselves, enables a discreet way of conveying fairly accurate information about strengths and weaknesses without intruding on our privacy, which tends to occur when 360° multi-rater procedures are used in organizations.

3. The EQ-i is **empirically based** on numerous studies that have been conducted over a period of many years. Bar-On (2004) has recently summarized more than 60 validity studies that have been conducted on this instrument. The findings demonstrate that this instrument provides a valid and reliable way of measuring what it purports to measure, that is, EI. Its psychometric robustness enables it to have great impact on the types of interventions that appear in Figure 13.2. Moreover, the instrument is useful in creating models of star performers that can be and are being used in hiring, training and succession planning. Lastly, other EI instruments that are less comprehensive in nature tend to be less discriminating and provide less information for the above mentioned applications in the organizational setting.

Practitioners can use the above list as criteria for comparison with the EI measures that are available to them.

Ensuring that methods are not limited by the skill of the coach

An extremely important dimension of individual and group EQ coaching is the amount of structure related to the intervention, and this is partly reflected in the amount of contact time that is involved. Furthermore, it is imperative that we ensure that the coaching methods we use are not limited by our skill.

Most coaching programs involve a relatively brief coaching period. An upfront two-hour diagnostic phase is typically followed by 12 hours of coaching and then two additional hours of review, totalling 16 hours. EQ coaching usually involves a 90-minute upfront conversation followed by 35 hours of group workshops delivered as five days of seven blocks—an initial two-day block followed by a three-day block—over three months, and a final evaluation conversation for a further 90 minutes. This totals 38 hours, or approximately five days. In my experience, shorter programs do not have the same impact, and longer programs rely unduly on the staying power of the individual client beyond the useful shelf-life of the program.

A highly structured approach to coaching is consistent with the EI Consortium's guidelines for implementing EI interventions (see the website at www. eiconsortium.org). This is expanded upon by Orme and Cannon (2000a; 2000b; 2001 a; 2001 b) in a series of articles covering the four phases of intervention:

1. Needs assessment.
2. Design.
3. Delivery.
4. Evaluation.

In planning these types of interventions, it is essential for us to ensure that the reasons are appropriate, that the right advocates are involved, and that we conduct a careful needs assessment before beginning the actual coaching. During the design phase, clear learning outcomes need to be defined and learner-centered approaches that will support emotions-based learning need to be built in. During the implementation or delivery phase, this means using experiential methods that involve providing feedback with care, role models for success and an ability to learn both on and off the job. During the evaluation phase, this means articulating a clear purpose for evaluation and using clear strategies for evaluation and stakeholder communication.

Based on the broad guidelines presented by the EI Consortium, four key features have been identified to ensure that the coaching is not limited to the qualities and skills of the coach:

1. Clear goals.
2. Pre- and post-intervention assessments.
3. Predefined structure and accountability.
4. Involved stakeholders.

Let us examine these features, along with an action plan for implementing each component of the coaching process.

The Impact of Coaching

We address these questions in this section:

- Which performance parameters are meaningful to individuals and organizations?
- What are the best ways of maximizing personal commitment and organizational benefit?

Pre- and post-intervention assessments—designed to identify changes in EI, individual and organizational performance are the integral components of an effective intervention. In other words, these assessments are the best way of scientifically examining not only whether the intervention has made a difference but also the extent of that difference. This holds true for every form of EI intervention—be it at home, in school, in the workplace or in health care.

Meaningful performance parameters

Kirkpatrick's (1994) four levels of training evaluation are an essential starting point:

1. Reaction.
2. Learning.
3. Behavior.
4. Results.

These levels provide an effective way to both structure evaluation at the outset and to conduct evaluation during the course of an intervention. Ideally, all four levels should be described at the beginning of the coaching process as part of an evaluation strategy so that all key stakeholders are aware of how the success of the EQ coaching will be measured. This is a logical step to take but it can often be overlooked in the haste to get a new intervention up and running.

Reaction level evaluation involves the collection of customer satisfaction feedback and must not be confused with outcomes evaluation. Typically, this level of evaluation examines how participants reacted to various aspects of the training rather than to the learning or the outcomes of the learning. Examples of aspects are the venue, the structure of the learning and the material used.

This level of evaluation addresses the question of whether the participants enjoyed the EQ coaching experience. It primarily yields feedback that is related to learner satisfaction, providing important input at the end of each learning module. If the satisfaction rating is 'high', that is, when 80% or more of the learners rate the coaching experience as valuable, enjoyable and well presented, then the intervention can continue as is. However, if there is any dissatisfaction, this needs to be addressed immediately or it will adversely influence the emotional climate within which the learning takes place.

Learning level evaluation involves gathering information about the learning accomplished during the EQ coaching in terms of both skills and knowledge. I have found that this is vital to the specific changes that the individual is trying to make. This evaluation is typically based on the use of a questionnaire designed to directly assess achievement by comparing the learning objectives defined at the outset of coaching with what has actually been achieved. The development plans created at the outset are also reviewed to see what has been achieved. When teams are taking part in group-based EQ coaching, the plans will be in the form of collective development plans and will typically summarize the team's actions. When the intervention involves individual EQ coaching, the plans will be in the form of coaching goals.

At this level of evaluation, it is essential that clear learning outcomes are formulated from the outset and reviewed at a later stage. Sometimes the learning will go beyond the stated goals, but it is more important for the EQ coach to be able to demonstrate that learning has been accomplished.

This level of evaluation can also take the form of knowledge tests and/or interviews, in which participants report back on how situations were approached. The latter is usually more intensive and time-consuming than the former.

Behavior change level evaluation involves gathering information about changes that the participants experience on a daily basis at work as a result of the coaching. For most programs involving EQ coaching, I have found that one of the strongest measures of success is how someone uses their daily calendar. This is something that I would encourage all practitioners to consider. When new skills are learned, they have an impact on how individuals use their time and to what they pay attention.

Another rich source of information is feedback received from other people. EQ coaching programs often involve two reference points at which up to six people are asked a set of questions about the individual, framed in the context of performance prior to the coaching experience. For example, for a client named James, people were asked these questions:

- In three words, how would you describe James?
- What is the strongest quality that James brings to his daily interactions?
- What is James's purpose in his current role?
- What is James's biggest development need?
- What is your highest aspiration for James?

A third source of information focuses on the quality of relationships. I ask all EQ coaching clients to complete a 'stakeholder analysis' at the outset and identify where each person is in relation to where others would ideally like them to be. This helps to generate a map of the relationships that surround the individual, so that the priorities for change can be easily located within certain key work relationships.

I also ask clients to audit their current meetings and use this as a benchmark for what they want to improve. For interventions involving leadership style and working with leaders of an organization, it is highly useful to conduct staff focus groups before and after a coaching intervention in order to obtain highly specific details of what the desired leadership changes look like from a co-worker's perspective, and then to repeat the focus groups after the intervention to see if the changes have indeed occurred.

These five areas—calendar, feedback, stakeholder analysis, meetings and focus groups—are genuine locations where change occurs and which provide the coach with a strong practical basis for demonstrating results.

Results level evaluation involves collecting information about the tangible results that emanate from changes and differences in daily functioning. It is this information that is going to interest the stakeholders the most for any intervention. It is recommended here that the EI measurement completed at the outset be repeated some six, nine or 12 months later. Two valuable sources of information are:

1. a comparison of pre- and post-coaching EQ profiles for the participating group versus a control group of non-participants
2. a review of the changes in EI in the participating group over time.

This kind of data is useful for isolating what our coaching program is addressing and what it is not addressing in order to focus on areas that need to be improved. This helps to demonstrate the competencies and skills that were influenced the most through coaching, and the others that still need to be addressed.

Additional important information at the results level of evaluation is based on documenting changes that occur in the workplace following coaching. These can be grouped into:

- **personal results**—often revealed in areas of health and personal relationships
- **physical results**—including whether or not the mission of the organization is clear
- **team-oriented results**—including ways in which team members interact and collectively contribute to organizational productivity.

Frequently, it proves useful to apply a strengths, weaknesses, opportunities and threats (SWOT) analysis at the end of program to identify changes and improvements that have been achieved. Through coaching, a number of weaknesses should be addressed, opportunities tapped and threats overcome.

Personal commitment and organizational benefit

The potential benefits from EQ coaching are realized only if the participants and their stakeholders are fully engaged in the learning process and the evaluation. It is important to get full approval from key stakeholders for the evaluation method at the outset of coaching. It is also useful to conduct mini-reviews and disseminate the findings. One of the most effective ways of doing this is to work with someone within the organization who is identified as a key advocate of the program. Such a person will typically act to support the overall learning process as either a co-facilitator or a program support person. This approach has been used by many organizations in the UK, and it represents an important facilitating feature of EQ coaching. It ensures that the intervention is not viewed as being foreign to the organization, and it increases the credibility of the results presented at the end of the process.

Coaching to Obtain the Best Results

In this section, we are occupied with answering the question of which are the most critical elements to 'get right' in implementing coaching. Above, I mentioned four essential features of the planning of EQ coaching that will impact on the results. Here, I combine each feature with an action plan for incorporating the feature into an intervention.

Key feature 1: Clear goals

I suggested above that in an organizational context, EI is an *essential mix of emotional, personal and social competencies* that influence our ability to be personally effective and organizationally productive. Such a mix dictates the necessity of clearly establishing personal efficacy and organizational productivity goals before coaching begins. We should ask the participants the following four questions early on in both individual and group EQ coaching interventions:

1. What do you wish to achieve in terms of personal efficacy over the next three to six months?
2. What will be the evidence that you have succeeded in achieving your goals? What will you *see* as proof of success, what will you *hear,* and how will you *feel* if you are successful in fulfilling these goals?
3. What would your organization's key stakeholders want you to achieve in terms of organizational productivity over the next three to six months?
4. What will prove to the stakeholders that you have succeeded in achieving these goals? What will they *see* as evidence of success, what will they *hear,* and how will they *feel* if you are successful in accomplishing this?

Table 13.1 provides some clear goals. Notice that the evidence is conveyed in highly specific terms.

Key feature 2: Pre- and post-intervention assessments

This is the 'heart' of EI coaching; it is here that the impact of our intervention is measured and felt. Comparing the difference between pre- and post-intervention assessments provides a way for us to scientifically demonstrate how successful or unsuccessful the coaching was.

Table 13.1   Example of clear goals for individual- and group-based EQ coaching

Personal efficacy goals	Organizational productivity goals
A stronger sense of comfort with regard to how I am prioritizing and directing efforts in what I am currently doing. *Evidence:* My diary is organized and reflects priorities.	Team member should leave my interactions feeling energized and not enervated, disappointed or deflated. *Evidence:* The results of a spot survey of the team after a key interaction.
Increased knowledge of the business. *Evidence:* I can make full contributions to business meetings involving multi-disciplines.	Take the lead on truly defining what leadership means in this organization, and the behaviors, practices and attitudes which support inspiring leadership. *Evidence:* A presentation to my peers.
Better communication skills. *Evidence:* My updating of team meetings is more succinct and focused.	Influencing change, be it process or behavior, across peer group, that is, senior managers. *Evidence:* Specific suggestions that I prepare beforehand and offer in every senior team meeting.

As mentioned above, we must determine a measured starting point or baseline before the coaching begins. Moreover, we should base specific assessments on a combination of the following:

- The administration of a psychometric instrument designed to measure EI and the receipt of focus group input, or specific feedback on the individual.
- A SWOT analysis.
- Personal diary analysis.
- Stakeholder analysis.
- Analysis of information regarding team efficacy.

We need to repeat these assessments identically at the end of the intervention. We should attempt to incorporate most, if not all, of these assessments in order to increase the robustness of the evaluation. The greater the difference between the pre-and post-intervention assessments, the more successful the coaching was. We should hold the assessments at least six months apart, with intervals of six, nine and 12 months.

Key feature 3: Predefined structure and accountability

In both individual and group EQ coaching, it is important that we clearly stipulate the time commitments and the responsibilities of each party before coaching begins. Ideally, we would detail the learning curriculum with objectives, potential workplace outcomes, topics to be covered, preparation tasks, follow-up activities and deliverables. This level of structure typically has a

This is what you, the client, can expect of me, your EQ coach:

1. I will challenge you to focus on the areas you are ignoring consciously or unconsciously.
2. I am fully on your side and interested in what is important to you.
3. I will keep all details of our conversations confidential. The content of our sessions are confidential between you and me.
4. I will be on time and will have respect for your time.
5. I will be as flexible as my diary allows for rescheduling if we have to postpone sessions.
6. When a session is cancelled, we will reschedule in the earliest possible time-frame.
7. You can expect me to write and email notes to you that come out of each session.
8. To provide value, I am fully accountable for everything we do.
9. You can expect me to be a resource to you and to share skills, knowledge and expertise as appropriate.
10. I will review the themes of our conversations with my supervisor with whom I review all my client work. This is one of my internal safeguards to ensure that my work with you is based on the highest possible professional level.

This is what I, the EQ coach, can expect of you, my client:

1. We agree on clear goals and deliverables at the outset.
2. You will be on time and fully prepared for our coaching sessions.
3. You shall accept and willingly work on any feedback received and be open to trying new methods and approaches.
4. You feel totally comfortable making telephone contact with me on my cellphone or, in the case of any last-minute schedule changes, the office landline. You return my calls and my text messages, and respond to my emails at your earliest convenience.
5. While short-notice cancellations are sometimes inevitable – through illness, urgent priorities, etc. – I expect us both to keep our meeting commitments.
6. You will reflect carefully before and after each session.
7. While there is a lot that I will do to stay on track with your goals, we have joint responsibility for making those goals happen.
8. We will review our work together regularly, and you will alert me to any changes to our work that would be beneficial – I am open to your feedback.
9. At the end of our time together, you will evaluate our work and provide feedback to your key stakeholders within your organisation.
10. You shall alert me to any personal or professional event that may compromise our work.

Client signature: _____   Coach signature: _____

Figure 13.3   Example of accountability in individual- and group-based EQ coaching

two-fold effect: as well as raising the motivation level of the participant, it also forces us as the coach to be prepared for the whole program from the beginning rather than simply for each current element at any particular time.

Part of the process of creating clear structure and accountability involves ensuring that the roles of coach and client are properly defined and agreed upon by both parties before coaching begins. Figure 13.3 is an example of the form that the list of respective responsibilities of coach and client frequently takes. Ideally, we should compile the list and present it to the client for comment.

Key feature 4: Involved stakeholders

This extremely important feature entails involving the appropriate internal organizational sponsors so that the value of the EQ coaching is realized and agreed upon.

To implement this feature, we should ensure that the stakeholders are involved:

- in setting goals
- in participating in mid-program progress reviews
- in designing the intervention by drawing in key people from the outset.

This helps to influence the entire learning context of the individual or group being coached. At the beginning, we must build in time for these activities. Failing this, questions will inevitably arise regarding confidentiality and how the intervention can provide organizational value, and so forth. In my experience, it is useful to note the dates of important business meetings that are scheduled and then to secure a slot in the meeting agenda entitled 'Recent results from the EQ program', for example.

The goal of the above mentioned features is to ensure that EQ coaching remains a highly visible topic in the organization in order to facilitate the dissemination of results while staying within the bounds of confidentiality agreed upon with the participants.

Conclusion

I use the metaphor of a life raft to summarize this chapter on EQ coaching. Every individual carries a life raft that contains survival equipment used, for better or for worse, every moment of every day. Many individuals are surviving with a life raft that has damaged sections with no regular maintenance plan to keep them fully afloat. As people in organizations do not need to use their rafts to deal with life-threatening crises each day, the damaged sections and survival equipment may not always be visible to the innocent passenger; the damages can 'hang around' for many years without being obvious or creating any immediate, serious problem. After all, the individuals involved can still perform their jobs; they continue to be employed and the organization continues to function.

If properly structured, EQ entails a process that enables the life raft to be fully inflated so that the individual can thrive, and not merely survive, on a daily basis...even in an emergency. In order for EQ coaching to provide this service, and to have a sustainable impact for individuals and the organizations that support its implementation, we must take the four key features, explored above, into consideration in the design, renewal and maintenance of the life raft:

1. **Clear goals:** Which parts of the life raft need to be inflated, and which emergency situations will it be able to cope with that could be problematic if they occurred today?

2. **Pre- and post-intervention assessments:** How do we test the strength of the life raft now before we do anything to repair it, and how can we test its strength and the way it functions after we have repaired it?

3. **Predefined structure and accountability:** Who needs to be involved in repairing the life raft? What do we have to do? What is the optimal time and framework for the maintenance schedule?

4. **Involved stakeholders:** Who will pay for the maintenance of the life raft? How will the funding be supported? What will happen if it needs more repair work than was predicted? How often do we need to examine its condition? Who is best positioned to do this? How will others be informed?

Many individuals are drowning in their organizations—they lack a well-functioning life raft with clear survival strategies. Perhaps the development of EI via coaching is this life raft. Perhaps EQ coaching is about throwing a life raft to individuals so that they can survive and, even better, thrive.

The territory of executive education and development has remained unchallenged for several years. Hopefully, the ideas in this chapter will serve to deepen your understanding of the importance and value of EQ coaching. I believe that the future of EQ coaching lies in this systematic approach designed to enable coaches to make an impact that will be sustained by their clients for years.

References

Bar-On, R. 1997. *Bar-On Emotional Quotient Inventory (EQ-i) Technical Manual.* Toronto: Multi Health Systems.

———. 2000. Emotional and social intelligence: Insights from the Emotional Quotient Inventory (EQ-i). In *Handbook of emotional intelligence.* Ed. R. Bar-On and J.D.A. Parker. San Francisco: Jossey-Bass.

———. 2004. The Bar-On Emotional Quotient Inventory (EQ-i): Rationale, description and summary of psychometric properties. In *Measuring emotional intelligence: Common ground and controversy.* Ed. G. Geher, pp. 111–42. Hauppage, New York: Nova Science Publishers.

———. 2006. The Bar-On model of emotional-social intelligence (ESI). *Psicothema* 18.

Bharwaney, G., and C. Paddock. 2003. Emotionally intelligent helping. *Competency & Emotional Intelligence*, 11(1): 27–32.

Gallwey, T. 1986. The inner game of tennis, Pan. In *Coaching for performance: Growing people, performance and purpose.* 3rd ed. 2002. Ed. L. Whitmore. London: Nicholas Breadley.

Gunnell, B. 2004, September 6. The happiness industry.*New Statesman* (cover story).

Kirkpatrick, D.L. 1994. *Evaluating training programs: The four levels.* San Francisco, CA: Berrett-Koehler.

Orme, G., and K. Cannon. 2000a. Everything you wanted to know about implementing an EQ programme—1: Getting started. *Competency & Emotional Intelligence* 8(1): 19–24.

———. 2000b. Everything you wanted to know about implementing an EQ programme—2: Design. *Competency & Emotional Intelligence* 8(2): 18–25.

———. 2001a. Everything you wanted to know about implementing an EQ programme—3: Taking the show on the road. *Competency & Emotional Intelligence* 8(3): 17–24.

———. 2001b. Everything you wanted to know about implementing an EQ programme—4: Assuring the highest standards. *Competency & Emotional Intelligence* 8(4): 19–24.

—— 14 ——

Emotional Competence Development and the Bottom Line: Lessons from American Express Financial Advisors

Douglas Lennick

Introduction

In this chapter, we examine the way in which the financial services division of American Express used EI training to dramatically improve the sales performance of its financial advisors. We also consider how the idea of emotional skills training originated, how the program was designed and delivered, and what results were achieved.

At the time of writing, American Express Financial Advisors (AEFA) had just become an independent publicly traded Fortune 500 company named 'Ameriprise Financial'. As an operating unit of American Express, it was an undisputed industry leader in financial advisory services. A large part of the AEFA success story is its strategic use of EI as a core business competence. In the corporate universe where management programs quickly ignite and often as quickly evaporate, how did AEFA create a lasting emotional competence development program—and arguably one of the most compelling business cases for the impact of EI on sustainable business growth? In this chapter, I hope to answer that question, and explore lessons learned that may benefit others in the business world who want to use EI to enhance their competitive edge.

Background

Today, EI is embedded in the business lexicon; it is recognized as an important ingredient in business performance. Thirty years ago, when I developed a model for business performance that included 'coping effectively', the role of emotions in the workplace was not well understood. By the 1980s, my early model had evolved into the 'Alignment Model', which proposed significant links between management of emotions and business goal achievement. The model labelled an individual's ability to manage emotions and respond appropriately to other's emotions as 'emotional competence'. Emotional competence became a personal business tool, and I also incorporated it into the coaching of financial advisors whom I managed in a series of increasingly senior leadership roles within AEFA.

What I did not know at the time was that while I was exploring the business value of emotional skills, academic researchers were examining the same arena. Pioneers in the field of EI—such as Reuven Bar-On (2003), Peter Salovey and John Mayer (1990), and others—were developing and validating theoretical notions of the existence and benefits of this newly conceived form of intelligence. Ironically, it was not until the publication of Daniel Goleman's first book, *Emotional intelligence* (1995), that I learned about the scholarly research in the area of emotional skills. By this time the research and training we explore in this chapter were well under way. In the mid-1990s, I had the opportunity of speaking to Goleman as he was writing *Working with emotional intelligence* (1998), and was energized by the formal EI research to continue his sponsorship of emotional competence training and coaching. Goleman was also pleased to discover in AEFA a powerful case study of the application of EI in the workplace.

There has since been some scholarly debate about the relevance, or even the existence, of EI as a dimension of human behavior (see, for example, the collection of articles in the *Journal of Organizational Behaviour* (2005)). However, the AEFA experience, as well as that of other businesses, demonstrates undeniably that EI has 'face validity', or practical value, in business settings.

The Importance of EI in Business Performance

Cary Cherniss's (2004) report cites numerous studies that substantiate the contribution of EI to the workplace, including a study that found that partners in a multinational consulting firm who scored above the median on nine or more of 20 mostly EI competencies delivered US$1.2 million more profit from their accounts than their less emotionally skilled counterparts (Boyatzis 1999). A study by Hay/McBer (1997) (see also Goleman (1998)) determined that sales agents at a US-wide insurance agency who were weak in emotional competencies sold premiums with an average face value of less than half that sold by agents who were strong in at least five of eight key emotional competencies. Research conducted by the Center for Creative Leadership has determined that the primary cause of leadership career derailments stems from inadequate emotional competence (McCall, Lombardo & Morrison 1998).

The Impact of EI Skills Training on Business Performance

Given the demonstrated importance of EI to business performance, it would be helpful for corporate leaders not only to select workers with the requisite emotional competencies, but also to be able to train them in enhancing their emotional competence. A few studies have examined the relationship between EI training and subsequent business performance. Pesuric and Byham (1996) reported that a manufacturing plant saw a 50% reduction in lost-time accidents and their productivity goals rose by US$250,000 after supervisors received training in how to listen better and help employees to resolve their own problems. Porras and Anderson (1981) found that production increased 17% in groups whose supervisors were trained in EI skills, while productivity did not increase at all in groups whose supervisors had not received EI training. Most recently, Luskin, Aberman and Delorenzo (2005) reported on a study of the efficacy of emotional competence training among financial services advisors. They found productivity increases of 25% post-training when compared with a 10% increase in sales for the non-trained group (Luskin et al. 2005).

The Business Imperative for EI Development

To understand the origins of EI training at AEFA, picture yourself as a prospective financial services client. You are making quite a lot of money. You have a family who depends on you continuing to do this. You are thinking about the future, and you have some big ideas. You want to give your children some choice about where they go to college. If they qualify, you want to be able to send them to one of the best schools. You want the option of retiring, or at least slowing down, when you are young enough to try new things or do the things you have always wanted to do. You want to get your money working *for you* so that you no longer have to work so hard for it.

You have a well-funded retirement account, and you own some stocks. Now you have been referred to a financial advisor from American Express. You have agreed to an appointment and are thinking about a few things. You are excited about saving more money and perhaps investing further in the stock market. But you hope this advisor does not want to talk about insurance. You hate insurance. You already have some, and you do not like talking about it—especially life insurance.

Now imagine the same scene from the vantage point of the financial advisor. It is not easy to get new clients. You have been referred to a prospective new client, and you have an appointment set. Several things are going through your mind. You are fairly sure that your prospective client will be excited about discussing the accumulation and preservation of capital and assets. You are also confident that they will have little or no interest in talking about insurance. And frankly, you do not like talking about insurance anyway. It makes you uncomfortable; after all, no one likes talking about dying or becoming disabled. So you decide that unless they bring it up, you are not going to mention it. That way you will not risk upsetting them.

The two scenarios—the client's and financial advisor's respective experiences of the selling process—posed a seminal challenge for me; Jim Mitchell, the CEO of the life insurance company and the executive vice-president of products and marketing; and other field and corporate leaders of AEFA. By 1992, we knew that 72% of our clients whose financial plans showed that they needed life insurance failed to buy it. Mitchell commissioned a team to *research the problem* by interviewing clients and financial advisors about their experience of the selling process. The research team learned that neither buyer nor seller was satisfied with the process. Moreover, the reasons had little to do with cost or product features— they were largely emotionally based.

Financial advisors had been taught how to bombard clients and prospective clients with objective evidence of insurance needs, but the emotions of both clients and advisors were frequently ignored. Thus, we discovered the true culprit behind lost sales opportunities: our advisors did not know how to deal with their own emotions or those of their clients and prospects. Remember that this was in 1992, three years before Goleman's (1995) first book on EI was published, and six years before Goleman's (1998) second book on the application of EI in the workplace became available. At the time, AEFA leaders were not aware of research on emotional skills and business performance; they simply knew that they had to find a way of removing the emotional obstacles to successful selling. It was only in 1995, following the publication of Goleman's book and when I had the opportunity to begin a series of conversations with him, that I discovered that what we had found through our research on EI was consistent with the ideas that Goleman was writing about.

We will now explore these ideas.

Origins of the EI training design

Our findings about the need for better emotional skills among financial advisors led to a business-shaping question: Could AEFA do anything to change the way its advisors managed emotions? To help answer the question, human resources (HR) executive Kate Cannon engaged several performance psychologists, including Rick Aberman, Darryl Grigg, Dwight Moore and Therese Jacob-Stuart, who assured us that people could indeed learn to be more emotionally intelligent. A comprehensive workshop was developed and was tested on two groups: financial advisors and field managers. The training focused on self-awareness, self-management and interpersonal efficacy. The expectation was that as a result of the program, workshop participants would improve their decision-making skills and increase their business results.

Pilot program results

Numbers 'wizard' John Bromley was assigned the task of tracking performance and comparing it with control groups. The results, published in Goleman (1998), were impressive. Advisor groups in the program achieved an 18% greater increase in sales than the control group. Just under 90% of leaders who completed the training reported it as important to their job performance, and 91% reported personally experiencing a positive effect.

What accounted for these differences? An examination of EI scores of training participants sheds light on their enhanced performance. The EI of the emotional competence training participants increased significantly when compared with those who did not participate, that is, the control group. Competencies that increased the most, based on pre- and post-workshop assessments with the EQ-i (TSI Consulting Partners 2000), were the following:

- **Self-regard**—to accurately perceive, understand and accept ourselves.
- **Assertiveness**—to effectively and constructively express our feelings.
- **Empathy**—to be aware of and understand how others feel.
- **Reality-testing**—to objectively validate our feelings and thinking with external reality.
- **Self-actualization**—to strive to achieve personal goals and actualize our potential.

Each of these factors exhibited statistically significant increases as a result of the workshops, as did overall EQ. Overall EQ increased from 94 to 100, self-regard from 97 to 103, assertiveness from 92 to 99, empathy from 97 to 105, reality-testing from 94 to 100, and self-actualization from 96 to 104. Significantly, the financial advisors who entered workshops with the lowest EQ scores made the most progress. This is an important finding because of the potential to turn substandard, and therefore expensive, employees into strong business contributors.

Moving from pilot project to company-wide asset

It is one thing for a pilot training program to produce positive results; it is another thing to get a whole company to change its view of its most fundamental process—selling products to implement the clients' financial plans. But AEFA's emotional competence training did just that, and soon migrated from a promising pilot project to influence the business practices of American Express as a whole. The benefits of emotional competence training have been confirmed time and time again with thousands of AEFA employees who have completed these workshops over the years (Bar-On 2003; 2004).

Long-term results of EI development

Unlike many 'flavor of the month' management fads, emotional competence development—now a 15-year-old venture at American Express—continues to be recognized as a key ingredient in the company's long-term success. In 2000, AEFA commissioned a comprehensive independent evaluation of the business impact of the company's EI development programs. Conducted by management consulting firm TSI Consulting Partners Inc., the evaluation focused on EI training participants from programs held in 1999, including 27 field leaders, 34 veteran advisors and 40 new advisors. Participants reported the results of increased revenue generation, improved client acquisition and increased business from existing clients (Bar-On 2004). For instance, in the Central New England market group, productivity increased in April 2000 to 6% above the national average, and in May 2000 to 11 points above the national average. The Kansas and Oklahoma market group moved from well below average prior to emotional competence training to achieve above-average sales in each of the first six months of the year 2000. In the Seattle, Tacoma, Hawaii market group, overall retention exceeded the national average by at least three percentage points in each of 12 months following their training. These increases may not sound impressive, but in a field sales force of 17,000, even modest percentage increases in productivity and retention translate into enormous financial gains.

Forces for Change

What accounts for the longevity and impact of emotional competence development at American Express? Emotional competence development would likely not have begun, let alone persisted, without the alignment of several 'planets': Mitchell, myself and our respective senior management teams.

Active engagement by senior field leaders

Throughout my career, I recognized the importance of emotional skills in helping advisors to achieve their personal goals through helping clients to achieve *their* goals. I saw that advisors who experienced either too much adversity or too much excitement became immobilized. I realized that extreme emotions, whether positive or negative, had a detrimental impact on personal activity and productivity. I set out to develop techniques for helping financial advisors to expand their emotional comfort zone so they could continue to perform at a high level regardless of what was happening externally. During weekly one-to-one meetings with my direct reports, we spent the majority of time dealing with the emotional issues that impede performance. For example, I would ask each direct report to prepare for the outcome of a sales call by deciding how they planned to deal with getting the business or being rejected. The correct response was the same, regardless of the outcome of the call: make another call. Because my direct reports were better able to anticipate events and decide in advance how they would respond in the face of negative and positive emotions alike, they were able to maintain momentum and their business results soared. And the more success they had as a result of effective self-management, the more committed they became to introducing self-management techniques into their leadership approach with others.

Senior corporate sponsorship

Although I had considerable success as a *missionary* for the importance of emotional skills within the financial advisory process, emotional competence development would never have reached critical mass at AEFA without the leadership of Jim Mitchell. Jim and the product companies that he oversaw were persuaded by the work of his research team as well as by the financial results produced by advisors and leaders who had participated in pilot emotional competence training. Jim and his team, already at the helm of successful enterprises, proclaimed: 'We can do even better, and we will.'

Getting ready for prime time

Building on the early success of the pilot programs, AEFA launched its Emotional Competence Training Program company-wide to help managers and advisors to develop better awareness of their own and clients' emotional reactions, and to more fully understand the role of emotions in the workplace.

Training elements

The training was based on the five levels of EI identified by Goleman (1998):

1. Self-awareness.
2. Managing emotions.
3. Motivation.
4. Empathy.
5. Social skills.

Getting the Emotional Competence Training Program off the drawing board and into the regular training curriculum for financial advisors was not easy. Until the early 1990s, job training at AEFA was conventional: it focused on making advisors more knowledgeable about financial planning, products and services as well as more proficient at making phone calls, conducting interviews and overcoming objections. Now, in addition to objective formulas, we would be teaching advisors how to handle themselves emotionally once they picked up the phone or were in an interview with a client or prospective client. They would have to learn how to perform well on the next call no matter how frustrating the last one had been. They would need to learn how to manage their discomfort and anxiety about talking to an underinsured client about death and life insurance, and discuss the topic constructively. And they would have to do all of this with passion and intensity in order to help the client to understand the actions they needed to take to achieve their financial goals.

Pairing inside and outside expertise

Kate Cannon and her dedicated team of internal and external experts did a remarkable job not only of developing the program and orchestrating its delivery, but also of overcoming the typical resistance associated with making major changes in an already successful large company. Independent psychologists Rick Aberman and Darryl Grigg conducted the initial workshops and coached internal trainers. Eventually, the bulk of the training responsibility was transferred to internal staff.

From Stand-Alone Training to Integrated Development

The positive impact of emotional competence on business results is well understood throughout the company. Despite such recognition, EI development programs have always been in competition for resources with other worthy performance-enhancement projects. Initially the AEFA Emotional Competence Program consisted of an intensive and comprehensive five-day training program. By 2001, decision-makers believed that emotional competence was sufficiently integrated into the company's culture to warrant emotional competence training being streamlined by incorporating it into the general training that new advisors receive. Emotional skills were introduced in conjunction with technical skills, and the overall amount of training time devoted to emotional competence was reduced from five days to five hours.

Rob Montella, AEFA director of leadership effectiveness, chronicles the evolution of the program:

> There was a push-pull. The push was that time and financial constraints made a stand-alone program less desirable. The pull was that it allowed us to take bite-sized chunks from the original emotional competence program and weave it into our functional training. That would allow us to highlight the importance of emotional skills in the context of the sales process. We focused on the central concept of the experiential triangle [of thought, emotion and action] during client transactions in several ways. For example, we retained the freeze game [a self-awareness exercise in which people learn to be highly conscious of what they are thinking, feeling and doing] and the reframing exercise [deciding to think differently about the challenge at hand]. We dropped reframing/self-talk into the training session on referral prospecting and the freeze game into the session on client service.

Advantages and Disadvantages of Integrated Development

Some people might bemoan the apparent 'watering down' of emotional competence training at American Express. It is important to note, however, that formal emotional competence training was and is only a part of American Express's commitment to emotional competence development. Emotional skills such as self-awareness, self-management and interpersonal efficacy continue to play a key role in the way in which managers coach their direct reports. Business units regularly request dedicated sessions on emotional competence. And emotional competence topics are also regular features of the annual CEO summit meetings of American Express global leaders focusing on the development of high potential executives.

While emotional competence is clearly a signal part of the American Express culture, not every leader at American Express is an active advocate. And as new employees enter the organization, they may get a weaker 'inoculation' in emotional skills than was the case ten years ago. But it is a testament to the power of the concept that when American Express prepared to transform AEFA into a separate company in the third quarter of 2005, many AEFA leaders called for a renewed focus on emotional skills. This is because major organizational change creates uncertainties that breed strong emotions. Employees now wonder: 'Is my job safe?'; 'Will I be able to succeed in the new company?'; 'Will the new company be successful?'; 'How well will leaders lead when beset by the same strength of emotions as their workforce?'. Another concentrated dose of emotional competence training may be just what is needed to protect and spur high performance during the launch of the new enterprise.

Implications

Weaving 'soft skills' development into the organizational fabric is difficult for most companies. Businesses are driven to produce exceptional growth and typically value only those skills that produce positive tangible results. Our success in integrating emotional competence development into AEFA depended primarily on our ability to demonstrate such results. Other factors that contributed to the introduction and sustained impact of emotional competence development include the following:

1. Build a compelling business case. To marshal the resources needed to mount an effective emotional competence development program, the organization needs to be convinced of the positive impact of emotional skills on business performance. At AEFA, we were fortunate to generate both informal and formal data that demonstrated the emotional underpinnings of lost business opportunities. Although examples from other companies may be helpful in selling the need for enhanced emotional skills, internal research is key to helping the organization to appreciate the return on investment in emotional competence development.

An effective business case for EI training will rest heavily on pre- and post-training assessments of individual and organizational EI and performance parameters. Such assessments are essential to empirically demonstrate that EI training programs make a difference in increasing EI as well as the organization's bottom line.

2. Rely on senior executive champions. Every organization's change protocol mentions the need for top-level support. At AEFA, we found that senior executive support must extend far beyond 'public relations' pronouncements about the importance of EI. Mitchell's support was critical. He was an effective champion because he initiated and understood the business case. His sponsorship enabled the corporate financial support that was vital to creating the emotional competence program. I was, I hope, an effective champion both because I tried to model emotional competencies to the best of my ability, and because I proactively coached my direct reports to increase their self-awareness, self-management and interpersonal skills.

3. Enlist support from HR executives. Business leaders may expect EI to be an 'easy sell' to HR staff. Our experience demonstrates that HR must endorse the program and also play a key role in sourcing expertise, advocating for budget, managing logistics and conducting program assessment. Only HR executives with strong business sensibilities and pre-existing productive partnerships with line executives will be able to meet the demands of managing such a major organizational intervention. Two senior HR executives illustrate this critical capacity: former AEFA senior vice-president of HR Susan Kinder, who recently retired as president of American Express Travellers' Cheques, and former vice-president of HR Judy Skoglund. Not only did they endorse the need for the program, they also ensured adequate financial support and enlisted good people to design, deliver and manage the program.

4. Recruit senior leader role models. An extension of the need for senior champions is the importance of creating senior leadership teams that demonstrate emotional competence and help to develop emotional skills among their direct reports. At AEFA, I needed field leaders on the ground who supported such development. I actively recruited leaders who 'got it', that is, who fully understood the importance of this idea. My direct reports were accountable for implementing the emotional competence tools and integrating them into the way they led their teams. My team also acted as role models by supporting the training program itself. My senior managers and I went through the original five-day program; our participation was instrumental in assuring understanding and competence at the highest levels of field leadership.

5. Create a partnership of internal and external experts. When implementing development programs in new skill areas, there is often a debate about who is qualified to 'teach' those concepts. Some organizations believe that only outside experts have the 'pedigree' to train people in sophisticated cognitive skills, for example. Other companies have a 'not invented here' mentality and rely exclusively on in-house trainers regardless of their level of expertise. We found that the most effective approach was to partner with both internal and outside development experts.

When we first identified the need for improved emotional skills among financial advisors, it was critical to have the assistance of independent performance experts in the design and delivery of the early programs. But we also recognized the danger of positioning emotional skills as so complex that only PhD-level psychologists could train people about them. It was therefore important to us to grow in-house experts who could blend their deep knowledge of the business with an understanding of how to develop and use emotional competence tools.

6. Emphasize development, not just training. Earlier, I mentioned the financial and time pressures that led to modifications in the way emotional competence training was delivered. Training is indeed time-consuming and expensive. But apart from training costs, 'classroom' training in any skill will not improve performance unless it is successfully applied in real work settings. Formal training programs can help to get emotional competence into the corporate bloodstream and certainly are necessary, but they are no substitute for the daily practice and reinforcement in emotional skills that needs to happen on the front lines. We found that field teams that emphasized emotional competence development consistently outperformed those who did not.

7. Weave emotional skills into the fabric of performance management. American Express is an acutely finance-driven company. Nevertheless, formal performance appraisal includes assessment of leadership skills. Leaders are accountable, and rewarded, not only for financial results—they are also evaluated on how they work through others to achieve those results. Moreover, AEFA recognizes that effective talent management is largely a function of emotional competence. This is because leaders who reveal their own emotions and encourage others to share theirs invariably come across as more 'real' than those who choose not to reveal their feelings. Emotional competence is a trust-builder. Leaders who display EI communicate to others that employees can feel safe when it comes to facing challenges and taking risks. Finally, emotional competence creates bonds. Leaders who are not afraid of discussing emotions are simply more likeable—and employees would much rather be around them than their 'zipped-up' counterparts.

Conclusion

Evidently, I am proud of what our company has accomplished in pioneering corporate EI training and in demonstrating the training's business impact so convincingly. But we are not resting on our EI laurels. We recognize the danger of counting too much on 'our culture' to magically inculcate emotional competencies into our workforce. The ongoing challenge is for us to balance formal training with leader-led emotional competence development. And our newest challenge will be to refine these development processes so that they help our workforce to thrive during our upcoming transformation into a new company. As Rob Montella commented, 'The great thing about emotional competence is that you get to use it every day.'

This AEFA story highlights the power of emotional competence as a business and leadership tool. More than 15 years ago, senior leaders at AEFA understood the barriers that negative emotions created in the sales process. And we believed, as do all optimistic sales leaders, that we could do something to build positive emotional capacity among our employees. And we did; but it took a skillful convergence of many factors:

- Field and corporate executive support.
- Pairing the skills of internal HR experts with those of external psychologists.
- Capitalizing on EI assessment tools and productivity analysis to make the ongoing business case for emotional competence development.
- Finding ways to sustain EI development over the long term by building it into the fabric of our overall training for financial advisors and managers.

It is our hope that the AEFA findings will provide useful insights for others who plan to introduce EI development into their organizations.

References

Bar-On, R. 2003. How important is it to educate people to be emotionally and socially intelligent, and can it be done? *Perspectives in Education* 21(4): 3–13.

Bar-On, R. 2004. The Bar-On Emotional Quotient Inventory (EQ-i): Rationale, description, and summary of psychometric properties. In *Measuring emotional intelligence: Common ground and controversy.* Ed. Glenn Geher, pp. 111–42. Hauppauge, NY: Nova Science Publishers.

Boyatzis, R.E. 1999, September 27. From a presentation to the Linkage Conference on Emotional Intelligence, Chicago, IL.

Cherniss, Cary. 2004. The*Business Case for Emotional Intelligence, Research Report.* The Consortium for Research on Emotional Intelligence in Organizations, www.eicon
sortium.org.

Goleman, D. 1995. *Emotional intelligence.* New York: Bantam Books.

Goleman, D. 1998.*Working with emotional intelligence.* New York: Bantam Books.

Hay/McBer Research and Innovation Group. 1997. In Goleman, 1998.

Luskin, F, R. Aberman, and A. Delorenzo, Jr. The Training of Emotional Competence in Financial Services Advisors. Consortium for Research on Emotional Intelligence in Organizations report, www.eiconsortium.org, 2005.

McCall, M., M. Lombardo, & A.M. Morrison. 1998. *The Lessons of Experience: How Successful Executives Develop on the Job.* Lanham, MD: Lexington Books.

Pesuric, A., and W. Byham. 1996, July. The new look in behavior modeling. *Training and Development*:25–33.

Porras, J.I., and B. Anderson. 1981. Improving managerial effectiveness through modeling-based training. *Organizational Dynamics* 9:60–77.

Salovey, P., and J. Mayer. 1990. Emotional intelligence. *Imagination, cognition, and personality* 9(3): 185–211.

TSI Consulting Partners, Inc. 2000, April. *An Evaluation of the Business Impact of American Express Financial Advisors' Emotional Competence Development Programs, Executive Briefing,* internal AEFA document

—— 15 ——

Applying Emotional Intelligence in Understanding and Treating Physical and Psychological Disorders: What We Have Learned from Alexithymia

Graeme J. Taylor and Helen L. Taylor-Allan

Introduction

Since ancient times, physicians and philosophers have expressed the idea that emotions, in particular unmodulated and excessive levels of emotion, can adversely influence mental and bodily health. Although the emphasis given to this idea has ebbed and flowed through the different eras, research studies over the past two decades have yielded empirical evidence that an impaired capacity to regulate emotions through mental processes is associated with many common medical and psychiatric disorders. Not surprisingly, this evidence has invited questions as to whether people with high EI, and therefore a greater awareness of and ability to regulate emotions, are less vulnerable to illness and disease, and whether the resilience of people with low EI, and their response to medical and psychiatric treatments, can be improved by methods aimed at raising EI. Although the research that explores the relations between EI and health is just beginning, much has been learned from investigations of **alexithymia,** a personality construct that overlaps conceptually with EI. As we will show in this chapter, the rapidly expanding knowledge of links between alexithymia and health is providing a strong incentive for educating people to be emotionally intelligent.

We begin the chapter with a description and definition of the alexithymia construct, and a summary of findings from empirical studies that examined relations between alexithymia and the EI construct. Then we explore the question of how alexithymia might influence health by describing a theoretical model of emotional processing and considering pathways by which poorly differentiated and unregulated emotions might lead directly to physical or psychological symptoms or to behaviors that may be damaging to health. We summarize empirical evidence of associations between alexithymia and various medical and psychiatric disorders, and then review studies that explored the potential influence of alexithymia on medical and psychiatric treatments. Finally, we describe some therapeutic interventions that are being used to reduce alexithymia and thereby raising a person's EI and potentially benefiting their health.

The Alexithymia Construct

This construct was introduced more than 30 years ago and is based on a cluster of cognitive and affective characteristics that were observed initially among patients with classic psychosomatic diseases, such as essential hypertension and ulcerative colitis (Nemiah, Freyberger & Sifneos 1976). The relevant features of the construct include:

- difficulties in identifying and describing subjective emotional feelings
- a limited imaginal capacity
- an externally oriented style of thinking (Taylor, Bagby & Parker 1997).

Although difficulty in monitoring the feelings and emotions of others is not included in the definition of the construct, there is empirical evidence that individuals with high degrees of alexithymia show a limited capacity to recognize emotional states in others and empathize with them (Taylor & Bagby 2000). As we will elaborate later, there is also evidence that individuals with high levels of alexithymia engage in maladaptive behaviors to cope with distressing emotional states (Taylor 2000). Thus, alexithymia overlaps conceptually, albeit inversely, with Salovey and Mayer's (1990) definition of EI as the ability to monitor one's own and other's feelings and emotions and to use this information to guide one's thinking and actions. Moreover, alexithymia converges with Gardner's (1983) concept of intrapersonal intelligence—that is, the ability to identify, label and discriminate among feelings—which is considered as the precursor to the concept of EI and a key component in Bar-On's (2000) broad conceptualization of emotional and social intelligence.

Alexithymia and EI

Alexithymia is most commonly measured by the self-report 20-item Toronto Alexithymia Scale (TAS-20), which has three factor scales for assessing difficulty identifying feelings, difficulty describing feelings to others, and externally oriented thinking (Taylor, Bagby & Luminet 2000). The TAS-20 has demonstrated reliability and factorial validity in many different languages and cultures. Although some researchers argue that a self-report alexithymia scale assesses a person's *beliefs* about their ability to identify and describe feelings, rather than the person's actual ability, the TAS-20 shows good agreement with the modified Beth Israel Hospital Questionnaire (BIQ) (Taylor et al. 2000), which is an observer-rated measure of alexithymia, and with the recently introduced Toronto Structured Interview for Alexithymia (Bagby, Taylor, Parker & Dickens in press).

Several studies have examined relations between the alexithymia and EI constructs. Predictably, there is empirical evidence that high alexithymia is closely related to the lower pole of EI. The TAS-20 correlates strongly and negatively with self-report measures of EI, including both the original and a modified version of the Emotional Intelligence Scale (EIS) (Schutte, Malouff, Hall et al. 1998) (*r* ranges from $-.52$ to $-.65$, *p*< .001), and long and short forms of the EQ-i (Bar-On 1997) (*r* ranges from $-.49$ to $-.64$, *p*< .01) (Austin, Saklofske & Egan 2005; Dawda & Hart 2000; Parker, Taylor & Bagby 2001; Saklofske, Austin & Minski 2003; Schutte et al. 1998; Taylor & Bagby 2000). Lumley and colleagues (Lumley, Gustavson, Ty Partridge & Labouvie-Vief 2005) examined relations between alexithymia, measured with both the TAS-20 and the BIQ, and the MSCEIT) (Mayer, Salovey & Caruso 2002). In a sample of young adults (*N*= 140), the TAS-20 and the BIQ correlated significantly and negatively with the total score on the MSCEIT (*r*= $-.37$, *p*< .001 and *r*= $-.38$, *p*< .001 respectively) and with the four subscales that assess the ability to:

1. perceive emotions accurately
2. use emotions to facilitate thought
3. understand emotions
4. regulate emotions in ourselves and others.

To summarize, the conceptual overlap and empirical relationship between the two constructs indicate that higher scores on one dimension tend to be associated with lower scores on the other. Let us now consider some of the possible processes and potential pathways by which alexithymia or low EI might influence health.

Alexithymia and Emotion Dysregulation

Taylor et al. (1997) proposed that the features comprising the alexithymia construct reflect deficits in the cognitive processing and regulation of emotions. This idea is consistent with a theoretical understanding of the development and organization of emotion schemas, and of how these schemas may be disrupted, which was developed by Wilma Bucci in the context of current work in cognitive science, emotion theory and neuroscience. As outlined by Bucci (1997; 2002), emotion schemas are comprised of non-verbal and verbal representations. The **non-verbal** schemas develop first and are comprised of subsymbolic processes—that is, patterns of sensory, somatic, visceral and kinesthetic sensations that are experienced during states of emotional arousal—as well as symbolic representations in the form of images, such as the person associated with an emotion. The **verbal** representations develop later and are organized according to the symbolic format of language. The verbal and non-verbal representations are linked by 'referential connections' such that dominant emotion schemas from the non-verbal mode can be translated into logically organized speech.

Normal emotional development and the acquisition of EI depend on the integration of somatic and motoric elements in the emotion schemas together with images and words. This developmental process is influenced strongly by the parents' ability to be attuned to and to regulate their child's emotional states, and to gradually translate states of emotional arousal into nameable feelings that the child can think about and communicate to others. Moreover, 'in normal development, emotion schemas, like all memory schemas, are continually being reconstructed and revised by new experience' (Bucci 2002:60). In pathology, this continuous reconstruction does not occur, as referential connections are either disrupted or have not been formed, and the components within or between the verbal and non-verbal emotion schemas are then dissociated (Bucci 2002). Such pathology may arise when there is neglect or other trauma during childhood, or when parents are unable to function as reliable external regulators of their developing child's emotional states.

Trauma or threatening conflicts during adolescence or adulthood may also disrupt referential connections within emotion schemas. In these situations, the absent or weak connections between subsymbolic processes and images and words can result in alexithymia and an impaired ability to reflect on and regulate states of emotional arousal. There is preliminary evidence that young adults with high alexithymia show significantly weaker referential connections than those with low alexithymia (Taylor 2003), and there is accumulating evidence that a history of childhood abuse or neglect is associated with a high degree of alexithymia (Moorman, Bermond, Albach & Van Dorp 1997; Zlotnick, Mattia & Zimmerman 2001).

Without regulation by connections to symbolic representations, subsymbolic processes in the emotion schemas continue to operate and are likely to generate prolonged and repetitive states of physiological arousal. These states may be experienced as unpleasant somatic sensations and/or bodily tension, the meanings of which are unknown to the person (Bucci 1997; 2002). People experiencing dissociated somatic sensations and bodily tension may attempt to provide meanings for them, but substitute meanings—such as 'these are symptoms of disease'—can be misleading and result in hypochondriasis and illness behavior. Although causal explanations cannot be inferred from cross-sectional studies, there is now substantial empirical evidence of an association between alexithymia and the reporting of somatic symptoms and hypochondriacal concerns (De Gucht & Heiser 2003; Taylor et al. 1997).

The failure to cognitively process emotions may contribute also to maladaptive emotion-regulatory behaviors that have an impulsive or compulsive quality and are potentially damaging to health. Such behaviors include alcohol and drug abuse, bingeing on food and restricting food intake, which over time may lead to substance-use and eating disorders (Taylor 2000; Taylor et al. 1997). Empirical studies have not only demonstrated associations between alexithymia and maladaptive modes of affect regulation (Taylor 2000), they have also found that as many as 50% of patients with substance-use disorders, and 50–70% of patients with eating disorders, manifest a high degree of alexithymia (Taylor et al. 1997). In contrast, recent studies of adolescents and university students found that high levels of EI, assessed with either self-report or ability measures, were associated negatively with alcohol consumption and/or illegal drug use, especially in males (Austin et al. 2005; Brackett, Mayer & Warner 2004; Trinidad & Johnson 2002).

Other impulsive behaviors related to deficits in emotion regulation include self-cutting or burning, which define characteristics of borderline personality disorder and are linked often with a history of childhood trauma. A recent study found that the association between childhood trauma and self-injurious behaviors is mediated by alexithymia (Paivio & McCulloch 2004). These findings are consistent with the view that the development of emotion schemas and the acquisition of EI are strongly influenced by the ways in which emotions are communicated, understood and regulated within the family environment.

When there is more extreme dissociation within emotion schemas, prolonged activation of the subsymbolic affective core may dysregulate other physiological systems and thereby contribute to the onset of a variety of somatic illnesses and diseases, the specific nature of which is determined by constitutional and other vulnerability factors (Bucci 1997; Taylor 2000). Functional gastrointestinal disorders (FGIDs), essential hypertension and panic disorder, for example, involve problems in autonomic regulation and have been found to have strong associations with alexithymia (Taylor 2000).

Whereas emotionally intelligent individuals have the skills to cope successfully with emotions evoked by stressful experiences, alexithymic individuals are deficient in the capacity to attend to, think about and understand distressing emotions. Moreover, these people are less able to seek support by talking about their feelings with others. It is not surprising, therefore, that researchers have found an association between alexithymia and quality of life among patients with chronic medical illnesses. For example, in a study of 74 patients suffering from inflammatory bowel diseases (IBDs), those with high alexithymia complained of more bowel and systemic symptoms and worse emotional functioning than those with low alexithymia (Verissimo, Mota-Cardoso & Taylor 1998).

Conversely, IBD patients with a tendency to actively control their emotions complained of fewer bowel and systemic symptoms and reported better emotional functioning than patients who were less disposed to controlling their reactions when they experienced distressing emotions. Alexithymia may impact also on quality of life in patients with coronary heart disease (CHD). In a study of 153 men with CHD, high alexithymia patients were more depressed and more incapable of working, and they expressed less life satisfaction, than other CHD patients of similar age and somatic status (Valkamo, Hintikka, Honkalampi et al. 2001).

Notwithstanding the potential pathways to illness and disease we have outlined above, because of the cross-sectional design of most studies, it is not possible to make any causal connections between alexithymia and the various disorders with which it is strongly associated. Indeed, the extent to which alexithymia is a predisposing risk factor can be evaluated only by prospective studies in which the construct is assessed before the onset of any medical or psychiatric disorder. In this regard, a prospective epidemiological study of more than 2,000 middle-aged Finnish men found that alexithymia predicted mortality by any cause over five years, independently of other well-known behavioral and physiological risk factors; aside from suicide, homicide and accidents, however, specific causes of death were not reported (Kauhanen, Kaplan, Cohen et al. 1996). Many more longitudinal studies are needed that not only track changes in health but also examine the influence of alexithymia and EI on physiological parameters and coping behaviors when people are experiencing stressful life events.

The Influence of Alexithymia on Medical and Psychiatric Treatments

There is accumulating evidence that alexithymia influences patients' responses to some medical and psychotherapeutic treatments and may even predict treatment outcome. In a recent study, for example, Porcelli and colleagues evaluated alexithymia as a predictor of medical treatment outcome for patients with FGIDs such as irritable bowel syndrome and functional dyspepsia (Porcelli, Bagby, Taylor et al. 2003). A group of these patients (N= 112) received the usual medical treatment and were followed for six months after which strict criteria were used to determine which patients had improved. Although both depression and alexithymia emerged as significant predictors of treatment outcome, alexithymia was the stronger predictor.

Clinicians have long recognized that alexithymic patients do not respond well to interpretive psychotherapy. This is usually attributed to a lack of psychological mindedness (PM), a characteristic that is believed to enhance a patient's prospects of engaging in and benefiting from insight-oriented forms of psychotherapy (Taylor 1995). There is now some empirical support for these clinical impressions. In a recent study, McCallum and colleagues evaluated both alexithymia and PM as predictors of outcome for four forms of short-term psychotherapy

(McCallum, Piper, Ogrodniczuk 2003). The therapies were 12 weekly sessions of short-term group therapy, either supportive or interpretive, for 107 outpatients with complicated grief, and 20 weekly sessions of short-term individual psychotherapy, either supportive or interpretive, for 144 outpatients with mixed diagnoses. Both low alexithymia and high PM were associated with a favorable outcome for all four forms of therapy.

Although there was an additive relationship between alexithymia and PM in predicting outcome, the investigators noted that these variables accounted for a relatively small portion of the total variance, which indicated that other factors also influenced outcome. Nonetheless, the present findings should encourage psychotherapists to include measures of alexithymia or PM when assessing the suitability of patients for psychotherapy. Indeed, this is an interesting and potentially valuable application of EI in the clinical setting. Although there are gradations of the three constructs, the idea of an EI continuum with alexithymia at the pathological end and PM at the eupsychic end needs to be seriously studied (Bar-On personal communication February 2004).

The finding that alexithymic patients had a similar unfavorable outcome from supportive therapy as they did from interpretive therapy was surprising, since most psychotherapists recommend a supportive approach for these patients. However, some researchers have wondered if alexithymic patients might benefit more from cognitive-behavior therapy (CBT). A recent study evaluated the potential role of alexithymia in predicting outcome in a sample of 42 inpatients with obsessive-compulsive disorder who were treated with multimodal CBT for an average of 70 days. Twenty-five of the patients, or 60%, also received a selective serotonin reuptake inhibitor (SSRI) antidepressant medication (Rufer, Hand, Braatz et al. 2004). Although obsessive-compulsive and depressive symptoms decreased substantially, alexithymia did not predict treatment outcome; nor did depression scores or the concomitant use of SSRI medication.

These findings suggest that obsessive-compulsive patients with high alexithymia will benefit as much from CBT as those with low alexithymia, even though the degree of alexithymia may not change. Similar findings were obtained in an earlier study of female rape victims with post-traumatic stress disorder (PTSD) who were treated with CBT (Kimball & Resnick 1999). Although 49% of the women had high alexithymia scores prior to treatment, alexithymia did not interfere with successful treatment—both PTSD symptoms and alexithymia scores were reduced after 12 weeks of either cognitive processing therapy or prolonged exposure therapy. Thus, it appears that alexithymia is not a contraindication for CBT.

The different outcomes from the treatment studies to date suggest that clinicians need to consider the degree of alexithymia when selecting treatments for their patients. Some patients' response to medical or psychiatric treatment, as well as their quality of life, might be improved by interventions aimed at increasing EI.

Reducing Alexithymia and Raising EI

Several clinicians have devised psychotherapeutic approaches that attempt to reduce alexithymia and thereby raise EI and potentially benefit a person's health. Although most of these approaches were devised before Bucci (1997) introduced her theory of emotional processing, the interventions can be understood in terms of her conceptualization of referential activity within emotion schemas. Krystal (1979), for example, recommends first educating patients about the nature of their affect deficits, and then using interventions to help them recognize, differentiate, label, tolerate and manage their subjective emotional feelings. Because images play a pivotal role in organizing emotion schemas, and because a restricted imagination is a salient feature of alexithymia, it is important to teach patients to use their imaginations. Images and fantasies can sometimes be prompted by deconstructing alexithymic patients' externally oriented language and exploring their experience of bodily sensations (Kuriloff 2004).

These and other techniques that promote imaginal activity are likely to strengthen referential links between symbolic and subsymbolic elements within a patient's emotion schemas (Bucci 2002). Increasing referential activity renders the patient more aware of feelings and therefore better able to reflect on and regulate states of emotional arousal. Other strategies include helping patients to become aware of how their emotional limitations can be linked to the 'rules' within their family of origin for experiencing and expressing emotion (Kennedy & Franklin 2002).

For the purpose of evaluating the efficacy of these strategies, patients can be administered self-report measures of alexithymia and EI before and after a period of treatment. These scales can be completed and scored quickly. In an exploratory study with three patients, Kennedy and Franklin (2002) evaluated the efficacy of a skills-based therapy that employed most of the above mentioned techniques. The patients received 16–24 weekly sessions of therapy and were administered the TAS-20, the Trait Meta Mood Scale (TMMS) (Salovey, Mayer, Goldman et al. 1995), which assesses a person's ability to attend to their moods and emotions, to discriminate clearly among them and to regulate them, and several other questionnaires at five time intervals. At the end of treatment, TAS-20 scores were reduced markedly for two patients and slightly for the third, and all three patients showed increased scores on the TMMS Attention to Feelings Scale. However, the reduction in alexithymia scores was maintained at a one-year follow-up for only the first two patients.

In a single case report, Taylor (1995) used a similar modified form of psychotherapy to treat a 31-year-old man who complained of a lifelong tendency to experience high levels of emotional distress and an absence of pleasurable feelings. This patient also suffered from frequent migraine headaches, reported a history of duodenal ulceration and major depression, and at times abused alcohol or marijuana to regulate distressing and poorly differentiated emotional states. He scored in the high range of the TAS-20. He was treated with weekly psychotherapy that encouraged imaginative activity, taught ways to identify and regulate emotions, and fostered the development of interests that generated positive emotions. After two years of treatment, the patient was less alexithymic in clinical interviews, less prone to somatization, and better able to tolerate and modulate his affective states. As his EI and mental health improved, he was able to establish an intimate and mutually satisfying relationship with a woman whom he subsequently married. Five years after completing treatment, the patient advised the therapist that he remained in good health and was enjoying being the father of two children, a role he previously resisted as he had felt emotionally ill-equipped for it.

Group therapy can also be modified to incorporate techniques aimed at reducing alexithymia and raising EI. In a preliminary study, 20 patients who had suffered a recent myocardial infarction (post-MI) and had moderate to high alexithymia scores received weekly group therapy for a period of four months (Beresnevaité 2000). The therapy techniques included relaxation training, role-playing and promoting non-verbal communication, as well as interventions to facilitate affect awareness and imaginative activity. A comparison group of 17 post-MI patients with moderate or high alexithymia scores received two educational sessions over one month that focused on information about CHD. Whereas the mean alexithymia scores of the two patient samples were not significantly different at the start of the study, the therapy group showed a significant reduction in the mean alexithymia score by the end of treatment, which was maintained over a two-year follow-up period; the educational group had no significant changes in mean alexithymia scores between the initial testing and later follow-up periods. Over the course of two years, patients whose degree of alexithymia had decreased from high to moderate or from moderate to low in response to group therapy experienced fewer cardiac events—re-infarction, sudden cardiac death or re-hospitalization for rhythm disorder or severe angina—than did patients whose degree of alexithymia had remained unchanged. Although this study needs to be replicated by other investigators, it suggests that a reduction in the degree of alexithymia influences favorably the clinical course of CHD.

There is accumulating evidence that alexithymia can negatively influence a person's response to the emotional disclosure writing task. This task was developed by Pennebaker (1997) for managing emotionally stressful experiences, and has been shown to benefit physical and mental health. In some disclosure studies, alexithymia even predicted increased pain and impairment among patients with rheumatoid arthritis, pelvic pain or migraine headaches (Lumley 2004). But it has been demonstrated that alexithymic patients may benefit from emotional disclosure if they are given more time and practice and special guidance. In an experimental study lasting four days, Lumley (2004) taught a group of physically symptomatic students how:

- to identify stressful experiences in their lives
- to identify and label various negative emotions, including the situations that elicit these emotions

- stressful experiences can change their thoughts and beliefs about themselves and others
- to change their thinking about a stressful experience.

A comparison group of students received only standard disclosure instructions, which are brief and provide little direction for how to engage in the task. The results showed that guided disclosure led to reduced reports of gastrointestinal symptoms compared to standard disclosure. Moreover, baseline alexithymia predicted decreases in anxiety and depression in the guided disclosure group and increases in these affects in the standard disclosure group. These findings support the idea that educating people to recognize, appraise and utilize emotional information can improve their ability to benefit from emotional disclosure.

Conclusion

In this chapter we have shown how alexithymia research and a current theory of emotional processing are providing new ways of understanding the way in which unregulated emotions might influence psychological and physical health. Substantial evidence from empirical studies shows that high alexithymia is situated at the lower pole of the EI continuum, and that it is associated strongly with several common medical and psychiatric disorders. Most of the studies linking alexithymia and illness are cross-sectional in design, however, and they rely on self-report measures to assess alexithymia. Future studies need to employ prospective, longitudinal designs and multiple methods for assessing both alexithymia and EI to establish definitively whether or not high alexithymia, or low EI, is an independent risk factor for illness and disease. In addition, more research is needed to evaluate the physiological, cognitive and behavioral pathways that are thought to mediate between alexithymia and changes in health. At the present time, however, there is sufficient empirical evidence to show that individuals with high alexithymia tend to engage in maladaptive coping behaviors that are potentially damaging to health, and furthermore that they are prone to somatization and illness behavior.

These findings indicate a need for educating people to be emotionally intelligent. Acquiring or enhancing EI skills enables people to cope more effectively with emotions generated by stressful experiences. There is evidence also that patients with high alexithymia may be less responsive than those with low alexithymia to interpretive psychotherapy and to certain standard medical treatments. Educating physicians and psychotherapists to be more aware of high alexithymia and low EI in their patients can guide their selection of treatments and sometimes lead to modified interventions that are more likely to reduce symptoms and improve quality of life among their patients.

References

Austin, E.J., D.H. Saklofske, and V. Egan. 2005. Personality, well-being and health correlates of trait emotional intelligence. *Personality and Individual Differences* 38:547–58.
Bagby, R.M., G.J. Taylor, J.D.A. Parker, and S. Dickens. in press. Development of the
Toronto Structured Interview for Alexithymia: Item selection, factor structure, reliabil-
ity and concurrent validity. *Psychotherapy and Psychosomatics.*
Bar-On, R. 1997. *The Bar-On Emotional Quotient Inventory (EQ-i): A test of emotional
intelligence.* Toronto: Multi-Health Systems.
———. 2000. Emotional and social intelligence: Insights from the Emotional Quotient
Inventory. In Bar-On and Parker, pp. 363–88.
Bar-On, R., and J.D.A. Parker, Eds.. 2000. *The handbook of emotional intelligence.*
San Francisco: Jossey-Bass.
Beresnevaité, M. 2000. Exploring the benefits of group psychotherapy in reducing
alexithymia in coronary heart disease patients: A preliminary study. *Psychotherapy
and Psychosomatics* 69:117–22.
Brackett, M.A., J.D. Mayer, and R.M. Warner. 2004. Emotional intelligence and its rela-
tion to everyday behaviour. *Personality and Individual Differences* 36:1387–1402.
Bucci, W. 1997. Symptoms and symbols: A multiple code theory of somatization. *Psycho-
analytic Inquiry* 17:151–72.
———. 2002. From subsymbolic to symbolic—and back: Therapeutic impact of the
referential process. In *Symbolization and desymbolization: Essays in honor of Norbert
Freedman.* Ed. R. Lasky, pp. 50–74. New York: Other Press.
Dawda, D., and S.D. Hart. 2000. Assessing emotional intelligence: Reliability and validity
of the Bar-On emotional quotient inventory (EQ-i) in university students. *Personality
and Individual Differences* 28:797–812.
De Gucht, V., and W. Heiser. 2003. Alexithymia and somatisation: A quantitative review
of the literature. *Journal of Psychosomatic Research* 54:425–34.
Gardner, H. 1983. *Frames of mind: The theory of multiple intelligences.* New York: Basic
Books.
Kauhanen, J., G.A. Kaplan, R.D. Cohen, J. Julkunen, and J.T. Salonen. 1996. Alexithymia
and risk of death in middle-aged men. *Journal of Psychosomatic Research* 41:541–49.
Kennedy, M., and J. Franklin. 2002. Skills-based treatment for alexithymia: An explora-
tory case series. *Behaviour Change* 19:158–71.
Kimball, L.A., and P.A. Resnick. 1999. Alexithymia in survivors of sexual assault:
Predicting treatment outcome. Poster presented at the International Society for
Traumatic Stress Studies Conference, Miami, FL.
Krystal, H. 1979. Alexithymia and psychotherapy. *American Journal of Psychotherapy*
33:17–31.
Kuriloff, E. 2004. When words fail: Psychosomatic illness and the talking cure. *Psycho-
analytic Quarterly* 63:1023–40.
Lumley, M.A. 2004. Alexithymia, emotional disclosure, and health: A program of
research. *Journal of Personality* 72:1271–1300.
Lumley, M.A., B. Gustavson, R. Ty Partridge, and G. Labouvie-Vief. 2005. Assessing
alexithymia and related emotional ability constructs using multiple methods: Interrela-
tionships among measures. *Emotion* 5:329–42.
Mayer, J. D., P. Salovey, and D.R. Caruso. 2002. Mayer-Salovey-Caruso Emotional
Intelligence Test (MSCEIT). Toronto: Multi-Health Systems.

McCallum, M., W.E. Piper, J.S. Ogrodniczuk, and A.S. Joyce. 2003. Relationships among psychological mindedness, alexithymia and outcome in four forms of short-term psychotherapy. *Psychology and Psychotherapy: Theory, Research and Practice* 76:133–44.

Moorman, P.P., B. Bermond, F. Albach, and I. van Dorp. 1997. The etiology of alexithymia from the perspective of childhood sexual abuse. In Vingerhoets, van Bussel, and Boelhouwer, pp. 139–53.

Nemiah, J.C., H. Freyberger, and P.E. Sifneos. 1976. Alexithymia: A view of the psychosomatic process. In *Modern trends in psychosomatic medicine,* vol. 3. Ed. O.W. Hill, pp. 430–39. London: Butterworths.

Paivio, S.C., and C.R. McCulloch. 2004. Alexithymia as a mediator between childhood trauma and self-injurious behaviors. *Child Abuse and Neglect* 28:339–54.

Parker, J.D.A., G.J. Taylor, and R.M. Bagby. 2001. Relationship between emotional intelligence and alexithymia. *Personality and Individual Differences* 30:107–15.

Pennebaker, J.W. 1997. Health effects of the expression (and non-expression) of emotions through writing. In Vingerhoets, van Bussel, and Boelhouwer, pp. 267–78.

Porcelli, P., R.M. Bagby, G.J. Taylor, M. De Carne, G. Leandro, and O. Todarello. 2003. Alexithymia as predictor of treatment outcome in patients with functional gastrointestinal disorders. *Psychosomatic Medicine* 65:911–18.

Rufer, M., I. Hand, A. Braatz, H. Alsleben, and S. Fricke, and H. Peter. 2004. A prospective study of alexithymia in obsessive-compulsive patients treated with multimodal cognitive-behavioral therapy. *Psychotherapy and Psychosomatics* 73:101–6.

Saklofske, D.H., E.J. Austin, and P.S. Minski. 2003. Factor structure and validity of a trait emotional intelligence measure. *Personality and Individual Differences* 34: 707–21.

Salovey, P., and J.D. Mayer. 1989/1990. Emotional intelligence. *Imagination, Cognition, and Personality* 9:185–211.

Salovey, P., J.D. Mayer, S.L. Goldman, C. Turvey, T.P. Palfai. 1995. Emotional attention, clarity, and repair: Exploring emotional intelligence using the trait meta-mood scale. In *Emotion, disclosure and health.* Ed. J.W. Pennebaker, pp. 125–54. Washington, DC: American Psychological Association.

Schutte, N.S., J.M. Malouff, L.E. Hall, D.J. Haggerty, J.T. Cooper, C.J. Golden, and L. Dornheim. 1998. Development and validation of a measure of emotional intelligence. *Personality and Individual Differences* 25:167–77.

Taylor, G.J. 1995. Psychoanalysis and empirical research: The example of patients who lack psychological mindedness. *Journal of the American Academy of Psychoanalysis* 23:263–81.

———. 2000. Recent developments in alexithymia theory and research. *Canadian Journal of Psychiatry* 45:34–142.

———. 2003. Somatization and conversion: Distinct or overlapping constructs? *Journal of the American Academy of Psychoanalysis and Dynamic Psychiatry* 31:487–508.

Taylor, G.J., and R.M. Bagby. 2000. Overview of the alexithymia construct. In Bar-On and Parker, pp. 40–67.

Taylor, G.J., R.M. Bagby, and O. Luminet. 2000. Assessment of alexithymia: Self-report and observer-rated measures. In Bar-On and Parker, pp.301–19.

Taylor, G.J., R.M. Bagby, and J.D.A. Parker. 1997. Disorders of affect regulation: Alexithymia in medical and psychiatric illness. Cambridge University Press: Cambridge.

Trinidad, D.R., and A. Johnson. 2002. The association between emotional intelligence and early adolescent tobacco and alcohol use. *Personality and Individual Differences* 32:95–105.

Valkamo, M., J. Hintikka, K. Honkalampi, L. Niskanen, H. Koivumaa-Honkanen, and H. Viinamäki. 2001. Alexithymia in patients with coronary heart disease. *Journal of Psychosomatic Research* 50:125–30.

Verissimo, R., R. Mota-Cardoso, and G.J. Taylor. 1998. Relationships between alexithymia, emotional control, and quality of life in patients with inflammatory bowel disease. *Psychotherapy and Psychosomatics* 67:75–80.

Vingerhoets, A., F. van Bussel, and J. Boelhouwer, Eds. 1997. *The (non)expression of emotions in health and disease.* Tilburg: Tilburg University Press.

Zlotnick, C., J.I. Mattia, and M. Zimmerman. 2001. The relationship between posttraumatic stress disorder, childhood trauma and alexithymia in an outpatient sample. *Journal of Traumatic Stress* 14:177–88.

— 16 —

Applying Emotional Intelligence in Treating Individuals with Severe Psychiatric Disorders: A Psychotherapeutic Model for Educating People to Be Emotionally Intelligent

*Lana Stohl, David Dangerfield, Jeremy Christensen,
David Justice and Douglas Mottonen*

Introduction

Researchers have identified EI as a critical component for success in relationships, education and employment (Bar-On 2004; 2006). However, most of the research has been focused on the general normative population and not on specific clinical samples such as individuals with severe psychiatric disorder (SPD), including schizophrenia, bipolar disorder and major depression.

According to the World Health Organization (WHO) (2005), 450 million people worldwide are affected by psychiatric, neurological and/or behavioral disorders at any give time. People with these disorders are often subjected to social isolation, poor quality of life and increased mortality. These disorders also necessitate staggering private and public expenditures to fund the ever-increasing cost of treatment.

In the US, treatment for individuals suffering from SPD is provided by a vast array of service providers such as community mental health centers, hospitals and charitable organizations. Valley Mental Health (VMH) is one such provider. Located in Salt Lake City, Utah, VMH serves approximately 20,000 adults and children with SPD annually. VMH's goal for treatment is to ensure the client's maximum participation in community life. The essential elements of this participation include education, employment and community living.

With the advent of the recovery movement, VMH's leadership became interested in developing an innovative approach to treatment utilizing the assessment and enhancement of EI. As a result of this endeavor, the Community Computer Education Program (CCEP) was created for clients with SPDs to assess, develop and monitor their EI. To facilitate recovery, moreover, we helped them to develop technology skills outside the traditional mental health environment and attempted to create meaningful employment opportunities.

Three fundamental questions arose from a review of the literature regarding EI and its application in the psychiatric health care setting:

1. Do individuals with SPD score lower than the general population on EI as measured by EI instruments such as the EQ-i?

2. Can individuals with such severe disorders benefit from efforts to improve their EI skill deficits as identified by the EQ-i?

3. Do improved EI skills result in an increase in employment, pursuit of higher education, and a reduction in treatment services and costs?

EI as a Foundation for Mental Health Treatment

Until fairly recently, SPDs were viewed as incurable illnesses with little hope for recovery. Individuals with these disorders were often institutionalized, stigmatized and distanced from educational and employment opportunities. In the 1950s and '60s, advances in medication and the de-institutionalization movement made it possible for individuals with SPD to live in the community.

As psychiatric health care agencies attempted to put together appropriate community-based treatment programs, the individuals who had once lived in institutions found themselves in communities with few skills or resources to adapt to their new environment. Many of the services provided focused on stabilization: keeping clients safe and trying to avoid hospitalization. This treatment paradigm was grounded in the negative belief that recovery from psychiatric illnesses was difficult, if not impossible. The belief became embedded in the individuals suffering from these disorders, their families, treatment professionals, and the general public and media (Spaniol 2001).

Current research indicates that recovery from SPD is not only possible, but also possible for the *majority* of the individuals who suffer from these disorders. According to WHO (2005), cost-effective treatments exist for most disorders and, if correctly applied, could enable those affected to become functioning members of society.

The idea of rehabilitation and recovery necessitated a new treatment paradigm and innovative approaches to treatment that successfully integrate psychiatric health care clients into the fabric of society. Many mental health professionals consider that the integration process involves:

1. the existence of meaningful interpersonal relationships
2. employment opportunities
3. the pursuit of educational goals.

The critical link between EI and success in each of these three areas served as a catalyst in the formulation of VMH's new treatment approach: the CCEP.

A Working Definition of Recovery

Recovery is defined as the act or process of 'bringing back to a normal position or condition' *(Merriam-Webster's Collegiate Dictionary* 2001). Medical professionals have long used the term to describe the process of returning patients to a healthy state.

Health care professionals have variously described recovery as a process, an outlook, a vision and a guiding principle (Anthony 1993; Deegan 1988; Spaniol, Gagne & Koehler 1997; Stocks 1995). There is neither a single agreed-upon definition of recovery nor a single way to measure it. Wilma Thompson (2004), a leader in the consumer recovery movement, defines recovery as 'a process by which an individual with mental illness recovers self-esteem, dreams, self-worth, pride, choice, dignity and meaning'. The overarching message is that hope, optimism and the restoration of a meaningful life—that is, self-actualization—are possible, despite SPD.

Because the symptoms of SPD often appear in late adolescence or early adulthood, they negatively impact on the acquisition of a number of competencies and skills that support the development of interpersonal relationships, educational pursuits and employment opportunities.

In light of the fact that the EQ-i measures a number of important emotional and social factors associated with EI that contribute to performance in various areas as well as general efficacy and success in life, this instrument was utilized in the study we describe in this chapter. Based on the above mentioned definition of recovery, two EI factors appear to be critical to the recovery process. The first is optimism. **Optimism,** as measured by the EQ-i, is the ability to maintain a positive or hopeful attitude and is considered to be especially helpful in handling difficult and stressful situations that are integrally associated with SPD. The second EI factor that we thought would play an important role in the recovery process is **self-actualization.** This important facilitator of EI, which is also measured by the EQ-i, is defined as the drive needed to achieve our full potential and to pursue meaningful activities in life. For individuals with SPD, their illness often becomes their identity; and for them to see other roles as possibilities is a major step toward recovery, in our opinion.

Employment and Recovery

There is a growing consensus among mental health consumers and psychiatric health care professionals that meaningful employment is an important component of recovery (Hutchinson, Anthony & Massaro 2001). The World Federation for Mental Health engaged in a two-year campaign with the theme of 'Mental Health and Work' for World Mental Health Day in 2000 and 2001. This extended campaign recognized and highlighted the important link between work and mental health. Employment is a vital way for people who have suffered SPD to reclaim their social roles, build self-management skills and take control of the major decisions affecting their lives. And this, in turn, has a positive impact on a person's feelings of confidence, self-esteem and overall sense of dignity. Furthermore, we thought that the competencies, skills and facilitators associated with EI are necessary for securing and retaining employment.

Of all persons with disabilities, those with SPD face the highest degree of stigmatization in the workplace and the greatest barriers to employment, as was previously mentioned. Some of the many reasons for this include:

- gaps in work history
- limited employment experience
- lack of self-confidence
- fear and anxiety
- workplace discrimination
- the rigidity of existing social support and benefit programs (Routes to Work 2005).

Employment rates for individuals with SPD are discouraging. According to the Resource Center to Address Discrimination and Stigma, Substance Abuse and Mental Health Services Administration (2005), the unemployment rate for people with SPD in the US is shockingly as high as 90%. Other sources of employment data from around the world report unemployment rates ranging from 50% to 90%.

Another barrier to re-entry into the workforce in the US is the inability of publicly funded vocational rehabilitation systems to effectively serve the needs of people with SPD (National Alliance for the Mentally Ill 2001). The majority of jobs available to these individuals are typically low-paying, entry-level positions in janitorial, clerical and food services (Ellison, Russinova, Massaro & Lyass 2001). Higher status and higher-paying jobs often require social and technical skills such as the ability to use computers and knowledge of software programs that individuals with SPD typically do not possess.

Employment, Recovery and the 'Digital Divide'

According to Judy Primavera and colleagues, 'over the course of the past two decades, America has become an increasingly technologically-based society where the ability to use a computer has become as fundamental to a person's ability to successfully navigate through society as traditional skills such as reading, writing, and arithmetic' (Primavera, DiGiacomo & Wiederlight 2001:2). The same can be said for other developed countries as well as for a growing number of developing countries around the world.

Computer technology and the internet have tremendous potential to enhance the lives of individuals with SPD by decreasing social isolation and providing access to information about health care, social events, education and employment opportunities, and by increasing employability and self-esteem. According to the Disability Statistics Abstract, however, people with disabilities in the US are less than half as likely as their non-disabled counterparts to own a computer, and they are about one-quarter as likely to use the internet. The gap between the people who can make effective use of IT and those who cannot has been termed the 'digital divide'. While there is no consensus on the extent of this divide and on whether it is growing, researchers are nearly unanimous in acknowledging that some sort of divide does indeed exist (The Digital Divide Network 2004).

The vast resources available through the use of technology have gone largely untapped. Kaye stresses that 'the computer revolution has left the vast majority of people with disabilities behind' (2000:1). Moreover, he feels that people with disabilities are those who could gain the most from computer use, despite the difficulty in accessing computers. He concludes his analysis of this challenge by stating that 'it seems clear that, in order to clarify the benefits that this technology can offer to the disabled, a concerted program of education will be needed, along with training and support in the use of the hardware and software' (Kaye 2000:13). While access to technology and computer literacy does not guarantee educational or occupational success, it does change the odds considerably (Primavera et al. 2001). Many individuals with SPD are caught in a vicious cycle in which low levels of education, poverty and a lack of knowledge of and access to technology relegates them to low-paying, entry-level jobs with little opportunity for advancement and improvement in their socioeconomic status.

EI, Recovery and Computer Technology

The CCEP aimed to help clients with SPD to:

- span the digital divide
- learn marketable computer skills and develop general occupational skills
- enhance their EI competencies and skills by combining their new knowledge of computers with an e-learning website, the EQ University, designed to improve EI, which increases the potential for being successful in various aspects of life
- move from a patient to a student role.

This approach has not yet been described in the literature, to the best of our knowledge. Several programs have been designed to teach computer skills to individuals with SPD, but none of them are combined with a web-based EI development curriculum premised on EI assessment and aimed at increasing employability.

The CCEP

VMH designed this project to address the above mentioned issues of recovery—to enhance EI, increase knowledge of and use of technology, and improve employment and educational opportunities—in collaboration with several community partners. The partners included:

- Behavioral Health Strategies, a consulting and training firm that markets EI products and services
- EQ University, a provider of online courses designed to enhance EI skills
- the Salt Lake City School District and its affiliate, the Horizonte Training and Instruction Center
- the George S. and Dolores Dore Eccles Foundation
- Dr. Reuven Bar-On
- Dr. Rich Handley.

The data we present in this chapter emerged from the two years that this project was conducted—from 2002 to 2003. The project is continuing and has been expanded to include other treatment populations such as women with substance-abuse problems, geriatrics and refugees.

In addition to utilizing EI assessment and skill development as the foundation for the CCEP, three other underlying principles were paramount to this project:

1. The professional staff should view and relate to the participants as *students* instead of patients.
2. The location of the project should be situated in a non-clinical environment.
3. The evaluation of the project's efficacy should be based on objective criteria, such as:

   a. improvement in EQ-i scores

   b. increase in employment rates

   c. reduction in treatment costs

   d. enhanced levels of consumer satisfaction.

Mental health advocates have stressed the importance of education as both a normalizing process for people in recovery and as a way out of the poverty and dependency frequently associated with SPD (Mowbray 2000). Having a productive role, such as being a student in an educational program or being employed at a meaningful job, is one of the most important factors in recovery (Hutchinson et al. 2001).

In order to reinforce the concept of clients with SPD as student learners, we located the CCEP in a hi-tech educational environment, separate from the traditional psychiatric health care center. We secured a computer lab through a collaborative relationship with a local non-traditional high school, the Horizonte Instruction and Training Center, which was well known in the area for delivering high-quality, professional adult and youth education to disadvantaged populations in Salt Lake City. The program was also modelled after the academic school year. Classes started in the fall and continued for nine months divided into three semesters; they ran for two hours a day, three days a week. Each day focused on two subject areas, which included self-guided practice time in order to facilitate student improvement in areas where they were struggling with or simply had particular interests.

Curriculum

The development of a curriculum that emphasized the enhancement of EI, in conjunction with learning basic work skills, computer skills and social interaction skills, was one of the major tasks for this project. The ability of clients to more effectively manage their own emotions and to more accurately to understand the impact of their emotions and behavior on others, as well as others' behavior on them, was seen as critical to workplace success for the participants. The program staff wrote a unique curriculum to address workplace skills, supplemented by online courses on EI through the EQ University. The curriculum, Recovery in the Workplace, consisted of straightforward, single-page lessons for building professional emotional-social skills for the workplace. The same EI curriculum, utilizing different teaching techniques, was taught during all three semesters for two hours a week and provided the foundation for the program.

In addition to EI, computer and job-related topics selected for the first year included the following courses: Microsoft Windows, internet basics, email, basic computer hardware, Microsoft Word, Microsoft Excel, Microsoft Access, Microsoft PowerPoint, Adobe Photoshop, Mavis Beacon typing and résumé writing. These courses were selected to provide students with a broad array of fields from which to choose possible employment opportunities including computer maintenance, graphic design, data entry, software support and jobs requiring basic computer knowledge.

Student selection

The CCEP was originally designed for 15 students, and 17 students were initially enrolled based on the possibility of attrition. Selection criteria were necessary, because twice as many individuals wanted to attend the program as there were places available. Selection criteria included:

- status as an active VMH client
- an expressed desire on the part of the client to participate in an educational program geared toward return to work and recovery
- an interest in learning computer technology
- a desire to move beyond the traditional psychiatric health care services on which the client had become dependent and by which they had been restrained
- the desire to pursue more mainstream educational and socially valuable roles.

Furthermore, students were screened for a willingness to participate in the EI assessment and courses. Prospective students also needed to be stable on medications and able to manage their psychiatric disorder.

So that the services could be offered to the clients most in need, applicants had to qualify as 'severely disturbed' according to the Utah State Division of Mental Health and Substance Abuse definition, and be receiving some form of government assistance including state welfare or social security disability.

Upon completing a formal application, prospective participants were invited to attend a four-day screening procedure in a computer lab. They were taught computer skills and were observed by the instructors. After the mock classroom exercise, applicants were invited to a personal interview with an instructor and rated on motivation, goals, commitment and functionality. Based on a systematic review of the applications, assessment of classroom participation and the interview, students were selected for the program.

EI evaluation and intervention

The next task was to administer interviews and the pre-intervention assessments.

Each student was asked to report on their current involvement in work, school and/or volunteer activities; and they discussed their goals regarding being employed, going to school or doing volunteer work in the future. They then completed a quality-of-life questionnaire and the EQ-i assessment. At the end of the project, as well as at subsequent 3-, 9- and 24-month intervals, students were asked the same series of questions to ascertain the progress they may have made in these activities.

As was previously mentioned, the Bar-On EQ-i was selected as the EI assessment tool (Bar-On 1997a). This instrument contains 133 brief items, and employs a five-point response set ranging from 'not true of me' to 'true of me'. The EQ-i takes approximately 30 minutes to complete. The assessment is multidimensional and yields a total EQ scale score, five EQ composite scale scores and 15 EQ subscale scores. Refer to Table 1.1 for a complete description of what the composite scales and subscales assess.

After completing the pre-intervention assessment with the EQ-i, the students were provided with individual feedback on their results. An EI improvement plan, based on personal preferences for improvement and the students' lowest scores, was developed.

A group report for the class was generated and used to identify skill deficits for the entire class; it provided the EI focus of the curriculum. During the first semester, in each class session, an individual EI skill was highlighted. Students discussed the definition of the EI skill and practical applications in real-life experiences. Afterwards, they were given time to write about how the skill could be applied in their personal lives. They completed their writing assignments utilizing computer word-processing programs, thus reinforcing their computer knowledge while addressing critical emotional-social skill development.

In the second semester, the students were given real-life scenarios for which a particular EI skill was applicable. They spent time role-playing the scenario and receiving feedback from their peers and instructors. Then they role-played from the other person's perspective, which gave them the opportunity to develop empathy in addition to the other important EI competencies and skills.

Finally, students were given time to take online EQ University courses in the specific emotional-social areas that were identified in their EI assessment as needing improvement. These courses gave them an overview of the EI skills being studied as well as of specific methods for enhancing the skills in daily life. Students were encouraged to work further on their particular skill deficits with family, friends, caseworkers and staff in their regular treatment sessions.

The students' progress with the web-based EI courses and the Recovery in the Workplace activities were tracked and compared with their individual development plans.

Data collection

The final phase of the project was the collection of data and evaluation of the results. One of the goals of this project was to develop a model that could be replicated both within our health care agency and in other similar locations.

On the first day of class, as was previously mentioned, students were administered the EI assessments and the structured interviews to ascertain employment status, volunteer work, use of the computer in non-classroom settings and educational pursuits. When the classes ended, the structured interviews and the EQ-i were administered once again. The students then had another debriefing session with a certified EQ-i professional to receive feedback on the progress they had made in improving their EI skills. Their individual EI development plan was revised, if necessary, to identify areas of focus for improving EI skills in the future.

In order to determine if there had been an increase or reduction of services and treatment costs, students' mental health service records were examined for a nine-month period both before and after graduation. Attendance for the program itself was also tracked. Students with an attendance record of more than 80% were offered a free computer to encourage participation. Students significantly exceeded this requirement, and have continued to do so in subsequent classes even without the incentive of receiving a free computer for attending classes.

A significant amount of qualitative data, consisting of comments before, several times during and after the program, was also collected from the students about every aspect of the CCEP.

Results

During the first two years, 50 students initially enrolled in the CCEP, and 42 successfully completed the program. The attendance record for the two years averaged 94.5%. The reasons for attrition included physical health problems, exacerbation of psychiatric conditions, obtainment of full-time employment and enrollment in other educational programs, such as university studies, occupational training and so on. Most of the individuals who dropped out of the program did so in the first semester.

In light of the fact that complete data were not obtained from two individuals, 40 rather than 42 cases were statistically analyzed in the end; this included 15 students who attended in 2002 and 25 in 2003. In order to determine if these two groups could be combined and treated statistically as one group, a non-parametric statistical examination was conducted, taking into account the relatively small and potentially skewed samples being compared (Siegel 1956). A Mann-Whitney U test revealed that there was no significant difference on any of the EQ-i scores between the students who began the program in 2002 and those who began in 2003—the p-level was .529 for the overall EQ scale score comparison.

Based on this outcome, both groups were combined for the purpose of continued statistical analysis. The results were as follows:

Pre-intervention results related to EI

The pre-intervention group report revealed that the participants scored lower than average on all of the EQ-i scales and subscales. Moreover, they scored one to two standard deviations lower than the US normative sample on the overall EQ score, on four out of the five composite scale scores (80%), and on nine out of the 15 subscale scores (60%). These results indicate that this sample scores significantly lower than the normative population for the most part. This finding validates the first premise of our pilot study, indicating that individuals with SPD score lower than the general population on EI. The lowest scores were obtained on the following EQ-i subscales:

- Self-regard—80.8.
- Independence—82.7.
- Self-actualization—80.7.
- Stress tolerance—79.9.

- Reality testing—83.1.
- Flexibility—84.7.
- Problem-solving—85.5.
- Optimism—79.7.
- Happiness—79.9.

Not only do these results make psychodynamic sense regarding individuals suffering from SPD, they also confirm key findings from existing studies that demonstrate the relationship between EI and psychological well-being (Bar-On 1997; 2000; 2004; 2006).

While these findings raised some concerns about the efficacy of VMH's traditional treatment strategies designed to promote recovery, it also reinforced our decision to use EI assessment and development as the foundation of the study we describe here. Without the data generated by the EQ-i, we would not have known that these particular factors needed to be addressed within a therapeutic framework, in spite of the fact that these individuals had received an average of 12.5 years of psychiatric treatment.

Post-intervention improvement in EI

The post-intervention results were even more intriguing than those described above. Taking into consideration the multivariate nature of the data, it was imperative to apply multivariate statistics (Tabachnick & Fidell 2001) to analyze the results. As such, a one-way Analysis of Covariance (ANCOVA) was used to examine the pre- and post-intervention EQ-i scores for significant differences. The results revealed that the post-intervention overall EQ score (88.3) was significantly higher than the pre-intervention score (77.6), based on an F value of 6.85 and a p level of .011 after the potential age and gender effect (Bar-On 1997) was neutralized by identifying them as covariates in this analysis. This finding indicates that the program is capable of increasing EI. Also using age and gender as covariates, a one-way Multivariate Analysis of Covariance (MANCOVA) revealed that three out of the five composite EQ scores increased significantly from what they were when the students began the program:

- Interpersonal EQ increased from 88.9 to 95.8—F= 4.23, p= .043.
- Stress management EQ increased from 85.0 to 91.7—F= 4.51, p= .037.
- Adaptability EQ increased from 80.7 to 91.7—F= 9.43, p= .003.

One of the most significant findings here is that the students' adaptability was the factor that revealed the most improvement, which has obvious implications for dealing with challenges in the real world. Table 16.1 compares the 15 pre- and post-intervention EQ-i subscale scores. The EI factors that showed the most improvement are the ones that, once again, make sense

Table 16.1   Comparison of pre- and post-intervention CCEP EQ-i scores ($N = 40$)

EQ-i	Pre-CCEP	Post-CCEP	F	p
Self-regard	80.8	88.4	3.67	.060
Emotional self-awareness	91.1	99.0	3.16	.080
Assertiveness	88.0	92.9	1.40	.241
Independence	82.7	87.9	1.88	.174
Self-actualization	80.7	89.2	4.67	.034
Empathy	91.5	99.1	4.92	.030
Social responsibility	94.3	99.0	3.18	.079
Interpersonal relationship	88.3	93.6	1.98	.164
Stress tolerance	79.9	87.4	4.55	.036
Impulse control	93.2	97.6	1.22	.273
Reality testing	83.1	92.8	6.07	.016
Flexibility	84.7	93.6	7.59	.007
Problem-solving	85.5	93.5	4.62	.035
Optimism	79.7	87.8	4.80	.032
Happiness	79.9	87.2	4.21	.044

regarding the nature of the SPD from which this particular sample suffers, and most likely the ones that are of key importance for their recovery. For example, symptomatic of psychosis are severe disturbances in reality testing and problem-solving (American Psychiatric Association 1994). The treatment should therefore address ways of strengthening these particular EI factors.

The psychodynamic driving force behind neurosis, by contrast, is a combination of an inability to handle stress and extreme rigidity in neurotic behavioral patterns (American Psychiatric Association 1994). Therefore, treatment needs to focus on stress tolerance and flexibility. By contrast, the typical signs and symptoms of people suffering from depression are:

- severe unhappiness
- pessimism
- lack of drive
- loss of meaning in life
- a cessation of involvement in things that interested them
- an inability to actualize their potential for growth.

(American Psychiatric Association 1994)

The road to recovery should thus concentrate on happiness, optimism and self-actualization.

Lastly, a lack of empathy typically drives the breakdown in interpersonal relationships that occurs in most psychiatric disturbances and is more directly symptomatic of avoidant, schizoid and especially antisocial personality disorders (American Psychiatric Association 1994). Clearly, an integral part of treatment should therefore focus on empathy.

Post-intervention improvement in educational, volunteer and occupational activity

A pre- and post-intervention analysis of the data showed that the CCEP was also successful in increasing employment as well as educational and volunteer activity. After combining the occurrence of these three types of pro-social activity and comparing them before and after the program, it was revealed that only 18 out of the 40 participants (45%) were employed, doing volunteer work or studying before they participated in this program. In sharp contrast, 34 of the participants (85%) were involved in at least one of these activities following completion of the CCEP. Based on a more in-depth analysis, a one-way ANCOVA confirmed that the participants were significantly more involved in work, volunteer work or an educational program by 119% ($F= 16.55$, $p< .001$). Moreover, a multiple regression analysis indicated that EI has a strong impact on these types of pro-social activities. More precisely, assertiveness, flexibility and independence were shown to be the strongest predictors of employment, volunteer work and getting involved in an educational program, based on beta scores of .327, .306 and .247 respectively. These findings suggest that the rehabilitation of individuals suffering from SPD should focus on these specific EI factors, in addition to strengthening specific occupational skills, to help increase their return to the community as productive and contributing citizens.

Post-intervention reduction in clinical, hospital and residential treatment cost

The results also revealed that the average clinical, hospital and residential treatment cost per person decreased from $10,666 to $4,213, representing a decrease of 60.5% for the same time period. A one-way ANCOVA confirmed the statistical significance of this finding after neutralizing the potential age and gender effect ($F= 26.77$, $p< .001$).

Conclusion

Based on the findings presented in this chapter, it has been shown that people who suffer from SPD have significantly lower EI than the general population. The findings also demonstrate that their EI competencies and skills can be greatly improved as a result of participating in programs such as the one we describe here, which has not been revealed in the health care or EI literature until now. It has further been shown that the 'digital divide' can be narrowed and employment rates enhanced for individuals with SPD. All of this increases the likelihood that people with SPD can recover and lead happy and productive lives. Lastly, programs such as the CCEP can succeed in substantially reducing the cost of clinical, hospital and residential treatment for these individuals; and this chapter represents the first scientific publication that demonstrates this vital point.

The findings regarding increased occupational and educational involvement by close to 120%, and a reduction in treatment costs by more than 60%, strongly suggest that the CCEP represents a tangible economic benefit for health care providers as well as for clients in utilizing EI as the basis for treatment services. Furthermore, the findings suggest that:

- EI instruments such as the EQ-i can serve as an important assessment tool in psychiatric health care settings to identify specific emotional-social areas for treatment focus
- individuals with SPD can benefit from treatment approaches emphasizing EI skill development
- clients can be involved in the process of recovery in a straightforward and non-threatening manner.

It is our opinion that the utilization of EI assessment as the foundation for developing interventions aimed at strengthening emotional and social deficits can greatly enhance the treatment services currently being provided to individuals who suffer from SPD and can help to ensure their eventual re-entry into society.

Future research needs to replicate this study on larger and more diverse clinical populations as well as to examine the long-term achievements such as less dependency on private and public health care services, continued employment and involvement in the community, and overall subjective well-being.

In closing, we wish to state that the personal benefits for individuals suffering from SPD, in terms of an overall improvement in quality of life and subjective well-being, cannot be overemphasized. In the words of one participant, who was unemployed at the beginning of the project and is now employed on a full-time basis:

> The EI component of this program offered me a clear way to measure my strengths and weaknesses. The end of the year post-intervention assessment showed me where I had improved and what still needed to be dealt with. I experienced a major shift in my own approach to recovery and now understand that wholeness is the appropriate aim.

References

American Psychiatric Association. 1994. *Diagnostic and statistical manual of mental Disorders,* 4th ed. Washington, DC: American Psychiatric Association.

Anthony, W.A. 1993. Recovery from mental illness: The guiding vision of the mental health service system of the 1990s. *Psychosocial Rehabilitation Journal* 16:11–23.

Anthony, W. 2000. Decade of the Person, editorial. *Psychiatric Rehabilitation Journal* Summer.

Bar-On, R. 1997a. *The Bar-On Emotional Quotient Inventory (EQ-i): A test of emotional intelligence.* Toronto, Canada: Multi-Health Systems.

———. 1997b. *The Bar-On Emotional Quotient Inventory (EQ-i): Technical manual.* Toronto, Canada: Multi-Health Systems.

———. 2000. Emotional and social intelligence: Insights from the Emotional Quotient Inventory (EQ-i). In *Handbook of emotional intelligence.* Ed. Reuven Bar-On and James D.A. Parker, San Francisco: Jossey-Bass.

———. 2004. The Bar-On Emotional Quotient Inventory (EQ-i): Rationale, description, and summary of psychometric properties. In *Measuring emotional intelligence: Common ground and controversy.* Ed. Glenn Geher, pp. 111–42. Hauppauge, NY: Nova Science Publishers.

———. 2006. The Bar-On model of emotional-social intelligence (ESI). *Psicothema* 18.

The Center for Psychiatric Rehabilitation. 1999. *The research and training center in rehabilitation for persons with long-term mental illness: Summary of research accomplishments, 1994–99.* Center for Psychiatric Rehabilitation: Boston University Sargent College of Health and Rehabilitation Sciences. Retrieved September 20, 2001 from the World Wide Web: http:/www.bu.edu/cpr/research/rtc1999/rtc1999sum.pdf.

Deegan, Patricia, 1988. Recovery: The lived experience of rehabilitation. *Psychosocial Rehabilitation Journal* 11(4): pp. 11–19.

Digital Divide Network, 2004, Digital Divide Basics. Retrieved December 14, 2004 from the World Wide Web: http:/www.digitaldividenetwork.org/.

Ellison, M., Z. Russinova, J. Massaro, and A. Lyass. 2001. Professional/Managerial Employment of People with Schizophrenia: Initial Evidence and Exploration. Unpublished Article. Boston University: Boston, MA.

Goleman, D. 1995. *Emotional Intelligence: Why it can matter more than IQ.* New York. Bantam Books.

Hutchinson, D., W. Anthony, J. Massaro. 2001. Fostering Computer Careers For Persons with Psychiatric Disabilities. Unpublished Article. Center for Psychiatric Rehabilitation: Boston University.

Jacobson, N., and L. Curtis. 2002. Recovery as Policy in Mental Health Services: Strategies Emerging from the States. *Psychiatric Rehabilitation Journal* Spring, 23(4): 333.

Kaye, H.S. 2000. *Computer and Internet Use Among People with Disabilities.* National Institute on Disability and Rehabilitation Research: U.S. Department of Education. Retrieved October 9, 2001 from the World Wide Web: http:/www.dsc.ucsf.edu/UCSF/pdf/REPORT13.pdf.

Mish, F.C., ed. 2001. Merriam-Webster's Collegiate Dictionary, 10th Edition, Merriam-Webster, Inc.

Mowbray, C. 2000. *Psychiatric problems as barriers to educational achievements.* Research Development Center on Poverty, Risk, and Mental Health. Retrieved November 8, 2001 from the World Wide Web. http./www.ssw.umich.edu/nimhcenter/Psychiatric.html.

National Alliance for the Mentally Ill (NAMI). 2001. *Employment, Work, and Income Supports for People with Brain Disorders.* Retrieved November 8, 2001 from the World Wide Web: http:/www.nami.org/update/unitedemploym.html.

Primavera, J, T.M. DiGiacomo, and P.P. Wiederlight. 2002, June. Closing the Digital Divide: Empowering Parents and Children with Computer Technology. Fairfield University. Presented at the 8th Biannual Meeting of the Society for Community Research and Action, Division 27 of the American Psychological Association. Atlanta, Georgia.

Resource Center to Address Discrimination and Stigma, U.S. Department of Health and Human Services, Substance Abuse and Mental Health Services Administration, Center for Mental Health Services, Employment Fact Sheet. http:/www.adscenter.org /topics_materials/employment.htm.

Routes to Work, Retrieved March 8, 2005 from the World Wide Web: http:/www.cmha.ca /english/routes/learned.htm.

Sands, R. 1991. *Clinical Social Work Practice in Community Mental Health.* New York, NY: Macmillan Publishing Company.

Siegel, S. 1956. *Nonparametric statistics for the behavioral sciences.* New York: McGraw-Hill Book Company.

Spaniol, L.J., C. Gagne, and M. Koehler. 1997. *Psychological and social aspects of psychiatric disability.* Boston, MA: Center for Psychiatric Rehabilitation, Sargent College of Allied Health Professions, Boston University.

Spaniol, L. 2001. Recovery. Unpublished Article. Boston, MA: Center for Psychiatric Rehabilitation, Sargent College of Allied Health Professions, Boston University.

Stocks, M.L. 1995. In the eye of the beholder. *Psychiatric Rehabilitation Journal* 19: 89–91.

Tabachnick, B.G., and L.S. Fidell. 2001. *Using multivariate statistics* 4th ed.. Boston, MA: Allyn and Bacon.

Thompson, Wilma. 2004, October 25. Making Recovery Real. Keynote address at the Valley Mental Health Annual Conference, Salt Lake City, Utah.

World Health Organization (WHO). 2005. Health Topics—Mental Health, The Bare Facts. Retrieved February 21, 2005 from the World Wide Web: http:/www.who.int/ mental_health/en/.

—— 17 ——

Assessing Emotional Intelligence in Children: A Review of Existing Measures of Emotional and Social Competence

Sarah Stewart-Brown and Laurel Edmunds

Introduction

Since the 1990s, reports on educational achievement in the UK have consistently highlighted the importance of early learning for lifelong achievement, and have identified the development of emotional and social competence as a key determinant of success in this process (Ball 1994; Department for Education and Employment (DfEE) 1997; Department for Education and Skills (DfES) 1998; National Commission on Education 1993).

Schools in the UK have been required to assess scholastic progress for many years, and there are now standardized approaches for this purpose for children two years of age and older. Since 1997, schools have also been required to conduct baseline assessments on children at school entry, and one of the assessment criteria is personal and social development (DfEE 1997). No standardized approaches have been recommended, and schools are required either to choose from approaches accredited by national criteria or to develop their own methods. There has therefore been a growing interest in methods of assessing emotional and social competence across the UK for more than a decade.

The new UK Foundation Stage Profile has proposed a number of items reflecting emotional and social development, such as the ability to display a sense of self-identity, to express a range of emotions and to form relationships (Qualifications and Curriculum Authority (QCA) 2002). However, the validity and reliability of this profile have yet to be evaluated. Teachers themselves are also seeking methods of assessing emotional and social competence. But many of them are concerned that the concepts are difficult to assess and that measures will address what is easy to measure rather than what is meaningful (Pascal & Bertram 2001). In this context, we were commissioned and funded by the UK DfES in 2001 to undertake a systematic review of measures of emotional and social competence suitable for use in pre-school and primary-school settings. We completed the review in 2003.

The concept of emotional competence is closely related to the concepts of emotional literacy and EI. Elias, Zins, Weissberg et al. (1997) define **emotional competence** as a person's ability to understand, manage and express the social and emotional aspects of their life in ways that enable the successful management of life tasks such as learning, forming relationships, solving everyday problems, and adapting to the complex demands of growth and development. This definition includes all of the attributes of emotional literacy as defined by Sharp and Faupel (2001) and most of the attributes of EI as defined by Mayer and Salovey (1997:10). Those who have studied the concepts concede that emotional competence, literacy and intelligence are important for lifelong achievement and for the development of emotional and social well-being and positive mental health (see, for example, Bar-On 2005; 2006; Bar-On, Handley & Fund 2005).

We have interpreted **social competence** as the behavior, attitudes and understanding that support the development of good relationships and enable children and adults to be successful in tasks involving others. We believe, moreover, that emotional competence plays an important part in the development of social competence, because it enables children and adults to identify and think about their feelings, to handle them appropriately and to make decisions about how to behave in light of both their feelings and their thoughts. The two concepts are widely recognized as being closely integrated (Bar-On 2000; 2006; Gardner 1983; Saarni 1990); and for the purposes of our review, it was considered unsuitable to separate them. For a more detailed discussion of our conceptualization of emotional and social competence, you can refer to Stewart-Brown and Edmunds (2003).

Measures of emotional and social competence are used for the early identification or screening, profiling and monitoring of weaknesses in this area:

- **Screening** instruments need to be capable of identifying children who require special support or intervention. As they are designed to assist practitioners in making appropriate professional judgements regarding intervention, these instruments are generally summative in nature. Because most, if not all, children will be screened at least once in their lifetime, the instruments need to be appropriate for a non-clinical population as well as quick and easy to administer. Furthermore, screening instruments need to have high sensitivity and specificity. This means that they will miss very few children who should be identified as having emotional and/or social problems, and they will not incorrectly identify problems in children who do not have them.

- Instruments suitable for **profiling** need to be able to describe a child from various perspectives in a way that enables individuals to identify what might be done to improve the child's emotional and social competence. Profiling is therefore formative, and ideally a number of observers are required to conduct this type of assessment.
- **Monitoring** instruments are designed to assess change in emotional and social competence over time. Therefore, they need to detect change accurately to assist practitioners in correctly assessing the extent of progress achieved as a result of the intervention that was initiated.

We can use all three of these assessment approaches for individual children, as well as for groups of children in a school and pre-school setting. In the latter case, the aim is to identify schools in need of special support (screening) to focus on specific weaknesses associated with a particular class or school, to suggest ways of supporting group development (profiling) and to track (monitor) progress.

Methods of Competence Assessment

The purpose of our review was to identify as many recent instruments for assessing emotional and social competence as possible. Instruments were identified through a variety of methods:

- Literature reviews were conducted by searching the following electronic databases from 1990 to 2002: ERIC, PsychInfo, Sociofile, Health Star, Medline and Embase.
- A notice was posted on the CASEL website notice board. The study was also described on the Focus Project website, which is dedicated to promoting effective practice in child and adolescent mental health services. The child database of the Oxford Outcomes Project was also searched; it is part of a larger database documenting the development and application of questionnaires, interview schedules and rating scales that measure health from the patient's perspective.
- Contact was made with academics known to be active in the field.
- All the local education authorities (LEAs) in the UK were contacted in an effort to identify approaches to assessment that were in current use. Letters were also sent to the Personal Social and Health Education (PSHE) advisors in all the LEAs, as well as to lead officers in Early Years Development and Childcare Partnerships.

The criteria for selecting instruments for inclusion in the review were:

- suitability for use with all children aged 3–11 years in pre-school and school settings
- test development based on non-clinical and general populations aged 3–11 years
- the existence of validity and reliability studies.

Exclusion criteria were:

- instruments developed with and for disease-specific populations
- instruments developed or published in languages other than English
- instruments developed before 1990.

We chose to restrict our searches to 1990 onwards, because there was minimal mention in the literature prior to this date of emotional competence, emotional literacy and EI.

We extracted the following information about each instrument:

- Contents.
- Method of development.
- Age group suitability.
- Who completes the instrument.
- In what setting it is applicable.

The purposes for which the instrument has been used. Instruments were evaluated on:

- the basis of their content, including the extent of negative and positive statements
- method of application
- evidence relating to their reliability and validity in relation to screening, profiling and monitoring.

Results of the Search

Following the electronic searches and critical appraisal, we excluded instruments that primarily focused on learning and those concerned only with self-esteem and related concepts. However, we included instruments in which at least one discrete scale focused on emotional or social competence, even though the entire instrument had a wider scope, as well as those in which the majority of items focused on emotional and/or social development. After these exclusions, we identified a total of 33 instruments developed since 1990 that were designed to measure various aspects of emotional and/or social competence. We were also notified of 26 instruments that were under development in 2003.

Of the 33 instruments described in this chapter, 21 were identified from peer-reviewed publications and 12 from contact with individuals who are active in this field. The details of the 33 instruments described here are available in tabulated form in an earlier publication by Stewart-Brown and Edmunds (2003).

Instruments identified from the peer-reviewed literature

All 21 instruments identified from the peer-reviewed literature were designed primarily to measure various aspects of social competence. Several focused entirely on specific social incompetencies. Although few were directly relevant to emotional competence, many covered at least some aspect of emotional behavior. Most of these instruments were well validated with reliability coefficients ranging between .70 and .90 for the most part.

We will now describe these instruments first for pre-school children and then for school-age children.

Three general instruments were designed for **pre-school children.** In two of these—the Infant and Toddler Social and Emotional Assessment (ITSEA) and the Penn Interactive Peer Play Scale (PIPPS)—social competencies and behaviors dominate the emotional components. The items in the ITSEA (Briggs-Gowan & Carter 1998; Carter, Little, Briggs-Gosan & Kogan 1999) were developed on the basis of clinical observations as well as existing checklists, and were piloted with parents from a pediatric clinic. The instrument takes an average of 40 minutes to complete, primarily by parents at home. Although designed for 1–2-year-olds, it can be used with 3-year-olds, and could be used by teachers or practitioners in pre-school settings. One of the five scales, the Competencies Scale, includes the emotionally relevant subscales of emotional positivity and emotional awareness. There are also empathy (social awareness), pro-social behavior and peer relations scales. The instrument includes attention skills as well as compliance. There are a number of positive items, but as a whole the ITSEA focuses on problematic behaviors.

The PIPPS (Fantuzzo, Suttonsmith, Coolahan et al. 1995) is a 36-item instrument to be completed by pre-school teachers and suitable for 3–5-year-olds. The instrument includes a small number of items recording emotional behavior as well as desirable social actions. The other items target a lack of social competence, particularly disruption and disconnection. Neither of these instruments is suitable for use in school settings because of the length of time needed to administer them.

The third measure potentially applicable to pre-school children is the teacher version of the Social Skills Rating Scale (SSRS-T) (Lyon, Albertus, Birkinbine & Naibi 1996). This is an adapted version of the SSRS for older children, which we describe below.

Six general instruments were designed for **school-age children.** One of these, the 18-item Interpersonal Competence Scale (ICS) (Cairns, Leung, Gest & Cairns 1995) for 8–16-year-olds, can be completed by teachers in 2–4 minutes. It measures:

- **social competencies,** for example 'popular with boys/girls', 'argues', 'fights'
- **emotional behaviors,** for example 'smiles a lot', 'cries'
- **academic competencies,** or example 'good at spelling', 'good at math'.

The Strengths and Difficulties Questionnaire (SDQ) (Goodman 1994; 1997) is also quick to complete and is applicable to children of 4–16 years of age. It was developed primarily for parents and clinicians to complete, but is also suitable for teachers. It includes positively phrased items, most of them reflecting problematic behaviors.

The School Social Behaviour Scales (Emerson, Crowley & Merrell 1994; Merrell 1993) also has a version to be completed by parents, which is the Home and Community Social Behaviour Scales (Lund & Merrell 2001; Merrell & Caldarella 2003; Merrell, Streeter, Boelter et al. 2001). This instrument has two scales: social competence with all items phrased positively, and antisocial behavior with all items phrased negatively. Each scale has three subscales, two of which relate to interpersonal and self-management skills, and hostile, irritable and antisocial behavior respectively. The other subscale in each scale relates to academic skills.

The SSRSs (Elliot, Sheridan & Gresham 1993; Gresham & Elliot 1990) also assess social skills, problematic behaviors and academic competencies. This instrument was designed as a screening tool to identify children of 5–18 years of age with significant problematic behaviors. It is relatively easy to complete by teachers and parents, and takes approximately 20 minutes to do so. A version for children of three to five years of age has also been developed (Lyon et al. 1996).

The fifth instrument, the Behavioral and Emotional Rating Scale (BERS) (Epstein 1999; Epstein & Sharma 1997; Epstein, Ryser & Pearson 2002) is suitable for 5–18-year-olds and is completed by teachers or parents. It has 52 items that load on five subscales, three of which are relevant to the measurement of emotional and social competence. The affective strength subscale is particularly relevant, including items such as 'identifies own feelings' and 'has the ability to give and receive affection'. The interpersonal and intrapersonal strength subscales are also relevant. Items on these subscales include 'shows concerns for the feelings of others' and 'manages anger effectively'. This instrument was developed on a sample of 250 parents and health care professionals who attended a mental health research conference. They were asked to generate statements describing emotional and behavioral strengths, and their responses were further refined by a group of health care professionals and researchers. Although primarily designed to identify children with emotional and behavioral problems who are in need of extra support, all the statements are positively phrased.

The sixth instrument is the 45-item Emotional Instability, Prosocial Behaviour and Aggression Scales (EIPBAS) (Caprara & Pastorelli 1993). Primarily, it assesses social interaction in 7–10-year-olds and can be completed by teachers, peers and parents as well as by the children themselves. The emotional assessment component of this instrument focuses on the child's capacity to refrain from impulsivity and excessive emotionality.

We will now discuss the other kinds of instruments.

We reviewed two instruments measuring **specific aspects of social competence.** The first is the Bully Victim Scales (Austin & Joseph 1996) for 8–11-year-olds; it examines perceived bullying and victimization and comprises two six-item self-report scales.

The items were developed on the basis of observed behaviors and are administered within an established instrument, the Harter Self-Perception Profile (Harter 1993). The format takes time to explain to children, and the analyses are time-consuming as well. The second instrument, the Social Ability Measure (Braza, Braza, Carreras & Munoz 1993), is rather different. It assesses social competence on the basis of observing time spent by the children in social contact using a range of social behaviors.

We identified two instruments that focus on **negative behaviors and social incompetence.** One of these, the Child Behavior Checklist, has three versions (Achenbach & Edelbroch 1991; Achenbach & Rescorta 2000; 2001; Costenbader & Keller 1990; Harris, Tyre & Wilkinson 1993). The other has only one version, which is the Pre-school Behavior Checklist (St. James-Roberts, Singh, Lynn & Jackson 1994). Both were characterized by their focus on negative behaviors typical of social incompetence. The former was developed to capture the things parents and teachers say about children exhibiting emotional and social incompetence, and the aim of both instruments is to identify psychopathology.

Some instruments were designed to detect **anxiety and social phobias.** Examples of these are the Dominic-R Pictorial Interview, the Social Phobia and Anxiety Inventory for Children (SPAI-C), the Penn State Worry Questionnaire for Children, and the Separation and Anxiety Test.

The Dominic-R Pictorial Interview (Valla, Bergeron & Smolla 2000) includes a series of pictures of 'Dominic', who can be either male or female, in varying situations. Children aged 6–11 years are asked to talk about the pictures, and their responses are used to enable the diagnosis of separation anxiety, over-anxiousness, depression, attention deficit hyperactivity disorder (ADHD), simple phobias and conduct disorders. The measure needs to be administered by a trained interviewer, and takes approximately 20 minutes to complete.

The SPAI-C (Beidel, Turner & Morris 1995) is a self-report instrument for 8–15-year-olds with 26 items that were generated from clinical interviews with phobic children as well as from their daily diaries. The Penn State Worry Questionnaire (Chorpita, Tracey, Brown et al. 1997) is a self-report instrument comprising 14 items for 6–18-year-olds. The children are asked to 'rate their worries' hypothetically and not in relation to specific circumstances. In the Separation and Anxiety Test (Duffy & Fell 1999; Wright, Binney & Smith 1995), children aged 8–12 years are presented with vignettes and photographs, and asked to say how they would feel if the stories were happening to them and how they think the people in the photographs feel. Responses are rated for the degree of attachment, specifically for self-reliance and avoidance. Therefore, the instrument is not appropriate for the assessment of emotional competence.

The FOCAL is another attachment-based instrument; it is designed for pre-school children (Mitchell-Copeland, Denham & DeMulder 1997). Moreover, the instrument serves as a research tool that records event-based emotional interchanges together with responses to others' emotions. The two subscales assess social competence and overall positivity.

The final measure that we identified from the peer-reviewed literature is quite different from the others. It assesses **whole-school or class competencies.** The Child Development Project instrument (CDP) (Solomon, Battistich, Watson et al. 2000) was designed to measure the social well-being of the class and school as a whole. It covers three key attributes of healthy interpersonal relationships: respect, trust and empathy. As such, the instrument does not directly assess emotional competence. One-third of the items are phrased negatively. Its development was based on a representative sample of 550 teachers and approximately 4,000 8–12-year-olds on the basis of classroom observation over a four-year period. The student version has 38 items and assesses perceptions of collaborative and supportive relationships among students, positive relations between students and teachers, as well as closeness and intimacy, student participation and influence. The teacher's version has 15 items and measures perceptions of collaborative and supportive relationships among staff, closeness, teacher participation and influence, and shared goals and values. This instrument is used to help teachers to create a caring community in the classroom and enhance the children's experience of school.

Instruments identified by contact with researchers and practitioners active in the field

The 12 instruments identified through contact with researchers and practitioners working in the field differ from those in the above mentioned group in that more of the content focuses on emotional competence. Some of these measures are designed to identify children who are suitable for specific educational programs aimed at promoting emotional and social development. Others have been developed in the context of whole school projects that are designed to support such aspects of development.

We will now describe these instruments for pre-school children and then for school-age children.

With regard to general instruments for **pre-school children,** the Devereux Early Childhood Assessment Program (DECA) (LeBuffe & Naglieri 1998) was developed in the US as part of an intervention program for 2–5-year-olds and has a version for teachers and parents. It is based on the identification of 'resilience' and 'protective factors' captured in 37 items organized into four subscales:

1. **Initiative,** which assesses the child's ability to use independent thought and actions to meet their needs.
2. **Self-control,** which is the child's ability to experience a wide range of feelings and to express those feelings in socially appropriate words and actions.
3. **Attachment,** which measures persistent relationships between child and significant adults.
4. **Behavior concerns.**

Teachers and parents complete the same version.

The DECA provides an individual and a classroom profile. For each, there are specific strategies appropriate for an individual child and for the class as a whole, addressing their respective needs. The instrument can also identify children who may be developing behavioral problems.

The Adaptive Social Behaviour Inventory (ASBI) (Hogan, Scott & Baven 1992) is a 30-item teacher rating scale that assesses social competence in 3–5-year-olds. It has three scales: express, comply and disrupt. The ASBI measures cooperation and conformity, peer sociability and antisocial behavior. It was developed on the basis of items found in current instruments with the aim of identifying children with emotional and behavioral disorders.

The Process-Oriented Monitoring System (POMS) (Laevers, Vandenbusshe, Kog & Depondt n.d.) was developed in the context of the Experiential Education Project in Belgium. Laevers and colleagues (n.d.) demonstrated that emotional well-being and involvement in class were two key indicators of learning. The instrument, which is suitable for 4–5-year-olds and completed by teachers, assesses various aspects of development—such as motor, language and under-standing—including emotional and social competence. It is administered in three stages. The first stage screens the entire class. The second stage involves a closer observation of individual children and the analysis of their behavior with the intention of identifying those with low well-being scores. The child's well-being is assessed in four domains of social activity covering aspects of emotional and social competence with family, peers, teachers and the children's play-, class- and school-world. Stage three sets the goals for action where the children are assessed in the context of the seriousness of problems and the areas to be addressed. The manual contains examples of well-being and involvement at each level, together with conclusions, interpretations and suggestions for interventions.

With regard to general instruments for **school-age children,** the youth version of the EQ-i, the EQ-i:YV (Bar-On & Parker 2000), directly assesses:

- **emotional competence,** for example 'It is easy to tell people how I feel' and 'I get too upset about things'
- **social competence,** for example 'I can tell when one of my close friends is unhappy'
- **impulse control,** for example 'I can wait my turn'
- **problem-solving,** for example 'I can come up with good answers to hard questions'.

The items in the EQ-i:YV were derived from the authors' clinical experience and literature review (Bar-On & Parker 2000). Final item selection was based on the items' psychometric properties and their appropriateness for capturing the construct being assessed, which is emotional and social intelligence. Self-completion and observer report forms are available in paper and computerized versions for adults and for children as young as seven years. There is a special response sheet for younger children, as young as six years, and those with young reading ages to whom statements can be read out.

The EQ-i, for adults, contains 133 items, while the EQ-i:YV for 7–18-year-olds has 60- and 30-item versions. The instrument can also be used to provide group scores allowing assessment of whole classes or schools. In addition to two validity indices—**positive impression** and **inconsistency index**—and the total **EQ scale,** the 60-item version of the EQ-i:YV has five primary scales:

1. **Intrapersonal**—which assesses the ability to understand and express feelings and needs.
2. **Interpersonal**—which assesses the ability to identify and respond to the feelings of others.
3. **Stress management**—which assesses the ability to manage and control emotions.
4. **Adaptability**—which assesses flexibility, reality-testing and problem-solving.
5. **General mood**—which assesses optimism and happiness.

The 30-item version comprises the same scales as the 60-item version except for the general mood scale and inconsistency index. The EQ-i:YV is commercially available and thus there are cost implications to its use. It can be used as part of personal development programs. This instrument was developed and standardized on nearly 10,000 children and adolescents in the US and Canada, and age- and gender-specific norms are available from 7–18 years of age. There are norms for other countries as well, including the UK, where extensive data collection has been conducted over the past two years. Each scale can be considered separately, and strategies are suggested to improve emotional and social competence in any area where a low score is achieved (Bar-On personal communication January 2003).

The Emotional Behaviour Scale (EBS) (Clarbour & Roger 2003) is a 65-item self-report questionnaire whose development was based on 7-year-old pupils' responses to what they think would most likely be their emotional and social reactions to a range of situations. It was designed to assess adolescent emotional coping strategies and focused on three subscales: social anxiety, malevolent aggression and social self-esteem. The instrument is applicable primarily to adolescents as old as 19, but can be used with children as young as eight years. The Emotional and Behavioural Development Scales (EBDS) (Riding, Rayner, Morris et al. 2002) is a 21-item teacher rating scale that can be completed in approximately four minutes and is applicable to children of 5–16 years of age. It was developed from the responses to a survey of educational psychologists working with emotionally and behaviorally disturbed children. There are three scales containing seven items each, all of which are phrased positively and designed to measure social development, emotional behavior and academic performance.

The Early Development Instrument (EDI) (Offord, Janus & Walsh 2001) was developed with an early-years action group and practitioners. It also includes a teacher rating scale and assesses readiness to learn in pre-school in five domains:

1. Physical health.
2. Social competence.
3. Emotional health.
4. Cognitive development.
5. Communication skills.

We will now explore other kinds of instruments that we reviewed.

Some instruments are associated with programs for children with **emotional and social problems.** The Boxall Profile (Bennathan & Boxall 1998) is based on the observation of deviant behaviors. It was developed to identify areas of difficulty in children entering school from severely disadvantaged backgrounds, and it is designed to help teachers plan focused interventions and to monitor progress. This instrument represents part of a program designed to support children with developmental disorders. It was standardized on 3–8-year-olds, but also works well with children up to 11 years of age (Bennathan personal communication February 2003), and is completed by teachers.

Two other instruments, developed in special education projects, focus on children's readiness for reintegration into mainstream schooling. These are the Coping in School Scale (CISS) (McSherry 2001) and the Reintegration Readiness Scale (Doyle personal communication 2002). The former contains general sections such as management of behavior, self and others. The short sections are designed to measure specific behaviors: self-awareness, confidence and organization, attitude, learning and literacy skills. Completed by teachers, the instrument is designed to help the reintegration of 8–12-year-old children before they transfer to secondary schools, as well as to monitor problems throughout this transition period. It contains positively phrased items and is child-centered. It highlights areas that require intervention, with the emphasis on self-management and learning, but has few items related to emotional competence. Its development was based on the author's experience and suggestions from teachers. The Reintegration Readiness Scale is based on the CISS but is shorter and can be used with 7–11-year-olds. It is quick and relatively easy to complete and has five scales:

1. Self-control and behavior management.
2. Social skills.
3. Self-awareness and confidence.
4. Learning skills.
5. Approach to learning.

The US Fast Track Program, which is an intervention designed primarily to prevent serious and chronic antisocial behavior, has been associated with the development of a series of instruments that identify and monitor children who need special help with their emotional and social development (Greenberg et al. n.d.). The series includes child interview and parent and teacher rating scales. The program uses the PATHS curriculum and social skills training. The instruments privilege social over emotional competence and tend to focus on negative behaviors.

The final instrument presented here assesses social and emotional problems in children and is interactive and attempts to identify gaps in emotional development in children with such problems. Thus, the instrument is designed to guide remedial work. It was developed iteratively as part of the Enable Project (Banks, Bird, Gerlach et al. 2001) with diverse populations in the UK. It is applicable to children of 3–16 years of age and can be completed by the teacher, parent and/or child. If the children are too young to complete the instrument, they are asked their opinion about the various statements. These statements are selected from various topic areas focusing on problem behaviors, and the items are phrased primarily in the negative. The six most relevant statements are chosen to identify strategies to repair missing developmental stages. The computer program suggests actions to promote development.

Conclusion

Based on a comprehensive search, we identified and reviewed 33 instruments that were designed to assess various aspects of emotional and social competence. Four instruments stood out as most promising.

The number of instruments reviewed found to be suitable for **pre-school** settings was small, and the most suitable at present appears to be the DECA. It can be used for the early identification and profiling of problematic emotional and social functioning, as well as for monitoring progress made as a result of targeted intervention. In light of the fact that we identified a number of instruments that were being developed and validated at the time, it is likely that there will be a wider choice available to researchers and practitioners in the future.

Among the instruments found to be suitable for use in **primary school** settings, two stood out as particularly relevant: the BERS and the EQ-i:YV. In addition to assessing social competence, the latter instrument focuses more on emotional competence than the former. Moreover, a 30-item version of the EQ-i:YV is available, in contrast to the 52-item BERS, which means that the administration, scoring and evaluation time is potentially less than the BERS. Additionally, the EQ-i:YV has been normed on a relatively large number of children in the US, Canada and in other countries including the UK. Both instruments provide a self-report assessment option as well as versions that are rated by parents and teachers. The adult version of the EQ-i could also be used to assess the emotional and social competence of parents and teachers, with the aim of assisting them in addressing this important aspect of their own development. This is a relatively important factor in light of the fact that the findings from one study have suggested that the more emotionally and socially competent educators prove to be the most effective (Haskett 2002).

These instruments are potentially useful in the promotion of emotional and social development in pre-school and school settings, because they can be used to:

- identify children who are in need of targeted intervention
- profile the specific aspects of emotional and social development that need to be improved
- monitor progress made by guided intervention.

Additionally, the DECA was developed primarily to promote emotional and social development among pre-school children, and the EQ-i:YV is suitable for use in the context of the personal development of older children.

All three instruments also facilitate the identification of the collective needs of a particular class, school or entire school district. In this capacity, they could all be used to assess the impact of class-based curricula in improving emotional and social competence. The fourth instrument we identified as showing promise, the CDP, was designed only with this purpose in mind. The CDP collects young people's views of the way in which they behave with one another. The CDP is a promising instrument in this specific regard.

While each of the above mentioned instruments shows promise, not one of them has been subjected to the ultimate test in which their usefulness in promoting emotional and social competence is empirically examined in pre-school and primary school settings based on a randomized controlled trial. Such research is necessary before the instruments could be recommended for widespread use in this context. Given the importance of emotional and social development outlined in other chapters in this book, such research should be undertaken with urgency.

References

Achenbach, T.M., and C.S. Edelbroch. 1991. *Manual for the child behavior checklist: 4–18 profile.* Burlington VT: University of Vermont Dept of Psychiatry.

Achenbach, T.M., and L.A. Rescorta. 2000. *Manual for the ASEBA preschool forms and profiles.* Burlington, VT: University of Vermont, Research Center for Children, Youth, and Families.

———. 2001. *Manual for ASEBA school-age forms and profiles.* Burlington VT: University of Vermont, Research Center for Children, Youth and Families

Austin, S., and S. Joseph. 1996. Assessment of bully/victim problems in 8 to 11 year-olds. *British Journal of Educational Psychology* 66:447–56.

Ball, C. 1994. *Start right; The importance of early learning.* London: The Royal Society for the Encouragement of Arts, Manufacturers and Commerce.

Banks, T., J. Bird, L. Gerlach, M. Henderson, and R. Lovelock. 2001. *ENABLE: Emotional Needs, Achieving, Behaving and Learning in Education.* Modbury, Devon, U. K.: The Modbury Group.

Bar-On, R. 2000. Emotional and social intelligence: Insights from the Emotional Quotient Inventory (EQ-i). In Handbook of emotional intelligence. Ed. R. Bar-On and J. D. A. Parker. San Francisco: Jossey-Bass.

———. 2005. The impact of emotional-social intelligence on subjective well-being. *Perspectives in Education* 23(2): 41–61.

———. 2006. The Bar-On model of emotional-social intelligence (ESI). *Psicothema* 18.

Bar-On, R., R. Handley, and S. Fund. 2005. The impact of emotional and social intelligence on performance. In *Linking emotional intelligence and performance at work: Current research evidence.* Ed. Vanessa Druskat, Fabio Sala, and Gerald Mount. Mahwah, NJ: Lawrence Erlbaum.

Bar-On R., and J.D.A. Parker. 2000. Bar-On emotional quotient inventory: Youth version (Technical Manual). New York: Multi-Health Systems Inc.

Beidel, D.C., S.M. Turner, and T.L. Morris. 1995. A new inventory to assess childhood social anxiety and phobia: The Social Phobia and Anxiety Inventory for Children. *Psychological Assessment* 7:73–79.

Bennathan, M. and M. Boxall. 1998. *The Boxall Profile. A guide to effective intervention in the education of pupils with emotional and behavioural difficulties.* London: Association of Workers for Children with Emotional and Behavioural Difficulties.

Braza P., F. Braza, M.R. Carreras, and J.M. Munoz. 1993. Measuring the social ability of preschool children. *Social Behaviour and Personality* 21:145–57.

Briggs-Gowan, M.J., and A.S. Carter. 1998. Preliminary acceptability and psychometrics of the Infant-Toddler Social and Emotional Assessment (ITSEA): A new adult-report questionnaire. *Infant Mental Health Journal* 19:422–45.

Cairns, R.B., M.C. Leung, S.D. Gest, and B.D. Cairns. 1995. A brief method for assessing social development: structure, reliability, stability, and developmental validity of the interpersonal competence scale. *Behaviour Research and Therapy* 33:725–36.

Caprara, G.V., and C. Pastorelli. 1993. Early emotional instability, prosocial behaviour, and aggression: some methodological aspects. *European Journal of Personality* 7:19–36.

Carter, A.S., C. Little, M.J. Briggs-Gowan, and N. Kogan. 1999. The infant-toddler social and emotional assessment (ITSEA): Comparing parent ratings to laboratory observations of task mastery, emotion regulation, coping behaviours, and attachment status. *Infant Mental Health Journal* 20(4): 375–92.

Chorpita, B.F., S.A. Tracey, T.A. Brown, T.J. Collica, and D.H. Barlow. 1997. Assessment of worry in children and adolescents: An Adaptation of the Penn State Worry Questionnaire. *Behaviour Research and Therapy* 35:569–81.

Clarbour, J. and D. Roger. 2004. The construction and validation of a new scale for measuring emotional response style in adolescents. *Journal of Child Psychology and Psychiatry* 45:3, 496–509

Costenbader, V.K., and H.R. Keller. 1990. Behavioural ratings of emotionally handicapped, learning disabled, and nonreferred children: Scale and source consistency. *Journal of Psychoeducational Assessment* 8:485–96.

Department for Education and Employment (DfEE). 1997. Baseline assessment schemes: Submission guidelines. London: DfEE.

Department for Education and Skills (DfES) 1998. Promoting children's mental health within early years and school setting. http://www.dfes.gov.uk/sen/documents/ UPDATE_8.htm (accessed on 12 June 2006). (Also available for order from DfES Publications, PO Box 5050, Sherwood Park, Annesley, Nottingham, NG15 0DJ, United Kingdom.).

Duffy, B., and M. Fell. 1999. Patterns of attachment: Further use of the Separation Anxiety Test. *Irish Journal of Psychology* 20:159–71.

Elias, M., J. Zins, R. Weissberg, K. Frey, M. Greenberg, N. Haynes, R. Kessler, M. Schwab-Stone, and T. Shriver. 1997. *Promoting social and emotional learning.* Alexandria, Virginia: ASCD.

Elliot, S.N., S. Sheridan, and F.M. Gresham. 1993. Behaviour rating scales: Issues of use and development. *School Psychology Review* 22:313–21.

Emerson, E.N., S.L. Crowley, and K.W. Merrell. 1994. Convergent validity of the School Social-Behaviour Scales with the Child Behaviour Check List and Teachers Report Form. *Journal of Psychoeducational Assessment* 12:372–80.

Epstein, M.H. 1999. The development and validation of a scale to assess the emotional and behavioural strengths of children and adolescents. *Remedial and Special Education* 20(5): 253–62.

Epstein, M.H., G. Ryser, and N. Pearson. 2002. Standardisation of the behavioural and emotional rating scale: Factor structure, reliability, and criterion validity. *Journal of Behavioural Health Services and Research* 29:208–16.

Epstein, M.H. and J. Sharma. 1997. *Behavioural and Emotional Rating Scale (BERS): A strength-based approach to assessment.* Austin, Texas: PRO-ED.

Fantuzzo, J., B. Suttonsmith, K.C. Coolahan, P.H. Manz, S. Canning, and D. Debnam. 1995. Assessment of preschool play interaction behaviours in young low-income children—Penn Interactive Peer Play Scale. *Early Childhood Research Quarterly* 10:105–20.

Gardner, H. 1983. *Frames of mind.* New York: Basic Books.

Goodman, R 1994. A modified version of the Rutter parent questionnaire including extra items on children's strengths: A research note. *Journal of Child Psychology and Psychiatry* 35:1483–94.

———— 1997. The Strengths and Difficulties Questionnaire: A research note. *Journal of Child Psychology and Psychiatry* 38:581–86.

Greenberg, M.L., L.J. Lengua, J. Coie, E.E. Pinderhughes, and the Conduct Problems Prevention Research Group. 1999. Predicting developmental outcomes at school entry using a multiple-risk model: Four American communities. *Developmental Psychology* 35:403–17.

Gresham, F.M. and S.N. Elliott. 1990. *Social Skills Rating System Manual.* Circle Pines, MN: American Guidance System.

Harris, J., C. Tyre, and C. Wilkinson. 1993. Using the Child Behaviour Checklist in ordinary primary schools. *British Journal of Educational Psychology* 63:245–60.

Harter, S. 1993. Causes and consequences of low self-esteem in children and adolescents. In *The puzzle of low self-regard.* Ed. R.F. Baumeister, 87–116 New York: Plenum.

Haskett, R. A. 2002. Emotional intelligence and teaching success in higher education Unpublished doctoral dissertation, Indiana University.

Hogan, A.E., K.G. Scott, and C.R. Baven. 1992. EPPE Project. Adaptive Social Behaviour Inventory Child Questionnaire. *Journal of Psycho-Educational Assessments* 10(3): 230–39.

Laevers, F., E. Vandenbusshe, M. Kog, and L. Depondt. no date. A process-oriented child monitoring system for young children. Leuven: Centre for Experiential Education.

LeBuffe, P.A., and J.A. Naglieri. 1998. Devereux Early Childhood Assessment Programme, DECA. Kaplan Companies.

Lund, J., and K.W. Merrell. 2001. Social and antisocial behaviour of children with learning and behaviour disorders: Construct validity of the Home and Community Social Behaviour Scales. *Journal of Psychoeducational Assessment* 19:112–22.

Lyon, M.A,, C. Albertus, J. Birkinbine, and J. Naibi. 1996. A validity study of the social skills rating system-teacher version with disabled and non-disabled preschool children. *Perceptual and Motor Skills* 83:307–16.

Mayer, J. D., and Salovey, P. 1997. What is emotional intelligence? In *Emotional development and emotional intelligence.* Ed. P. Salovey and D.J. Sluyter, pp. 3–31. New York: Basic Books.

McSherry, J. 2001. *Challenging behaviours in mainstream schools. Practical strategies for effective intervention and reintegration.* London: David Fulton Publishers.

Merrell, K.W. 1993. Using behaviour rating-scales to assess social skills and anti-social behaviour in school settings—development of the School Social-Behaviour Scales. *School Psychology Review* 22:115–33.

Merrell, K.W., and P. Caldarella. 2003. Home & Community Social Behaviour Scales. Assessment-Intervention Resources (Accessed at www.assessment-intervention.com).

Merrell, K.W., A.L. Streeter, E.W. Boelter, P. Caldarella, and A. Gentry. 2001. Validity of the home and community social behaviour scales comparisons with five behaviour-rating scales. *Psychology in the Schools* 38:313–25.

Mitchell-Copeland, J.,S.A. Denham, and E.K. DeMulder. 1997. Q-sort assessment of child-teacher attachment relationships and social competence in the preschool. *Early Education and Development* 8:27–39.

National Commission on Education. 1993. Learning to succeed: A radical look at education today and a strategy for the future. Report of the Paul Hamlyn Foundation, National Commission on Education. London: Heinemann.

Offord, D., M. Janus, and C. Walsh. 2001. *Population-level assessment of readiness to learn at school for five year olds in Canada.* Ontario: The Canadian Centre for the Study of Children at Risk, McMaster University.

Pascal, C., and T. Bertram. 2001. *The AcE Project. Accounting Early for Life Long Learning.* Worcester, U.K.: Centre for Research In Early Childhood Education.

Qualifications and Curriculum Authority (QCA). 2002. http:/www.qca.org.uk/ca/foundation/foundation_stage_profile.asp.

Riding, R., S. Rayner, S. Morris, M. Grimley, and D. Adams. 2002. Emotional and Behavioural Development Scales. Birmingham, U.K.: Assessment Research Unit, School of Education, University of Birmingham.

Saarni, C. 1990. Emotional competence: How emotions and relationships become integrated. In *Socioemotional development. Nebraska symposium on motivation* vol. 36. Ed. R.A. Thompson, pp. 115–82. Lincoln, NE: University of Nebraska Press.

Sharp, P., and A. Faupel. 2001. *Promoting emotional literacy. Guidelines for schools, local authorities, and health services.* Southampton, U.K.: Southampton City Council, Emotional Literacy Interest Group (SELIG).

Solomon, D., V. Battistich, M. Watson, E. Schaps, and C. Lewis. 2000. A six district study of educational change: Direct and mediated effects of the Child Development Project. *Social Psychology of Education* 4:3–51.

St. James-Roberts, I., G. Singh, R. Lynn, and S. Jackson. 1994. Assessing emotional and behavioural problems in reception class school children: Factor structure, convergence and prevalence using PBCL. *British Journal of Educational Psychology* 64:105–18.

Stewart-Brown, S., and L. Edmunds. 2003. Assessing emotional and social competence in preschool and primary school settings: A review of instruments. *Perspectives in Education* 21(4): 17–40.

Valla, J.P., L. Bergeron, and N. Smolla. 2000. The Dominic-R: A pictorial interview for 6 to 11 year-old children. *Journal of the American Academy of Child and Adolescent Psychiatry* 39:85–93.

Wright, J.C., V. Binney, and P.K. Smith. 1995. Security of attachment in 8–12 year-olds: A revised version of the Separation Anxiety Test, its psychometric properties and clinical interpretation. *Journal of Child Psychology and Psychiatry* 36:757–74.

—— 18 ——

Assessing Emotional Intelligence in Adults: A Review of the Most Popular Measures

David L. Van Rooy and Chockalingam Viswesvaran

Introduction

EI has been promoted as an individual difference variable that plays a major role in determining success in various types of human performance (see, for example, Bar-On 1997b; 2004; 2005; Bar-On, Handley & Fund 2005; Brackett, Mayer & Warner 2004; Goleman 1998). It has also been argued that EI could be more important than cognitive ability in predicting success in certain areas (Goleman 1995). Although this particular claim has remained largely unsupported empirically (Van Rooy & Viswesvaran 2004), it does not mean that EI has limited utility. EI has indeed demonstrated predictive validity comparable to other assessment techniques, including personality testing (Barrick, Mount & Judge 2001) and interview procedures (McDaniel, Whetzel, Schmidt & Maurer 1994). The measurement of EI is still in its infancy, and many questions remain unanswered since the recent re-emergence of this construct in the 1990s. However, if the current trend continues and if empirical research can adequately address a number of the more pertinent issues regarding EI measurement, EI may capture a respectable place among other widely accepted assessment techniques applied in selection, training and elsewhere. Given this potential, it is important that we address issues related to EI measurement as well as ways of enhancing EI itself.

In this chapter, we begin with a review of important measurement issues related to EI. We then examine six of the most commonly used measures and briefly summarize their properties. Owing to space limitations, the chapter is designed to provide a brief summary and is not intended to be a comprehensive appraisal. For a more detailed evaluation of these and other EI instruments, you can refer to texts such as Geher (2004); Geher and Renstrom (2004); and Matthews, Zeidner and Roberts (2002).

Measurement Issues in EI Assessment

For any construct to be useful, it should be measurable, and individual differences should be quantifiable (Schmidt 1992; Schmidt & Hunter 1996). In social sciences, unlike in physical sciences where concrete constructs such as weight and length are assessed, constructs are more abstract. With abstract constructs, there is no physical entity that can be directly described and identified; we can only *infer* the presence of the construct from assessing a subset of several potential manifestations of that construct. And although we infer in this way, we are generalizing to the entire content domain. As such, careful consideration should be given to measurement, and certain psychometric characteristics should be demonstrated.

Classical measurement theory (cf. Allen & Yen 1979/2002) provides a background for judging the adequacy of measurement of a construct. Although more recent measurement conceptualization methods such as latent trait models are available, the classical measurement theory framework adequately provides a basic understanding of what needs to be addressed regarding the measurement of constructs like EI. In this section, we describe some data that should be presented when advancing an EI measure in the literature. In the following section, we then review existing measures with an emphasis on whether they meet the criteria for sound measurement in our opinion.

Assessment models of EI can be split into 'mixed models' and 'ability models' (Mayer, Salovey & Caruso 2000). Mixed assessment models, which have also been described as 'trait-based models' (Petrides & Furnham 2000; 2001), are generally based on self-report. The term 'mixed model' denotes the idea that such EI measures assess aspects of personality and cognitive intelligence in addition to EI. In contrast, EI measurement based on 'ability models' uses a performance-based response format from which a 'correct' answer can be derived. A correct answer is based on the percentage of respondents who endorse a particular option, rather than on an absolute or definitive result (Van Rooy, Viswesvaran & Pluta in press).

The first step in the proper measurement of a construct is to define its content domain. The users of the construct should agree on what is included within the domain. Unfortunately, as our review in the next section shows, the label 'EI' has been used to denote quite different conceptualizations of the content domain. Consider, for example, the above mentioned division of EI conceptualization into the 'ability model' and the 'mixed model' of this construct (Mayer et al. 2000). On the one hand, there is presently only *one* measure that is based on the 'ability model' of EI, that is, the MSCEIT (Mayer, Salovey & Caruso 2002), which limits the content domain of this construct and oversimplifies its description and conceptualization. On the other hand, measures based on the 'mixed model' have emerged from a wide range of conceptualizations of EI, making it difficult to determine, describe and define the content domain involved. A similar scientific challenge has been encountered with other constructs that have been around for more than a century, such as intelligence and personality. As such, a *distillation* of the content domain of EI through factor analyses and a more detailed construction of nomological nets would represent a critical milestone in the conceptualization and measurement of this construct.

Once the content domain is defined, appropriate measurement methods have to be chosen. Methods such as self-reports, situational judgement tests and multiple-choice response formats have been typically employed.

Mayer and colleagues have argued that *if* EI is an actual ability and *if* self-report assessments typically correlate poorly with performance measures of ability, EI should not be measured with self-report instruments (Mayer, Salovey, Caruso & Sitarenios 2003). However, such a position fails to capture, inter alia, the rich idiosyncratic emotions experienced by the test-taker—emotions that may be accessible only to that person. A related concern is that when self-report instruments are used in high stakes testing, responses *could* be distorted intentionally (Hough & Ones 2001). This is certainly a possibility, especially if the self-report instrument does not include response bias indicators and a correction factor based on these indicators. Even though meta-analyses do not indicate that 'faking good' significantly distorts personality assessment (cf. Ones, Viswesvaran & Reiss 1996), specific studies of 'fakability' in EI assessment are needed (Alonso, Van Rooy & Viswesvaran 2004). When EI measures are based on self-reports, it is important that the test author and/or publisher provide data on the fakability of test scores. Moreover, it is imperative that such measures include validity scales to detect this type of test behavior; and appropriate norms should be developed to flag potentially invalid profiles. When such information exists for the measures being reviewed below, we indicate this.

When situational judgement tests are chosen as the measurement method, test-takers are presented with a scenario and asked to choose, from a set of given options, the option they would prefer. The test-takers' responses are scored on several dimensions, such as the correct identification of emotions in a particular scenario, the understanding of the emotions involved, and so forth. Several scenarios are presented, and scores on various dimensions are averaged across them. A related measurement issue in ability-based measurement has to do with scoring the responses. Three options have been used in EI assessment based on the 'ability model' of this construct. The first involves identifying the 'correct' response by having **experts** judge the response options. This approach is employed in various types of tests, but it has the potential limitation of being influenced by the culture of the experts. As such, cross-cultural generalizability is a concern with this method.

A second scoring method is the **consensus** method in which the correct response is the one with which most test-takers agree. The problem with this approach is its potential emphasis on conformity and the potential likelihood of the person high on EI being penalized for not adhering to the common response. It is possible that cultural differences exist and may impact on EI assessment. The approach is also influenced by the culture of the test-takers, which makes its generalizability across cultures questionable as well.

Finally, the third scoring approach is based on matching the responses to how the target feels, which is referred to as 'target scoring'. **Target scoring** relies on the self-report approach and may not be feasible in all circumstances, such as in high stakes testing. This is especially true if there is no method of response bias detection and a way of adjusting scores based on the direction of the response bias detected, such as 'faking good' or 'faking bad'. It is disturbing to note that the convergence across these three methods of scoring is low (Matthews et al. 2002).

Once the content domain has been specified and the assessment as well as the scoring methods have been chosen, items need to be selected to provide a representative sample of the content domain involved. A pilot test of the items with a representative sample—of the population of potential test-takers—needs to be conducted and item analyses then performed on the data. Item difficulty, discrimination indices and item-criterion correlations need to be assessed, and the best items are then chosen before the test can be finalized. Culturally laden items need to be identified and modified. Item bias should be evaluated with differential item functioning analyses, and culturally biased items need to be deleted. Group differences in gender, age and ethnicity should be noted, and separate norms should be provided if justified. Adequate norms need to be developed and explained in the test manual. It is imperative that test manuals describe, in detail, the choices made in the development phase. If the test is administered in more than one format, for example paper copies and computer-based, the cross-modal consistency should be presented.

Then, the psychometric properties of the measure need to be assessed. The first psychometric property that is typically examined is the reliability of the measure. **Reliability** is the consistency and stability of measurement. To the extent that we want to generalize EI scores, the relevant reliability coefficients need to be examined. Almost every conceptualization of EI presents it as a stable variable, which implies the need for assessing the stability, or the test-retest, reliability of the instrument. The appropriate time intervals to be examined depend on the underlying theory of how EI changes over time. Given that several items are used to measure any dimension, clarification of the extent to which the items cluster together and measure the same trait are needed as well. This means that internal consistency estimates, measured primarily by coefficient alphas, are also needed to be reported for EI measures. Following the sufficient establishment of the reliability of EI scores, issues of construct validity and nomological net arise. A key measurement concern when new constructs are proposed is to demonstrate how the focal construct is different from or similar to other traditional constructs, such as intelligence and personality. Convergent as well as divergent construct validity of psychometric instruments need to be established. Both of these requirements are important, and establishing just one of them is insufficient (Campbell & Fiske 1959). **Convergent** construct validity assesses the extent to which two or more measures of a construct correlate, while **divergent** construct validity assesses how measures of the construct, such as EI, differ from other constructs that are theoretically unrelated to it, for example personality and cognitive intelligence. Adequate sample sizes are also needed to address these issues. Furthermore, it is desirable to show that the new measures of EI explain behavior over and beyond traditional measures such as intelligence and personality. This **incremental** validation requires empirical evidence based on hierarchical regressions.

If the above measurement issues can be adequately addressed and *if* EI can be reliably measured and shown to be related to success in various life outcomes, it is *then* important to empirically explore ways of developing this construct and enhancing emotionally intelligent behavior in individuals. However, much of the evidence presently available is still anecdotal and generated by the measurement of competencies that some theorists do not consider to be part of EI (Mayer et al. 2000). Be that as it may, initial empirical evidence has suggested that EI can be developed to some extent when compared with cognitive intelligence, which is considered to be genetically determined. Cross-sectional research has indicated that EI increases naturally with age, even when this construct is measured by different assessment modalities based on different conceptual models (Bar-On 1997b; 2000; Mayer, Caruso & Salovey 1999). Emotional and social development begins during infancy (Zeidner, Matthews, Roberts & MacCann 2003) and progresses through childhood (Saarni 1999) to at least the fourth or fifth decade of life (Bar-On 1997b; 2000).

It is important, however, to isolate and empirically examine those particular aspects of emotional and social development that are specifically part of EI. The accurate measurement of the construct is essential to study this type of development and allow for targeted intervention programs aimed at enhancing it. Moreover, when EI is viewed from the 'mixed model' perspective, developmental progress seems more plausible. In contrast, when viewed from the 'ability' perspective, the implied cognitive component of this model may serve to limit the extent to which EI can be developed, enhanced and trained. If EI is indeed a multifaceted construct, it would make sense to design targeted programs focusing on areas of relative weakness, instead of simply trying to raise EI scores. As Goleman, Boyatzis and McKee (2002) have suggested, leadership is an area where EI may have great potential for improving performance. If this is the case, developmental programs should be designed to promote leadership in all walks of life as well as directed to enhance areas of weakness that most threaten successful performance in those roles.

In the next section, we summarize some of the most popular EI measures to be found in the literature. Wherever evidence is presented on item development, item analysis, content domain, reliability and validity, we summarize this information. At the outset, we wish to emphasize that none of the measures described below presently satisfies *all* of the criteria we have explored above. However, it is unreasonable to expect that in this early stage of development such a measure will be available. Instead, progress will continue to be made as more measurement and validation studies are conducted for existing and new measures of EI. The purpose of the above section was to list what is needed for an *ideal* EI measure, and the purpose of the following section is to sketch where we currently are. We discuss findings related to each measure in terms of the issues discussed above. We look forward to future research to address what we outline here.

Measures of EI

We will now describe six of the most well-known measures of EI. Only one of the measures, the MSCEIT, is framed as an 'ability-based' measure, and the remaining scales fall under the 'mixed model' framework. We do not discuss some measures, such as the Trait Meta-Mood Scale (Salovey, Mayer, Goldman, Turvey & Palfai 1995), because they do not fully capture the current conceptualizations of EI, in our opinion, and are rarely used in research or applied settings. Others, such as the TEIque (Petrides & Furnham 2003), are not reviewed because too little research currently exists.

The Mayer-Salovey-Caruso Emotional Intelligence Test

The Multi-factor EI Scale (MEIS) was the precursor to the MSCEIT (Mayer et al. 2002). Because the MSCEIT has undergone a number of rapid revisions, much of the existing research is based on the MEIS and earlier versions of the MSCEIT that are no longer used. Another reason for being careful when drawing inferences about this instrument is that little evidence of convergent construct validation, based on correlating the current published version of the MSCEIT with other EI measures, has been published to date (Bar-On 2004; 2005; Matthews et al. 2002).

The 141 items of the MSCEIT load onto four 'branches' of the authors' conceptualization of EI:

1. Perception of emotion.
2. Use of emotion to facilitate thinking.
3. Understanding of emotion.
4. Management of emotion.

An overall score, a score for each branch, and an experiential score (based on branches 1 and 2) and a strategic score (based on branches 3 and 4) are all derived. The reported reliabilities have improved with each iteration of the MEIS and are now above accepted guidelines. Brackett and Salovey (2004) reported overall split-half reliability coefficients of .93 and .91 for consensus and expert scoring respectively. The reliability coefficients for the four branches, based on both scoring methods, range from .76 to .91 (Mayer et al. 2003). As was previously mentioned, a 'correct' or 'best response' is based on choosing the answer endorsed most frequently by experts in the field of emotion. The MSCEIT have been shown to correlate poorly with other EI measures (Bar-On 2004; Brackett & Mayer 2003; Van Rooy et al. in press).

Of the available EI measures, the MSCEIT has demonstrated the highest correlation with measures of cognitive ability with an average correlation coefficient of .35 after reliability corrections have been made (Brackett & Mayer 2003; Van Rooy et al. in press). Moreover, in contrast to self-report measures, the ability-based MSCEIT correlates lower with personality (Van Rooy et al. in press). As such, and in light of the fact that personnel selection has traditionally relied on cognitive assessment for selecting job applicants, the MSCEIT could have an appeal in selection settings to the extent that group differences are minimal. The measure is presently being used in development and training within the corporate coaching context (see Chapter 12 with regard to this application). Scores on the MSCEIT have been shown to increase with age, and females appear to outperform males (Mayer et al. 1999). Using previous versions of the test, Roberts, Zeidner and Matthews (2001) found, however, that these gender differences depend on the scoring method employed, which was consensus versus expert; and the same was found for ethnic differences.

The Emotional Quotient Inventory

Bar-On's EQ-i (1997a) was the first commercially available and mass-marketed measure of EI to be published, and a large research base has subsequently used this 133-item instrument. As summarized in Table 1.1, the EQ-i has five composite scales that measure five meta-factors: intrapersonal, interpersonal, stress management, adaptability and general mood. These composite scales comprise 15 subscales based on a 15-factor structure that emerged from the factor analysis of the normative population sample (Bar-On 1997b). More recent factor analytic findings, based on a re-examination of the sample, have suggested an alternative factor structure justifying the use of 10 key subscales (Bar-On 2000); the remaining five subscales are now postulated as facilitators of emotionally and socially intelligent behavior.

Some of the EQ-i subscales, primarily those that are presently considered to be *facilitators* of emotionally and socially intelligent behavior, measure areas such as independence and optimism, which may explain the overlap with certain personality facets. Based on the normative sample upon which the EQ-i was standardized in the US (n = 3,831), the consistency coefficients of the 15 sub-scales range from .70 to .89 (Bar-On 1997b). A more recent re-examination of this normative sample indicates that the overall internal consistency of the EQ-i as .97 with the five composite scales ranging from .86 to .94 (Bar-On 2004). The EQ-i includes four scales designed as validity indices. These indices assess item omission, item inconsistency, positive impression (faking good) and negative impression (faking bad). A correction factor is used to adjust scale and subscale scores based on scores obtained on the positive and negative impressions scales.

Although the EQ-i technical manual reports no significant differences between males and females on the total EQ score, the subscale scores indicate that women are more adept at understanding how others feel and relating with people, while males are more adept at managing emotions (Bar-On 1997b; 2000; 2004). As such, the EQ-i scoring algorithm incorporates gender- as well as age-specific norms. In contrast to the MSCEIT, the EQ-i tends to correlate higher with measures of personality and lower with measures of cognitive ability. Moreover, studies have shown that EI assessed by the EQ-i is relatively distinct from cognitive intelligence (see, for example, Bar-On 2004; Bar-On, Tranel, Denburg & Bechara 2003; Derksen, Kramer & Katzko 2002), which makes this instrument appealing from a training and development perspective. The EQ-i is also used extensively in selection settings (Bar-On 2005; Bar-On et al. 2005).

The Emotional Intelligence Scale

Of the existing measures of EI, the EIS (Schutte, Malouff, Hall et al. 1998) has received the most published empirical attention. Part of this is owing to the fact that it is one of the only public-domain EI measures available. The scale was designed to be a short and easy-to-administer measure of EI based on the ability framework, although it uses a self-report methodology. The 33-item EIS has been shown to be extremely reliable, with internal consistency estimates frequently above .90 (Schutte et al. 1998).

The EIS has repeatedly been shown to be highly correlated with personality factors, suggesting that it is most likely a trait-based measure. It was originally described as a 'unifactorial' measure, but subsequent research has failed to consistently replicate the single factor solution (see, for example, Ciarrochi, Deane & Anderson 2002; Petrides & Furnham 2000; Saklofske, Austin & Minski 2003). The EIS has also been shown to be susceptible to test sabotaging such as faking good (Van Rooy, Alonso & Viswesvaran 2005). Although group differences have been found with the EIS (Van Rooy et al. 2005), these differences have largely favored protected groups. The measure is unlikely to be used in high stakes selection settings, but it could continue to be used in evaluating the convergent and discriminant validity of other EI measures.

The Emotional Competency Inventory

The ECI (Boyatzis, Goleman & Hay Group 2001) is another measure that conforms most closely to the trait-based model of EI, although the authors consider it to be a measure of emotional competency. The ECI 2.0 consists of 18 competencies comprising 72 items loading onto the four clusters of self-awareness, self-management, social awareness and relationship management (Boyatzis & Sala 2004). The technical manual reports marginal coefficient alpha values for self-report responses (Sala 2002). However, consistency reliability increases considerably when the respondent's EI ratings are provided by others, which is the most common use of the ECI as a multi-rater assessment. Self-ratings on the ECI tend to be inflated compared with other measures, but it has a built-in correction factor designed to adjust scores downward. Murensky (2000) conducted one of the few studies found in the literature that compares ECI scores with those of measures of personality and cognitive intelligence—the ECI was shown to be positively related to personality and negatively related to cognitive intelligence. The cluster scores overlapped the most with extroversion, openness to experience, and conscientiousness.

As with other EI measures, the ECI is positively correlated with age, and females tend to score higher than males on several of the scales. We were unable to locate any data reporting score differences across racial groups, but norms are reported for seven countries. The majority of the research on the ECI has been presented in its technical manual and in other non-peer-reviewed sources, typically with small sample sizes. A review of six studies using the ECI reveals a corrected validity coefficient of .23 (Van Rooy et al. 2005). The findings reported in the technical manual suggest that EI, as assessed by this instrument, may be related to several important behavioral outcomes, but peer-reviewed research on the ECI is needed to determine if these findings can be replicated. Furthermore, independent validation studies are needed to assess the convergent and discriminant properties of the ECI.

The Emotional Judgment Inventory

Another recently developed EI measure is the EJI (Bedwell 2003). Like the EIS and the ECI, the EJI does not conform clearly to an ability- or a trait-based assessment model. It is narrower in focus than the trait models and the cognitive underpinning that defines the ability model. The EJI consists of seven dimensions comprising 70 items. The dimensions are as follows:

1. Being aware of emotions.
2. Identifying one's own emotions.
3. Identifying others' emotions.
4. Managing one's emotions.
5. Managing others' emotions.

6. Using emotions in problem-solving.

7. Expressing emotions adaptively.

Raw scores for each of the scales are standardized. An additional ten items form an impression management index used to assess response distortion. Internal consistency reliabilities are reported to range from .75 to .90, while test-retest reliabilities range from .48 to .69 after an eight-week interval (Bedwell 2003).

Group differences have been found with the EJI, as reported in the technical manual (Bedwell 2003). Females tend to score better than males with large differences observed on the first and sixth dimensions, whereas males performed considerably better than females on the fourth dimension. No ethnic differences were reported based on the pooled average of the following groups: Caucasians, African Americans, Asians and Hispanics. At the individual level, however, effect sizes of up to .43 were found between the two largest groups, which consisted of Caucasians and African Americans. Age differences were also reported based on those less than 40 years of age and those equal to or greater than 40 years of age. In all instances, the older group scored better than the younger group, with the largest effect size equal to .46.

The Wong and Law Emotional Intelligence Scale

Of the EI measures discussed so far, the WLEIS (Wong & Law 2002) has been the least researched. We include it here because of the depth of the two studies that have been conducted to date (Law, Wong & Song 2004; Wong & Law 2002), and because it is a short public-domain scale that is easily accessible to researchers. This alone could make it a popular alternative given the lack of EI measures that can be obtained by researchers at no cost. The WLEIS consists of four dimensions, each consisting of four items that are rated on a seven-point Likert scale:

1. Self-emotion appraisal.

2. Uses of emotion.

3. Regulation of emotion.

4. Others' emotions appraisal.

The items were selected from an original pool of 36 that were factor analyzed. A total of eight factors were reduced to the four based on the largest eigenvalues, and the four items with the highest item loadings on each of the factors were selected.

This four-factor structure has held up in multiple samples within the two studies, with coefficient reliabilities ranging from .79 to .93.

Although the WLEIS's content domain has been described as relatively distinct from personality (Law et al. 2004; Wong & Law 2002), average correlations in excess of .30 have been found between the WLEIS and neuroticism as well as conscientiousness on the 'Big 5' personality test. Across the four WLEIS factors, Law and colleagues (2004) found an average correlation of .17 with cognitive ability. The WLEIS has been shown to predict several real-life behavioral outcomes including occupational performance ratings (.21), job satisfaction (.40) and life satisfaction (.41).

Although the studies reported by the authors have been conducted in English, they were based on population samples from Hong Kong and have not been replicated by other researchers using larger and more diverse samples. Moreover, these studies have precluded an examination of group differences and test bias. In the Multitrait-Multimethod Matrix (MTMM) approach, similar and dissimilar measures are correlated along with the same measures assessed with different methods, for example self-reports versus multi-rater ratings. MTMM results obtained by Wong and colleagues have also shown that peer, self- and supervisor ratings of the participants' responses are not as highly correlated as would be expected. This is an important factor in that MTMM is used to assess the convergent and discriminant validity of a construct. Future research needs to continue to explore this issue with the WLEIS and EI measures in general (Alonso et al. 2004).

Conclusion

In this chapter, we have pointed out key measurement issues that must be addressed if EI is to become an accepted and viable construct. We have also shown that some of the most consistent findings generated by existing EI measures are that:

- scores tend to increase with age
- females generally outperform their male counterparts.

Moreover, regardless of what type of measure is used, the total overlap with personality and cognitive ability is quite similar. What differs, however, is the specific derivation of the variance involved. Whereas the ability assessment model correlates more with cognitive ability and less with personality, the mixed model correlates more with personality and less with cognitive ability. Initial findings also suggest that EI plays a role in various aspects of occupational performance, such as leadership. Additionally, EI appears to predict other important outcomes including the enhancement or hindrance of life satisfaction, stress, and even deviant behavior.

With the potential to influence so many consequential aspects of human existence, it will become more important for researchers to continue to study the properties of EI and determine how it can best be assessed and utilized.

References

Allen, M.J., and W.M. Yen. 1979/2002. *Introduction to measurement theory*. Prospect Heights, IL: Waveland Press.

Alonso, A., D.L. Van Rooy, and C. Viswesvaran. 2004. *Emotional intelligence: An examination of self- and peer ratings*. Paper presented at the Society for Industrial and Organizational Psychology, Chicago, IL.

Bar-On, R. 1997a. *Bar-On emotional quotient inventory*. Toronto: Multihealth Systems.

———. 1997b. *Bar-On emotional quotient inventory: Technical manual*. Toronto: Multihealth Systems.

———. 2000. Emotional and social intelligence: Insights from the Emotional Quotient Inventory. In *The handbook of emotional intelligence*. Ed. R. Bar-On and J.D.A. Parker, pp. 363–88. San Francisco: Jossey-Bass.

———. 2004. The Bar-On Emotional Quotient Inventory (EQ-i): Rationale, description, and summary of psychometric results. In Geher, pp. 115–45.

———. 2006. The Bar-On model of emotional-social intelligence (ESI). *Psicothema* 18.

Bar-On, R., R. Handley, and S. Fund. 2005. The impact of emotional and social intelligence on performance. In *Linking emotional intelligence and performance at work: Current research evidence*. Ed. Vanessa Druskat, Fabio Sala, and Gerald Mount. Mahwah, NJ: Lawrence Erlbaum.

Bar-On, R., D. Tranel, N.L. Denburg, and A. Bechara. 2003. Exploring the neurological substrate of emotional and social intelligence. *Brain* 126:1790–1800.

Barrick, M.R., M.K. Mount, and T.A. Judge. 2001. Personality and performance at the beginning of the new millenium: What do we know and where do we go next? *International Journal of Selection and Assessment* 9:9–30.

Bedwell, S. 2003. *Emotional Judgment Inventory Manual*. IPAT, Champaign, IL.

Boyatzis, R.E., D. Goleman, and Hay Group. 2001. *The Emotional Competence Inventory (ECI)*. Boston: HayGroup.

Boyatzis, R.E., and F. Sala. 2004. The Emotional Competence Inventory (ECI). In Geher, pp. 147–80.

Brackett, M.A., and J.D. Mayer. 2003. Convergent, discriminant, and incremental validity of competing measures of emotional intelligence. *Personality and Social Psychology Bulletin* 29:1147–58.

Brackett, M.A., J.D. Mayer, and R.M. Warner. 2004. Emotional intelligence and its relation to everyday behavior. *Personality and Individual Differences* 36:1387–1402.

Brackett, M.A., and P. Salovey. 2004. Measuring emotional intelligence with the Mayer-Salovey-Caruso Emotional Intelligence Test (MSCEIT). In Geher.

Campbell, D.T., and D.W. Fiske. 1959. Convergent and discriminant validation by the multitrait-multimethod matrix. *Psychological Bulletin* 56:81–105.

Ciarrochi, J., F.P. Deane, and S. Anderson. 2002. Emotional intelligence moderates the relationship between stress and mental health. *Personality and Individual Differences* 32:197–209.

Daus, C.S., and N.M. Ashkanasy. 2003. Will the real emotional intelligence please stand up? On deconstructing the Emotional Intelligence 'debate'. *The Industrial Psychologist* 41:69-72.

Derksen, J., I. Kramer, and M. Katzko. 2002. Does a self-report measure for emotional intelligence assess something different than general intelligence? *Personality and Individual Differences* 32:37–48.

Geher, G., ed. 2004. *Measuring emotional intelligence: Common ground and controversy.* Hauppauge, NY: Nova Science Publishers.

Geher, G., and K.L. Renstrom. 2004. Measurement issues in emotional intelligence research. In Geher, pp. 3-19.

Goleman, D. 1995. *Emotional intelligence: Why it can matter more than IQ.* New York: Bantam.

———. 1998. *Working with emotional intelligence.* New York: Bantam.

Goleman, D., R.E. Boyatzis, A. McKee. 2002. *Primal leadership: Realizing the power of emotional intelligence.* Boston: Harvard Business School Press.

Hough, L.M., and D.S. Ones. 2001. The Structure, Measurement, Validity, and Use of Personality Variables in Industrial, Work, and Organizational Psychology. In *Handbook of Industrial, Work, and Organizational Psychology* Vol. 1. Ed. N. Anderson, D.S. Ones, H. Sinangil, and C. Viswesvaran, pp. 233–77. London, U.K.: Sage.

Law, K.S., C.S. Wong, and L.J. Song. 2004. The construct and criterion related validity of emotional intelligence and its potential utility for management studies. *Journal of Applied Psychology* 89:483–96.

Matthews, G., M. Zeidner, and R.D. Roberts. 2002. *Emotional intelligence: Science and myth.* Cambridge, MA: MIT Press.

Mayer, J.D., P. Salovey, and D.R. Caruso. 2002. *Mayer-Salovey-Caruso Emotional Intelligence Test (MSCEIT).* Toronto, Canada: Multi-Health Systems, Inc.

Mayer, J.D., P. Salovey, D.R. Caruso, and G. Sitarenios. 2003. Measuring emotional intelligence with the MSCEIT V2.0. *Emotion* 3:97–105.

McDaniel, M.A., D.L. Whetzel, F.L. Schmidt, and S.D. Maurer. 1994. The validity of employment interviews: A comprehensive review and meta-analysis. *Journal of Applied Psychology* 79(4): 599–616.

Murensky, C.L. 2000. *The relationship between emotional intelligence, personality, critical thinking ability, and organizational leadership performance at upper levels of management.* Dissertation: George Mason University.

Ones, D.S., C. Viswesvaran, and A.D. Reiss. 1996. The role of social desirability in personality testing in personnel selection: The red herring. *Journal of Applied Psychology* 81:660–79.

Petrides, K.V., and A. Furnham. 2000. On the dimensional structure of emotional intelligence. *Personality and Individual Differences* 29:313–20.

———. 2001. Trait emotional intelligence: Psychometric investigation with reference to established trait taxonomies. *European Journal of Personality* 15:425–48.

———. 2003. Trait emotional intelligence: Behavioral validation in two studies of emotion recognition and reactivity to mood induction. *European Journal of Personality* 17:39–57.

Roberts, R.D., M. Zeidner, and G. Matthews. 2001. Does emotional intelligence meet traditional standards for an intelligence? Some new data and conclusions. *Emotion* 1:196–231.

Saarni, C. 1999. *The development of emotional competence.* New York: Guilford.

Saklofske, D.H., E.J. Austin, and P.S. Minski. 2003. Factor structure and validity of a trait emotional intelligence measure. *Personality and Individual Differences* 34:707 21.

Sala, F. 2002. *Emotional Competence Inventory: Technical Manual.* McClelland Center For Research: Hay Group.

Salovey, P., J.D. Mayer, S. Goldman, C. Turvey, and T. Palfai. 1995. Emotional attention, clarity, and repair: Exploring emotional intelligence using the Trait Meta-Mood Scale.

In *Emotion, disclosure, and health*. Ed. J.W. Pennebaker. Washington DC: American Psychological Association.

Schmidt, F.L. 1992. What do data really mean? Research findings, meta-analysis, and cumulative knowledge in psychology. *American Psychologist* 47:1173–81.

Schmidt, F.L., and J.E. Hunter. 1996. Measurement error in psychological research: Lessons from 26 research scenarios. *Psychological Methods* 1:199–223.

Schutte, N.S., J.M. Malouff, L.E. Hall, D.J. Haggerty, J.T. Cooper, and C.J. Golden. 1998. Development and validation of a measure of emotional intelligence. *Personality and Individual Differences* 25:167–77.

Van Rooy, D.L., A. Alonso, and C. Viswesvaran. 2005. Group differences in emotional intelligence test score: Theoretical and practical implications. *Personality and Individual Differences* 38:689–700.

Van Rooy, D.L., and C. Viswesvaran. 2004. Emotional Intelligence: A Meta-Analytic Investigation of predictive Validity and Nomological Net. *Journal of Vocational Behavior* 65:71–95.

Van Rooy, D.L., C. Viswesvaran, and P. Pluta. in press. An examination of construct validity: What is this thing called emotional intelligence? *Human Performance*

Wong, C.S., and K.S. Law. 2002. The effect of leader and follower emotional intelligence on performance and attitudes: An exploratory study. *The Leadership Quarterly* 13:243–74.

Zeidner, M., G. Matthews, R.D. Roberts, and C. MacCann. 2003. Development of emotional intelligence: Towards a multi-level investment model. *Human Development* 46:69–96.

—— 19 ——

The Anatomy of Emotional Intelligence and Implications for Educating People to be Emotionally Intelligent

Antoine Bechara, Antonio R. Damasio and Reuven Bar-On

Introduction

Recent years have witnessed a surge in research focusing on the important role that emotions play in daily life. This represents a dramatic shift in neuroscience research, which has largely ignored the part emotions play in areas such as problem solving, personal judgement and decision making. There remains a popular notion that logical calculation forms the basis of sound decisions, and many people continue to believe that emotions can only cloud the mind and interfere with good judgement. But what if these notions were wrong and had no scientific basis? What if good decision making, in fact, *depended* on the effective processing of emotions? The study of decision making in neurological patients, who can no longer process emotional information normally, suggests just that. Given the importance of emotion in many aspects of human behavior, the understanding of cognition and performance requires a far greater knowledge of the neurobiology of emotion and of EI.

Although there are many competing conceptualizations of EI (Mayer, Salovey & Caruso 2000), the *Encyclopedia of Applied Psychology* (Spielberger 2004) suggests that the three most popular conceptual models are those proposed by Bar-On (1997), Goleman (1998), and Mayer and Salovey (1997). We have selected the Bar-On model to conceptually frame our discussion in this chapter because this comprehensive conceptualization of the EI construct offers an accurate description of the psychosocial domain of our research in this area (see, for example, Bar-On, Tranel, Denburg & Bechara 2003; Bechara & Bar-On in press; Bechara, Damasio & Damasio 2000; Bechara, Tranel & Damasio 2000). Based on the Bar-On model (Bar-On 1997b; 2000; 2006), EI is defined as a multifactorial cross-section of interrelated emotional and social competencies that influence our ability to cope with daily demands and challenges effectively. These competencies have been described fully in preceding chapters in this book. The concept of EI is closely related to the concept of social intelligence, and the literature reveals various attempts to combine the emotional and social components of the underlying construct (see, for example, Bar-On 1988; 1997b; 2000; Gardner 1983; Saarni 1990). In this chapter, we therefore interchangeably refer to this wider construct as 'emotional-social intelligence' as well as 'emotional intelligence', which is currently in more popular usage.

In the current chapter, we review the scientific evidence for a neural system that governs emotional intelligence that is distinct from cognitive intelligence. We present research findings demonstrating that:

- the neural systems that govern emotional intelligence overlap with neural systems subserving the processing of emotions but not with the neural systems associated with cognitive intelligence

- damage to the neural structures that subserve emotions and feelings, but not those subserving cognitive intelligence, is associated with changes in emotional processing, emotional intelligence, personal judgement in decision-making, and social functioning.

We also address the role of development and education in strengthening these neural systems—neuroplasticity—as they form the basis of emotional and social behavior which is driven by emotional intelligence.

The Anatomy of Emotions and Feelings

Suppose that a person you are in love with brings you flowers. This simple act may cause your heart to race, your skin to flush and your facial muscles to contract into a smile, which is the physical expression of happiness. The encounter may also be accompanied by bodily sensations such as hearing your own heartbeat, sensing butterflies in your stomach and the like. There is an additional kind of sensation that accompanies these physical sensations, which is the *emotional feeling* of love and elation directed towards your loved one. Neuroscientists and philosophers have long debated whether these two sensations—that is, bodily sensations or **emotions,** and emotional feelings or **feelings**—are fundamentally the same or different.

From a psychological viewpoint, James-Lange (James 1884) proposed that emotions and feelings are essentially the same and inseparable, while philosophers have traditionally argued that they are different. More recent neuroscientific evidence, such as that provided by Craig (2002), has empirically confirmed the theoretical view of James-Lange that neural systems supporting the perception and sensation of bodily states (emotions) provide a fundamental and inseparable ingredient for the subjective experience of emotions (feelings). More specifically, these findings suggest that the anterior insular cortex plays an important role in mapping bodily states and translating them into emotional feelings.

The view of Damasio (1999; 2003) is consistent with this notion, although it suggests further that emotional feelings are not just about the body but about things in the world as well. In other words, sensing changes in the body requires neural systems in which the anterior insular cortex is a critical substrate. However, the feelings that accompany emotions require additional brain regions. Damasio (1994; 1999; 2003) suggests that feelings emerge into conscious awareness through the representation of bodily changes in relation to the object or event that has triggered those changes. This **second-order mapping** of the relationship between organism and object occurs in brain regions that can integrate information about the body with information about the world.

According to Damasio (1994; 1999; 2003), there is a distinction between emotions and feelings in spite of the fact that they are governed by the same neural circuitry. Emotions are a collection of changes in body and brain states triggered by a dedicated brain system that responds to the content of our perceptions of a particular occurrence. The physiological changes range from those that are hidden from an external observer—such as heart rate, smooth-muscle contraction and endocrine release—to those that are perceptible to an external observer, for example skin color, body posture and facial expression. The signals generated by these changes in the brain produce additional changes that are mostly perceptible to the individual in whom they are enacted and which provide the essential ingredients for what is ultimately perceived of as a 'feeling'. Thus, emotions are what an outside observer can see or measure; and feelings are what the individual senses or subjectively experiences.

An emotion begins with the perception of an emotionally competent stimulus, which is the object of our emotion. Images related to this object are first represented in the brain's sensory processing systems. Regardless of how short this presentation is, signals related to its presence are then made available to a number of emotion-triggering sites in the amygdala and in the orbitofrontal/ventromedial prefrontal cortex. The amygdala is more involved in triggering emotions when the emotionally competent stimulus is in the immediate environment, while the orbitofrontal/ ventromedial prefrontal cortex is thought to be more engaged when the emotional object is recalled from memory (Bechara, Damasio & Damasio 2003). Laboratory experiments suggest that the amygdala represents a critical substrate in the neural system necessary for triggering emotional states from primary inducers (Bechara et al. 2003). **Primary inducers** can be either pleasant or aversive in nature; and once they are activated, they automatically, quickly and obligatorily elicit an emotional response. **Secondary inducers,** by contrast, are activated by the recall of an emotional event, that is, by thoughts and memories about the primary inducer. When they are brought to working memory, they gradually begin to elicit an emotional response.

With regard to Figure 19.1, information related to the emotionally competent object is represented in one or more of the brain's sensory processing systems. This information is made available to the amygdala and the orbitofrontal cortex, where emotions are triggered. The activation sites include the hypothalamus, the basal forebrain and nuclei in the brainstem tegmentum. Visceral sensations reach the anterior insular cortex by passing through the brainstem. Feelings result from the re-representation of changes in the viscera in relation to the object or event that prompted them. The anterior cingulate cortex is the site where this second-order map is realized.

In order to create an emotional state, the activity in the triggering sites must be transmitted to activation sites by means of neural connections. These sites are situated in **visceral motor structures** found in the hypothalamus, basal forebrain and brainstem tegmentum.

Feelings result from neural patterns that represent changes in the body's response to an emotional object, which is the emotionally competent stimulus.

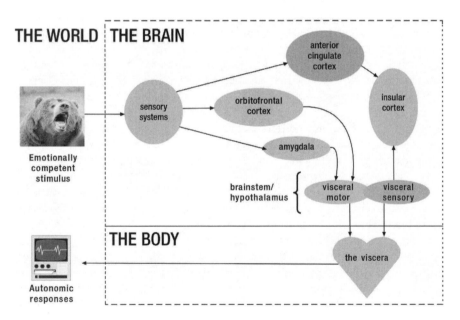

Figure 19.1   Information related to the emotionally competent object passes the brain's sensory processing systems and is made available to the amygdala and the orbitofrontal cortex, where emotions are triggered. The activation sites include the hypothalamus and nuclei in the brainstem. Visceral sensations reach the anterior insular cortex by passing through the brainstem. Feelings result from the re-representation of changes in the viscera in relation to the object that prompted them. The anterior cingulate cortex is the site where this second-order map is realized.

Signals from bodily states are relayed back to the brain, and neural representations of these states are formed in **visceral sensory structures** found in the brainstem tegmentum.

Representations of these bodily signals also form in the insular and somatosensory cortex primarily on the right side of the brain, as shown in Figure 19.1. The anterior insular cortex plays a special role in mapping visceral states and in bringing signals to conscious awareness.

As touched on above, in Damasio's view (1994; 1999; 2003), feelings arise into conscious awareness through the neural representation of bodily changes in relation to the emotional object, present or recalled, that triggered the bodily changes. A **first-order mapping** of 'self' is supported by structures in the brainstem, insular cortex and somatosensory cortex. Additional regions, such as the anterior cingulate cortex, are required for the above mentioned second-order mapping of the relationship between organism and emotional object, as well as for the integration of information about the body with information about the world.

Disturbances in Emotional Experience Related to Focal brain Damage

There are various disturbances affecting emotional experience that are associated with focal lesions found in the above mentioned structures; these disturbances demonstrate the role of the specific neural structures in processing information about emotions, feelings and social behavior. Figure 19.2 illustrates the locations in which the following disturbances are to be found.

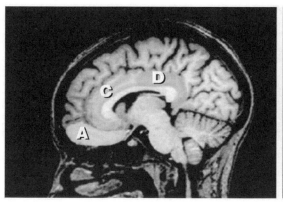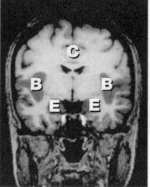

Figure 19.2   Brain regions implicated in emotional experience include orbitofrontal cortex (A), insular cortex (B), and anterior (C) and posterior (D) cingulate cortices. The amygdala is E.

(Source: modified from Dolan 2002.)

Disturbances associated with damage to the amygdala (E in Figure 19.2)

Clinical observations of patients with bilateral amygdala damage reveal that these patients express emotional 'lopsidedness', in which negative emotions such as anger and fear are less frequent and less intense than are positive emotions (Damasio 1999). Several laboratory experiments have also identified similar problems in these patients that are related to processing emotional information (Adolphs, Tranel & Damasio 1998; Adolphs, Tranel, Damasio & Damasio 1995; LaBar, LeDoux, Spencer & Phelps 1995; Phelps, LaBar, Anderson et al. 1998). When the damage occurs early in life, the individuals grow up to exhibit abnormal social behavior (Adolphs et al. 1995; Tranel & Hyman 1990). Amygdala damage also interferes with the emotional response to cognitive information. Examples of this type of response are learned reactions to 'winning' or 'losing' something of value that immediately, automatically and involuntarily elicits an emotional response. Patients typically fail to trigger emotional responses in reaction to winning or losing money, for example (Bechara, Damasio, Damasio et al. 1999).

Findings from functional neuro-imaging studies corroborate those from lesion studies with respect to consistently revealing amygdala activation in response to winning and losing various sums of money (see, for example, Zalla, Koechlin, Pietrini et al. 2000). When subjects are asked to solve a series of problems, amygdala activation is also found to be associated with the 'aha!' reaction to finding the correct solution to a given problem (Parsons & Oshercon 2001).

Disturbances associated with damage to the insular and somatosensory cortex (B in Figure 19.2)

The typical symptom of patients with damage to the right insular/somatosensory cortex is anosognosia (see Figure 19.3), which is reduced self-awareness and denial of the patients' physical condition. They are typically apathetic and placid, and appear unconcerned about the severity of their condition. Moreover, numerous studies have noted that these patients experience difficulty in identifying emotions in the facial expressions of other people (see, for example, Adolphs, Damasio, Tranel & Damasio 1996). The patients also show severe impairment in judgement and failure to observe social conventions (Damasio 1994).

Evidence from functional neuro-imaging studies also suggests that the insular/somatosensory cortex is activated in experiments involving the generation of feeling states (Damasio, Grabowski, Bechara et al. 2000; Dolan 2002; Maddock 1999).

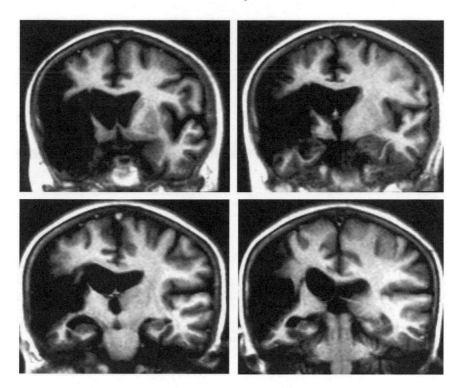

Figure 19.3   Coronal sections through the brain of a patient suffering from anosognosia. This section shows extensive damage in the right parietal region that includes the insular and somatosensory cortex (SII, SI).

Disturbances associated with damage to the orbitofrontal/ ventromedial prefrontal cortex and anterior cingulate cortex (A and C in Figure 19.2)

Patients with orbitofrontal/ventromedial prefrontal cortex damage exhibit varying degrees of disturbances in emotional experience, depending on the location and extent of the damage. If the damage is localized, especially in the anterior orbitofrontal region, the patient typically exhibits various changes in emotional experience and social functioning. Previously well-adapted individuals become unable to observe basic social conventions and to decide advantageously on personal matters; their ability to effectively experience emotions and express feelings in a socially appropriate manner also becomes compromised (Bechara et al. 2000; Bechara, Tranel & Damasio 2002). If the damage is more extensive, especially when it involves parts of the anterior cingulate cortex, patients exhibit additional problems of impulse control, lack of inhibition and antisocial behavior.

Findings from functional neuro-imaging studies are also consistent with the lesions' results. These studies have consistently shown activity in the orbitofrontal/ventromedial prefrontal cortex and anterior cingulate cortex during the recall and imagery of personal emotional events (Damasio et al. 2000; Lane 2000; Lane, Reiman, Ahern et al. 1997; Lane & McRae 2004; Mayberg, Liotti, Brannan et al. 1999).

Development of the Neural Systems Governing Emotions and Feelings

The normal development of the amygdala represents a logical, necessary step in the normal development of the orbitofrontal system, which is of key importance in generating emotional states from secondary inducers and converting emotions into feelings. When the amygdala is damaged, primary inducers cannot transmit signals to secondary inducers in the insular/somatosensory cortex and begin to convert internal emotional states into conscious feelings about ourselves and the world around us.

There are two types of developmental abnormalities that lead to distorted brain representations of emotional/feeling states, which in turn lead to abnormal cognition and behavior, especially in the areas of personal judgement and decision-making:

1. **Neurobiological abnormality** may be associated with:

    a. abnormal receptors connected with the triggering or detection of emotional signals at the level of the viscera and internal milieu

    b. abnormal peripheral neural and endocrine systems related to the transmission of emotional signals from the viscera and internal milieu to the brainstem tegmentum

    c. abnormal neural systems involved in the triggering or building of representations of emotional/feeling states.

2. **Environmental abnormality** relates specifically to social learning, that is, learning how to interact with others and to observe acceptable social conventions.

Although both types of abnormalities are difficult to discern from each other at the behavioral level, they are distinguishable at the physiological level. We argue that individuals with environmental abnormalities are capable of triggering emotional states, because they possess the basic *capacity* to empathize, feel remorse and fear the potentially negative consequences of their actions. By contrast, individuals with neurobiological abnormalities are unable to trigger emotional states because they lack the basic neurological capacity to do so. Such individuals cannot:

- effectively understand and control emotions
- express feelings constructively
- empathize with others

- solve problems of a personal and interpersonal nature
- relate well with people and adhere to basic social conventions.

The distinction between the two abnormalities has important social and legal implications. Individuals whose abnormal neural representations of emotional/ feeling states relate to inefficient social learning might be able to reverse this abnormality and theoretically 'unlearn' antisocial behavior once they are exposed to proper learning contingencies. However, individuals with underlying neurobiological abnormalities are expected to demonstrate repeated and persistent failures to learn from mistakes; and it follows that they are unlikely to benefit from rehabilitation.

Emotions, Feelings and Decision-Making in the Context of Emotional and Social Functioning

Personal and interpersonal situations are strongly associated with positive and negative emotions. Reward and punishment, pleasure and pain, happiness and sadness all produce changes in physical states, and these changes are expressed as emotions. Such emotional experiences often come into play when we are deliberating a decision and solving a problem of a personal or interpersonal nature. The emotions and resulting feelings provide the 'go', 'stop' and 'turn' signals needed for making advantageous decisions in life. In other words, the activation of these relevant brain representations of physical and emotional states provides biasing signals that identify various options and scenarios. The signals assist in the selection of advantageous responses from among an array of available options. Deprived of these signals, response options become more or less equalized, and the distinction between them becomes blurred. In the end, the result is often an inadequate and ineffective solution to a problem—quite simply, a bad choice. This explanation strongly suggests that decision-making is a process guided by emotions.

Our early studies employed an instrument known as the 'Iowa Gambling Task' (IGT) to assess the ability to exercise personal judgement in decision-making (Bechara, Damasio, Damasio & Anderson 1994; Bechara, Damasio, Tranel & Damasio 1997a; Bechara, Tranel, Damasio & Damasio 1997; Bechara et al. 1999; Bechara, Tranel & Damasio 2000). Briefly, the IGT comprises four decks of cards labelled A, B, C and D. The goal is to maximize profit in play money. Subjects are required to make a series of 100 card selections and are free to choose from any deck they wish. Every time the subjects select a card from decks A or B, they get $100; and every time they select a card from decks C or D, they receive $50. However, in each of the four decks, the subjects encounter unpredictable punishments in the form of monetary loss. The punishment is set to be higher in the high-paying decks A and B, and lower in the low-paying decks C and D. Decks A and B are disadvantageous, or risky, because they cost more in the long run—that is, the subject loses $250 every ten cards. Decks C and D are advantageous, or safe, because they result in an overall gain in the long run—that is, the subject wins $250 every ten cards.

In a number of seminal studies in this area (Bechara et al. 1994; Bechara et al. 1997a; Bechara et al. 1997b), we investigated the performance on the IGT of healthy individuals and of patients with brain lesions along the neural circuitry that governs emotional experience and processing. The non-clinical sample learned to avoid the risky decks A and B and choose the safe decks C and D. In sharp contrast, patients with damage in brain regions that are critical for processing emotions did not avoid the risky decks A and B. They continued to choose decks A and B and make disadvantageous choices. Based on these results, we suggested that the patients' performance profile is comparable to their real-life inability to decide advantageously.

In follow-up studies, we determined that the reason for the brain-damaged patients' failing to learn to make the right decisions was not due to cognitive deficit or limitation, but rather due to a deficit they have in processing emotional information linked to prior experience with reward and punishment (Bechara, Tranel, Damasio & Damasio 1996). To determine this, we added a physiological measure to the IGT study. The goal was to examine the generation of emotional signals while the subjects were making decisions. We compared a non-clinical control group with patients with damage to the orbitofrontal/ventromedial prefrontal cortex as they performed the IGT while we recorded their electrodermal activity. As the body begins to change after a thought, and as a given emotion begins to be enacted, the autonomic nervous system starts to increase the activity in the skin's sweat glands. Although this activity is relatively small and not observable by the naked eye, it can be amplified and polygraphically recorded, thereby providing an indirect measure of the emotion experienced by the subject.

Both the controls and the brain-damaged patients generated electrodermal activity after they were told that they had won or lost money. However, the most important difference between the two groups was that the non-clinical sample, as they became experienced with the task, began to generate electrodermal activity *prior* to the selection of a card, that is, during the time when they were pondering from which deck to choose. This anticipatory electrodermal activity was more pronounced before they picked a card from the risky decks A and B. We argue that this represents a 'gut feeling' that warned the controls against selecting cards from the risky decks. The brain-damaged patients failed to generate such anticipatory electrodermal activity before selecting the risky cards. These findings support the notion that decision making is indeed guided by emotional signals, or gut feelings, generated in the anticipation of future events.

The Neurological Substrate of EI

Almost every patient with damage to the brain regions that we describe here as important for processing emotional information—that is, the amygdala, insular/

somatosensory cortex, orbitofrontal/ventromedial prefrontal cortex and anterior cingulate cortex—tends to exhibit problems in:

- experiencing emotions and expressing feelings
- exercising good judgement and making advantageous decisions
- observing social convention.

By contrast, patients with damage in areas that are not included in this specific neural circuitry may express a variety of problems related to perception, memory and cognition. However, they seldom experience the problems listed above. Based on these observations, we decided to conduct a study to test the hypotheses that EI is different from cognitive intelligence and that damage to the neural structures that govern emotions and feelings, but not those that are directly associated with cognitive intelligence, are expected to lead to low scores on measures of EI, personal judgement in decision-making and social functioning but not on measures of cognitive intelligence.

In this study (Bar-On et al. 2003), the experimental group consisted of patients with focal brain lesions in areas known to be critical for the processing of emotions and feelings; and the control group consisted of patients with similar-size lesions outside of those critical areas. The experimental and control groups were matched with respect to gender, age and level of education. We used four types of measures in examining these patients:

1. The EQ-i for assessing EI (Bar-On 1997a; 1997b; 2004).
2. Standardized neuropsychological tests for assessing cognitive intelligence, perception, memory and executive functioning (for details, see Bar-On et al. (2003)).
3. The IGT for assessing personal judgement in decision-making (Bechara et al. 1994).
4. Semi-structured interviews for assessing social functioning (Tranel, Bechara & Denburg 2002).

The results of this study were interesting. In addition to a lack of significant difference between the experimental and control groups regarding the level of cognitive intelligence, no significant correlation was found between cognitive intelligence and emotional intelligence for the clinical sample examined. In striking contrast to their unimpaired cognitive intelligence, post-morbid emotional and social functioning was found to be significantly worse for the experimental group when compared with the control group. Most importantly, the experimental group subjects exhibited significantly lower EI than those in the control group. The findings furthermore demonstrated that EI is significantly related to the ability to exercise personal judgement in decision-making. We also found that the experimental group's personal judgement got worse rather than better as time passed—that is, they were making increasingly disadvantageous decisions.

The findings from the lesion studies summarized here are supported by functional neuro-imaging studies that have identified activity related to key aspects of EI, such as emotional self-awareness in the same area of the orbito-frontal/ventromedial prefrontal cortex and anterior cingulate cortex (Lane 2000; Lane & McRae 2004). While this confluence of findings indicates that the orbito-frontal area of the ventromedial prefrontal cortex governs key aspects of EI, the site of major activity associated with cognitive intelligence appears to be situated primarily in the dorsolateral prefrontal cortex (Duncan 2001). Not only are the neural circuitries that govern emotional intelligence and cognitive intelligence situated in different areas of the brain, there also is a low degree of correlation between these two types of intelligence, as has been demonstrated here and elsewhere (Bar-On 2004; Van Rooy & Viswesvaran 2004; Van Rooy, Pluta & Viswesvaran in press). Both sources of evidence, neurological and statistical, indicate that emotional and cognitive intelligence represent different types of intelligence.

Conclusion

The findings presented in this chapter indicate that the neural circuitry that governs emotional experience and processing also subserves key aspects of EI. Additionally, these findings offer strong evidence that there is a difference between emotional intelligence and cognitive intelligence. Both aspects of human intelligence are not only governed by different neurological areas of the brain, as was shown, but they also fail to demonstrate a statistically strong correlation. We have also shown that patients with injury to the neural circuitry subserving emotions and feelings exhibit low EI according to the research findings presented, which additionally suggests that this circuitry governs EI.

Based on the studies presented, the four key elements of the neural circuitry that governs EI are the:

1. amygdala
2. insular and somatosensory cortex
3. orbitofrontal/ventromedial prefrontal cortex
4. anterior cingulate cortex.

We now summarize the major findings related to these specific neural structures.

Amygdala (E in Figure 19.2)

The amygdala is 'wired', or programmed, to respond immediately to potentially dangerous threats in the individual's environment. It is the central neurological component of the human alarm system dedicated to survival in that it is capable of initiating the 'fight or flight' reaction to threat. The amygdala is the key element in the neural circuitry integrally associated with the **emotional self-awareness** component of EI. It is the first link between the initial awareness of emotions, the creation of feelings related to those emotions, and the control of emotions and expression of feelings. As such, the amygdala represents the neurological foundation of EI.

Insular and somatosensory cortex (B in Figure 19.2)

The right insular cortex and adjoining lateral somatosensory cortex map emotions and convert them into feelings. This is one of the vital sites for enhancing emotional self-awareness, which begins in the amygdala; and it represents the neurological basis for empathizing with others as well as adhering to social conventions. These neural structures provide the anatomical basis for the social awareness component of EI often referred to as **'empathy'**.

Orbitofrontal/ventromedial prefrontal cortex (A in Figure 19.2)

This structure is the neurological site that governs the expression of feelings, social interaction and behavior, as well as interpersonal problem-solving, which includes the ability to exercise personal judgement in decision-making. These emotional-social intelligence factors correspond, respectively, to what is often referred to as **'emotional expression'**, **'social interaction and behavior'** and **'interpersonal problem-solving'** in the EI literature.

Anterior cingulate cortex (C in Figure 19.2)

This is the cortical site where feelings develop into full conscious awareness through the representation of bodily changes that are detected in and transmitted from the insular/somatosensory cortex. In addition to contributing to the **emotional regulation** component of EI, the anterior cingulate contributes to the non-destructive expression of feelings and adherence to social conventions. Together with the orbitofrontal/ventromedial prefrontal cortex, the anterior cingulate cortex represents the 'intelligence' component of emotional intelligence more than any other element of the neural circuitry that governs emotions.

The above findings offer neurological support for most of the key components of the Bar-On model of emotional-social intelligence (Bar-On 2000). As such, the neurological mapping of the key components of this model appear to be as follows:

- **Emotional self-awareness** is governed primarily by the amygdala together with the insular/somatosensory cortex and anterior cingulate cortex.
- **Impulse control** is governed by the anterior cingulate cortex.
- **Assertiveness** is governed primarily by the orbitofrontal/ventromedial prefrontal cortex together with the anterior cingulate cortex.

- **Empathy** is governed primarily by the insular/somatosensory cortex together with the orbitofrontal/ventromedial prefrontal cortex.
- **Problem-solving** is governed by the orbitofrontal/ventromedial prefrontal cortex.
- **Interpersonal relationship** is governed primarily by the orbitofrontal/ventromedial prefrontal cortex together with the anterior cingulate cortex.
- **Social responsibility** is governed primarily by the orbitofrontal/ventromedial prefrontal cortex together with the anterior cingulate cortex.

This neurological mapping of the Bar-On model appears to support the existence of a more compact and generic six-factor model of EI comprising:

1. emotional self-awareness (Emotional self-awareness)
2. emotional control (Impulse control)
3. emotional expression (Assertiveness)
4. social awareness (Empathy)
5. social problem-solving (Problem-solving)
6. social interaction (Interpersonal relationship and Social responsibility).

The findings presented in this chapter could be applied to help people become more emotionally and socially intelligent.

For example, the findings might be applied in psycho-diagnostic assessment to pinpoint those emotional-social intelligence competencies that need to be strengthened in order to increase performance in various areas of life. As such, EI instruments could be included in the test battery administered by neuropsychologists as well as clinical and educational psychologists, in order to assess the individual's general level of emotional-social intelligence and to rule out or identify significant deficits in the specific areas of emotional self-awareness, emotional control, emotional expression, social awareness, social problem-solving and social interaction. Significantly low scores in any of these areas, especially if cognitive intelligence is found to be in the normal range, would suggest the need to further rule out brain damage in the neural circuitry governing these areas.

If such brain damage can be ruled out, it is reasonable to assume that the individual who has received low scores on the relevant scales could benefit from guided remedial intervention designed to enhance the specific emotional-social competencies involved.

Parents and educators should begin working, as early as possible, with young children to develop and strengthen the above mentioned key components of emotional-social intelligence. Schools should emphasize not only the enhancement of cognitive skills but also the development of these particular EI competencies and the improvement of performance in other areas of life in addition to scholastic performance. Several chapters in this book outline in detail how to implement such educational programs.

Irrespective of the specific didactic technique applied, it is of key importance to educate children at home and in the school to be more aware of:

- bodily sensations and what causes them
- how various emotions make us feel
- how to control emotions so they work for us and not against us
- how emotions contribute to personal and interpersonal problem-solving in order to make the right decisions and improve overall efficacy in various areas of life.

If applied from an early age, these activities could help to shape and strengthen important neural connections within the circuitry that governs emotional-social intelligence.

References

Adolphs, R., H. Damasio, D. Tranel, and A.R. Damasio. 1996. Cortical systems for the recognition of emotion in facial expressions. *The Journal of Neuroscience* 16(23): 7678–87.

Adolphs, R., D. Tranel, and A.R. Damasio. 1998. The human amygdala in social judgment. *Nature* 393(6684): 470–74.

Adolphs, R.,D. Tranel, H. Damasio, and A.R. Damasio. 1995. Fear and the human amygdala. *The Journal of Neuroscience* 15:5879–92.

Bar-On, R. 1988. The development of a concept of psychological well-being. Unpublished doctoral dissertation, Rhodes University, South Africa.

———. 1997a. *The Bar-On Emotional Quotient Inventory (EQ-i): A test of emotional intelligence.* Toronto, Canada: Multi-Health Systems.

———. 1997b. *The Bar-On Emotional Quotient Inventory (EQ-i): Technical manual.* Toronto, Canada: Multi-Health Systems.

———. 2000. Emotional and social intelligence: insights from the emotional quotient inventory (EQ-i). In Bar-On and Parker, pp. 363–88.

———. 2001. Emotional intelligence and self-actualization. In *Emotional intelligence in everyday life: A scientific inquiry.* Ed. J. Ciarrochi, J. Forgas, and J. Mayer. New York: Psychology Press.

———. 2004. The Bar-On Emotional Quotient Inventory (EQ-i): Rationale, description, and summary of psychometric properties. In *Measurment of emotional intelligence: Common ground and controversy.* Ed. G. Geher, pp. 111–42. Hauppauge, New York: Nova Science Publishers.

———. 2006. The Bar-On model of emotional-social intelligence (ESI). *Psicothema* 18.

Bar-On, R. and J.D.A. Parker, eds. *Handbook of Emotional Intelligence.* San Francisco: Jossey-Bass.

Bar-On, R., D. Tranel, N. Denburg, and A. Bechara. 2003. Exploring the neurological substrate of emotional and social intelligence. *Brain* 126:1790–1800.

Barrash, J., D. Tranel, and S.W. Anderson. 2000. Acquired personality disturbances associated with bilateral damage to the ventromedial prefrontal region. *Developmental Neuropsychology* 18:355–81.

Bechara, A., and R. Bar-On. in press. The neurological substrates of emotional and social intelligence: Evidence from patients with focal brain lesions. In *Essays in social neuroscience*. Ed. J.T. Cacioppo and G.G. Bernston. Cambridge, MA: MIT Press.

Bechara, A., A.R. Damasio, H. Damasio, and S.W. Anderson. 1994. Insensitivity to future consequences following damage to human prefrontal cortex. *Cognition* 50:7–15

Bechara, A., H. Damasio, and A.R. Damasio. 2000. Emotion, decision-making, and the orbitofrontal cortex. *Cerebral Cortex* 10(3): 295–307.

———. 2003. The role of the amygdala in decision-making. In *The Amygdala in Brain Function: Basic and Clinical Approaches* vol. 985. Ed. P. Shinnick-Gallagher, A. Pitkanen, A. Shekhar, and L. Cahill, pp. 356–69. New York: Annals of the New York Academy of Science.

Bechara, A., H. Damasio, A.R. Damasio, and G.P. Lee. 1999. Different contributions of the human amygdala and ventromedial prefrontal cortex to decision-making. *The Journal of Neuroscience* 19(13): 5473–81.

Bechara, A., H. Damasio, D. Tranel, and A.R. Damasio. 1997a. Deciding advantageously before knowing the advantageous strategy. *Science* 275:1293–95.

Bechara, A., D. Tranel, and A.R. Damasio. 2000. Poor judgment in spite of high intellect: Neurological evidence for emotional intelligence. In Bar-On and Parker.

———. 2002. The somatic marker hypothesis and decision-making. In *Handbook of Neuropsychology: Frontal Lobes* 2nd ed., vol. 7. Ed. F. Boller and J. Grafman, pp. 117–43. Amsterdam: Elsevier.

Bechara, A., D. Tranel, H. Damasio, R. Adolphs, C. Rockland, and A.R. Damasio. 1995. Double dissociation of conditioning and declarative knowledge relative to the amygdala and hippocampus in humans. *Science* 269:1115–18.

Bechara, A., D. Tranel, H. Damasio, and A.R. Damasio. 1996. Failure to respond autonomically to anticipated future outcomes following damage to prefrontal cortex. *Cerebral Cortex* 6:215–25

Bechara, A., D. Tranel, H. Damasio, and A.R. Damasio. 1997b. An anatomical system subserving decision-making. *Society for Neuroscience Abstracts* 23:495.

Craig, A.D. 2002. How do you feel? Interoception: the sense of the physiological condition of the body. *Nature Reviews Neuroscience* 3:655–66.

Damasio, A.R. 1994. *Descartes' error: Emotion, reason, and the human brain.* New York: Grosset/Putnam.

———. 1999. *The feeling of what happens: Body and emotion in the making of consciousness.* New York: Harcourt Brace & Company.

———. 2003. *Looking for Spinoza: Joy, sorrow, and the feeling brain.* New York: Harcourt, Inc.

Damasio, A.R., T.G. Grabowski, A. Bechara, H. Damasio, L.L.B. Ponto, J. Parvizi, et al. 2000. Subcortical and cortical brain activity during the feeling of self-generated emotions. *Nature Neuroscience* 3(10): 1049–56.

Dolan, R.J. 2002, November 8. Emotion, cognition, and behavior. *Science* 298:1191–94.

Duncan, J. 2001. An adaptive coding model of neural function in the prefrontal cortex. *Nature Reviews Neuroscience* 2:820–29.

Gardner, H. 1983. *Frames of mind.* New York: Bantam Books.

Goleman, D. 1998. *Working with emotional intelligence.* New York: Bantam Books.

James, W. 1884. What is an emotion? *Mind* 9:188–205.

LaBar, K.S., J.C. Gatenby, J.C. Gore, J.E. LeDoux, and E.A. Phelps. 1998. Human amygdala activation during conditioned fear acquisition and extinction: A mixed-trial fMRI study. *Neuron* 20:937–45.

LaBar, K.S., J.E. LeDoux, D.D. Spencer, and E.A. Phelps. 1995. Impaired fear condition-ing following unilateral temporal lobectomy in humans. *Journal of Neuroscience* 15(10): 6846–55.

Lane, R.D. 2000. Levels of emotional awareness: Neurological, psychological, and social perspectives. In Bar-On and Parker, pp. 171–91.

Lane, R.D., K. McRae. 2004. Neural substrates of conscious emotional experience: A cognitive-neuroscientific perspective. In *Consciousness, emotional self-regulation and the brain.* Ed. Beauregard M. Amsterdam and John Benjamins, pp. 87–122.

Lane, R.D., E.M. Reiman, G.L. Ahern, G.E. Schwartz, R.J. Davidson. 1997. Neuroana-tomical correlates of happiness, sadness, and disgust. *American Journal of Psychiatry* (154): 926–33.

LeDoux, J. 1996. *The Emotional Brain: The mysterious underpinnings of emotional life.* New York: Simon and Schuster.

Lee, G.P., J.G. Arena, K.J. Meador, J.R. Smith, D.W. Loring, and H.F. Flanigin. 1988. Changes in autonomic responsiveness following bilateral amygdalotomy in humans. *Neuropsychiatry, Neuropsychology, and Behavioral Neurology* 1:119–29.

Lee, G.P., A. Bechara, R. Adolphs, J. Arena, K.J. Meador, D.W. Loring, et al. 1998. Clinical and physiological effects of stereotaxic bilateral amygdalotomy for intrac-table aggression. *The Journal of Neuropsychiatry and Clinical Neurosceinces* 10:413–20.

Maddock, R.J. 1999. The retrosplenial cortex and emotion: new insights from functional neuroimaging of the human brain. *Trends in Neurosciences* 22(7): 310–20.

Malkova, L., D. Gaffan, and E.A. Murray. 1997. Excitotoxic lesions of the amygdala fail to produce impairment in visual learning for auditory secondary reinforcement but interfere with reinforcer devaluation effects in rhesus monkeys. *Journal of Neuroscience* 17(15): 6011–20.

Mayberg, H.S., M. Liotti, S.K. Brannan, S. McGinnis, R.K. Mahurin, P.A. Jerabek, J.A. Silva, J.L. Tekell, C.C. Martin, J.L. Lancaster, and P.T. Fox. 1999. Reciprocal limbic-cortical function and negative mood: Converging PET findings in depression and normal sadness. *American Journal of Psychiatry* (156): 675–82.

Mayer, J.D., P. Salovey, and D. Caruso. 2000. Models of emotional intelligence. In *Hand-book of intelligence.* Ed. R.J. Sternberg. Cambridge: Cambridge University Press, pp. 396–420.

Parsons, L., and D. Oshercon. 2001. New evidence for distinct right and left brain systems for deductive versus probabilistic reasoning. *Cerebral Cortex* 11:954–65.

Phelps, E.A., K.S. LaBar, A.K. Anderson, K.J. O'Connor, R.K. Fulbright, and D.D. Spencer. 1998. Specifying the contributions of the human amygdala to emotional memory: a case study. *Neurocase* 4(6): 527–40.

Saarni, C. 1990. Emotional competence: How emotions and relationships become inte-grated. In *Socioemotional development, Nebraska symposium on motivation* Vol. 36. Ed. R.A. Thompson. Lincoln, NE: University of Nebraska Press, pp.115–82.

Spielberger, C., Ed. 2004. *Encyclopedia of Applied Psychology.* San Diego, California: Academic Press.

Tranel, D., A. Bechara, and N.L. Denburg. 2002. Asymmetric functional roles of right and left ventromedial prefrontal cortices in social conduct, decision-making, and emotional processing. *Cortex* 38:589–612.

Tranel, D., and B.T. Hyman. 1990. Neuropsychological correlates of bilateral amygdala damage. *Archives of Neurology* 47:349–55.

Van Rooy, D.L., and C. Viswesvaran. 2004. Emotional intelligence: A meta-analytic investigation of predictive validity and nomological net. *Journal of Vocational Behavior* 65:71–95.

Van Rooy, D.L., C. Viswesvaran, and P. Pluta. in press. An examination of construct validity: What is this thing called emotional intelligence? *Human Performance.*

Whalen, P.J. 1998. Fear, vigilance, and ambiguity: Initial neuroimaging studies of the human amygdala. *Current Directions in Psychological Science* 7(6): 177–88.

Zalla, T., E. Koechlin, P. Pietrini, G. Basso, P. Aquino, A. Sirigu, et al. 2000. Differential amygdala responses to winning and losing: A functional magnetic resonance imaging study in humans. *European Journal of Neuroscience* 12(5): 1764–70.

20

Integrative Summary

Peter Salovey

It is my pleasure to offer these final words to this book, *Educating People to Be Emotionally Intelligent,* with its focus on the application of EI in school, the workplace and clinical settings. The contributors here—many of whom I am proud to count as friends—represent some of the most enlightened researchers, writers and educators in the fields of EI and SEL, and closely associated areas of inquiry. Their chapters are stimulating and inspiring.

Let us review what we have learned in this illuminating collection.

Chapters 1 and 2 are offered by Reuven Bar-On and Carolyn Saarni respectively. Bar-On has championed the idea of an 'EQ' since his days in graduate school and has developed a useful set of self-report, and other, measures designed to assess what he has collectively referred to as 'non-cognitive intelligence' (Bar-On 1997) and more recently as 'emotional-social intelligence' (Bar-On 2006). These measures predict important outcomes in myriad domains. In his chapter, Bar-On presents research findings showing that it is important to be emotionally intelligent and that such intelligence can be developed in various educational settings. In 1999, Saarni offered one of the first comprehensive theories of the development of children's emotional competencies, published in a highly lucid text. In her chapter, Saarni delineates the set of skills that need to be learned as children grow up in order to be considered emotionally intelligent. These skills represent an appropriate curriculum for any intervention effort.

In Chapter 3, Robin Stern and Maurice Elias extend our understanding of the development of EI to include the role of parenting. Their work indirectly addresses the controversy over the importance of parenting, as opposed to socialization by our peers, in the socio-emotional domain.

While Saarni focuses primarily on individual children, and Stern and Elias address the part played by parents, Patrikakou and Weissberg, in Chapter 4, look at the interactions between schools and families in promoting children's learning of all kinds—from traditional academics to social and emotional development. These authors also provide a useful set of core competencies for the socio-emotional area, namely, self-awareness, self-management, social awareness, relationship skills and responsible decision-making. Significantly, these competencies are arranged hierarchically, which suggests that it is difficult to imagine possessing the latter competencies without some proficiency in the ones that precede them.

Jonathan Cohen and Sandra Sandy, in Chapter 5, provide a view of SEL and its development that is complementary to the one provided in Chapter 6. Cohen and Sandy's view emphasizes skill-building, psychodynamics and character education, to some extent. They point out the importance of and challenges to high-quality, systematic evaluation of intervention efforts, and warn us of the dangers of piecemeal curricular programming. Moreover, Cohen and Sandy's CSEE has advanced the cause of teacher education for SEL, the development of school-based interventions, and resiliency training through their edited and authored books and other publications and programs.

It is Elias, Weissberg and their colleagues and students—together and in their individual capacity as investigators—who have advanced our understanding of SEL through school-based, skills-oriented programs, and via CASEL. I recommend that you refer to its comprehensive website (www.casel.org) for additional information. In Chapter 6, Joseph Zins, Maurice Elias and Mark Greenberg discuss CASEL's approach to working with schools directly as well as the range of possible intervention styles.

Similarly to Cohen and Sandy, Norris Haynes describes, in Chapter 7, some of the special challenges confronting those who aspire to intervene in inner-city schools with underserved communities and provides insight into the influential Comer School Development Program. Designed by Yale's James Comer, the program argues for overall school reform and systems change, and not merely new curricula. In his chapter, Haynes presents evidence demonstrating that SEL programs achieve positive personal, social and academic results.

In Chapter 8, Anabel Jensen, Karen McCown and Joshua Freedman describe the development of one of the earliest educational curricula, called 'Self-Science', which focused primarily on the advancement of emotional and social skills and competencies at the Nueva School in Hillsborough, California. These ideas have been disseminated worldwide through the authors' praiseworthy publications and outreach organization, Six Seconds. They provide many useful 'tips' that maximize the chances of the introduction of a new curriculum being successful.

As an investigator who has come to SEL more recently, Marc Brackett argues in Chapter 9, with Bruce Alster, Charles Wolfe, Nicole Katulak and Edward Fale, that the development of EI in school-based curricula occurs through the building up of specific skills. The authors' approach is rooted in the EI model that John Mayer and I published some years ago—Brackett was Mayer's graduate student and is currently affiliated with my laboratory—and is especially note-worthy with regard to the assessment of learned competencies. Brackett has developed and published a well-received curriculum for middle-school students, Emotional Literacy in the Middle School, which is accompanied by a set of workshops for teachers and administrators. Preliminary data from several schools both in the US and the UK suggest that Brackett's approach will add meaningfully to interventions with middle-school populations—a group at particular risk for coping difficulties (Maurer, Brackett & Plain 2004). In line with the views of many other contributors to this book, Brackett and colleagues propose that directly working with teachers in an effective and professional way is critical to the success of EI intervention efforts.

Jacobus Maree and Queen Esther Mokhuane, in Chapter 10, provide observa-tions from the multicultural experiment that is contemporary South Africa to help us to understand the factors that facilitate or inhibit the adoption of new SEL curricula. These authors have adapted the principles promoted by CASEL and other groups in an attempt to meet the unique challenges of the South African educational scene.

Perhaps you have noticed that at this point the book shifts focus, to some extent, from the traditional social and emotional learning of children in schools to developing EI among adults in the workplace. Richard Boyatzis has argued for decades that competencies not well captured by traditional notions of intelli-gence or technical skills determine success at work, especially in management contexts. In Chapter 11, he describes the role of coaching in developing EI and, ultimately, leadership skills in such contexts. This baton then goes to Charles Wolfe, who describes in Chapter 12 how he uses the Mayer-Salovey model of EI in working with executives. His case studies are thought-provoking, and they complement more theoretical and empirical arguments for the importance of workplace EI.

Another well-known executive coaching approach is that taken by Geetu Bharwaney in the UK. In Chapter 13, she too provides useful exercises and suggestions for successful intervention and appropriate evaluation, but this time from the perspective of the Bar-On model of EI. One of the better-known examples of the way in which EI can be used company-wide to change a work-place culture is that of American Express. In Chapter 14, Doug Lennick provides a description of how this was done under the leadership of HR executive Kate Cannon in the 1980s. It is noteworthy that Lennick adds this important historical note: 'Cannon's work took place before more formal statements of the impor-tance of EI, a crisp definition of it or measures of individual competencies had appeared in the scientific literature'.

In the first article on EI that we wrote (Salovey & Mayer 1990), John Mayer and I argued that the usefulness of this construct would in part be determined by its providing a common language through which existing scholarship on indi-vidual differences in the ways in which individuals deal with their emotions and the emotions of other people could be discussed. One of the examples we used was alexithymia, an idea that had become popular in psychiatry and in the field of psychosomatic medicine but had not yet made its way over to mainstream psychological research on emotions, let alone school curricula or executive coaching. Yet, as Graeme Taylor and Helen Taylor-Allan comment in Chapter 15, alexithymia has been described and measured for more than fifty years and clearly represents a coping style that is 'at the lower pole of the EI continuum'. Its role in potentially diagnosing and treating various medical and psychiatric conditions is convincingly demonstrated in their chapter.

It is an idea that Lana Stohl, David Dangerfield, Jeremy Christensen, David Justice and Doug Mottonen pick up in Chapter 16. They present interesting findings demonstrating that EI can be applied in treating individuals with severe psychiatric disturbances. Stohl and her colleagues' use of computer skills training as the vehicle for developing emotional and social competencies is quite clever. The authors also show that their program significantly reduces the cost of psychiatric treatment.

This book draws to a close with two extremely useful chapters on the measurement of EI. Sarah Stewart-Brown and Laurel Edmunds, in Chapter 17, provide tools for assessing emotional and social competencies in pre-school and primary-grade children. And in Chapter 18, David Van Rooy and Chockalingam Viswesvaran present a similar survey of the adult assessment literature. Finally, in Chapter 19, Antoine Bechara, Antonio Damasio and Reuven Bar-On summarize a decade of neurological research, suggesting that the abilities and skills underlying EI are processed along a specific neural circuitry in the brain. These authors conclude with a fascinating idea of how this information might be used to educate people to be emotionally intelligent. It is Damasio, perhaps more clearly than anyone else, who has argued that the continued conceptual separation of emotion and cognition—especially the differentiation of them as irrational and rational, respectively—makes no neurological sense (Damasio 1994).

What is left that has not been said? Since our earliest article on EI (Salovey & Mayer 1990), we have been arguing that schools, families and employers should encourage the development of the following competencies:

- Perceiving emotions in ourselves and others.
- Understanding and expressing our emotions.
- Managing our emotions.
- Using our emotions as sources of creativity, problem-solving, decision-making and motivation.

(Salovey & Grewal 2005; Salovey & Sluyter 1997)

Moreover, it has been our contention that those of us who are able to master these competencies will deal better with the stresses of the classroom and school-yard and, eventually, the real world. We have also lobbied for the development of ways to assess these competencies and have made our own contributions to the growing arsenal of measurement tools (Mayer, Salovey & Caruso 2002; Mayer, Salovey, Caruso & Sitarenios 2003). At various points along the way, however, we have worried about the proliferation of tests, interventions and exuberant claims in the absence of convincing research findings (see, for example, Mayer and Cobb (2000)).

In the spirit of cautious optimism, I thought that in these closing comments I might suggest avenues for future work. It seems quite likely that well-designed SEL programs effectively promote children's emotional and social adjustment, and that EI can be developed among adults in the workplace through coaching, group-based interventions, or perhaps personal exploration. This much we know. What we now need to explore is exactly what it is about these programs that makes them effective. What are the active ingredients of programs that work? What kinds of school-based contexts allow programs to thrive or, alternatively, to ruin the best-designed programs? How long do these benefits last? And perhaps most significantly, can we generalize SEL competencies developed through school-based programs to other settings and life-tasks? Similar questions can be asked about interventions designed to improve EI in the workplace and in clinical settings.

Certainly CASEL, among others, has outlined some principles for effective programs (Payton, Graczyk, Wardlaw et al. 2000; Zins, Elias, Greenberg & Weissberg 2000). Such programs need to be theoretically based, comprehensive, multi-year and well integrated into the existing curriculum—or, I would add, workplace, organizational development and HR management programs. Successful programs are those that promote a caring school or organizational climate, teach a broad range of skills, and are implemented by a well-trained staff with adequate support from families and the larger community. Less clear, though, is precisely which skills we should promote. Programs range from working at the molecular level (by identifying emotional expressions in faces, for example), at the molar level (by resolving social conflicts through social problem-solving, for example), or at the global level (by developing character-based attributes such as honesty and trustworthiness, for example). Perhaps work at all of these levels is necessary.

Elsewhere, we have argued that a common denominator in every program might be a particular focus on skills that allow people to process and interpret emotion-laden information (Lopes & Salovey 2004). There is some evidence that the development of these skills is associated with lower levels of aggressive behaviors among young children (Rubin 1999), reduced substance abuse among teenagers (Trinidad & Johnson 2002), and enhanced psychological well-being and effective interpersonal relations among college students (Bar-On 2005; Brackett & Mayer 2003; Lopes, Salovey & Straus 2003; Lopes, Brackett, Nezlek et al. 2004). There is accumulating evidence showing that when children learn how to process emotions in themselves and in others—in other words, to read emotions in faces, understand emotional vocabulary and regulate their emotional expressions—peers, parents and teachers notice associated improvements in their social competence, resilience and adaptation (Eisenberg, Fabes, Guthrie & Reiser 2000; Halberstadt, Denham & Dunsmore 2001; Saarni 1999).

My colleagues and I have collected similar data, as have many others, showing that individuals who have these skills perform better at work (Lopes, Grewal, Kadis et al. in press). For example, employees of a US health insurance company, who worked in teams that were headed by a supervisor, completed measures of their EI. Later, these employees were asked to rate each other on the qualities they displayed at work, such as handling stress and conflict as well as displaying leadership potential. Supervisors were also asked to rate their employees. Employees with higher EI were rated by their colleagues as easier to deal with and more responsible for creating a positive work environment. Their supervisors rated them as more interpersonally sensitive, more tolerant of stress, more sociable and having greater potential for leadership. Furthermore, greater EI was related to a higher salary and to their ability to move up within the company.

Although the programs developed by the contributors to this book are well conceived and have been successfully implemented throughout the world, I would like to see teachers continue to consider ways of enhancing their students' emotional and social intelligence without necessarily having to rely on a program and little else. The same can be said for HR professionals. Teachers could use everyday classroom and schoolyard situations, and managers could use their daily interactions with the individuals who report to them to promote a richer appreciation of the importance of emotion and a more sophisticated repertoire of emotional and social skills. Naturally occurring conflicts and arguments represent one kind of teachable moment. But literature or history, too, can provide examples of bravery, persistence or equanimity in the face of intense stress and challenges. Athletics presents a wealth of opportunities: What better place than the gym or the sports field to learn how to win gracefully and to cope with the agony of defeat, not to mention learn more effective ways of working as a team?

I would like to close with a suggestion made by one of my collaborators, Paulo Lopes, who proposes that we help youth to relate to others by promoting a deeper understanding of the complexity of human nature and the challenges of difficult social situations that will hopefully produce social and emotional learning of more lasting value than will practicing a limited set of circumscribed skills. I suspect that the contributors to this book share this view, along with the hope that many of the challenges of postmodern society—such as gun violence, ethnic and racial prejudice, and international conflict—might be effectively addressed by focusing on the development of competencies in the youngest among us as well as reinforcing these skills in our co-workers.

References

Bar-On, R. 1997. *The Bar-On Emotional Quotient Inventory (EQ-i): A test of emotional intelligence.* Toronto, Canada: Multi-Health Systems.

————. 2005. The impact of emotional intelligence on subjective well-being. *Perspectives in Education* 23:41–61.

————. 2006. The Bar-On model of emotional-social intelligence (ESI). *Psicothema* 18.

Brackett, M.A., and J.D. Mayer. 2003. Convergent, discriminant, and incremental validity of competing measures of emotional intelligence. *Personality and Social Psychology Bulletin* 29:1147–58.

Damasio, A.R. 1994. *Descartes' error: Emotion, reason, and the human brain.* New York: Grosset/Putnam.

Eisenberg, N., R.A. Fabes., I.K. Guthrie, and M. Reiser. 2000. Dispositional emotionality and regulation: Their role in predicting quality of social functioning. *Journal of Personality and Social Psychology* 78:136–57.

Halberstadt, A.G., S.A. Denham, and J.C. Dunsmore. 2001. Affective social competence. *Social Development* 10:79–119.

Lopes, P.N., M.A. Brackett, J.B. Nezlek, A. Schütz, I. Sellin, and P. Salovey. 2004. Emotional intelligence and social interaction. *Personality and Social Psychology Bulletin* 30:1018–34.

Lopes, P.N., D. Grewal, J. Kadis, M. Gall, and P. Salovey. in press. Evidence that emotional intelligence is related to job performance and affect and attitudes at work. *Psicothema.*

Lopes, P.N., and P. Salovey. 2004. Toward a broader education: Social, emotional, and practical skills. In *Building school success on social and emotional learning.* Ed. J.E. Zins, R.P. Weissberg, M.C. Wang, and H.J. Walberg. New York: Teachers College Press.

Lopes, P.N., P. Salovey, and R. Straus. 2003. Emotional intelligence, personality, and the perceived quality of social relationships. *Personality and Individual Differences* 35:641–58.

Maurer, M., M. Brackett, and F. Plain. 2004. *Emotional literacy in the middle schools.* Port Chester, NY: Dude Press (an imprint of National Professional Resources, Inc.).

Mayer, J.D., and C.D. Cobb. 2000. Educational policy and emotional intelligence: Does it make sense? *Educational Psychology Review* 12:163–83.

Mayer, J.D., P. Salovey, and D. Caruso. 2002. *Mayer-Salovey-Caruso Emotional Intelligence Test (MSCEIT), Version 2.0.* Toronto, Canada: Multi-Health Systems.

Mayer, J.D., P. Salovey, D.R. Caruso, and G. Sitarenios. 2003. Measuring emotional intelligence with the MSCEIT V2.0. *Emotion* 3:97–105.

Payton, J.W., P.A. Graczyk, D.M. Wardlaw, M. Bloodworth, C.J. Tompsett, and R.P. Weissberg. 2000. Social and emotional learning: A framework for promoting mental health and reducing risk behavior in children and youth. *Journal of School Health* 70:179–85.

Rubin, M.M. 1999. Emotional intelligence and its role in mitigating aggression: A correlational study of the relationship between emotional intelligence and aggression in urban adolescents. Unpublished manuscript, Immaculata College, Immaculata, PA.

Saarni, C. 1999. *Developing emotional competence.* New York: Guilford Press.

Salovey, P., and D. Grewal. 2005. The science of emotional intelligence. *Current Directions in Psychological Science* 14:281–85.

Salovey, P., and Mayer, J.D. 1990. Emotional intelligence. *Imagination, Cognition, and Personality* 9:185–211.

Salovey. P., and D. Sluyter, eds. 1997. *Emotional development and emotional intelligence: Educational implications.* New York: Basic Books.

Trinidad, D.R., and C.A. Johnson. 2002. The association between emotional intelligence and early adolescent tobacco and alcohol use. *Personality and Individual Differences* 32:95–105.

Zins, J.E., M.J. Elias, M.T. Greenberg, and R. P. Weissberg. 2000. Promoting social and emotional competence in children. In *Preventing school problems—promoting school success: Strategies and programs that work.* Ed. K.M. Minke and G.C. Bear, pp. 71–99. Washington, DC: National Association of School Psychologists.

Index

The letter *f* following a page number denotes a figure.

About the Authors

BRUCE ALSTER began his educational career as a sixth-grade teacher in New York. Since then he has served as curriculum coordinator and assistant principal in a large urban district, and was the principal of the Brooklyn Avenue School on Long Island. He has also taught at Brooklyn College and Adelphi University. Currently he is middle-school principal of General Studies at the Flatbush Yeshiva in Brooklyn, supervises student teachers at Adelphi University, and consults with various schools on emotional intelligence. In his capacity as principal, he has applied emotional intelligence strategies to create educationally sound and emotionally secure learning environments.

REUVEN BAR-ON holds a research position at the University of Texas Medical Branch and has been involved in studying various aspects of emotional intelligence since 1980. He coined the term "EQ" (emotional quotient) in his doctoral dissertation submitted in 1985. This approach to describing emotional–social competence culminated in the creation of the Bar-On Emotional Quotient Inventory, the first measure of this construct to be published by a test publisher. The Bar-On model is described in the *Encyclopedia of Applied Psychology* as one of three major ones in the field of emotional intelligence. He has authored more than 20 publications on this topic.

ANTOINE BECHARA has focused his research on understanding the neural processes underlying decision-making. Together with Antonio and Hanna Damasio, he has conducted lesion studies on patients with amygdaloid, somatosensory-insular and prefrontal damage. His development of the Iowa Gambling Task has enabled investigators to detect these patients' elusive neurological impairment in the laboratory, measure it and investigate its possible causes. This research has drawn attention to the potential value of studying the neural basis of decision-making and emotional intelligence, and the relationship between them. It has facilitated this line of research in the laboratory through the use of structured tasks and psychometric instruments.

GEETU BHARWANEY is founder and managing director of EI World, a UK-based organization working in educational, health care and corporate settings. She is one of Europe's leaders in the field of emotional intelligence through building EI programs and proving measurable results with individuals and groups. Her work includes measuring emotional intelligence, researching the EI characteristics of high achievers and providing EI-based coaching and development. She is the author of *Emotionally Intelligent Living*.

RICHARD E. BOYATZIS is currently professor in the departments of Organizational Behavior and Psychology at Case Western Reserve University, and human resources at ESADE (Spain). He has consulted to a number of Fortune 500 companies and government agencies on selection, succession planning, management competencies and leadership development. He has authored and co-authored numerous publications on these and other topics, including *Primal Leadership: Realizing the Power of Emotional Intelligence* with Daniel Goleman and Annie McKee (2002), and *Resonant Leadership* with Annie McKee (2005).

MARC A. BRACKETT is an associate research scientist in the Department of Psychology at Yale University. He is also the associate director of Yale's Health, Emotion, and Behavior Laboratory, and a faculty fellow of the Edward Zigler Center in Child Development and Social Policy. He is the author, co-author or editor of more than three dozen scholarly publications, including three educational curricula: Emotional Literacy in the Middle School, Emotional Literacy in the Elementary School, and The Emotionally Intelligent Teacher. He regularly works with school systems and corporations worldwide in the areas of assessment, training and leadership development.

JEREMY CHRISTENSEN is the executive director of Alliance House and the former program coordinator for the Community Computer Education Program (CCEP) with Valley Mental Health. He is currently a consultant for CCEP and a clinical instructor in social work at the University of Utah. He has also been extensively involved in administering the Bar-On EQ-i to severely disturbed psychiatric patients, providing them with feedback and enhancing their emotional intelligence skills. He has presented research findings related to this work at various professional conferences.

JONATHAN COHEN is president of the Center for Social and Emotional Education, adjunct professor in Psychology and Education in Teachers College at Columbia University, founder and editor of the Teachers College Press *Social Emotional Learning* series, and a practicing clinical psychologist and psychoanalyst. Currently, he is focusing his research on school climate assessment and social, emotional, ethical and academic school improvement processes. He is the author of several publications, including *Educating Minds and Hearts* (1999) and *Caring Classrooms/Intelligent Schools* (2001), which both won the American Library Association's Best Academic Book award. He lectures and consults nationally and internationally.

ANTONIO R. DAMASIO is the David Dornsife professor of Neuroscience and director of the Brain and Creativity Institute at the University of Southern California. He was formerly at the University of Iowa as the Van Allen Distinguished Professor and head of the Department of Neurology. He is a member of the Institute of Medicine of the National Academy of Sciences, and a fellow at the American Academy of Arts and Sciences, the Bavarian Academy of Sciences and the European Academy of Sciences and Arts. He has authored numerous publications including *Descartes' Error, the Feeling of What Happens* and *Looking for Spinoza.*

DAVID E. DANGERFIELD is currently the CEO of Valley Mental Health, a community mental health centre serving over 20,000 individuals annually that has successfully applied the Bar-On Emotional Quotient Inventory as an assessment tool and intervention guide with severely disturbed psychiatric patients. He has served on many national and regional organizations, including the Mental Health Corporations of America, Utah Health and Hospital Association, and the Mental Health Risk Retention Group. He has also been on the faculty of three major universities and is a frequent consultant, guest lecturer and keynote speaker at mental health conferences across North America.

LAUREL EDMUNDS has worked as a teacher in the United Kingdom for over 16 years. Her doctoral research in childhood obesity prevention won the ASO Researcher Prize in 1999. Over the past 12 years, she has focused on the psychosocial aspects of childhood weight management and obesity prevention. She was a specialist advisor to the House of Commons and to the National Institute for Clinical Excellence. While at the University of Oxford, Dr. Edmunds, together with Dr. Sarah Stewart-Brown, was commissioned by the British Department of Education and Skills to survey measures of emotional-social competence for applicability nationwide.

MAURICE J. ELIAS is a professor in the psychology department at Rutgers University, director of the Rutgers Social-Emotional Learning Lab and the Developing Safe and Civil Schools prevention initiative, and acting chair on the Leadership Team at the Collaborative for Academic, Social and Emotional Learning. Among his many writings are *Emotionally Intelligent Parenting* (2000), *Raising Emotionally Intelligent Teenagers* (2002), *Social Decision-Making/Social Problem-Solving Curricula for Elementary and Middle School Students* (2006), *Bullying, Peer Harassment, and Victimization in the Schools:*

The Next Generation of Prevention (2003), and *The Educator's Guide to Emotional Intelligence and Academic Achievement: Social-Emotional Learning in the Classroom* (2006).

EDWARD M. FALE began his career in education as a high-school mathematics teacher. Since that time, he has served as an assistant high-school principal, junior-senior high-school principal and assistant superintendent, as well as superintendent of schools, a position he has held at Valley Stream for the past eight years. He also held an adjunct professorship in educational administration as well as supervision in safety education and mathematics. He has co-authored educational articles related to school boards and superintendence, and regularly presents at educational conferences.

JOSHUA M. FREEDMAN is director of the Six Seconds' Institute for Organizational Performance, which assists schools and businesses in applying emotional intelligence. Developing a worldwide network of emotional intelligence practitioners, he has helped launch EI programs in many countries, including Singapore, China, Indonesia, the Philippines, Mexico, Canada, the United States, Italy, Switzerland, the United Kingdom, Belgium and India. He is a co-author of the *Six Seconds Emotional Intelligence Assessment* and the *Organizational Vital Signs Climate Assessment*, and related training curricula including EQ for Families, The EQ Leader, The Inside Path to Change and Selling with EQ.

DANIEL GOLEMAN is co-director of the Consortium for Research on Emotional Intelligence in Organizations at the Graduate School of Applied and Professional Psychology at Rutgers University. He is one of the co-founders of the Collaborative for Academic, Social and Emotional Learning at the University of Illinois at Chicago. He wrote *Emotional Intelligence* (1995); *Working with Emotional Intelligence* (1998); *Primal Leadership: Learning to Lead with Emotional Intelligence* (2001); and, more recently, *Social Intelligence* (2006).

MARK T. GREENBERG holds the Bennett Endowed Chair in Prevention Research at Penn State's College of Health and Human Development. He is currently the director of the Prevention Research Center and serves in a leadership capacity for the Collaborative for Academic, Social, and Emotional Learning (CASEL). His research has focused on the role of individual, family and community-level factors in prevention and the role of emotional development in children's health and well-being. He received the Research Scientist Award from the Society for Prevention Research in 2002.

NORRIS M. HAYNES is professor and chairperson in the Counseling and School Psychology Department at Southern Connecticut State University and the founding director of the Center for Community and School Action Research. He is associate clinical professor at Yale's Child Study Center and a member of the CASEL Leadership Team. He was director of Research for the Comer School Development Program. Among his many publications are *Pathways to School Success: Leaving No Child Behind*; *How Social and Emotional Development Adds Up: Getting Results in Math and Science Education*; and *Rallying the Whole Village: The Comer Process for Reforming Education.*

ANABEL L. JENSEN is a professor at Notre Dame de Namur University and founding president of Six Seconds. Under her leadership, Six Seconds has delivered EQ certification courses in 20 countries, published elementary- and secondary-level affective education curricula, and launched Nexus, a series of international EQ conferences providing opportunities for e-networking for education and business audiences. In addition to authoring a number of books, articles and EI assessment tools for education and business, she has written a series for *Priorities* magazine and was interviewed on the Discovery Channel.

DAVID H. JUSTICE is a research specialist in the Research and Program Evaluation Department at Valley Mental Health (VMH). He has been involved in mental health data analysis for 13 years and has participated in the development of a state-wide mental health data system as well as the subsequent analysis and reporting of mental health service data. He is responsible for the analysis of service, cost and client outcome data for VMH clients. Since 2002 he has completed the data analysis for VMH's CCEP classes based on a comparison of pre- and post- EQ-i scores.

NICOLE A. KATULAK is a research associate in the Health, Emotion and Behavior Laboratory in the Department of Psychology at Yale University. She has co-published on emotional intelligence and health behavior motivation, and also facilitates in the training, implementation and quality assurance of emotional literacy programs.

DOUG LENNICK is a founding member of Lennick Aberman and formerly served as a senior advisor to Ken Chenault, CEO of American Express (AMEX). Although no longer employed full time, he retains the title of executive vice-president at American Express, where he successfully introduced a pioneering EI programme for 20,000 AMEX financial advisors. In addition to being a sought-after keynote speaker, he is frequently interviewed and quoted by the broadcast and print media including *Fortune, Wall Street Journal,* and *The New York Times.* His third book, *Moral Intelligence: Enhancing Business Performance and Leadership Success,* was released in 2005.

JACOBUS G. MAREE is a Professor of Education at Pretoria University and Editor of *Perspectives in Education.* He is internationally acknowledged for his work in career counselling, and his research focuses on optimizing the achievement of disadvantaged learners and providing cost-effective career facilitation. He is a highly rated researcher with the National Research Foundation in South Africa and was recently honoured with Exceptional Achiever status. As the author and co-author of more than 36 books and 80 articles and as the recipient of numerous awards for his research, he is frequently interviewed on radio and television.

KAREN MCCOWN founded the pioneering and world-renowned Nueva School in California in 1967 to demonstrate that emotional development and academic achievement can flourish together. With a background in health education, she has worked with educators from around the world to create schools where students pursue both knowledge and wisdom. She was honoured as Educator of the Year by the California Association of the Gifted, and has presented at hundreds of symposia and conferences. She has served on a broad range of trustee and advisory boards for educational and mental health organizations.

QUEEN ESTHER M. MOKHUANE is professor of Psychology and head of the Department of Clinical Psychology at MEDUNSA (South Africa). Involved in teaching medical students and training clinical psychologists, her clinical interests and work with children led to her appointment to the Committee on the Rights of the Child (Geneva) where she served as vice-chairperson from 1999 to 2001. She is currently chairperson of both the Professional Board for Psychology and the Health Committee of the Health Professional Council, and is interim executive director of student affairs at the University of Limpopo in South Africa.

DOUG MOTTONEN is a licensed clinical social worker and currently associate director of Adult Services for Valley Mental Health (VMH) in Utah. He has served as the senior supervisor of the Community Computer Education Program (CCEP) at VMH since its inception. He is an adjunct faculty member of the Graduate School of Social Work at the University of Utah. He has been instrumental in demonstrating the applicability and usefulness of the EQ-i to a wide variety of clinical populations. Based on this extensive experience, he has presented his research findings to local and state conferences.

EVANTHIA N. PATRIKAKOU is a professor in the School of Education at DePaul University. She is also the director of the School-Family Partnership Program and a member of the Scientific Council of the Center on Innovation and Improvement. Her professional interests focus primarily on parent involvement and its effects on children's emotional, social and academic development, as well as the development of school-family programming to enhance home-school relations and children's growth. In addition to numerous peer-reviewed articles, she has recently authored a book entitled *School-Family Partnerships: Promoting the Social, Emotional, and Academic Growth of Children* (2005).

CAROLYN SAARNI has served as professor of Counseling at Sonoma State University in California since 1980. She is an internationally recognized scholar in developmental psychology, specializing in emotional development. Her social constructivist orientation is evident in her approach to emotional competence, defined as the demonstration of self-efficacy in emotion-eliciting social transactions. She has authored and co-authored numerous publications on emotional competence, the most recent being 'Emotional development: Action, communication, and understanding' in the *Handbook of Child Psychology*.

PETER SALOVEY is the Chris Argyris Professor of Psychology and the dean of Yale College at Yale University. His research has focused on the psychological significance and function of human moods and emotions, as well as on the application of social psychological principles motivating people to adopt behaviors that protect their health. He has published more than 250 articles and chapters, and he has authored, co-authored or edited 13 books including, most recently, *The Wisdom in Feeling: Psychological Processes in Emotional Intelligence, Key Readings in the Social Psychology of Health* and *The Emotionally Intelligent Manager*. He also co-authored the MSCEIT.

SANDRA V. SANDY is currently the director of Research for the Center for Social and Emotional Education. Previously, she was the director of Research for the International Center for Cooperation and Conflict Resolution and has taught graduate-level courses in conflict resolution theory. She developed the Peaceful Kids Educating Communities in Social Emotional Learning (ECSEL) program. She also serves as a consultant to a number of organizations on social-emotional education and conflict resolution, and has authored many peer-reviewed publications in this area. She is currently completing a book entitled *What the Heart Knows, the Brain Will Learn*.

ROBIN STERN is an educator, psychotherapist, author and consultant who has developed and implemented programs designed to promote personal and professional growth through self-awareness, emotional competence and ethical leadership. She is on the faculty at Teachers College (Columbia University) as well as at Hunter College's Leadership Center, where she teaches courses on emotional intelligence. She is the social-emotional learning specialist at The School at Columbia University, and serves on the board of directors of Educators for Social Responsibility and the Woodhull Institute for Ethical Leadership.

SARAH STEWART-BROWN is professor of Public Health and director of the Health Sciences Research Institute at Warwick Medical School in the United Kingdom. She is a fellow at the U.K. Faculty of Public Health and at the Royal College of Pediatrics and Child Health. Her research interests have included the measurement of emotional-social competence and learning as well as school- and family-based interventions supporting SEL development. Her article, 'A systematic review of universal approaches to mental health promotion in schools' in *Health Education* (2003), won a Literati Club Award for Excellence.

LANA STOHL is CEO of Behavioral Health Strategies, which is a healthcare organization that provides EQ-i certification training in addition to providing individual and group assessment, coaching, leadership enhancement and clinical program development based on emotional intelligence. Since 1990, she has served as clinical instructor in the Graduate School of Social Work at the University of Utah. She has also provided assessment feedback, coaching and training for a number of individuals, groups and organizations in a variety of settings including the U.S. military, correctional officers, corporate executives, leadership teams, educational institutions, and private as well as not-for-profit organizations.

GRAEME J. TAYLOR is professor of Psychiatry at the University of Toronto Medical School and a staff psychiatrist at Mount Sinai Hospital in Toronto. He is internationally recognized for his theoretical contribution and research in the area of alexithymia, and has co-authored several articles and chapters relating this work to emotional intelligence. In 2005, he received a Mary S Sigourney Award for distinguished contributions to the field of psychoanalysis, in particular for his application of psychoanalytic concepts to medicine, and his research and theoretical conceptualizations concerning the role of emotions and alexithymia in illness and disease.

HELEN L. TAYLOR-ALLAN is a psychoeducational consultant at the Chisholm Educational Centre in Oakville, Ontario. Her fields of expertise are human development and applied psychology, based on work at the Ontario Institute for Studies in Education at the University of Toronto. She is co-author of a chapter on alexithymia in an edited book on psychological mindedness.

DAVID L. VAN ROOY is a senior manager of Talent Selection and HR Research with Marriott International. His interests include leadership development, performance management, personnel selection and organizational surveys. He has published articles and chapters on a variety of topics including emotional intelligence, commuter stress and models of organizational performance. He is a member of several organizations including the American Psychological Association, the Society for Industrial and Organizational Psychology, and the Consortium for Research on Emotional Intelligence. Together with Chockalingam Viswesvaran, he conducted the first meta-analysis of emotional intelligence and psychometric instruments that measure this construct.

CHOCKALINGAM VISWESVARAN is professor of Psychology at Florida International University. His research interests include meta-analysis, personnel selection and human resource management. He has published in the *Journal of Applied Psychology, Organizational Behavior and Human Decision Processes,* and the *Psychological Bulletin*. He has served on five editorial boards and currently serves as an associate editor of the *International Journal of Selection and Assessment*. He is an elected fellow of the Society for Industrial and Organizational Psychology as well as for Divisions 5 (Measurement) and 14 (Industrial–Organizational Psychology) of the American Psychological Association.

ROGER P. WEISSBERG is professor of Psychology and Education at the University of Illinois at Chicago. He is also president of the Collaborative for Academic, Social, and Emotional Learning. For 25 years, he has trained scholars and practitioners to design, implement and evaluate family, school and community interventions. He has authored over 200 publications focusing on positive youth development and preventive interventions with children. He received the American Psychological Association's Distinguished Contribution Award for Applications of Psychology to Education and Training, and the Society for Community Action and Research Distinguished Contribution to Theory and Research Award.

CHARLES J. WOLFE is CEO of Charles J Wolfe Associates, a result-driven consulting firm committed to making a meaningful difference in the lives of others. In addition to being an internationally sought-after speaker, he has published and is quoted in a number of professional journals. He has also created the Emotion Roadmap, which is a methodology designed to help individuals and organizations enhance performance based on his adaptation of the Salovey-Mayer model of emotional intelligence. His expertise is in executive coaching, leadership development and team-building for a range of clients.

JOSEPH E. ZINS passed away suddenly on March 1, 2006 at the age of 56. He was professor and director of the Doctoral Program in Special Education at the University of Cincinnati. He was internationally respected for his expertise in social and emotional learning, prevention, and individual and organizational consultation. He contributed over 150 scholarly publications, including *Building Academic Success on Social and Emotional Learning* (2004) and *Bullying, Peer Harassment, and Victimization in the Schools* (2003). Colleague Timothy Shriver said of Professor Zins:

> He was a man of such enormous warmth. He was never without humility, never without openness, and never without a certain wonder. In his voice, I could always hear the hint of a child's voice regardless of what he was saying.

He is deeply missed by colleagues, students and his foremost love—his family.